INTEGRATION NOW

INTEGRATION
—NOW—

Alexander v. Holmes

and the End of Jim Crow Education

❀

WILLIAM P. HUSTWIT

The University of North Carolina Press

Chapel Hill

Designed by April Leidig

Set in Arno by Copperline Book Services, Inc.

The University of North Carolina Press has been
a member of the Green Press Initiative since 2003.

Cover illustration: gavel icon © iStockphoto.com/palau83;
close-up of blank blackboard © iStockphoto.com/triloks.

Library of Congress Cataloging-in-Publication Data
Names: Hustwit, William P., author.
Title: Integration now : Alexander v. Holmes and the
end of Jim Crow education / William P. Hustwit.
Description: Chapel Hill : University of North Carolina Press, [2019] |
Includes bibliographical references and index.
Identifiers: LCCN 2018038927 | ISBN 9781469648552 (cloth : alk. paper) |
ISBN 9781469668741 (pbk : alk. paper) | ISBN 9781469648569 (ebook)
Subjects: LCSH: Alexander, Beatrice—Trials, litigation, etc. | Holmes County
(Miss.). Board of Education—Trials, litigation, etc. | School integration—
Mississippi—Holmes County—History—20th century. | School integration—
Law and legislation—United States—History—20th century. | African
Americans—Civil rights—United States—History—20th century.
Classification: LCC LC214.22.M7 H87 2019 | DDC 379.2/6309762625—dc23
LC record available at https://lccn.loc.gov/2018038927

For my friend and mentor,
Charles W. Eagles

There is a school of thought that holds that
these legal victories are empty. They are not. At the
very least, they provide the ground upon which
we make our stand for our rights.
—James Weldon Johnson

———

Education is the one thing the white
man can't take from you.
—Otis Campbell, Holmes County farmer

CONTENTS

MAP AND FIGURES

ACKNOWLEDGMENTS

Scholarly work requires the contributions of many people. At Birmingham-Southern College, several individuals provided help and encouragement. First, thanks to my friends at BSC, particularly in the history department. From the beginning, Mark Lester, Matthew Levey, Randy Law, Victoria Ott, and Mark Schantz had confidence in the project. Every professor should be fortunate to work alongside such wonderful colleagues who, in spite of their life sentences to the salt mines of academe, remain committed to the insane asylum of higher education. I can always count on fellow inmates Bill Myers, Fred Ashe, Steve Hendley, Barbara Domcekova, Jody Stitt, Melinda Thompson, and Lucas Johnson. Dave Ullrich is a brilliant Fitzgerald scholar, an inspirational teacher, a gifted artist, and a dear friend. Deb Smith, the fearless Girl Friday of humanities and the other pea in my pod, makes each day better on the Hilltop. Pam Venz did her best to make me look presentable for the book jacket. I would also like to thank BSC for its financial support, including a January sabbatical and, at the behest of Sandra Sprayberry, supplemental funding for copyright permissions covered by Provost Brad Caskey.

From the start, I intended to write a historical narrative that would appeal to a wide audience and be true to primary sources. Librarians and archivists are vital to historical research, and several across the country assisted me. At BSC, Pam Sawallis, Janice Poplau, and Nancy Colyar diligently retrieved materials. In Oxford, Mississippi, Jennifer Ford's and Leigh McWhite's staffs at the University of Mississippi's archives gathered manuscript collections and photographs on short notice. In Jackson, the Mississippi Department of Archives and History staff found obscure newspaper microfilm and television segments. In Washington, D.C., the National Archives and Library of Congress extended every professional courtesy. Though not an archivist or a librarian, Stephen Black, grandson of Hugo Black, granted access to the justice's papers at the Library of Congress.

A number of Birmingham-Southerners and people elsewhere gave good counsel and improved the manuscript. Mark Schantz, a recovering provost, read drafts of the manuscript and didn't think twice (it's all right) about its merits. My friend Mark Lester educated me on legal terms and matters. Guy Hubbs pried himself loose from Crimson Tide football to comment on early versions of the manuscript. I am especially grateful to Guy and his wife, Pat, for the generous use of their beautiful cottage near Sewanee, Tennessee, to hammer out most of the book. My students deserve thanks as well, notably the happy few who survived my historical methodology and intensive-writing seminar. When the hunter became the hunted, they chomped at the bit to spill red ink on their taskmaster's pages. Outside the academy, Ken Rutherford, an Oxford attorney, put me in contact with several Mississippi lawyers. Dr. Sylvia Reedy Gist reviewed individual chapters, arranged interviews for me, and imparted her intimate knowledge of Holmes County's race relations and school system. Mel Leventhal took time from his own work to critique the manuscript and saved me from dozens of errors. Sue Lorenzi Sojourner provided invaluable insights into the Holmes County movement and vignettes of several local activists. Bob Corley answered questions related to the legacy of school desegregation. Additionally, I benefited enormously from the prudent revisions suggested by Alan Draper, John Charles Boger, and the anonymous referee at the University of North Carolina Press. Among the press's indefatigable staff, Anna Faison, Cate Hodorowicz, Dino Battista, Dylan White, Jay Mazzocchi, and Julie Bush spurred on the publishing process. Chuck Grench has again proved to be a superb editor and has made working with UNC Press an enjoyable and rewarding experience. None of the aforementioned bear responsibility for any mistakes, sins of omission, and annoying or dissatisfying arguments in this book, but I am more than happy to share the credit with them.

I would never have known to study *Alexander v. Holmes* had it not been for Charles Eagles. Charles represents the history profession at its very best. Since graduate school, he has challenged me to write simply, think clearly, and take seriously the perspectives of both civil rights activists and their segregationist counterparts. I could not have asked for a better adviser and role model as a historian. If I can excuse Charles for "crushing my puppies" along the road, maybe he can forgive me for dedicating the book to him. I am also grateful to his wife, Brenda, for her support, friendship, criticisms, recipes, and copyediting.

My family and friends, in their own ways, also inspired this project. Mum and Dad, thank you. They say it takes a village to raise a child, but it really takes a family. Holls, our bond is special. Ronnie and Heather, no matter where you roam, I love you both. To Liam, my favorite nephew, and Molly, the newest member of the Hustwit family circus, your uncle has good news:

after a parboiling debate, we decided not to return you to the gypsies, unless, of course, you turn into Stalinist teenagers, in which case all bets are off.

In Alabama, my hiking buddy, T. C. McLemore, stresses the importance of finding a "third place"—a home away from home and work. I'm thankful for Father Jon Chalmers and the community at Holy Rosary Catholic Church in Birmingham for being my third place. "The light shines on in the dark, and the darkness has never mastered it" (John 1:5).

INTEGRATION NOW

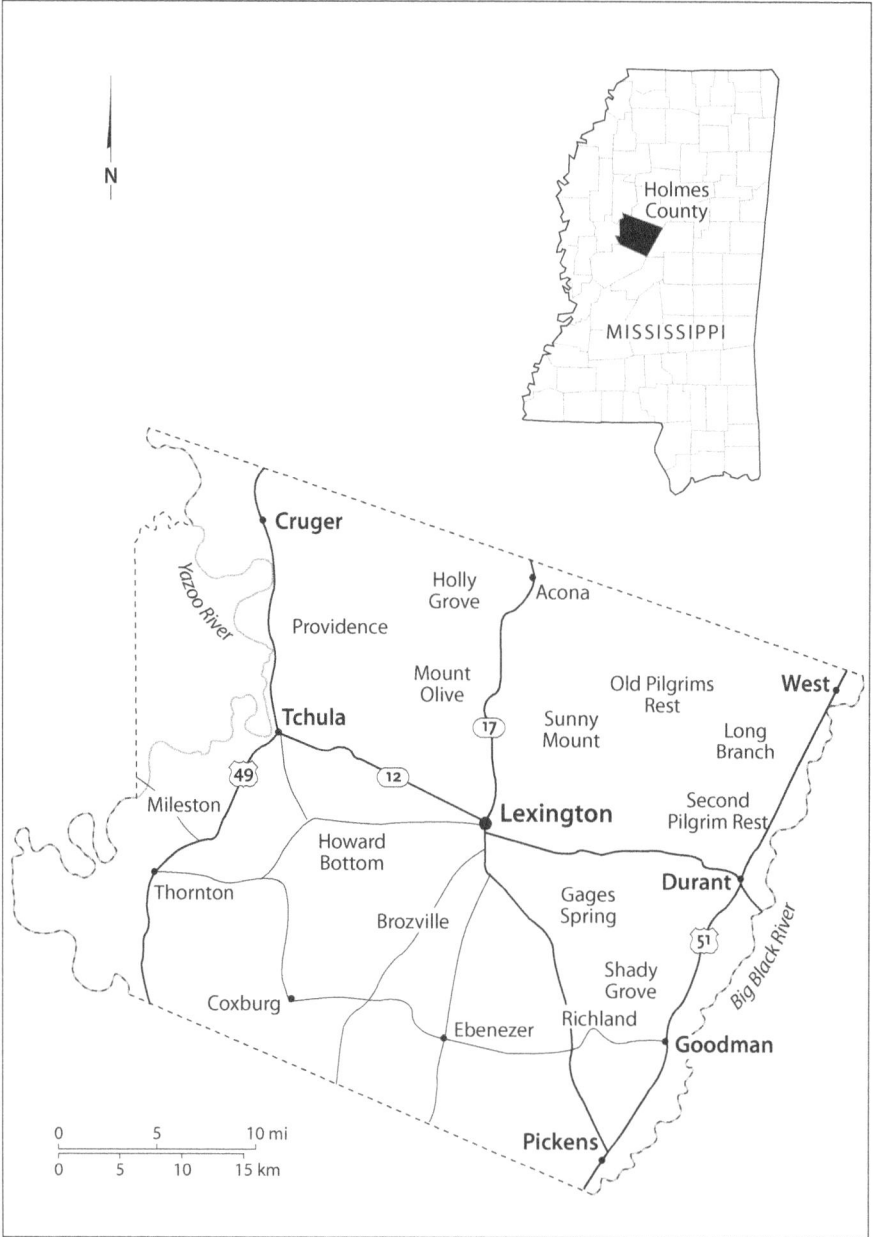

N

Holmes
County

MISSISSIPPI

Cruger

Yazoo River

Holly
Grove

Acona

Providence

Mount
Olive

Old Pilgrims
Rest

West

17

Sunny
Mount

Long
Branch

Tchula

49

12

Mileston

Lexington

Second
Pilgrim Rest

Howard
Bottom

Durant

Thornton

Gages
Spring

51

Big Black River

Brozville

Shady
Grove

Coxburg

Ebenezer

Richland

Goodman

Pickens

0   5   10 mi

0   5   10   15 km

Holmes County, Mississippi.
(Adapted from Youth of the Rural Organizing
and Cultural Center, *Minds Stayed on Freedom*)

Introduction

✿

Let us now sing the praises of famous men.
—Ecclesiasticus 44:1

O N THE MORNING of January 5, 1970, a new day and a new world dawned in a sleepy town nestled on the banks of the murky Pearl River in southern Mississippi. The era of massive integration had begun in Columbia. A few blocks from the river, a principal addressed the black and white student body at Columbia High. "You people are in a history-making situation," B. J. Oswalt announced to the student assembly at the now biracial high school. "It can happen only once and you are part of it. Now, what are you going to do?" The question hung in the air across Mississippi and the entire region as the first generation of southerners adapted to wide-spread school desegregation.[1]

Curiously, most Americans know nothing about the milestone U.S. Su-preme Court decision that struck down racially segregated public schools once and for all and thrust thousands of students into integrated classrooms for the first time. *Brown v. Board of Education of Topeka* in 1954 was the salient legal step in combating discriminatory education, but the ruling's signifi-cance lay as much in the wrangling over how to enforce it as in the ways that it changed American society. What followed in the decade and a half after *Brown* did more to invalidate Jim Crow education conclusively. To be sure, *Brown* served as a crucial intervention that addressed the problem of de jure segregation in schools and created a new phase of the civil rights movement. Only after a painstaking campaign by black plaintiffs and their attorneys, however, did the justices insist on an immediate transition to nonsegregated public schooling.

The real effort to desegregate occurred after the Court's implementation order on October 29, 1969, in *Alexander v. Holmes County Board of Education*. Following the ruling, southern schools went through the most audacious social upheaval and prolific change ever required of any educational system in the United States. In the fall of 1968, fourteen years after *Brown*, 68 percent of African-American children in the South still attended all-black schools. Within a year of *Alexander v. Holmes*, that figure subsided to 18 percent. The story of the struggle to erase the stain of school segregation involved white resistance as well as black defiance of patently unequal education. In the buildup to *Alexander*, flashpoints had erupted over desegregation across the South.[2]

Seven years before the Court announced its capacious decision in *Alexander v. Holmes*, a leader arose among local blacks in a secluded Mississippi county. Born in 1916, the tenth of thirteen children, stout and copper-skinned, Mrs. Anger Winson Hudson's eyes emitted her unflinching resolve. Hudson's intense gaze revealed a good deal about her, wrote novelist Alice Walker, "for she is one of the 'sleepless ones' found in embattled Mississippi towns whose fight has been not only against unjust laws and verbal harassment, but against guns and fire bombs as well." On more than one occasion, the Ku Klux Klan sprayed her house with bullets for her civil rights activism, but Winson "Winnie" Hudson and her husband, Cleo, stood their ground.[3]

Myriad characters, including the Hudsons, contributed to what the Supreme Court decided in October 1969. *Alexander v. Holmes* involved thirty-three Mississippi school desegregation lawsuits folded into a single case that bubbled up from the hothouse activism of unsung multitudes of blacks. The often-neglected named plaintiffs who braved bombings, gun-toting night riders, and ostracism by white and black neighbors in beleaguered communities over a protracted slog ultimately persevered and spoke truth to power on behalf of African Americans across the South. *Integration Now* is their story.[4]

Winson Hudson's cameo in that drama began in remote Leake County in the dead center of Mississippi and sixty miles northeast of Jackson, the state capital. Ensconced within rural and isolated Leake was the all-black town of Harmony—"a black Brigadoon in the heart of Klan country," as one historian described it. Once called Galilee, Harmony dated back to the Reconstruction era when former Negro slaves acquired farmland from their previous masters. In the late nineteenth century, blacks purchased more property deemed unsuitable by whites, sometimes for only a dollar an acre, and grew cotton. The black farmers of Harmony prospered and formed a tiny but vibrant African-American enclave. Harmony was an aptly named safe haven, "a together community," wrote the *New York Times*' John Herbers. The cloistered town embodied what could happen if blacks owned land in Mississippi: they took charge of their lives, rolled up their sleeves, and fought for their civil rights.[5]

The black freedom struggle arrived in Harmony in the late 1950s when Medgar Evers, state field secretary for the National Association for the Advancement of Colored People (NAACP), set up a local branch. Winnie Hudson was a natural choice to chair the county chapter. She and her sister, Dovie, both married to men named Hudson, were pillars of the Harmony community and ahead of their time. Since 1937, the Hudson sisters had tried to register to vote just "for the heck of it." To announce herself, Winson usually marched in a bright red dress to the art deco courthouse in Carthage, the county seat. The Klan noticed. One day, someone slipped her a note with two glaring red eyes and the message, "The eyes of the White Knights of the Ku Klux Klan are upon you." In 1962, despite the intimidation, she finally registered to vote.[6]

In March 1963, Winnie and Dovie Hudson, along with nearly fifty other blacks, brought the first school desegregation lawsuit in rural Mississippi after county administrators shuttered the Negro school in Harmony as part of a consolidation plan. The action named Diane Hudson, Dovie's daughter, as lead plaintiff in *Diane Hudson et al. v. Leake County School Board*. The school had been built in 1922 with a charitable gift from the Julius Rosenwald Fund. Harmony's blacks helped to erect the single-story building and took great pride in their little schoolhouse. "So, we really got mad and rallied together when whites started messing with our Harmony School," Winson Hudson remembered. Rather than bus their children thirteen miles to Carthage, a handful of families filed a suit to integrate Leake County's schools. If white officialdom wished to close their beloved school, the stalwart band of plaintiffs decided to sue for the end of segregated education itself—a quantum leap beyond keeping the Harmony school open. They joined with NAACP litigants in Jackson, by far the largest school district in the state, and Biloxi to desegregate their school systems.[7]

Whites warded off the challenge. Bent on undercutting the Negro position, segregationists pressured individual plaintiffs to drop their names from the case. One of Governor Ross Barnett's cousins in Leake, the Barnetts' home county, threatened that desegregation would only happen over students' dead bodies: "Little children's blood will run in the streets like water." All but a dozen signatories had their names removed from the suit. Undaunted, the indomitable Hudson matriarchs, the "Big Women of Leake County," pressed on and eventually won their case. On the opening day of school in the fall of 1964, a black first-grader, Debra Lewis, integrated Leake's formerly white elementary schools. In 1965, desegregation expanded to the high school. Diane Hudson began her senior year, but she never finished at Leake High. White students pestered her constantly, calling her names, spitting on her, and roughing her up.[8]

The school suit inflamed racial tensions in the county, and Harmony's blacks suffered for their boldness. Some parents who sent their children to previously all-white schools got fired from their jobs. Others lost credit lines at banks. Tiny Harmony no longer felt harmonious. White police failed to prevent the Klan from burning a cross within the city limits and from booby-trapping the dirt road into Harmony with a bed of tire-shredding nails. White supremacists put a bomb in Dovie Hudson's mailbox, but her sons caught the culprits in the act and peppered the getaway car "with bullets up and down." The terror proved too much for the more docile element in Harmony. Blacks who refused to join the school litigation case said the plaintiffs "had no business getting into such a mess" and should stay in their place, Winson Hudson recalled. Characteristically, the Hudson sisters met their opponents head-on. "We knew we could be blown away any time," Winnie wrote. "The more they did to us," she swore, "the meaner we got."[9]

About one hundred miles west of Leake, another rural hotspot flared up near the southern tip of the Delta in thinly populated, majority black, and achingly poor Issaquena County. Most blacks there picked cotton. None voted. One dark-skinned daughter of sharecroppers, a recent arrival in the county, was "pickin' and choppin' cotton at three dollars a day" when she decided to register to vote. Years later, Unita Blackwell would be the first black female mayor in Mississippi. "I'm sure my mother never thought that her black, barefoot child would become in a position of power," Blackwell reminisced. When she and seven other blacks decided to register to vote at the county courthouse in Mayersville, the circuit clerk turned them away. Spurned and insulted, Blackwell contacted the Student Nonviolent Coordinating Committee (SNCC). By 1964, she worked for SNCC as a full-time field secretary. Blackwell and Issaquena would never be the same.[10]

The black freedom struggle consumed Unita Blackwell and changed her whole outlook. "When I got into the civil rights movement, I got a new kind of education," she later reflected. Blackwell lost little time getting into the fray, helping to instigate a voter registration drive in the county and then challenging Issaquena's segregated schools. In the spring of 1965, she and her husband, Jeremiah, pushed for a desegregation suit against the county school board after the principal at Henry Weathers High School suspended over 300 black students, including their son, Jerry, for wearing SNCC "freedom pins" show-ing black and white hands clasped in racial solidarity.[11]

Plaintiffs sued the school board to defend the students' freedom of speech and to address gross deficiencies in the county's educational system. Black parents knew their schools were substandard in important ways. Black stu-dents read outdated textbooks, and their teachers received dismal pay, lower than white faculty salaries. From August to October, the demands of the cot-ton harvest truncated the length of the school year at picking time and inter-rupted students' studies. In Jackson, the federal district court ruled in the plaintiffs' favor that Issaquena's school system must begin desegregation by the fall of 1965. The court, however, also sided with the school board's disci-plinary action to squelch student activism and upheld the ban on the SNCC buttons. Jerry Blackwell and nearly fifty other high schoolers boycotted in protest. Many black teens attended "freedom schools" organized by local Af-rican Americans until the demise of the dual-education system.[12]

The desegregation of Issaquena's schools represented one small piece of the larger legal campaign by black Mississippians to eliminate racially discrimi-natory education during the 1960s that came together in *Alexander v. Holmes*. To the northeast of Issaquena, Holmes County straddled the Mississippi Delta and the hill country. Holmes resembled other impoverished, mostly black counties in rural Mississippi. In the mid-1960s, Negroes accounted for more than 70 percent of the county's population of 27,000. Holmes had the unenviable distinction of being one of the poorest counties in the poor-est state in America. Only twenty blacks had ever registered to vote there. Many black farmworkers eked out a hardscrabble existence on plantations, yet nearly 800 African-American farmers owned 50 percent of the land in the county. One civil rights worker estimated that almost 90,000 acres belonged to Negroes. The abnormally high concentration of black yeomen gave the Holmes movement special power in its fight against school segregation. As veteran activist Susan Lorenzi Sojourner corroborated, "Probably no other of Mississippi's 82 counties . . . developed a comparable political organization, sophistication, and level of accomplishment."[13]

The county's base of independent black farmers supplied what sociologist Jay MacLeod italicized as "the critical resource" in pressing for racial reform. Black landholding traced back to a New Deal–era redistribution program. In 1940, the Farm Security Administration purchased over 9,000 acres of Delta bottomland around the all-black community of Mileston and subdivided it into 106 farms. The experimental project unfettered hundreds of black sharecroppers and farm laborers from planter dependency and made land ownership possible. "Always since I was a young man," said Ralthus Hayes, one beneficiary of the program, "I thought of buying land but there was no ways I could have done it. There was no ways to make enough on shares to ever get land." In 1941, he applied for a federal loan to buy fifty-four acres and received the necessary funding to get construction materials for a home, mules, and farm tools. His hard work earned Hayes enough income to acquire sixty-four additional acres ten years later, which meant more than economic autonomy to him and other native farmers. Owning land gave African Americans social standing above black plantation laborers and put them atop the rural class structure as a kind of petite bourgeoisie. Mileston farmers formed the repository of the county's black leadership, and their community coalesced into an important staging ground during the civil rights movement.[14]

During the spring of 1963, Mileston's black landholders and their families initiated a voter registration drive that disseminated the movement throughout the county. The franchise remained a priority until the passage of the 1965 Voting Rights Act, but the Holmes movement's goals dilated to include school desegregation. As they battled for the vote, African Americans also locked horns with the county's all-white school board. In 1965, Holmes blacks cooperated enthusiastically with civil rights attorneys and filed a lawsuit that later reached the Supreme Court as *Alexander v. Holmes*.[15]

The outcome of the historic *Alexander* case, packaged together with the suits from Leake and Issaquena counties and thirty other school districts from across the state, would change the South profoundly. The wrong it sought to right had lingered since the *Brown* decision, but justice delayed would not be justice denied. *Alexander* crowned the long ordeal of desegregating southern public education that began fifteen years earlier with *Brown*. In 1970, after numerous delays, elisions, and last-ditch attempts to block black enrollment, a tidal wave of integration hit school districts across the Lower South. Jim Crow education rapidly receded.

───────────────

THE LARGELY OVERLOOKED case of *Alexander v. Holmes* illustrates two approaches to civil rights movement scholarship. Scholars have typically contrasted the more gradual approach stemming from precedent-based litigation in the courts with protests flowing from sit-ins, marches, boycotts, and rallies. A close reading of the historical record renders any simple dichotomy false and too limited a view of the dynamics of change. At the core of *Integration Now* are the civil rights lawyers and reformist jurists who crafted a strategy for harrying segregation in public education and the ordinary citizens who joined them in the fight. Tributaries of legal agitation and black activism merged together in a confluence of law and protest. More importantly, school segregation would never have ended without work on each front. Even Dr. Martin Luther King Jr., a proponent of direct action, conceded, "The law itself is a form of education." Discerning the symbiotic relationship between law and local movements proves critical to interpreting how the Supreme Court and nation moved from *Brown* to *Alexander*. "A crucial aspect of the civil rights litigation pioneered by the NAACP," commented historian Waldo Martin, "was the guiding assumption that the legal battles were part and parcel of the collective struggle of African Americans." Mel Leventhal, one of the lead plaintiff attorneys in *Alexander*, later credited "a potion, a combination of things, grassroots leadership and a court system that's responsive," for winning school desegregation. "It's best to understand it as a collaborative result." Legal scholar Randall Kennedy has also emphasized the law's centrality in the movement's success. Lawsuits supplemented boycotts, sit-ins, and marches and performed "valuable functions apart from helping to shape the legal issues at stake. Courtrooms provided one of the few contexts in American history in which a cadre of Negroes—the Movement's black lawyers—bested whites in an intellectual-professional setting on a consistent and highly public basis." Activists, he continued, often "reaped the best of both extra-legal protest and litigation, the grassroots participation generated by the former and the official legitimation bestowed by the latter." An assessment of the *Alexander* case will consider the background and motivations of the plaintiffs and their inventive lawyers who brought the case to fruition, peruse the ideology and reactions of southern whites, and place the varying perspectives within the wider context of the black freedom struggle.[16]

Students of the movement have also, by consensus, cheered *Brown* as a turning point for black civil rights but have lamented Americans' lack of commitment to sustain racially balanced school integration. As Tamar Jacoby wrote in her 1998 book, *Someone Else's House*, "If integration is still most Americans' idea of the goal, few of us talk about it any more. The word has a quaint ring today—like 'gramophone' or 'nylons.'" Due to de facto resegregation in school districts and because the larger national racial dilemma remains unresolved, many scholars depict school desegregation in failed terms. Historian James Patterson has accentuated *Brown*'s "troubled legacy," and Peter Irons regards the Court's opinion as an unfulfilled promise. Gary Orfield and Susan Seaton have documented the "quiet reversal" of *Brown* in *Dismantling Desegregation*. Political scientist Gerald Rosenberg has claimed that the breakthrough in school desegregation did not occur within the courts but with the 1964 Civil Rights Act, which empowered the executive branch to shave federal funds from school districts that practiced segregation. Other legal historians have divested *Brown* of its primacy in inaugurating the civil rights movement. In perhaps the most controversial critique of the decision, Michael J. Klarman argues that strong links existed between the Court ruling and the mobilization of white southern resistance to racial change. Historian Raymond Wolters also offers an intriguing, yet contentious, thesis in the debate about *Brown*. In *Race and Education*, he distinguishes between desegregation, which required an end to state-sanctioned discrimination, and integration, which insisted upon racial balance but never won support from the majority of Americans. Wolters's delineation helps to clarify the meaning and scope of *Alexander v. Holmes*. Viewing *Alexander* from its past rather than its future recaptures its significance by relating how much sacrifice occurred to produce the case and how much progress it represented at the time.[17]

Although scholars have previously dealt with aspects of *Alexander v. Holmes*, no dedicated monograph has been written on the case. Soon after the ruling, one prosaic article appeared in a law journal. Otherwise, no scholar has drawn on archival research, delved into court records, trolled newspaper coverage, interviewed lawyers, or compiled a narrative of *Alexander* from its genesis in Holmes County to the Supreme Court in Washington. Histories of the civil rights movement, Supreme Court justices, and school desegregation have also included fleeting discussions of *Alexander* as part of their larger subjects, but most scholarly literature has gravitated toward *Brown*. In the annals of integration's fate, *Alexander* proved more functionally decisive in actuating school desegregation than *Brown v. Board of Education*. In key respects, in terms of engineering a Court order that restored *Brown*'s intent and made desegregation immediate and irreversible, *Alexander v. Holmes* ranked as a success. This study treats *Alexander* for what it was—the regional touchstone in abolishing segregated public education.[18]

Appreciating *Alexander v. Holmes* weaves together three strands in the historical fabric of a capstone Supreme Court ruling. One concerns the actions of black Mississippians in a distinctive and fascinating county to break up the segregated school system in a state referred to by one historian as "the most southern place on earth." Holmes was hardly a microcosm of the entire South—the durability of the grassroots movement and higher concentration of black landholders alone made it exceptional. The experiences of black Holmes Countians may not have been exactly normative for the region as a whole, but their lives were the lives of their times. From 1954 to 1969, many rural and majority-black communities throughout the South had much in common with Holmes. The county epitomized challenges facing integration in the locales that brought the group of court suits collectively decided in 1969 as *Alexander v. Holmes*. Focusing attention on one of the thirty-three "*Alexander*" cases should provide insight into the potent forces colliding in the broader movement for equal rights in Mississippi and the South. Another thread tracks the efforts of conservative whites to preserve the culture of racial segregation and white supremacy. A third examines how civil rights lawyers pursued a winning legal strategy in the federal courts. Throughout, the narrative tours southern and American history as it analyzes the ways race, education, and the law guided school desegregation at the local and national levels.[19]

The chronicle of *Alexander v. Holmes* is both triumphant and troubling, inspiring and disquieting. It is the saga of an extraordinary case that advanced school desegregation on the national stage and reaffirmed *Brown*'s insistence that separate and unequal education was unconscionably wrong and unconstitutional. The strength and courage of the black plaintiffs who toppled the racial order defined a new era in American life. By starting not with the case itself but with the people at the bottom of the process, this story makes clear that the Supreme Court decision grew out of a tradition of struggle. *Alexander*'s proper backdrop originated in the dark journey of Mississippi's past, a gothic terrain that provided too many sadistic reminders for black activists ever to forget that they worked in the belly of what Roy Wilkins, executive secretary of the NAACP, eviscerated as "the most savage, the most brutal state" in America. No other state matched Mississippi's record "in inhumanity, murder, brutality, and racial hatred," he concluded. As one leader of the Holmes movement suggested, any history about black Mississippians' confrontation with the state's racial caste system must begin by showing where they came from and how they suffered for their defiance:

> You need to tell how it was before the movement, what led up to it. Write about back before the movement come and how life was for a Negro in Mississippi. Take the man on the plantation, how he get up at five in the morning and get behind that mule and work in the field until they ring that bell at twelve o'clock noon and he stop for dinner. Then he go back to work at one o'clock when they ring the bell again, but then they don't ring that bell no more after that because he know to stay out working 'til the sun go down. You gotta tell all that and how they was lynching and beating Negroes and just what life was like down here. And then how it built up to the movement that come.[20]

— CHAPTER ONE —

Race and Education before *Alexander*

❀

The only effect of Negro education is
to spoil a good field hand.
—Mississippi governor James K. Vardaman

I N MARCH 1941, President Franklin Delano Roosevelt received a letter
from a forlorn mother. Her son, a twenty-year-old black man, had been
killed two years earlier and dumped in a river near Pickens, Mississippi,
a small town in southeastern Holmes County. When the sheriff pulled the
swollen corpse onto the bank, he noticed that the dead man's neck had been
snapped by an iron weight used to sink the body. "I am sending a contract in
regards to the lynching of my son Willie Jack Heggard," wrote Jane Heggard.
In desperation and outrage, she "tried every way to have a trial, but no lawyer
will accept the case, because a white man killed an innocent man. Is that the
law in Mississippi[?]" Roosevelt's assistant attorney general, O. John Rogge,
lamely referred the matter to local authorities. Despite her plea, no one investigated the crime. Her son became one of many victims of racial violence in
Holmes, a macabre tradition that characterized the county for generations.[1]
   During the Jim Crow era in Mississippi, black men like Willie Heggard
had to learn their place. Anyone who refused to conform to the code of racial
orthodoxy either had to leave posthaste or face retaliation. Often sudden and
unprovoked, violence engendered an inveterate fear of whites that intimidated African Americans and contributed to their subordination. Ingrained
violence lay at the heart of white supremacy, slavery, disfranchisement, and
segregation. It occurred most viciously perhaps in lynchings, but physical
punishment was only one form of suppression prevalent in Holmes County.

The killing of Willie Jack Heggard was not some flash of promiscuous violence—in many ways, it had been building for more than a century, from the antebellum period to the gestation of the *Alexander* case.

On February 18, 1833, the Mississippi legislature carved Holmes County out of 820 square miles of Yazoo County and named it in honor of the state's first and fifth governor, David Holmes. Located sixty-five miles north of Jackson, the lopsided county has the Yazoo River, snaking toward Vicksburg and the Mississippi River, as its western edge. On its ragged eastern border, the Big Black River divides Holmes from Attala and Madison counties. Between 1826 and 1836, the first farm settlements cropped up, including Lexington, the county seat and largest town, near the middle of Holmes. In the countryside, outlying villages—Durant, Tchula, Ebenezer, West, Cruger, Goodman, Pickens, and Mount Olive—soon dotted the county.[2]

Indians originally inhabited what Americans called Holmes County. The Chickasaw and Choctaw tribes resided in the region, but whites encroached on their domain after the American Revolution. The area that would constitute Holmes joined the United States in 1804 as part of the Mississippi Territory and after 1817 as part of the state of Mississippi. Statehood ignited a Mississippi land fever. As whites traversed Indian country and plundered aboriginal land, they clashed with Native Americans. The Choctaw ceded their land in the treaties of Doak's Stand (1820) and Dancing Rabbit Creek (1830). With the expulsion of the Indians, whites arrived with their black slaves to cultivate the prime real estate. One of the first homesteaders to enter Holmes furnished Negro bondsmen to clear the site on which the courthouse in Lexington now stands. Most of the settlers hailed from worn-out farm communities in the Carolinas, Georgia, Virginia, Kentucky, and Tennessee. The land rush attracted farm families as well as speculators.[3]

Of the rich land left behind by the Choctaw, the westernmost section of Holmes County was some of the most coveted earth in the antebellum South. Alluvial Delta soil, silted and black, lay within the western bottoms of Holmes. Less desirable red clay hills, trellised by abundant groves of hardwood forests and muddy creeks, dominated the eastern two-thirds of the county. The dividing line between the two physiographic portions consisted of bluffs that rose seventy-five to 200 feet above the level of the Yazoo-Mississippi Delta. Holmes County was a good place to grow things: corn, cotton, oats, wheat, field peas, sugar cane, and sorghum. Peaches, pears, apples, figs, plums, blueberries, and strawberries ripened in the wild. Stands of large ribbon cane (native bamboo) lined the rivers and gullies. Old-growth forests of oak, pine, walnut, poplar, willow, sycamore, sassafras, ash, hickory, tupelo and sweet gum, hackberry, and cypress canopied Holmes. An expanse of virgin timber, imposing swamps, and impenetrable canebrakes teemed with wolves, black bears, panthers, white-tailed deer, alligators, snakes, birds, and biting insects. The ground gurgled with artesian wells and mineral springs that gushed potable water. According to local folklore, the land was so naturally productive that a good seed of cotton started taking root before it hit the ground.[4]

The unusually fertile county needed more reliable access to external markets. Waterways provided the earliest and best method to export crops. The river port in Vicksburg, nearly a hundred miles down the meandering Yazoo, serviced the county. A few roads connected farmers to the world beyond Holmes, but they could turn soggy and impassable during the rainy winter and spring deluge. Only in the summer's sun did the arteries of dirt harden for travel. By 1858, the Mississippi Central Railroad (later the Illinois Central Railroad) clacked through Durant and linked Holmes to New Orleans and Memphis. Once settlers discovered the suitability of the land for agricultural production, bottlenecks in transportation did not prevent the county from developing and populating. More farmers came and planted fruit trees, corn, wheat, oats, and small amounts of tobacco. They also raised hogs and beef cattle for their families' subsistence. Planters, however, were not raring to grow food and graze livestock. Cotton became the key money crop. Dark, rich soil made much of western Holmes County optimal for a plantation economy, and the lucrative cotton market's ever-increasing demand for labor led to a larger black population.[5]

Planters wasted no time in amassing gangs of slaves to exploit the acreage. Prior to the Civil War, Negro slaves constituted the majority of the county's inhabitants and outnumbered whites nearly two to one. Whites brought into the county their bound laborers, who transformed the land into a cotton paradise for their masters. They felled trees, drained swamps, and cultivated fields to replace the forests, canebrakes, and marshes. By 1860, Holmes had roughly 5,800 white residents and almost 12,000 slaves.[6]

Cotton fast became king in the Old South, but its dividends accrued unevenly. One might envision spacious plantations with hundreds of slaves, but in reality plantations in Holmes were smaller and counted fewer slaves than ones in nearby Hinds and Carroll counties. Muddy roads, distance from trading centers, and hilly land hindered the growth of expansive plantations. Slave ownership, therefore, varied greatly in the Delta. In 1860, dozens of farms in the surrounding counties could boast at least one hundred enslaved laborers per plantation. Holmes County tallied a mere seven, and no planter owned more than 200 slaves. Of the 806 slave masters in the county, 185 possessed twenty or more bondsmen, accounting for over 7,700 enslaved people, or 64 percent of the county's total population. Perhaps 430 slaveholders claimed twenty or fewer slaves.[7]

One ravenous thread of the "Old South" did run through Holmes County: the acquisition of land for cotton. In their preoccupation with wealth, many planters became careless about their farm implements and methods. Crude farming techniques hurt the planters' progress and bruised the land, especially on estates in the hill country. In the eastern portion of the county, fields had been plowed and planted quickly after clearing the hillocks of timber. The flat bottomlands along the Yazoo began to germinate with intensive work that required draining wetlands and building levees but supported continuously profitable cotton crops. Prior to 1850, only a smattering of plantations operated in the Delta. In the hills, farmers cultivated the land in an undisciplined and wasteful manner, ripping up the earth and allowing the topsoil to wash away each spring. When the soil lost its fertility, planters uprooted and leapfrogged across Holmes to find greener pastures. Cotton production in the county, therefore, remained comparatively lower than in other more prosperous areas of the Delta. In 1850, Holmes planters ginned only 12,635 bales. By 1860, that figure improved to 40,000 but sagged ten years later to barely 19,000. Because of inferior cotton yields, limited transportation, and slower growth, antebellum Holmes County remained what one historian described as a "plantation frontier" until the Civil War. On the southwestern frontier, the "planter elite" were only moderately wealthy farmers, far from the aristocratic plantation fantasy. Well into the twentieth century, most whites did not fit the iconic image of the sumptuous planter. About 621 slaveholders, nonetheless, presided over the county.[8]

The planting class had brought most of the original blacks in Holmes as slaves from outside Mississippi. In the late 1930s, a Works Progress Administration federal program gathered many "slave narratives," or oral histories with former slaves. Ninety-four-year-old Elvira Boles spoke about her enslavement on a plantation near Lexington. "Marster was good to slaves," she told her interviewer. Relations between white masters and their Negro bondsmen ran the gamut from inhumane to what slaveholders perceived as compassionate and paternalistic. Whatever kindness some slaveholders may have shown, slavery in Holmes still amounted to a zero-sum world where planters measured success on the backs of black men and women. Even Elvira Boles could not reconcile her master's "good" side with his cruelty. Elihn Boles, her owner, "Don't believe in just lashing 'em [slaves]. He'd not be brutal, but he'd kill 'em dead right on the spot. Ova-seers'd git after 'em and whop 'em down."

Payton Archer, who grew up as a slave on a plantation near Tchula, recalled a master who walloped him for no other reason than to remind him "who was the boss."⁹

Establishing a tradition of white supremacy, slaveholders held the economic, political, and social levers. They made the rules and the decisions that governed both their own fortunes and the fates of their human chattel. The white owners defrayed shelter, food, clothing, fuel, and medical attention for their slaves, and they organized and directed their daily toil. In exchange, slaves like Elvira Boles spent long, grueling years doing physically arduous jobs. Purchased as a slave girl, Elvira washed dishes in the Boles family's big house, but when she got older and stronger, "Den dey put me in the fields," she said, and "I worked in the field and brick yard. . . . Toted brick, six bricks each load all day. . . . I'se worked to death. I had to work evva day." Enslaved women performed backbreaking labor alongside their bound brethren. Boles "done evvy thing but split rails," she remembered. "I've cut timber an' ah ploughed. Done evvy thing a man could do." The slave system depended on white subjugation and exploitation because slavery existed for whites to profit from black work. Masters also raped slave women to propagate the servile labor force. Elvira Boles's oldest child, "he boy by Boles, almost white," she disclosed. "I had to work evva day" for whites: a reprise that summed up the experience of many blacks in Holmes before and after the curtain fell on slavery.¹⁰

When emancipation came after the Civil War, slaves left one world behind and entered a topsy-turvy one. Elderly, now former, slave Elvira Boles recollected a certain gloom about her new life of freedom in the days after word traveled to her Holmes County plantation that slavery had ended: "Dey turn us loose in the world. Not a penny. Oh, dey was awful times. We just woked [walked] about from place to place after freedom. Hiahd [hired] to white people by month, week, day."¹¹

In the years after 1865, blacks shed slavery in part by attending school and in part by participating in politics. The Reconstruction era inaugurated a capsule period of black political experimentation and social mobilization. In Holmes County, newly enfranchised blacks worked a number of county jobs: sheriff, tax assessor, circuit clerk, and coroner. Born a slave, Benjamin Hoover became Holmes's first Negro county supervisor and held the office for six years. Another freedman, Buck Trueheart, won election to the Mississippi Senate. Shortly afterward, Ed Scarborough, a former slave who organized black Methodist meetinghouses throughout the area, entered the Mississippi House of Representatives. Between 1870 and 1880, six African Americans served Holmes in the state legislature.¹²

Reconstruction in Holmes County jutted beyond modest black political gains. More than holding office, freedpeople desired education for their children. Before Reconstruction, Mississippi had no formal system of education. In 1870, the federal Freedmen's Bureau founded the first public school district in Holmes. Enacted by Congress in March 1865 to assist freed slaves in the war-torn South, the Freedmen's Bureau encouraged blacks to find work with local whites, and its agents tried to arbitrate labor disputes between former masters and slaves. In Holmes County, the Freedmen's Bureau stewarded an extensive school construction program that helped people of color establish public primary education. Negro and white missionary teachers from northern states traveled to the county and staffed the new schools, commonly referred to as Freedmen's Schools. The first Freedmen's School began at the old Lexington Male Academy, a private school for wealthy whites deserted during the war when students joined the military. The bureau renovated the building for black students and renamed it the Lexington Colored School. Later that year, a second Freedmen's School opened in the Richland community. By 1872, Holmes counted five Freedmen's Schools, including two that instructed students through the fourth grade and three through grade 8.[13]

The demands of the cotton kingdom and scant resources, however, handicapped blacks who strove to build an educational system. Of the nearly 13,000 blacks in Holmes, only 221 went to school. The county's heavy dependence on an agricultural labor force meant that blacks had little time for schooling, and the few who did learned a curriculum of basic reading, writing, math, bookkeeping, and accounting. Children of both races attended classes in segregated, usually one-room, shanties with semiliterate teachers.[14]

Conditions were primitive, but some blacks, nevertheless, acquired skills for success. The schools set up by the Freedmen's Bureau in Holmes continued to educate the children of former slaves into the twentieth century. One graduate credited his white northern teacher with imparting the academic and business acumen necessary to work a lucrative farm at the turn of the century. Between 1870 and 1877, the Freedmen's Schools hired an integrated faculty, but they abided by local customs. In Negro schools, the bureau typically assigned black teachers less prestigious jobs as instructors. Whites acted as principals and county school superintendents. In deference to community mores, the Freedmen's Bureau managed separate facilities for white and black pupils. Prone to racial proprieties and paternalism and never adequately staffed, the bureau's schools still left an indelible mark on Mississippi and the South by birthing the public education system. Outside the black church, schoolhouses served as hallowed halls where African Americans had the most control over their lives. Black public schools were both a venerated place and a lightning rod.[15]

White residents opposed black education from the beginning and did not drop their claims to the buildings they had abandoned during the war that now housed the bureau's schools. The man responsible for organizing the county's black schools, Robert Augustus Simmons, a mulatto and Dartmouth University graduate, responded to white animus in a show of cussed pride at the Richland Colored School. On convocation day, he led black students in a defiant march through Richland and the nearby town of Goodman.[16]

Blindsided by the advances of blacks, Holmes County whites rallied to throw Negroes out of power. Conservative white Democrats soon controlled the county once again through lethal force and intimidation at the polls. Whites in Holmes relied heavily on brute violence to rein in African Americans and roll back Reconstruction. The Reconstruction era lasted a brief time in Holmes as white resistance stooped to terrorism. Holmes County turned into a battleground after the war ended.

The Civil War had barely drawn to a close when white paramilitary groups emerged to counter emancipation and Reconstruction. Mississippi spawned numerous vigilante outfits and secretive societies—the Ku Klux Klan, the Pale Face Brotherhood, the White League, and the Knights of the White Camellia, to name a few. The Klan and its imitators may have gone by various nomenclature, but their objectives overlapped: to maintain white supremacy. Heggie's Scouts, one of Mississippi's first terrorist organizations, surfaced in Carroll County immediately following the surrender of Confederate armies. The Scouts metastasized in Holmes and Montgomery counties, and some accounts traced the formation of the armed gang to "Major Heggie," a mysterious figure from the town of Vaiden. Other sources attributed its founding to the paroled Confederate general and Klan patriarch Nathan Bedford Forrest. Despite the presence of a nearby federal garrison in Winona, north of Holmes, blacks incurred the wrath of Heggie's Scouts. Before long, unreconstructed rebels enlisted in the Scouts and swelled the group's ranks to nearly a hundred. Each recruit joined with the expectation that "he must do his duty or die." The Scouts' mission, noted one saccharine history, mirrored the Klan's: "to make the negroes humble by visiting terrible punishment upon them." Their warpath coincided with efforts to repeal black freedom at the state level.[17]

During Reconstruction, blacks faced physical retaliation for any perceived, hinted, or actual assertion of their newfound but fragile freedom. Eager to restore white control over black labor, in November 1865 the state legislature passed laws to abridge the rights of freemen. In fact, the new statutes mimicked Mississippi's old slave code. Under the Mississippi "Black Codes," African Americans could not lease land, carry arms, hunt or fish, bring lawsuits against whites, drink alcohol, or preach the Gospel. The Black Codes also aimed at hemming black rights, preventing Negro land ownership, and returning blacks' labor to their former masters. Planters anxious to harvest the fall cotton crop relied on local sheriffs and unofficial parties to enforce their will. Whites sought to keep their black field hands docile and sedentary through the Black Codes and beatings. Heggie's Scouts "often whipped negroes who refused to work," wrote one historian. Violence was routine in Holmes.[18]

On one occasion, the Scouts thwarted a suspected "negro uprising" in the Delta. Major Heggie reportedly came upon a freedmen's militia training in a cotton field north of Holmes, ordered a charge, and scattered them pell-mell. More an outright slaughter than a battle, his men killed 116 blacks and tossed them into the Tallahatchie River. Afterward, the Scouts engaged in a handful of other atrocities. Most African Americans quailed. For any freedpeople who dared to defy the parochial racial order, the Scouts had standing orders to "kill every one they met." By 1866, federal authorities decided to apprehend the Scouts. Forty-eight members stood trial in federal court in Oxford, where a lenient judge dismissed all charges. The Scouts disbanded thereafter, but the Klan absorbed them.[19]

The terror campaign waged by Heggie's Scouts and other white supremacist insurgents became a widely recognized and adopted tool throughout Mississippi. Running amok and murdering African Americans, especially ones involved in politics, became rife. Tormented by the dreaded tactics, blacks rarely appealed to the legal system for justice. When a U.S. Senate committee later investigated voter fraud and intimidation in the disputed presidential election of 1876, for example, no blacks from Holmes testified.[20]

Disfranchisement soon joined violence as central to white oppression of blacks in Holmes County. Following federal efforts to curb the Klan's reign of terror and the enactment of the Fourteenth and Fifteenth Amendments to the Constitution, blacks momentarily felt more empowered. For years, African Americans continued to vote in Holmes County in spite of harassment and affliction. To reduce the impact of black ballots in the county, white supremacists developed a strategy to cripple black political activism that other areas in the state imitated. In October 1875, W. J. Taylor of Goodman telegraphed the head of the Mississippi Democratic Party, requesting freight costs to ship a cannon to Lexington. Once delivered, before the November election, they positioned the artillery in front of the courthouse and demarcated a firing line. Any Negro who dared to vote would be blown to kingdom come. The maneuver worked. During the 1875 state and county elections, no blacks in Holmes won election or reelection to office. After 1880, no African Americans represented the county in the legislature. White supremacist cabals in other parts of the state implemented analogs. Commonly known as the "Mississippi Plan," the state's Democratic Party devised a bloodthirsty overthrow of the Republican Party in Mississippi by coercing or bribing blacks not to vote. To reinforce their furious and determined opposition, Holmes Democrats also formed rifle clubs, or "Red Shirts," to blunt the black electorate. As one reporter attested, "The Klan terrorized . . . by night, but the bolder red shirts kept their colors flying by day."[21]

Reconstruction in Mississippi ended politically in 1875 when southern Democrats doggedly clawed their way back into power through force, outright fraud, assassinations, and persistent pressure to deter black voting. White supremacists swept blacks and their Republican allies out of county and state offices. In January 1877, the last Freedmen's Bureau school superintendent in Holmes County, J. L. Dyson, truckled and resigned his position. A local white, W. F. Cross, replaced him. African Americans continued to lose ground and incumbencies across Mississippi after the inauguration of President Rutherford B. Hayes and the withdrawal of federal troops from the South.[22]

Dishonesty and violence had won the day, at least for a while. Not all blacks in Holmes and the Delta capitulated to worsening conditions. The Populist-agrarian movement in the late 1880s and 1890s once again threatened conservative Democratic hegemony and prompted moves to collar suffrage. At that time, sundry and systemic problems encumbered southern farmers with rising agricultural costs and credit rates, falling crop prices due to overproduction, and rural isolation. During the 1880s, cotton prices plummeted. Local merchants responded by restricting loans and raising interest rates on farmworkers and plantation owners alike. Many landholders went into debt or foreclosure. By 1890, Negro farmers in Holmes reacted by organizing the Tchula Cooperative Store on the Mississippi Delta's eastern periphery. Adopting the cooperative vision of the Farmers' Alliance and Colored Farmers' Alliance movement, blacks pooled their resources; bought food, supplies, and seed; secured cash advances; and marketed their crops through the Tchula cooperative. Unlike other lenders, the co-op did not charge steep interest on debts or loans. The cooperative movement also tested planter influence over commerce, agriculture, and politics and white authority over black labor.[23]

Hidebound Democrats trounced the Populist challenge and inscribed their power by rewriting the Mississippi Constitution. In 1890, the state constitutional convention enacted restrictive voter registration laws, including a literacy test and the poll tax, that deprived the Populists of a constituency. The voting requirements of the new straitjacket of a constitution disfranchised poor illiterate whites as well as blacks, but the repercussions were most devastating for African Americans. Segregationist ordinances dealt democracy a mortal blow for blacks. During the 1870s, more than 180,000 African Americans had voted in Mississippi. Statewide, in 1888, black voter turnout was estimated at 29 percent. In 1892, that figure nosedived to 2 percent, or fewer than 1,300 blacks. By 1895, no African Americans appeared on voter rolls. Particularly in the rural areas of the state, black voter registration would remain at historic lows or virtually nonexistent until the mid-1960s. Prohibitive voting laws and ubiquitous racial violence successfully kept blacks subservient to whites. After Mississippi's 1890 constitution, blacks in Holmes and other Delta counties had no voice in politics or government. They could not vote for the superintendent of schools, for justice of the peace, for county commissioner, or for sheriff. Blacks would also not be called to serve on juries. The white elite had tightened its grip.[24]

Whites in Holmes found that overt violence proved just as effective at taming African Americans. Blacks faced physical retaliation if they did anything to annoy whites or deviated from the accepted order. Any transgression of the prevailing racial customs and habits required correction, and any whiff of black equality necessitated a heavy-handed response. Even a frivolous provocation, including dressing nicely in public or buying a soft drink, could be misconstrued as impudent behavior. One elderly black woman in Holmes recalled, "You wasn't allowed to wear white shirts in town. If you did, the white people would whoop ya. Also couldn't buy a coca cola. . . . They say niggers didn't have no reason with no coca cola." Such racial subjection rested on a bedrock of violence.[25]

Racially aggravated killings and murder enhanced Holmes County's reputation for brutality. The racial decorum imposed by the powerful white minority bullied Negroes into submission and required them always to be obsequious. If a black stepped outside the sublimated boundaries established by whites or acted in an unacceptable or disrespectful manner, whites often reacted with a vengeance. The ordinary smack or punch usually sufficed but sometimes proved insufficient or inappropriate punishment. Whites also resorted to a lurid ritual of extralegal violence—lynching. Between 1889 and 1945, the county recorded at least eight lynchings. In 1893, whites caught an accused black murderer, Sloan Allen, and made him dig his own grave and build a fire to broil him alive. Such butchery instilled fear in African Americans and maintained white control for decades. In October 1923, an African-American boy borrowed fifty cents from a white planter, but when he repaid the debt a few days later, the black youth refused to pay ten cents for interest. After armed whites hunted him in vain near Pickens, they settled for an eighteen-year-old black woman and shot her to death. Interracial sex was the crime most likely to arouse the furor of a southern lynch mob. Whites in Holmes referred to the children of mixed-race trysts as "half-white niggers." In 1936, the appetites of the flesh cost one black man his life when whites uncovered Booker T. Burch's dalliance with a white woman. For his offense, a mob tortured and castrated Burch before they tied him in chains and drowned him in a pond.[26]

Lynch law and disfranchisement were only two forms of oppression that Holmes County blacks experienced around the turn of the century. Important changes wrought by the Civil War and Reconstruction affected King Cotton, still regnant in the Delta but over a less impressive domain in Holmes County. Cotton production declined during and immediately after the war. Although the local farming economy rebounded somewhat from the conflict by the mid-1880s with the introduction of the railroad and access to Chicago, the agricultural sector bounced back at the expense of black workers. Landless freed blacks still needed work on the farms owned by whites, and many white landlords still depended on the labor of their former slaves. An uneasy exchange of work for payment developed. Slaves turned into sharecroppers and tenants after the Civil War as agriculture remained Holmes County's focal point.[27]

Holmes blacks exemplified the African-American scholar and civil rights leader W. E. B. Du Bois's claim in 1901 that most Negroes had "emerged from slavery into a serfdom of poverty and restricted rights." By the twentieth century, farm tenancy and sharecropping thrived in the Delta as in few other places. A 1908 Department of Agriculture study provided considerable insight into the plantation and tenancy systems as they existed in Holmes County on the eve of World War I. For their livelihoods, Negroes and whites continued to rely on cotton, the perennial source of most income and wealth in the Delta. The county maintained two distinctive cotton-growing areas. In the hillier, less fertile country to the east, the farms remained smaller than ones in the Delta, and landowners worked their fields alongside their tenants and sharecroppers. They hauled their crop to market by rail spurs that trundled through the county's interior, and a single cotton gin met the needs of a whole community. In the western, low-lying Delta, larger, wealthier tracts proliferated, and each planter owned a gin. Premium staple cotton blossomed on almost 360,000 acres. The size of the landholdings varied from twenty to 5,000 acres and averaged seventy acres. From the Civil War to the turn of the century, however, agricultural production in Holmes had been rather stagnant. Farmers clear-cut as they went, and the soil eroded and lost its nutrients. The market price of cotton had also remained low. Cotton was still king, but for many blacks in Holmes, life was bleak. They suffered the detrimental effects of a tenancy system that tripped up their stride toward freedom.[28]

By 1900, most of the nearly 28,700 blacks in Holmes County labored in agriculture. Although some blacks avoided farming and preferred to work in sawmills or for the railroads, which offered higher wages, the majority remained tethered to the land through tenantry and peonage. The largest plantations in Holmes had been apportioned into small plots, or "cuts," among the black tenants who operated under the direction of a white manager. Some blacks rented land, ranging from four to nine dollars an acre in the Delta to a lower price in the hills, or they worked for a daily wage that varied from fifty cents to a dollar, depending on the plantation. Most tenants entered into more complicated transactions with the landholders. Under the share system, landless tenants and landowners signed yearly or semiannual agreements to ensure work and cotton production. The planter furnished everything but the labor and typically got half the crop. Planters drew up legal contracts that stipulated the amount of financial support the owner would provide, the number of acres to be farmed, the crops to be raised, and the owner's oversight regarding other farming practices. At the end of the year, landlord and tenant divided the crop. Sharing the crop with the landowner became known as a sharecropping.[29]

Most black tenants found the life of Sisyphean toil and debt little better than slavery. Landless black farmers exercised more personal autonomy than had slaves, but the various tenancy arrangements incapacitated black freedom and real economic independence. Sharecropping and renting acreage enabled black families to escape gang labor and farm for themselves but reflected the inability of African Americans to acquire land of their own. From the time a Holmes tenant or cropper, whether black or white, agreed to a contract with a planter until the fall harvest, he and his family had to live on credit from a landlord or a storekeeper in town. Lacking any collateral except the future crop, the sharecropper or tenant gave the creditor a lien on a marketable cash crop, ordinarily cotton. Until the end of the crop year, a running tab mounted on the supplies, fertilizer, seed, food, and interest charged to his account. At settling time, the farmhand usually owed more than he pocketed, compelling him to deal with the same landowner or merchant for still another season. If unable to repay the loan in full, the debtor-tenant borrowed again for the next year, and the downwardly spiraling cycle of debt became as routinized as the work performed. By the early twentieth century, a new form of economic tyranny had vacuumed up many.[30]

Sharecropping and chronic debt set a pattern of near-servitude for blacks in Holmes County and across the Delta that continued until the mid-twentieth century. While the black population in the Delta continued to rise to meet labor demands, their political power had been sapped, and opportunities had dried up. African-American life in Holmes between Reconstruction and the 1930s was difficult and, for many, dreary. Most blacks worked as tenants or sharecroppers on white plantations and farms. By 1925, tenant farmers and sharecroppers cultivated 90 percent of the land. Blacks, usually the descendants of slaves, made up 94 percent of all tenants. Sharecropping had become a trough of inescapable poverty. After forty years of tenancy in Holmes County, Catherine Jefferson sighed, "It seems like I just been a slave all the way from down then til now." The longer the ruling planter class maintained a dependent, stationary labor force, the more autonomy, educational advancement, and dreams for blacks faded. Segregation seemed immutable. Only the crisis in agriculture during the Great Depression of the 1930s began to reverse the trend of black disempowerment.[31]

As the 1930s unfolded, the Great Depression plunged Holmes County's economy into dire straits. So acutely had the downturn ravaged the county by the time President Franklin Roosevelt took office in 1933 that one elderly couple remembered "whole families" going "bare-footed all winter because they couldn't get shoes." The Roosevelt administration's recovery efforts reintroduced the presence of the federal government, largely absent in the region since Reconstruction. The New Deal unleashed forces that would drastically alter the Delta's agricultural labor system and disturb the county's race relations. Although Holmes emerged from the Depression and the Second World War with its rural character and racial hierarchy intact, an innovative land-redistribution program challenged the county's traditional caste and economic arrangements.[32]

Several New Deal projects tried to mitigate depressed economic conditions in Holmes County. Foremost among them in the Delta, the Agricultural Adjustment Administration (AAA) implemented acreage-reduction plans to take cotton out of production and stabilize tumbling crop prices. Planters administered the program and received federal subsidies for their cooperation.

Although AAA guidelines required landowners to reallocate federal payments among planters and sharecroppers, landlords often refused to comply. Planters instead kept the money, bought mechanical cotton-pickers and tractors with federal loans, and fired their excess manual labor. Thousands of sharecroppers lost their jobs. Planters evicted them, pushed or burned down their cabins and barns, and plowed them under. Clearly, the landowners benefited, but the AAA had a lasting and harsh impact on Delta blacks. Landless and penniless, farmworkers had few safeguards against the planter class and market forces. The displaced migrated north as nearly 300,000 African Americans fled Mississippi. Over the next twenty years, Holmes County hemorrhaged population from 39,710 in 1940 to just over 27,000 in 1960. As more sharecroppers got put off the plantations, disaffection and problems beset Holmes.[33]

As tenants' troubles multiplied, the federal government responded with projects designed to empower the landless. The New Deal's Resettlement Administration and Farm Security Administration (FSA) floated the radical idea of extending money directly to would-be landowners or relocating tenants in model communities where they received housing and industrial employment. In 1937, the FSA began to oversee rural rehabilitation, farm loans, and subsistence homestead programs. Unlike the AAA, which coddled the big planters and exacerbated the plight of tenants, the FSA promoted land ownership for poor whites and blacks who aspired to own farms but could not obtain credit elsewhere. Loans fastened at 3 percent interest provided farm families with the means to become self-sustaining. By early 1941, 16,000 tenant families nationwide participated and whetted their appetite for land. The FSA was "the most adventurous liberal experiment" of the New Deal, according to one historian of the Delta. In Holmes, the FSA had profound and unintended consequences.[34]

One of the most successful efforts at stimulating black land ownership among former tenants derived from the FSA's purchase and redistribution of several failing plantations in Holmes, including the Marcella, Dawson, Choctaw, and Mileston estates, south of Tchula. In 1940, the FSA partitioned over 9,000 acres of vacant bottomland into 106 farms and leased plots to sharecropping families on long-term, low-interest mortgages that the new landholders paid off annually with profits from crops. Some seventy of the farms went to African Americans, of which thirty-six were originally co-owned and co-operated. Outfitted with a general store, a repair shop, a modern school, a cannery, and a cotton gin, the experimental all-black resettlement community, one of thirteen created during the New Deal, opened. When some

congressmen argued that the cooperative nature of the venture smelled so-
cialist, the FSA sliced the communal plots into individual family spreads.
Parcels typically ranged from forty to eighty acres and included a home with
indoor plumbing, a smokehouse, a henhouse, an orchard, and a barn with
stalls for livestock. Farmsteads also came replete with seed, tools, mules, can-
ning jars, and other supplies. The FSA even provided health care and technical guidance to families for the improvement of their farms and households.
With FSA assistance, the former tenants founded the Mileston Community
Organization with an all-black board of directors to supervise and coordinate with FSA officials. Otherwise consigned to subsisting on someone else's
land, Mileston farmers worked for themselves and increased their equity.
Living with fewer constraints from local whites, a viable African-American
community, locally known as "the project," developed with a modicum of
independence.[35]

White planters did not initially regard the Mileston project as an affront
to their authority. They had dismissed the land acquired by the FSA as de-
void of agricultural potential. Forested and swampy, most of the tract looked
unfit for farming. Deep-seated racial prejudice also convinced whites that
Negroes could not seriously manage their own farms and affairs. One planter,
while deeding his land to the FSA, predicted derisively that he would have
his property back in ten years. Mileston farmers never competed with the big
plantations and lived just above the subsistence level, but even pitiable turf
gave them their first taste of freedom since Reconstruction.[36]

The novel arrangement left a tremendous psychological and economic impression on Mileston blacks. One participant reflected decades later on his
ability to buy land and a home: "This was the best thing that the government
could have done for us. It gave us a home and land to live on and a way to pay
for them and to make a living." Even a little landholding boosted morale and
created insulation from white strictures. "Excitement abounded," exhilarated
the pert child of a black farmer near Tchula.[37]

The enthusiasm spilled over into benefits that helped rectify the county's
grossly deficient educational facilities for African Americans. Between 1870
and 1930, a racially segregated public education system had emerged in Holmes,
but black schools depended on church tithes or the generosity of northern
philanthropy. Because most Mississippi whites regarded black schooling
as a waste of labor—or worse, a Trojan horse for Negro advancement—the
county school board choked black institutions of financial resources. The federal government, in contrast, expanded education for blacks in the Mileston
community. In October 1941, the FSA opened the Mileston Colored School,

a model for Negro primary education in Holmes County. Unlike the county's many single-room schools with their rustic wood stoves and outhouses, Mileston's now modern elementary featured seven rooms, indoor plumbing, and a cafeteria. By 1950, the school extended through the twelfth grade—one of four black high schools in Holmes and the first in the Delta portion of the county.[38]

Another special departure from white planter dominance arose nearby at Providence Cooperative Farm, an experiment in Christian socialism and biracial living. Comprising 2,700 acres of Delta land in the northwest tier of the county, Providence nuzzled the loess bluffs. Arising from an earlier failed cooperative to the west in Bolivar County, Providence Cooperative Farm opened in 1938. The commune was the brainchild of Sherwood Eddy, a Christian evangelist and author, and his assistant, the Reverend Sam Franklin, a Presbyterian missionary. Inspired by Eddy's friend, renowned theologian Reinhold Niebuhr, the two men yearned to help some of the poorest people in the nation. In response to the injurious effects of mechanized farming and plantation consolidation on sharecroppers, Eddy and Franklin purchased land near Tchula and christened their agrarian enterprise "Providence." Later that year their colleague A. Eugene Cox, a native Texan, took over the project along with Dr. David R. Minter, who returned to the farm after serving in World War II and established a free clinic.[39]

By the late 1940s, ten families lived on Providence Cooperative Farm. Cox kept inventory and ran the property. Minter provided health care, assisted by his wife, Lindsey Hail, a nurse from Boston General Hospital. The missionaries risked defamation and death to usher in the kingdom of God and attempt their Christian witness on behalf of the indigent African Americans surrounding Providence. The farm's racial egalitarianism stood as a radically different way for whites and blacks to coexist in the violent cauldron of an intolerant society. Cox and Minter, along with their families and a tiny but intrepid staff, tried to improve the lives of tenants and the dispossessed with basic necessities. Black patients came to the farm on foot, by mule, or by tractor to receive medical treatment and other assistance at Minter's clinic. Providence also offered educational programming, a library, religious services, and a summer work camp for black youth. Cox managed a cooperative store and credit union to boot. For a one-dollar membership fee, anyone could join the co-op and buy affordable farm and home supplies. Provisions could be purchased on credit and repaid at low-interest rates at the end of the harvest. The farm's numerous breaches of local racial etiquette did not go unnoticed.

Many whites branded Cox and Minter as troublemakers and suspected them of preaching racial integration.[40]

Across the long regime of Jim Crow before the *Alexander* case, Holmes County whites preserved strict racial separation and a deficient dual-school system. Black and white students and teachers stayed rigidly segregated in the public schools. Overall, education in the county lagged. Holmes blacks typically completed about six years of education in shabby facilities. The county average attendance hovered around eight years. According to one report, 25 percent of adults had achieved no more than four years of education, and slightly over 40 percent of Negroes were functionally illiterate. Although the state upgraded some county schools through consolidation, teacher salaries in Holmes remained among the lowest in the nation. Throughout the 1940s and early 1950s, the district spent a pittance on black students but approximately fifteen-fold more on white ones. Prior to the 1960s, as historian Neil McMillen noted, Mississippi's effort at black education amounted to a "mere faint gesture."[41]

The first significant overhaul in black education trailed the 1954 *Brown* ruling. To maintain separate schools, county officials frantically built black "attendance centers" in Lexington, Tchula, and Durant. Despite the tardy spate of equalization, segregated, unequal, and inadequate schools continued to perpetuate the inferior status of blacks by diluting their opportunities for education and advancement. Generation upon generation, the ensuing cycle of crippling poverty and ignorance had ensnared many and limited black horizons. Whites cared more about fertilizing their cotton than cultivating black minds. Year by year, little had changed, just as the county's white rulers intended.[42]

Because of their intense and long-standing commitment to the cotton crop and the racial caste system that kept planters and other whites on top and blacks at the bottom of the economic, social, and political ladder, whites refused to brook challenges to their way of life. For most of the white businessmen, professionals, planters, store clerks, mechanics, politicians, and their families, the good life rolled onward. Holmes County, observed a white woman who grew up in Lexington during the 1960s, "was marked by manners, a sense of place, a taste for liquor and religion, and the knack for telling stories." The local sheriff, the leading official in the county, ensured white happiness and control.[43]

Sheriff Walter L. Ellis, a reputedly honest and decent man, kept the peace and made sure Holmes was a safe place to live for whites despite the misery of the Depression. At the height of World War II, however, according to one journalist, "there was trouble brewing in paradise." By 1944, bootlegging flourished off the main highways in spite of the state's alcohol prohibition. Moonshining had become a profitable yet shady business. Nightclubs, filling stations, and honky-tonks with slot machines, craps tables, and illegal liquor pocked the county. Some bars could afford bands from Chicago. In the remote western part of Holmes, liquor agents sometimes disappeared. Only ambitious or foolhardy lawmen interfered with the alcohol trafficking and gambling. On the other side of the county, Durant's "liquor establishments outnumbered churches and businesses," estimated one investigator, and catered to railroad workers, military personnel from Mississippi army bases and airfields, and out-of-town mobsters. Bootleggers hired teenage prostitutes for their juke joints and drove fancy Cadillacs. "And everyone knew about it," wrote one snooping newspaperman, "including the sheriff."[44]

Between the end of World War II and the late 1960s, three notable men and one woman occupied or abused the office of Holmes County sheriff. In 1944, Walter J. Murtagh held the office. Murtagh owned a Ford auto dealership in Pickens before putting on the badge. Well-liked and better known for his laid-back demeanor than for his rigorous law enforcement, Sheriff Murtagh permitted, and was probably complicit in, the racketeering and traffic in alcohol that drenched the county. In 1952, Richard F. Byrd, a former scoutmaster and Chevrolet salesman, won election by promising to rid the county of alcohol, gambling, and cattle rustling. Three and a half years later, legendary *New York Post* columnist Murray Kempton visited Sheriff Byrd in Holmes County to assess his performance. True to his word, Byrd had shut down every gin distillery in his jurisdiction. "A little while later," Kempton reported, "a fresh cluster opened under new management." The sheriff's friend Bluford Taylor owned the resurrected gin mills. In 1956, Andrew P. Smith followed Byrd as sheriff and also nosed around in booze trafficking. Shortly after election, he raided the clubs owned by Tillman Branch, the seedy "juke joint king of the Mississippi Hills" with Chicago mafia ties. Angered by the dragnet, Branch allegedly stormed into Smith's office one day and nearly shot the sheriff. After a tense staring contest, Smith backed down, and Branch reopened shop. When Smith's tenure ended, his wife, Hattie "Hab" Coleman Cade Smith, replaced her husband. Since state law did not allow a sheriff to succeed himself in office, Hattie Smith stood in for her spouse until he won again in 1968. Such chicanery gave the county an aura of corruption for decades.[45]

Rather than cracking down on booze and crime, the sheriffs of Holmes County preferred to line their pockets with bribes and maintain the peace and racial equilibrium. In Holmes, the wages of alcohol and whiteness paid. An important unofficial duty of the sheriff was to tolerate extralegal violence against blacks. Whites periodically killed blacks not because they tried to assert their civil rights or protested racial discrimination but merely because they did something to irritate whites. Law enforcement usually ignored such barbarity, especially if the perpetrators expeditiously disposed of the victim in a creek, river, or ravine and did not carelessly or flagrantly dump the body alongside a road. In the summer of 1946, however, one group of local whites failed to camouflage their crime.

On July 22, 1946, Leon McTatie, a thirty-five-year-old black tenant farmer, died suddenly and savagely. The slight man had worked his entire life on the Dodd plantation, near the little country town of West. Jeff Dodd Sr., the plantation owner, had accused McTatie of stealing a saddle and had him arrested. After three days in jail, Dodd told Sheriff Murtagh that he wanted to drop the charges and post McTatie's bond. "I need him to help me make my cotton crop," Dodd schemed with the sheriff. The ruse succeeded. Murtagh released McTatie into Dodd's custody, and they returned to the plantation. That night, Dodd and five others, including his son, Jeff Dodd Jr., entered McTatie's flimsy shack and dragged him outside as his wife, Henrietta, watched them hurl her husband into a truck and barrel into the Mississippi night. After flogging McTatie to death with a leather strap and a buggy whip, they left his body in a Sunflower County bayou. Days later, two children on the Dodd plantation admitted to taking the saddle. When McTatie's bloated corpse turned up, the murder made national news. The NAACP picketed the White House and appealed to President Harry Truman for federal action. Truman expressed shock but offered only his condolences. Due to a national outpouring of disgust, Sheriff Murtagh investigated the case, arrested Dodd and his accomplices, and charged five of them with manslaughter. Two of the men confessed to lashing McTatie, but they denied killing him. On October 22, 1946, a jury of their white peers acquitted the defendants after ten travestied minutes of deliberations. McTatie's lynching numbered one of ten spanning a four-week carnival of violence during the long and bloody summer of 1946 in the Deep South.[46]

Though white Holmes Countians probably murdered an untold number of African Americans in the obscurity of the rural county's fields, swamps, and forests, only two more racially motivated killings received public scrutiny in the postwar era. Both deaths occurred during a pivotal and tumultuous year in civil rights history. In January 1954, Eddie Noel, a World War II veteran, returned to Holmes after the U.S. Army deemed him unfit to serve and discharged the short, quiet young man. On the evening of January 13, the twenty-eight-year-old Noel and his cousin Percy Cobbins confronted Willie Ramon Dickard, white owner of a juke joint and general store near Ebenezer, about a suspected extramarital affair with Noel's wife, Lu Ethel, who waited tables at the roadhouse. Interracial paramours were not unheard of in Holmes. After all, as one Mississippi journalist pointed out the hypocrisy of the southern way of life, integration "has always been practiced between the sheets and in the bushes." Dickard's attraction, however, proved fatal. He and Noel brawled in the bar until Dickard chucked Noel out the front door. Noel then retrieved a .22-caliber rifle from his vehicle and shot two bullets into the honky-tonk owner's chest. After killing Dickard, eyewitnesses watched Noel walk back into the country store, grab more ammunition, and head to his home, just north of Brozville. On that cold, rainy evening, Eddie Noel loaded his rifle with hollow-point cartridges and waited for whites to revenge Dickard.[47]

Under the cover of night, white vigilantes came for Noel, but the former sharpshooter ambushed them, wounding two and killing one—Richard Byrd's deputy sheriff, John Pat Malone. Now, two white men had died at the Negro marksman's hands. Noel melted into the sleet, and perhaps the largest manhunt in Mississippi history ensued. A 400-man posse, many drunk on moonshine whiskey, tracked Eddie Noel in the frozen wilderness of western Holmes County. Not even bloodhounds from Parchman Farm, the state penitentiary, and aerial surveillance could catch the fugitive in the tangle of sloughs, bayous, deadenings, and oxbows. On the lam, Noel eluded capture by the mob for eighteen days. Once, when they came too close, Noel opened fire with his bolt-action rifle, killed yet another white man, and wounded three more. Only after Noel surrendered to a livestock inspector did the search for the killer end.[48]

Authorities carted Noel to jail in Jackson, but his case took a surprising turn. Returned to Holmes County to answer for his crimes, Noel underwent a psychiatric examination. Doctors declared him mentally unfit to stand trial, and Noel landed in the state sanitarium in Whitfield rather than in the electric chair. "But the story had more twists," reported political journalist Bill Minor. Why the court did not sentence Noel to death remains a mystery. "Neither Hollywood nor a fiction writer could have concocted the many bizarre factors that converged in how a black man could have survived in the dark era of Jim Crow Mississippi after killing three white men," wrote Minor. The truth may have been stranger than fiction. Minor speculated that a judge spared Eddie Noel's life because of his illustrious namesake and white ancestor, Edmund Faver Noel, a Holmes County politician and Mississippi's governor from 1909 to 1913.[49]

White Holmes Countians would not so easily forgive Noel's shooting spree or forget his pernicious example. Whatever fear and loathing generated by the January killings among whites soon dissolved in larger and more audible outrage about the Supreme Court's monumental school desegregation decision in May. During the same month that doctors found Noel legally insane, the Court struck down segregated schools in *Brown v. Board of Education*. From Brookhaven, Mississippi Circuit Court judge Thomas P. Brady mourned the day of the ruling as "Black Monday." Writing in Jackson's *Clarion-Ledger*, Edwin White, a member of the Mississippi legislature from Holmes, damned the Court edict and invoked the Bible to whip up white supremacist fervor. He would not "abide by the Supreme Court Decision" because segregation kept white people white. "It's God's law."[50]

In the Holmes County sheriff's office, Negrophobia and clangorous talk of "Russian communists and stirring up the niggers" filled the halls. Still upset about watching his deputy die as Eddie Noel pumped bullets into him, Sheriff Byrd had had about enough. Byrd was a tough man and fit the stereotypical rural, southern mold of a sheriff. He carried a pearl-handled pistol and wore steel sunglasses, and a thick vein throbbed in his neck when riled up. Byrd stockpiled a cache of weapons in his desk drawer to keep law and order: a second revolver, two blackjacks, and a "sap" or small leather club studded with lead on one end. The sheriff had taken to cruising the county with his deputies, pulling over cars with Negroes, and manhandling the passengers with the blackjack, his cane, or a flashlight. When he spotted his quarry, noted Murray Kempton, Byrd's eyes narrowed "like a basilisk." His victims rarely sought legal redress because no lawyer would accept their cases. In Holmes, the best bet for any blacks who ran afoul of Byrd or local whites was to keep quiet or flee the county.[51]

Unfortunately for twenty-seven-year-old Henry Randle, there was no warning to take cover. On the Fourth of July weekend in 1954, Byrd went on a bender and roamed the county for a victim. Sufficiently limbered up, he surprised Randle and other young black men standing outside a roadside café near Tchula. When he ordered his hapless prey to "get goin'" and scatter for dark sport, the sheriff shot Randle in the leg. The injured man's friends raced him to David Minter's clinic at Providence Cooperative Farm to suture his bullet hole.[52]

At least one white person in Holmes County stood up to the sheriff's predatory mayhem. Someone had to speak on behalf of the good citizens in the county, regardless of their color. The female editor of the *Lexington Advertiser* drove to Tchula the day after the incident and listened to stories of Byrd's carousals of hate. She heard about his evening rampages; she examined victims' scars from his blows; she scanned the shards of flashlight that Byrd busted when he decked a young black teacher at a crossroads gas station. Appalled, she ran an astringent front-page editorial against Sheriff Byrd: "The laws in America are for everyone—rich and poor, strong and weak, white and black.... Byrd has violated every concept of justice, decency, and right. He is not fit to occupy office." She typed her name: Hazel Brannon Smith. For Hazel Smith and her husband, Walter, life had begun to change even before Henry Randle's shooting.[53]

In 1936, Smith came to Holmes from Gadsden, Alabama, to operate the county's faltering weekly newspaper, the *Durant News*. By 1943, the "saucy, pretty woman," remarked one admirer, with a curly head of hair and a laugh like a "debutante" bought the *Lexington Advertiser* and established herself as a muckraking journalist. In 1940s and 1950s Mississippi, Hazel Smith was a peculiar and tenacious woman. Only a brave man could "look Hazel in the eye," commented Murray Kempton. Smith caused a stir in 1946 when she interviewed the widow of Leon McTatie at the trial of his executioners. The judge berated Hazel Smith in chambers and fined her fifty dollars for contempt of court. Frustrated with the liquor racket inebriating Holmes County, she burst into Sheriff Richard Byrd's office another day and demanded to know why the gin joints had reopened on his watch. "Richard," she said, "you're not keeping your promises." After the sheriff squirmed in his chair, Smith went to her typewriter and reprimanded him in her editorial column, "Through Hazel Eyes." For nearly four decades, the crusading editor waged a one-woman war against crooked officials and injustice in Holmes County.[54]

Smith's column generated more buzz in 1954 when she excoriated Richard Byrd after the Randle shooting and called for his resignation. Byrd sued her for $57,500, claiming libel, and a jury awarded him $10,000. Smith appealed the decision, and the state supreme court ruled in her favor. Many Holmes whites wished she would tone down her writing and quit making the county look so bad. Most considered Smith a nuisance or a gadfly, and her mettlesome sins accumulated. Living like "a latter-day Scarlett O'Hara," wrote historian Jim Cobb, she motored around Lexington in a Cadillac convertible and lived in a gorgeous antebellum mansion. As the civil rights movement intensified and her commitment to fairness never waned, Smith's vexing columns pitted her against the white establishment in Holmes County. Her editorials continually deviated from what most southerners expected of a proper white lady. In September 1957, when President Dwight Eisenhower deployed the 101st Airborne to break up the segregationist mob at Little Rock's Central High School, she refused to dislike Ike. When Mississippi governor J. P. Coleman objected to closing public schools as a way to subvert the *Brown* decision and ridiculed massive resistance as legal gibberish, Hazel Smith applauded him. When the white supremacist Citizens' Council formed in the Delta after *Brown* and organized the spoiling fight against school desegregation in Mississippi, she lampooned them as demagogues. Smith's candor won her devotees outside the county, but at home, the plucky editor met vehement opposition.[55]

Hazel Smith wrote the truth and paid for it. Her husband lost his job as county hospital administrator because Citizens' Councilors controlled the board of trustees. The Citizens' Council had briskly established chapters throughout Holmes County in Lexington, Durant, West, Goodman, Pickens, Coxburg, and Tchula. Teenage boys, including the son of Lexington's council president, set off firecrackers and burned a cross on the Smiths' lawn. The next day, she penned a blistering editorial, "A Cross Burns—Symptom of Community Illness." The Citizens' Council also launched an advertising boycott of the *Advertiser* and, in 1958, opened the rival *Holmes County Herald*. Smith now had to fight for her economic survival. Her unswerving determination sustained Smith, but the situation worsened. The stifling conditions in Holmes hung "like a dark cloud," she wrote, and darkened "every facet of public and private life. None speaks freely without being afraid of being misunderstood. Almost every man and woman is afraid to try anything to promote good will . . . between the races."[56]

Smith's editorial stance, she clarified, "is not to favor Negroes any more than anyone else, but to uphold equal protection of the law for all people, including Negroes. Unfortunately, some of my fellow Mississippians do not look upon Negroes as 'people,' although they would be shocked if you told them that." In 1963, the year before she won the Pulitzer Prize for editorial writing, Smith tabulated that nine years of blowback and the loss of her husband's job cost them $200,000.[57]

By the 1960s, despite Hazel Smith's efforts, white supremacists ran Holmes County almost as completely as they had in 1880. Not only did whites own most of the land, but they also dictated local governance and practiced what could only be described as thought control. Smith's forthright columns failed to loosen their clutch on the county, and their reaction to her writing nearly bankrupted the *Advertiser*. Her friend and colleague Hodding Carter, editor of Greenville's *Delta Democrat Times* and the region's best-known apostate, devoted an entire chapter to Hazel Smith in his memoir, *First Person Rural*. Smith's "war on bigots" entangled her with men who had as much "chivalry" as "a cottonmouth moccasin," Carter polemicized. The ruthless but powerful gentry of Holmes County embodied "the worse rather than the better qualities" of southern manhood. Their indefensible anachronism and huffy ancestor worship represented "the arrogant feudalism and reactionary outlook of the old-time, life-and-death masters of vast acres; and the provincial suspicion, the racial and religious bigotry and the predilection for violence which have traditionally been part of the character of hillmen everywhere." By attacking white supremacy, Carter and Smith had insulted Mississippi and sold out the South, according to the Delta's most influential segregationists, the Citizens' Council.[58]

Two months after the *Brown* decision, the segregationist elite in Indianola, about forty miles north of Tchula, had founded Mississippi's prototype Citizens' Council. Derided by Hodding Carter as an uptown Ku Klux Klan, the council organized intimidation of civil rights advocates and coordinated with state officials to save the Jim Crow system. Holmes County formed the state's second chapter of the council and counted Hillery Edwin White and Wilburn Edwin Hooker Sr. as distinguished members. Born in 1907 in Lexington, White studied at Southwestern at Memphis (now Rhodes College) and earned a law degree from the University of Mississippi. He practiced law in Lexington and, after World War II, served two terms in the state legislature. The younger of the pair by six years, Wilburn Hooker descended from old Holmes County stock. Hooker, his father, and his grandfather all graduated from Ole Miss. After college, he returned home to manage the family's immense 4,000-acre plantation and then run for state legislator. In 1955, he joined White in the Mississippi House. Even though they lived next door to each other, Hooker and White were not friends. White was soft-spoken, bookish, and obsessed with interracial sex and eugenics. Hooker was a gregarious insurance salesman and fanatical politician. Despite their dissimilar personalities, opposites attracted. Hooker and White shared an ideology and worked to rid Mississippi of race-mixers and socialists. Both men defended segregation through the Citizens' Council.[59]

For the Holmes County affiliate of the Citizens' Council, exposing and expunging the integrationist do-gooders at Providence Cooperative Farm became a priority. For nearly twenty years, Eugene Cox and David Minter, both white southerners, had dedicated themselves to the sea of poverty-stricken Holmes tenants and sharecroppers surrounding their farm. Local whites had always been puzzled by Cox and Minter's adherence to the social gospel and their minimalist lifestyle. Providence Farm's simplicity and rejection of profit stood in stark relief to the Delta's plantation ethos. Many Holmes blacks regarded Providence Farm as a sanctuary from the inbred racism and farm tenancy that smothered their hopes. For one African-American woman, Fannye Booker, Cox and Minter's liberal project evoked black nostalgia for the Civil War and Reconstruction. "Well it's like when the Yankees came through," she told one interviewer. "They was tired of people living in slavery and they was trying to let you come out on your own," Booker said. She added,

> And they was doing that to show you that you could make profits for yourself. You didn't have to be the underdog all the time. You could work for yourself and save yourself. You were being taught, you see. Naturally so, we just been taught that get what you want. I heard the saying, they say to them, "You keep you out of the grave, I keep you out of jail." And that means cause he'd be looking for you to work for them next week to keep him going. And there was somebody coming along enlightening you—how you could make profit for yourself, how you could come up and do. How you could be somebody one day. You never would be as long as you stay under. There's some white people interested in people. They're not interested in who you are, nothing like that. But they just want everybody to have equal—equal share.[60]

Holmes whites wanted to shellac any fond black memories of abolitionism and Reconstruction. Over the years, David Minter and Gene Cox had roused considerable consternation among segregationists. The local rumor mill hummed busily about blacks and whites swimming together on the farm. After the shooting of Henry Randle, Minter had testified in court that he had stanched the man's gunshot wounds. In the reactionary firestorm following the *Brown* ruling, Holmes County Citizens' Councilors got anxious to weed out the undesirables on Providence Cooperative Farm.[61]

The council's paranoia about black equality at Providence spelled the farm's doom. Cox and Minter's dream of interracial Christian brotherhood could not withstand the whirlwind kicked up by the *Brown* decision. The two men soon fell victim to the Citizens' Council's malign tactics. One councilor, the insurance agent who managed the account for Providence, wiped out the farm's policy. Threats of violence were made against Cox, Minter, and their families. Afraid of planter retaliation, blacks stopped coming to the free clinic, and Dr. Minter's practice shrank by half. The minister at the church in Durant, where the Coxes and Minters worshipped, ignored the crucible of his fellow Presbyterians. White congregants also whispered that they practiced race-mixing at Providence and warned that any pretenses of social equality would get "a lot of good niggers . . . killed."[62]

In September 1955, white supremacists finally spied an opportunity to ferret out the outside agitators and ruin their mad experiment. A teenage white girl waiting for her school bus claimed that four black boys flirted with her. The accusation materialized just weeks after an all-white jury had ignominiously acquitted two white men for the kidnapping, torture, and murder of Emmett Till in Money, Mississippi. Sheriff Byrd rounded up the black adolescents for hard querying. The interrogation had less to do with maidenhood than it did with the activities at nearby Providence Cooperative Farm, where the boys sometimes went to play. News spread like wildfire that their tape-recorded answers exposed the farm's interracial improprieties and other "goings on." The following night, 500 people shoehorned into Tchula's high school auditorium to hear the "confessions." J. P. Love, state representative-elect and head of the Tchula Citizens' Council, officiated at the kangaroo court and informed everybody that he would preserve the "American Way of Life" and racial integrity. Everyone bowed their heads in prayer and then listened to two hours of audiotape. On edge after the Till lynching, one plainly terrified black youth had admitted to making "obscene remarks" to the white girl and clued in investigators about the biracial swimming parties that had occurred at Providence Farm's swimming hole.[63]

A current of anger swirled through the room. Unhinged by the intimation of interracial sex, retiring legislator Edwin White, soon to be replaced by J. P. Love, "fanned the emotions of the crowd with Hitler-like, fascist oration." Minter and Cox sat aghast and denied any wrongdoing. Cox attempted to calm the whitewater by assuring everyone that the farm did not endorse integration or racial intermingling. Unconvinced, the white people of Tchula bayed for his personal opinion on segregation. Cox finally relented. Racial segregation was incompatible with Christianity, he answered them. The last straw turned the rapt audience rancorous. A voice shouted over the madhouse din, "This isn't a Christian meeting!" When a local planter brought a motion to banish Cox and Minter from the county, only two people voted no. One dissenter, a blacksmith, asked for more thought and prayer before they exiled Cox and Minter. The other was the Reverend Marsh Calloway, minister of Durant's Presbyterian church. Calloway praised segregation, but he protested the inquisition as un-American and un-Christian. Afterward, his congregation forced him out of the pulpit for his heresy. On the way out the door, Minter overheard the hothead in front of him menace, "What we need for these S.O.B.s is a couple of grass ropes."[64]

The staff and residents of the Providence Cooperative Farm faced a grim future in Holmes County. Cox and Minter refused to buckle under the pressure and calumny, even while Providence felt more like a purgatory. Death and arson threats escalated. Cox stayed up all night for nearly a week with a rifle across his knees. The sheriff cordoned off the road at the farm's entrance and jotted down the license plate numbers of any visitors. Edwin White, who helped make the original dubious tape, rumbled, "We just can't afford to have them up there teaching what they are teaching—which will lead to violence unless it is stopped." Hodding Carter bolstered Cox and Minter to stick it out. In an open letter, he extolled "their guts" but quivered for the future if they fled the county. "Something else would leave with them, something very precious and American, something for which a great many Holmes County citizens apparently don't give a damn. That something is the Bill of Rights, the guarantees which alone distinguish us from the oppressed people of the totalitarian world."[65]

Nerves shot and spirits deflated, Minter and Cox left the farm. In July 1956, Minter headed to Tucson, Arizona. A month later, Cox departed for Memphis. Providence Cooperative Farm's pilgrimage in interracial harmony and Christian socialism had come to an end. Minter's clinic fossilized. The building sat empty in a field for years until a farmer converted it into a barn. Ever collaborative, Cox and Minter wrote a joint Christmas card in 1956 that read, "Only two members of our church wrote to us. A few others have voiced their faith in us, but above these small voices is the frightening SILENCE. It is frightening—not only for us, but for any Christian and American who may wake up some morning and find himself persecuted because of his beliefs, or for unfounded rumors of 'guilt by association.'"[66]

Long after its undoing, Providence Cooperative Farm continued to have a ripple effect in Holmes County. Some native blacks believed that the farm foreshadowed the organizing that took place during the civil rights movement in Holmes County. One local African-American woman suggested that the biracial alchemy at Providence "was something of a turning point to let them know that all white Americans were not aligned—that there were some friends among the Caucasian race. That could have made ... an imprint to let Afro-Americans know that there were some white Americans who were not against the races all the way through." Other blacks cherished Providence's role as an inclusive oasis where the written rules and informal codes of racial segregation did not seem to apply.[67]

A more sensational uproar over Negro empowerment soon eclipsed the threat of Providence Farm. In the post-*Brown* era, the denouement of the county's quaking racial climate resulted from a convergence of forces: a rich history of organized struggle and the validation of African-American rights by the federal government. When civil rights activity sprouted in Holmes, one offshoot would be the corollary decision of litigants and their lawyers to sue the county school board and make color-blind education the incontrovertible business of the federal courts. Forging Holmes blacks into a sturdy vanguard ready to carry out a school desegregation suit would depend upon harnessing the power of racial reform and the black community's deep resource base.[68]

— CHAPTER TWO —

The Holmes County Movement

❀

No one who puts a hand to the plow and looks back
is fit for service in the kingdom of God.
—Luke 9:62

DURING THE LONG, hot summer of 1964, national civil rights organizations and native blacks defied the repressive culture of segregation in Holmes County and nurtured a new spirit of resistance.
Mike Kenney, one of the 600 white northern college students who volunteered for the Mississippi Freedom Summer Project, arrived in Holmes in
June 1964 from the University of Iowa and rushed headlong into a nascent
struggle for black rights. When the movement did make its first tentative in-
roads, it encountered blinkered opposition from Holmes whites, who recognized, probably more intuitively than rationally, its phenomenal force and
revolutionary potential. More significantly and unusually, civil rights gained
traction among many blacks who imagined positive changes in the county's
racial and educational system despite retaliation from white supremacists.[1]

Mississippi's reputation as the most intransigently segregationist southern state, which did not prevent the movement's maturation, preceded Kenney. Holmes County was "not at all what I pictured Mississippi to be like,"
he wrote. "We are on the fringe of the Delta here." White planters' control
seemed tenuous to Kenney, however, and Holmes's black landholders, he
marveled, "are the backbone of the Movement" and "cower before no man."
Empowered by decades of land ownership and aided by numerous civil rights
groups and the federal government, blacks in Holmes spearheaded one of the
most electrifying local movements in the South. The black liberation struggle
grew quickly and mystified whites by exhibiting several characteristics

atypical of other grassroots civil rights campaigns. "Holmes County was an enigma to white Mississippians," maverick Baptist minister Will Campbell remembered. In spite of segregationist enmity and the county's rural isolation, black-led activism in Holmes animated the Negro community and precipitated the eventual *Alexander* suit.[2]

Reacting to developments outside the county, indigenous leaders pioneered the Holmes movement. In early 1963, an entourage of black farmers from Mileston drove thirty miles north to Greenwood, the marketing hub for cotton in neighboring Leflore County. The trip took the small caravan along back roads, hidden from the prying eyes of whites who might do them physical and economic harm. A spurt of recent protests in Greenwood had turned the Delta city into a destination for the interested visitors from Mileston and a flashpoint for civil rights activism. In the summer of 1962, civil rights groups had opened shop in Greenwood and launched a voter registration campaign. Unwilling to wait any longer for voting rights, organizers from the Congress of Racial Equality (CORE) and the Student Nonviolent Coordinating Committee streamed into Greenwood to make it the focal point of their activities. They coordinated area efforts through an umbrella network called the Council of Federated Organizations (COFO).[3]

Segregationists retaliated swiftly. Aspiring registrants faced retribution at work, police brutality, threats, and violence. Leflore was plantation country, and the majority of blacks there lived in poverty and subsisted on federal welfare. White officials pared down the relief rolls of African Americans who sought the vote. During the late winter and early spring, the registration effort in Greenwood had enticed some national media attention, but the effort had stalled without federal backing.[4]

Despite setbacks, enthusiasm for civil rights percolated throughout the Delta and won followers. Movement operatives spurred forward a vision of black enfranchisement in the predominantly African-American region. Voter registration drives became the primary battleground for black political influence in Mississippi. Civil rights figures Fannie Lou Hamer from Ruleville, Aaron Henry of Clarksdale, and Robert Moses from Harlem in New York City emerged as seminal leaders of the registration campaign in the Delta. Gentle and taciturn, Moses directed SNCC's voting rights projects in Mississippi. Just as SNCC's initiative in Greenwood petered out, Mileston farmers from Holmes County arrived at Moses's headquarters for help. Invited to town in early 1963 by Amzie Moore, a prominent NAACP activist in Bolivar County, they participated in mass meetings and discussed voter registration with SNCC staff. The roster of blacks from Holmes included Ozell Mitchell and his older sister, Alma Mitchell Carnegie; Hartman Turnbow; Ralthus Hayes; and Ben Square. Emboldened by the synergy with Greenwood, the Mileston farmers asked Moses to "bring the movement to Holmes County," and SNCC took the fledgling group under its wing.[5]

As civil rights in Leflore County teetered, the voting rights drive in Holmes ramped up. During the spring of 1963, Samuel Block, a patient and inspirational SNCC field secretary and friend of Amzie Moore, ventured into Holmes County and made contact with blacks about a voter registration effort. Block had grown up with Moore in Cleveland, Mississippi, a town in the heart of the Delta, had attended historically black Mississippi Valley State College, and had joined the movement after the school's administration expelled him for his civil rights participation. He toughed it out beside Bob Moses in Leflore County for about a year before relocating to Holmes. SNCC fieldwork appealed to Sam Block and other young organizers who embedded themselves in Holmes County regardless of the precarious situation.

In the late 1950s and early 1960s, black voting in Holmes, as elsewhere in Mississippi, was almost unheard of. Justice Department records indicated that by April 1963 perhaps twenty blacks had registered to vote in the county. SNCC and the Southern Christian Leadership Conference (SCLC), Dr. Martin Luther King's organization, helped to mobilize the Holmes movement. During the winter of 1962 and the spring of 1963, several Mileston farmers consulted with SNCC field staff in Greenwood. Afterward, local leaders Ralthus Hayes, Reverend Jesse Russell, and Willie James Burns attended a weeklong SCLC training program on the South Carolina Sea Islands. They learned to clear legal hurdles to voting and the "fundamentals of practical politics, democracy, community leadership and organizing, civil rights, and the strategies and tactics of resistance and struggle," wrote one county activist. When they returned, the Mileston activists established citizenship classes and urged their friends, kin, and neighbors to begin a regular Wednesday night meeting. Ozell Mitchell, a deacon at the Sanctified Church in Mileston, convinced the board of elders to open the sanctuary for mass meetings. Some black families agreed to secrete SNCC workers in their homes. Jack and Mattie Louie, who lived on the old Marcella Plantation, invited John Ball, a SNCC organizer from Itta Bena, Mississippi, onto their farm. Ball instructed the Mileston farmers about voter registration. Under his tutelage, blacks prepared for the voter application exam; studied how to pass its requirement to read, write, and interpret any of the 285 sections of the state constitution to the satisfaction of the registrar; and understood that their names would be published in the *Holmes County Herald*.[6]

By early March, local black leaders had stepped forward, and the ground-work had been laid to mount a registration challenge. Weekly voter education classes had taken place in churches and in the homes of Turnbow, the Rus-sells, the Mitchells, and others. The first Mileston mass meeting occurred in stealth. On April 8, about forty people at the Sanctified Church talked and prayed about what to do and decided to register to vote at the courthouse in Lexington. Two dozen had volunteered for the next day, but a night of second-guessing had thinned the ranks to fourteen. The untried but true convened at Ozell and Annie Bell Mitchell's farm a few miles north of Mileston and drove to Lexington. They became known as the "First Fourteen."[7]

For Negroes, trying to pass the voter registration exam at the county courthouse usually amounted to a fool's errand. One of the white circuit clerk's unofficial jobs was to prevent the county's 8,757 eligible black adults from voting. Circuit Clerk Henry B. McClellan was adept at stonewalling registration. He administered a voter test that consisted from six to twenty-one questions, including a section that required interpretation of the U.S. Constitution. If unsatisfied, McClellan had discretionary power to disqualify an applicant. McClellan's arbitrary and unfair treatment of blacks meant they almost never passed.[8]

Few blacks screwed up the courage to register. "Simply asking for the right to vote," wrote former Holmes activist Sue Lorenzi Sojourner, "was an al-most revolutionary step." Even a successful applicant could wait up to thirty days for McClellan's decision. On the infrequent occasions blacks tried to register, they came in individually or with one companion in the hopes of not drawing unwanted attention. Registering to vote stigmatized "a person as a troublemaker," Sojourner continued. African Americans knew that they could be beaten, lose their jobs, or even be killed. For years, Holmes whites had shrouded the voting process in secrecy. Many blacks assumed that they could not even register to vote. Such obfuscation did not quell the desire to vote, however. In early April 1963, the First Fourteen piled into cars and headed to Lexington to "redish," in the local black vernacular—to vote.[9]

Tuesday, April 9, began like most days in Lexington. On the north side of town stood the stately homes of the white middle class and upper crust. One longtime white resident described the manors as "huge and old, with white columns and intricate fences of wrought iron." Along Carrollton Ave-nue, well-appointed brick houses with manicured lawns and shiny auto-mobiles in the driveways showcased the neighborhood's affluence. Holmes County's two-story red brick courthouse anchored the town's dusty square. Beale Street, sloping downhill to the south, marked the border between white and Negro Lexington. White children dared not stray into the "forbidden 'niggertown.'"[10]

The prospective black voters parked away from the courthouse. John Ball led the trickling procession. Wary of alarming whites, they traipsed silently in pairs or threes. An organized march or protest might draw the ire of the Klan. All the potential registrants were over age forty, and Charlie Carnegie, at seventy-eight, was the oldest. Most of the group farmed in the vicinity of Mileston. A black Methodist minister, Nelson C. Trent, a newcomer to Lexington who pastored a church on Highway 17, was the only person not from the Delta. Three women accompanied the men. Standing at the courthouse door, Sheriff Andrew Smith and his deputies awaited them.[11]

Smith, corpulent and imposing in his cowboy hat, glowered at the First Fourteen from the courthouse steps. Thirty members of his posse flanked him. Tipped off by the Justice Department about an impending SNCC voter registration demonstration, Smith had deputized the men earlier that morning. The Federal Bureau of Investigation (FBI) had positioned agents with cameras in storefronts about a block away to monitor the situation. The sheriff and local white authorities did not want any publicity or disturbances of the peace. After Smith inquired about their intentions, Hartman Turnbow spoke for the group: "We's come to redish." Smith demanded, "All right now, who will be first?" According to Turnbow, the sheriff put one hand on his blackjack while the other ominously palmed his revolver. Smith taunted them again, "Who will be first?" Everyone glanced at each other and wobbled with fear; they knew the tough sheriff could settle a dispute with a skull-cracking blow. Turnbow meditated his next move carefully and thought to himself, "These niggers fixin' to run." Anything but craven, he piped up in his strangely high-pitched voice, "Me, I'll be first. Hartman Turnbow."[12]

Hartman Turnbow was not a man to be trifled with. Weighing almost 175 pounds, short and husky, he had blood on his hands. Turnbow had served time at Parchman Farm, the state prison, for killing his first wife near the town square in Lexington. In Turnbow's embellished retelling of the events on April 9, he and Smith looked each other up and down before the sheriff stepped aside and allowed Turnbow into the courthouse. The rest, so to speak, was history, or histrionics, depending on who told the story. Ralthus Hayes offered a more mundane version of the episode. Sheriff Smith never threatened anyone with his blackjack, and Hartman Turnbow never called his bluff. "Fact is we weren't thinking too much about who was first to go in or nothing," Hayes recalled about their lack of strategy. "It didn't matter. No one was worried about being first. The first was just whoever Smith let in first." The FBI's presence kept the situation calm, and Turnbow and John Daniel Wesley, another black farmer, walked into the circuit clerk's office to register. The other twelve applicants milled around under the big tree by the Confederate monument on the courthouse lawn. Hoping to go unnoticed, most black bystanders slinked or scooted by with their heads bowed down.[13]

Turnbow and Wesley could not take the registration exam until Henry McClellan returned from lunch. When he did, the circuit clerk told Turnbow that he would never pass. Over the next few days, each African American stood before McClellan and failed the examination. Even though none of the First Fourteen registered, they felt proud for trying and relieved for surviving the ordeal. Many blacks probably suspected that their troubles had only just begun.[14]

The registration effort made front-page news in the *Holmes County Herald*. The newspaper's headline scrolled, "Quiet Prevails Here after Tense Situation." The paper also published the names, ages, and hometowns of nearly all of the First Fourteen. Their pictures appeared along the bottom of the page to make them fodder for white retaliation. The *Herald* saluted Sheriff Smith and white authorities for maintaining law and order. "The time has come and the citizens of Holmes County have showed their mettle," the story read. "And the people of this peace-loving county have responded with one of the strongest weapons the world has ever known—sound thinking and responsible actions." Hazel Smith's description of events in the *Lexington Advertiser* credited the composure of both whites and blacks.[15]

Black news rarely graced the pages of the *Herald*, except for the police report. After the April registration attempt, the segregationist newspaper declared open season on the unwelcome civil rights presence in the county. The circuit clerk's office provided the newspaper with lists of African Americans who tried to register, and the *Herald* named names to identify the racial agitators. Holmes County's black activists faced considerable repression from the beginning as whites tried to cull their leadership. Nine days after the courthouse incident, Reverend Nelson Trent fled the county after receiving death threats. According to one black leader, T. C. Johnson, Trent's exodus "stopped a lot of the preachers" from aiding the Holmes movement.[16]

For all the First Fourteen, but for Hartman Turnbow specifically, their insubordination directly impacted them. Turnbow's temerity did not inoculate him from white venom. One month after the First Fourteen's foray into voter registration at the courthouse, night riders attacked his small white-frame house. Around 3:00 A.M. on May 8, unhooded Klansmen lobbed three Molotov cocktails into Turnbow's kitchen, the living room, and a bedroom.

The assailants had targeted him not only for his impertinence but also because John Ball had slept in the back bedroom. Turnbow's future second wife, "Sweets," and teenage daughter ran from the flames into the backyard, where two men snuck up on them and riddled the house with gunfire. As bullets hissed through his home, Turnbow rolled out of bed and grabbed his .22 Remington automatic rifle. He squeezed off several rounds and dispersed the intruders. Blacks hailed Turnbow as a hero. "They can't stand when a black man go to throwing fire," one Negro farmer later recalled. "When you stop and return fire, they moves." The Turnbow family somehow escaped unscathed and spent the night putting out the fire. Hazel Brannon Smith denounced the bombing as a "vicious and criminal act." The *Herald*, conversely, downplayed claims about white terrorism and glossed over the incident as "a trumped-up affair."[17]

The next morning, Bob Moses, John Ball, and two other SNCC workers arrived to survey the damage. As Moses snapped pictures of the smoldering debris, Sheriff Andrew Smith and a deputy pulled up. When Moses took Smith's photograph, the sheriff arrested him for "impeding an official investigation of the fire." Many blacks suspected that Smith and his deputies had participated in the previous night's attack. Capping it off, county officials accused Turnbow, Moses, and the other SNCC workers with setting fire to the Turnbow home and remanded them to a local grand jury. John Doar, a sympathetic attorney for the Justice Department's Civil Rights Division, traveled from Washington, D.C., to Holmes and Leflore counties and intervened in the matter. By May 13, he had the defendants released from jail. In October, a Holmes County grand jury cleared Turnbow of the farcical arson charges. Meant to raise the hackles of blacks, the firebombing of the Turnbow home had the reverse effect on the county's Negro population. Turnbow reflected, "This is the thing. They set my house on fire, but that just stirred it up. It just made the fire bigger. Them people that done it, they thought, if they burn me out, it would just squash it. But it made it worser." Turnbow probably exaggerated blacks' inclination to vote when he confidently said, "Everybody then was determined to go redish. They poured out. Didn't care what it cost."[18]

During the spring of 1963, Mississippi was a racially charged powder keg as the civil rights movement infiltrated what historian James Silver called the "closed society." The threat of fungible race relations disturbed white citizens. White southerners realized instinctively that civil rights challenges would mean genuine social and political changes, and they resisted the revolution. The prospect of black political power was sinister to whites. If blacks could register and vote, then whites would soon lose control of county politics.

African Americans would become sheriffs, superintendents of schools, voter registrars, and other public officials. Some considered extreme measures to prevent a black takeover. Violence, some of it random, some of it premeditated, reminded African Americans to keep their heads down.[19]

After the Klan firebombed Turnbow's home, a white police officer gunned down a black man in Lexington. Alfred Brown, a World War II Navy veteran and father of five, had recently been discharged from a veterans' hospital, where he had been treated for mental health problems. On the evening of June 8, Brown died after an altercation with the Lexington police. The *Holmes County Herald* buried the story in its back pages, blandly noting that Brown had pulled a knife on Officer W. R. McNeer, who shot Brown twice in the chest. In the *Lexington Advertiser*'s lead story, Hazel Smith reported the killing differently. Brown had been diagnosed with a psychological disorder. On suspicion of public drunkenness, the white patrolman chased the mentally ill man down the street. When Brown paused in front of a honky-tonk on Yazoo Street, he brandished a pocketknife. The officer fired instantly, and Brown bled to death on the sidewalk. When his family arrived, they could only watch from a distance and scream. Distraught by what seemed an excessive use of force, Smith tore into local lawmen for failing to notice Brown's medical wristband or recognize the veteran's symptoms of psychological distress. In a separate incident, four nights after Brown's shooting, a white sniper assassinated NAACP field secretary Medgar Evers at his home in Jackson. Throughout Mississippi, spasms of violence normally followed any Negro defiance to the Jim Crow system.[20]

Overcoming the danger, the burgeoning movement in Holmes steadily jelled and built on its first activity. Beginning in the spring and summer of 1963, countywide meetings on every third Sunday rotated among different locations in the black communities. By July, the regular mass meeting in Mileston drew anywhere from seventy-five to 200 people. The meetings commenced, like most in the civil rights era, with prayers and featured sermons. For further inspiration, the group sang popular movement anthems and black spirituals. As news of the movement circulated, blacks started to manage their fear and take a stand. "Meet, plan, then take the action" became their organizing refrain, stated Sue Sojourner. Nothing much about that mantra changed over the next few years. To guide their activism, Holmes blacks could rely on a deep pool of leadership.[21]

In many ways Hartman Turnbow already stood as a leader of the Holmes County movement. Born in 1905 in the Mileston community, he was the grandson of a Holmes County slave whose mother bore the child of her master. Turnbow's grandfather became the perverse beneficiary of interracial concubinage. After emancipation, he inherited property south of Tchula along the rim of the Delta from his white father. Hartman Turnbow's grandmother bequeathed her grandson the heirloom. Over the years, he accumulated seventy acres of rich Delta flatland, which predated the FSA project in Mileston by at least two generations. Although better off than most blacks, Turnbow lived in a simple farmhouse.[22]

Hartman Turnbow worked the land for most of his life. Landholding provided Turnbow and other black farmers in the Mileston area with a fiercely independent streak. Unlike some other Negroes, however, his harrowing experiences with racial violence hardened and prepared him to resist Jim Crow. While picking cotton on a white-owned Holmes plantation at the age of sixteen, two white employees bullied him. "They jus' grabbed me by the head and snatched me down," he remembered, "and put [a] pistol to the back of my neck and went to beatin' me with this strap." Turnbow also witnessed a lynching that haunted him for years. As a child, he watched whites roast a black man alive with an acetylene torch. The grisly spectacle, "a turning point" in Turnbow's life, "made a Negro mad," and got him "thinking he'd rather die any way but to be all burnt up with a torch while he's still living." Turnbow would tell that story to rouse blacks to take action despite their trepidation about white segregationist violence. "The Negro ain't gonna stand for all that beating and lynching and bombing," he would pump up black audiences. The more whites assaulted them or clipped their credit at stores and banks, it "just made him angry and more determined to keep on ... and get redished." By the time he reached adulthood, Turnbow packed the fortitude to lead civil rights efforts in his native county.[23]

Turnbow's bearing made him a formidable opponent. In an interview, journalist Howell Raines presented Turnbow as "a man who, as the Southern saying has it, covered all the ground he stood on. But where I had expected a big man, Hartman Turnbow was no more than five and a half feet tall." Other movement people had been awed by his moxie too, but Turnbow's reputation for being disagreeable and a loose cannon made whites and some blacks nervous. To complicate matters, Turnbow sported a handgun. During one civil rights meeting, a heated debate flared about SNCC's policy of nonviolence. Two or three men, including Turnbow, reacted automatically, "This is all academic. We been carrying guns." One, probably Turnbow, announced, "I got mine here." Dismayed, the SNCC staff repeated their organization's adherence to nonviolent tactics, but to no avail. Another man stood up and boomed, "Don't tell me I can't carry my gun. I been carrying this for a year."[24]

The pistols startled the gun-shy SNCC volunteers. Many rural families in Mississippi, regardless of race, owned a shotgun, a rifle, or both, but seldom handguns. Shotguns and rifles kept snakes out of the yard, vermin out of the garden, and foxes out of the chicken coop, put meat on the table, and guarded against trespassers. For black men in Holmes, observed one scholar, "guns were as customary in the homes for protection against burglary and for shooting game for food as the Big Ben clocks were for marking the hours." In the rural South, sparse or idle law enforcement left a void that some African Americans filled with firearms. After Emmett Till's lynching and the tumult of the movement years, more blacks grew concerned about their safety.[25]

The violence perpetrated by whites caused some blacks to shrink from nonviolence. Clad in his farmer's coveralls, muddy boots, and a beaten-up hat, Hartman Turnbow concealed a loaded army-issue pistol in his briefcase. One young Mileston activist, Rosie Head, witnessed the tense SNCC discussion about weapons and noted that many people balked at nonviolence. Tired of the debate, Turnbow fished out his handgun, plunked it on a table, and unapologetically exclaimed, "Let's vote!" Turnbow did "whatever he believed in and whatever he stood for," Rosie Head admired his seeming invincibility, and "he did it wholeheartedly, 100 percent. Wasn't scared of nobody!"[26]

Despite its proponents, self-defense did not commandeer the Holmes movement. Most people never broke with the central tenet of nonviolence and worked for change peacefully. Blacks overwhelmingly abstained from violence and stuck to marches, economic boycotts, voter registration, and federal lawsuits. As a precaution, though, some African Americans kept their weapons loaded and ready, especially in the isolated countryside. T. C. Johnson, a farmer near Lexington, argued that guns added a layer of security and deterred whites from violence. He respected Hartman Turnbow for shooting back at night riders: "He opened fire on them.... When you stop and return fire, they moves; they'd leave you alone then and says you's crazy or need treatment." Howard Taft Bailey, a local NAACP member who housed SNCC workers on his farm and chauffeured black voters to the courthouse, agreed. Bailey would not doff his hat for the sheriff and supposedly told him, "I'm gonna tote a gun and kill you quick as I would a snake" if Andrew Smith or any deputy laid hands on him. By the summer of 1964, blacks in corners of the county stationed patrols of night watchmen along rural roads to protect churches during civil rights meetings.[27]

Blacks knew better than to incite violence, however. A black caught with a firearm during an arrest could serve jail time or worse. One civil rights lawyer working in Holmes County insisted that African Americans craved peace and "couldn't win in a gunfight. The sheriff had more guns, and Holmes wasn't the O. K. Corral." When historian John Dittmer questioned Walter Bruce, a carpenter and activist from Durant, about Holmes blacks and weapons during the movement, Bruce made a critical distinction that many scholars later missed. Bruce could handle himself and a gun, but he did not want to harm anyone. "When we were meeting in Durant or something," he said, "some of them was trigger-happy. They were glad to [bring weapons], but that time I did ask them to bring them out there, you know, but, not to try to kill nobody but just let them know that by them shooting over the building wasn't going to stop us from meeting." Although some blacks stood ready for violence, very few vied openly with practitioners of nonviolence.[28]

At the Democratic National Convention in 1964, Hartman Turnbow and Martin Luther King Jr. exchanged verbal artillery about guns. In late August, King and Turnbow both arrived at the convention in Atlantic City, New Jersey. Turnbow attended as one of sixty-eight newly elected members of the Mississippi Freedom Democratic Party (MFDP or FDP), a voting rights group and political alternative to the state's regular-party segregationists. The MFDP formed after Mississippi's lily-white Democratic delegation, sent by state representative Edwin White, turned blacks away. At the convention, Turnbow and Fannie Lou Hamer publicly testified before a national party committee about trying to vote in Mississippi. During a private meeting among civil rights leaders, Turnbow and King engaged in a war of words about nonviolence. The black farmer chastised the preacher for his commitment to pacifism and civil disobedience: "This nonviolent stuff ain't no good. It'll get ya' killed. If you follow it long enough, it's gon' get *you* killed ... you finish up in a cemetery you just keep a followin' it." King asked him, in turn, what solution Turnbow favored. "It ain't but one thing that is good," he replied. "The Mississippi white man ... got to be met with ... whatever he pose with. If he pose with a smile, meet him with a smile, and if he pose with a gun, meet him with a gun."[29]

Though Turnbow remained an incandescent force, other African Americans in the county also demonstrated significant leadership in the Holmes movement. Ralthus Hayes, for example, attended the SCLC training course in South Carolina, taught citizenship and adult literacy classes in Mileston, and participated in the First Fourteen's voter registration attempt. His pensive nature stood in sharp relief to Turnbow's fiery persona. Hayes "had to think things out completely before he would do anything," recalled one Holmes activist, "but he was always willing to do what he could." Born in 1916, Hayes was polite and low-key. For years, he and his father sharecropped in the hills and Delta. After working as a hired hand on white-owned plantations, Hayes secured property through the Farm Security Administration program and took the giant leap from sharecropper to landowner. In 1941, he applied for a federal loan to buy fifty-four acres and bankroll start-up costs for a home, mules, and farm tools. His toil in the earth earned Hayes enough income to acquire sixty-four additional acres, which yielded other benefits.[30]

Ralthus Hayes's status as a man of property produced more than economic stability. The FSA program incubated a spirit of independence that shielded blacks in the Mileston-Tchula area from vengeful tactics by whites and sowed a seedbed of civil rights agitation. In 1951, nearly twelve years before the First Fourteen had come together, Hayes had tried unsuccessfully to register. Intrigued by the special quality of Hayes and other Negro farmers, SNCC transplanted its voter registration campaign from Greenwood to Holmes County in the spring of 1963. The Mileston community's solidarity and volition to endure bank foreclosures and physical intimidation from local whites inspired many of the county's other blacks. John Ball, who lived and worked in Holmes, described the difference between the movements in Greenwood and Holmes as "the difference between night and day." When African Americans in Holmes committed to a project, they followed through with it. In fact, wrote sociologist Charles Payne, "*More* people would show up for a march than had promised to."[31]

John Daniel Wesley, the most formally educated of the First Fourteen, was also one of the youngest leaders in the Holmes movement. Even though hundreds of men had left the county for jobs in the North, he stayed behind and tilled his land. Born in 1926, in Lincoln County, Mississippi, Wesley farmed with his father on a cousin's property and grew cotton, corn, peas, and other crops. With his family, Dan Wesley moved to Holmes and attended Mileston's black high school. In March 1945, he answered his army draft notice and served in occupied Germany. When Wesley came home in October 1946, he inherited land from his father.[32]

In the spring of 1963, Wesley heard talk of black voter registration at his Masonic lodge and decided to act. Wesley's version of the First Fourteen's coming-out on the courthouse lawn differed from Hartman Turnbow's David-versus-Goliath imagery. When the group arrived in Lexington, the direct and unpretentious Wesley recalled, Sheriff Smith discouraged them from making a public demonstration and ushered them to wait by a magnolia tree. Turnbow strode away from the makeshift holding area toward Smith to parley, but Wesley was not close enough to eavesdrop. Afterward, the sheriff addressed the voting initiates, asked who would be first to register, and shrugged, "Well, it doesn't make no difference." He gestured to Wesley to go inside. Black onlookers, too frightened to participate, peered around corners. In the beginning, very few African Americans had the gumption to exercise their rights. Wesley sensed the gravity of the situation on the courthouse lawn but stayed calm. He trusted the watchful Justice Department officials to keep the peace, and even Sheriff Smith "really acted pretty good." Wesley acknowledged the First Fourteen's amateurish preparation that day. "We moved too fast, without getting all the full details," he mulled over their neophyte performance. "But then I see now . . . that we didn't start soon enough."[33]

Another foot soldier in the Holmes movement, Shadrach "Crook" Davis, long refused to knuckle under to whites and provided muscle and backup anytime other civil rights leaders and workers called upon him. Davis was a big, powerful, dark-skinned man. In 1943, at about age twenty-one, he inherited 300 acres south of Tchula from his father and aunt and grew cotton. By then, the Delta started to empty as blacks headed out of state for cities and jobs, but Davis never wanted to leave. Besides, after his two brothers, Meshach and Abednego, drifted north to Detroit, somebody had to stay on the farm with their aging father and mother. After the war, the outmigration of blacks continued as the plantations introduced more farm machinery, particularly mechanical cotton pickers. Agricultural booms and busts, though, could not shake Crook Davis loose from his land. He shared a simple home with his schoolteacher wife, Sarah, and their children.[34]

In 1963, Shadrach Davis posted bond for Bob Moses's release after the sheriff arrested him for interfering with the arson investigation at Hartman Turnbow's home. Davis liked the younger, contemplative man from Harlem. The SNCC director's laissez-faire style of community organizing and nonhierarchical creed of participatory democracy suited local people. "Bob Moses was cool. He just come to meetings and sits back quiet and wouldn't say much, just let the people talk." In the early days, most blacks did not support the movement because they feared retaliation. "There wasn't too many that would go in there," Davis remembered. "You know, all them niggers around there were saying, 'You better not go in there, better not fool with that mess,' acting scared and the fool." Crook Davis embraced the civil rights movement from its advent in Holmes. He and many other black farmers in the county rejected the confines of suppression and intimidation and made the local push for civil rights possible.[35]

Grassroots organizations also tapped the wellspring of religious faith of Holmes blacks to galvanize them. Civil rights meetings began and ended with songs. Singing spirituals and prayers sustained, inculcated, and cradled everyone in the Holmes County movement. Music hoisted people's hearts during difficult times and incarnated them in freedom. Through Christianity, Holmes blacks found spiritual solace from a racially bellicose world. Inside God's house, they felt utterly free; outside, religion undergirded them for the struggle against Jim Crow's wicked ways.[36]

Ironically, "the biggest obstacle to the Holmes County Movement," remarked one scholar, "was the character of the rural church." Although organized religion acted as a critical refuge and reservoir of leadership for the national movement, the Negro church in Holmes was "a belated, reluctant convert" to the movement. Many clergy ministered only part time to Holmes's nearly one hundred black churches. Preachers often worked day jobs for white landowners and businessmen and depended on the white elite for their livelihood. Some congregations held worship services only on alternate Sundays or monthly. Other men of the cloth pastored to plantation tenants, who could be easily cowed by white overlords. "Some preachers were in good standing with the white community," remembered Walter Bruce, "and didn't want to be seen as disreputable rabble-rousers. We often forget simply how scared many people were." Most black ministers abjured civil rights activity, but not Reverend J. J. Russell. Movement people affectionately called him "the second Martin Luther King."[37]

Born in 1916, Jesse James Russell grew up in Holmes County. He and his wife, Erma, brought the desire for change out of the theological and into the temporal. Counted among the First Fourteen, they opened their home for movement gatherings. Russell paid a steep price to practice what he preached. Whites plagued him, and in 1964, they set a match to Bell Chapel, one of his churches. Other congregations that welcomed him had their windows shot out. When fellow parsons and deacons refused to let him deliver sermons in their sanctuaries, his house in Mileston became his pulpit. For safety, Russell drove at night with the lights off, and despite the threats, he never carried a gun. Reverend Russell believed his personal Bible would protect him from harm. Slowly, other black preachers came into the fold, but they too became casualties of vandalism and reprisals. North of Durant, Walter Bruce and other activists met at a small church near the community of Second Pilgrim Rest. Night riders strafed and firebombed the church to disrupt meetings.[38]

Russell and his flock withstood the violence and intimidation, and the reverend planned his moves carefully. In April 1963, when the First Fourteen decided to register at the courthouse, Russell described their thinking: "We drilled our people before we came up to Lexington. Y'see, Holmes County was a bull with long horns goin' in the movement. The way they was keeping us from going to the Courthouse to redishter. Most folks was afraid. We . . . dehorned the bull. . . . After you dehorned him, he can't do nothing." More people joined the movement. Russell glorified the coming of the movement as akin to the Second Coming of Christ. "The guards of Christ went to the government after Christ was resurrected and rose," he enthused to one compatriot. "When they told the government what had happened, the governors decided to explain it to all the people by deceit. They said some of the disciples had come and released Christ and taken him. He hadn't risen alone." He compared the biblical story to the way Sheriff Smith and the Citizens' Council had borne false witness against Hartman Turnbow at his arson trial. The Holmes movement had been baptized under fire. Danger and death excommunicated other black churchmen from the struggle. Outbreaks of violence kept many blacks from exercising their citizenship rights.[39]

Years earlier, in neighboring Humphreys County, Reverend George Washington Lee had started a NAACP chapter and organized an enfranchisement drive after the *Brown* decision. He became the first registered Negro voter in the county. In May 1955, two Citizens' Council members chased his car through Belzoni and blew off half his face with a shotgun. Lee died in a hospital. Neither gunman ever stood trial. The sheriff ruled his death the result of an argument with another black man over a woman. "That kept the other pastors back because they was organizing then and had been holding meetings, talking about registering," J. J. Russell recalled plaintively. "After Lee got killed, things went under a bit and there weren't so many meetings" in Holmes. When the Holmes movement crystallized eight years later, Mileston farmers approached Russell. "They said, 'Come with us, Reverend. We need a pastor with us.' And I said, 'Why don't you get some of those bigger men to go on up with you?' But I knew they probably wouldn't . . . and so I went."[40]

From the beginning, the Holmes County movement also involved women. Even though men usually dominated leadership roles, Alma Mitchell Carnegie and Bernice Montgomery were key exceptions. In April 1963, Carnegie was sixty-six years old, spirited, and a seasoned activist. She and her husband, Charlie, were the oldest of the First Fourteen. Her younger brother, Ozell, went to the courthouse too. Dating back to the 1920s, Alma Carnegie had acquired a reputation as a matron of the community. She stashed copies of the *Chicago Defender*, the militant black newspaper, in her home and treasured the provocative tabloid almost as much as her Bible. During the Great Depression, Carnegie wrote President Herbert Hoover letters about her plantation's poverty and requested humanitarian aid. She also hid tenant workers' organizers who tried to unionize Delta sharecroppers. In the 1940s and

1950s, Carnegie crisscrossed the state to attend an underground network of NAACP meetings and learned about the civil rights movement. When SNCC workers came to Holmes in the 1960s, she sheltered and cooked for them. During the April voter registration drive, she kept morale high.[41]

Like preachers, black teachers could lose their jobs and shied away from the movement. Educated at Rust College in Holly Springs, Mississippi, Bernice Patton Montgomery taught biology and math at the all-black Mount Olive Elementary and High School in eastern Holmes County. One of the early activists from that part of the country, and one of the rare but revered schoolteachers in the voting campaign, she lived and worked in the hamlet of Sunny Mount, to the northeast of Lexington. Her resolute leadership came as no surprise to anyone who knew Bernice or her brash husband, Eugene, and his family. The Montgomerys bowed to no one. Four brothers presided over the stiff-necked clan, which collectively owned hundreds of acres in the hill country. As in the Delta, the first African Americans to organize in the hills held land and, therefore, exercised considerable freedom from whites.[42]

On the second day of the First Fourteen's demonstration at the courthouse, Eugene Montgomery observed them on the lawn from a distance. "I was standing on the other side of the square watching them crazy folks," he recollected. "Word got around quick and everybody was talking about it. Yes, I thought they were fools," the farmer continued. "I didn't think nothing was wrong. I was doing fine myself. I had money and could get what I wanted." The example of the First Fourteen, however, moved blacks across the county to action and lifted the suffocating lid on racial reform. Something awakened within Eugene and Bernice Montgomery too. They got hooked on mass meetings in Mileston and spread the movement gospel to the eastern side of Holmes County. "We were constantly going from community to community, from church to church, asking people to allow us to come into your church," Bernice Montgomery remembered. The Montgomerys set up workshops on civic education and voting rights, and their farm doubled as a safe house for civil rights workers.[43]

During the 1963 Christmas holiday, Eugene and Bernice Montgomery tried to register to vote at the courthouse. They received a baleful reception from Henry McClellan. The clerk told Eugene to pay the poll tax and goaded him to count the number of bubbles in a bar of soap. He refused. McClellan next squared off with Bernice. When she claimed her right to vote, he said that since "she had the reputation of being a 'smart nigger,'" she would have to repeat the entire U.S. Constitution. Eternally optimistic, she vowed to return and studied for the registration exam each Saturday for months. In late January 1965, Bernice Montgomery came back, handed McClellan a copy of the Constitution, and, according to family lore, quoted any section of it flawlessly. White county officials allegedly gawked at her recital, and Henry McClellan approved her to vote. Montgomery's dubious audition held at least one kernel of truth: she became one of the first black women to register to vote in Holmes County.[44]

Hartman Turnbow, Ralthus Hayes, John Daniel Wesley, Shadrach Davis, J. J. Russell, Alma Carnegie, and Bernice Montgomery were only seven of more than a score of local activists—including Ozell and Annie Bell Mitchell, Joe Smith, Walter Bruce, Edith Quinn, Robert Head, Jodie "Preacher" Saffold, Sam and Laura Redmond, Daisy Montgomery Lewis, Mary Hightower, Howard Taft Bailey, and Rosebud and Norman Clark—who ignited the county's civil rights movement. Though they had never voted or held public office, many of them had earlier gained significant political preparation in local black organizations. The skills that they developed in church groups, fraternal lodges, and Masonic halls served as valuable stepping-stones toward civil rights activism. In addition, they shared important traits common to alumni of the Holmes movement: land and home ownership. The tradition of black landholding produced a foundation of resourcefulness and self-sufficiency after several families bought farms. Because they owned their homes, they could not be evicted by a white landlord for their effrontery.

Alma Mitchell Carnegie, Ralthus Hayes, and Dan Wesley could also draw on their respective adventures and experiences outside the repressive atmosphere of Holmes County. Whether overseas in war, attending NAACP meetings strewn across the state, or traveling to SCLC training sessions in South Carolina, they had learned about organizing as a guarantor of basic rights. In particular, as members of civil rights groups or the military, they soaked up possibilities for social change and racial justice that seemed previously unimaginable in Holmes. When Freedom Summer gave momentum to the civil rights struggle in their county, they were prepared.

In late 1963, planning began for Freedom Summer, or the Mississippi Freedom Summer Project, when SNCC and CORE drafted several hundred mostly white college students to work in Mississippi during the summer of 1964. They would register and educate black voters, establish a biracial political party (the Mississippi Freedom Democratic Party), and teach Negro history and civil rights in newly conceived Freedom Schools. Training students for Freedom Summer started in June 1964 with an orientation program at Miami University in Oxford, Ohio. SNCC seminars drilled summer volunteers in nonviolent tactics and primed them for the cunning realities of life in segregated Mississippi. Students from across the country answered SNCC's invitation, including one committed activist from the San Francisco Bay Area.[45]

Mario Savio, the future leader of Berkeley's Free Speech Movement, came to Oxford before departing for Holmes County and just days after the abduction of three Freedom Summer workers—Michael Schwerner, James Chaney, and Andrew Goodman. Their bodies would be recovered later that summer from an earthen dam outside Philadelphia, Mississippi. Born in Queens, New York City, in 1942, Savio grew up in an Italian Catholic family. As an altar boy, he discerned a vocation in the priesthood. After elementary school, Savio instead attended the prestigious Martin Van Buren High School, graduated at the head of his class, and glided through Manhattan and Queens Colleges. He spent the summer of 1963 working at a Catholic mission in Mexico, where he lived among the downtrodden and developed a heightened social conscience. Later that summer, Savio followed his parents to Los Angeles and transferred to the University of California, Berkeley. During his first semester, he felt a strong linkage to social justice and the civil rights movement and joined the University Friends of SNCC, a campus affiliate that raised funds for its parent group. Savio embraced even more of SNCC's cause when activists visited Berkeley and described the Mississippi situation. "Well, I mean, honest to God," he beamed, "this was like the sort of outlying church receiving some St. Paul's assistant or something. . . . There was . . . a tremendous cachet and glamour attached to the SNCC worker." Motivated by his religious convictions and his affinity for the oppressed, Savio applied for the Mississippi Freedom Summer Project.[46]

After finishing orientation in Oxford, Savio headed for the South. McComb, in southwest Mississippi, was his original destination, but the severity of Klan violence in that part of the state diverted Savio to Holmes County. The influx of summer volunteers elicited hostility from the county's white supremacists. Savio and nearly a dozen raw recruits had only just arrived in the Mileston area when the bomb threats started. They spent their first sleepless night in the pangs of "veritable paranoia. We crawled about on hands and knees fearing to be caught before a window. We kept watch all night." The vigil passed without incident, but Savio and other activists stayed cooped up in an abandoned farmhouse for several days.[47]

The white students soon understood that their lives depended on the Negro farmers who looked after them. Armed and vigilant, a local black watch group stood guard at night. Savio adhered to the principles of nonviolence, but he appreciated that his black hosts "are not as non-violent as we." He speculated that the community's self-defense tactics held night riders at bay and foiled terrorism. "If it were not very well known that the Negro farmers are not non-violent," he acknowledged, "I seriously doubt that a non-violent student movement would be possible in Mississippi." With blacks and whites both "armed to the teeth . . . Holmes County—as comparatively safe as it may appear—is the peaceful extension of a dangerously live volcano."[48]

In spite of the volatility, Mario Savio relished his time in Holmes. The courage of the African Americans in the county mesmerized, intrigued, and liberated him. In one enthralling letter he noted, "It's wonderful . . . to be part of such a change for good that's sweeping across our country. . . . The history of the world is pivoting on the internal changes that are going on today in America—and we are in part the agent of that change. A breath of freedom."[49]

Concluding that Mississippi society bred racism that debilitated blacks as well as whites in their youth, Savio hoped to eradicate the color prejudice that warped children's minds. Although he searched for opportunities to educate "the poor little white children whose hearts are not yet filled with fear and hate," he devoted his energy to uplifting Holmes's blacks. Savio intended his work at the local Freedom School to empower "black children who've not yet learned to cringe and shuffle and bend their heads and say 'yasir' and 'nosir' to every white they see." After overcoming his stage fright, and perhaps some latent white guilt, Savio had to grapple with racial customs that kept the benighted local black population crouched in subservience. He felt ashamed about adult blacks calling him "sir" and abhorred the poverty of the county's residents. Upset, he wrote, "Only in Mexico have I seen it as bad. Rarely in Mexico did I see it worse." Despite the hardships, Savio helped blacks qualify to vote and coaxed them to register.[50]

Voter registration in Holmes was a quintessential grassroots effort, and progress unfolded gradually and sometimes violently. Even with the assistance of the FDP and SNCC, Savio and other Freedom Summer volunteers had to move about the county cautiously because they knew that local whites would forcibly resist their campaign to organize Negroes. The civil rights workers could depend on the bastion of black farmers in the Mileston community, but other African Americans hesitated to assist with gaining the vote.

Landless farm workers, for example, suffered from a near-absolute reliance on white landlords for their employment. Charles Payne described their vulnerability: "One man controlled your work, told you what to plant and where, where to shop for groceries and what you could spend on them, where to take your children if they were ill, where you lived, and, of course, what if anything your labor had been worth during the year." If sharecroppers or tenants became identified as supporters of the civil rights movement, white bosses would retaliate against the black peasantry by attacking them, firing them, or forcing them off their land. As oppressed as blacks on the plantations were, the small towns had their share of challenges too. Black townspeople "sometimes turn us away before we can even get in the door," Savio complained. "They have been warned by the whites not even to speak to the 'northern agitators.'" Teachers and principals felt constrained as well because they depended on the white school superintendent and board of education for their jobs. Most black ministers, who exerted considerable influence over their congregations, also vacillated in aiding voter registration.[51]

Often without the assistance of the black clergy or apolitical schoolteachers, Savio and his coworkers blanketed the county door-to-door and farm-to-farm to introduce themselves to black housewives, woodcutters, sharecroppers, and other laborers. Trying to rekindle the spirit of the earlier April 1963 voting episode at the courthouse, they encouraged local Negroes to assert their latent political power by registering to vote. As Savio found out, however, mobilizing blacks to vote often proved futile. "I have had the agonizing experience," he commented, "of talking with a family for fully an hour without convincing them they should go down to the court house." Sue Lorenzi Sojourner, another white Summer Project worker, attended a meeting in the upstairs of a country store in Tchula. Twelve people sat and listened while the head of the local NAACP chapter underscored their citizenship rights and tried to prompt questions. When asked why so few had come, the group slouched in their chairs from fatigue after a long day of backbreaking work. Several spoke up, "They's afraid. No one will come." The assembly ended with singing "We Shall Overcome," but it did not feel inspired. Sojourner recalled, "The gathering was so pitiful it hurt. In the North, I'd sung that song stridently, energetically, even offhandedly. In Holmes, where the song was so clearly needed, it felt bleak." White supremacists compounded their disillusionment by disrupting the operation. In Tchula, the deputy sheriff and Citizens' Council antagonized blacks by driving through their neighborhoods and blaring threats about "uppity Negroes" from loudspeakers on trucks.[52]

Initially discouraged, Savio and other Freedom Summer recruits sought ways to stimulate interest in voter registration. Simply raising the issue of the vote presented a special set of problems. "After all," Savio racked his brain, "what can you tell these poor people when they say they may (or *will*) lose their jobs or have their welfare cut off if they agree to do what you ask?" Blacks, furthermore, hardly ever passed the literacy test at the circuit clerk's office. Even if they had the audacity to go, they would probably be turned away. The only upshot would be for SNCC to report cases of aborting black voter registration to the federal government for a possible voting-rights lawsuit. Such a remote prospect did little to boost morale or improve blacks' commitment to voting. Savio and SNCC had the difficult chore of motivating African Americans to jeopardize "their lives and livelihoods because of a suit the [Justice Department] *may bring* if enough people register."[53]

When Holmes blacks did gamble everything and tried to vote anyway, Savio's heart rejoiced. During his first few weeks in the county, his confidence grew as Freedom Summer made "some progress, however slow." Each person who agreed to register deepened Savio's missionary impulse, and he immersed himself in the struggle: "I'm ever more feeling this as a personal fight." The moral centerpiece of Savio's summer occurred when he escorted an old black farmer to vote at the courthouse. The white registrar sneered at the elderly Negro: "What do you want, boy?" The man responded, "I want to redish." The circuit clerk mocked his speech, "What's redish? What are you talking about, boy? . . . We don't got no redish around here." The two went back and forth until the farmer got the registration test. "He never gave up," Savio swelled with pride. The registrar "made him eat shit for it. . . . Here's somebody, who because of something I had done, was maybe risking his [life and his] family['s], facing that kind of humiliation," Savio wrote a friend. "He must have been afraid. I know I was afraid. Yet he stood his ground." After his summer in Mississippi, Savio returned to Berkeley for the fall term, but he came back a battle-tested activist.[54]

For the MFDP and SNCC workers who stayed in Holmes after the college students departed, the community center in Mileston proved essential to the freedom struggle's long-term success. Carpentered with volunteer labor and donations from California, the wood-framed center opened in October 1964 and included a kitchen, bathroom, and meeting hall. The Holmes County Community Center was soon the envy of movements in the surrounding counties. Richard Jewett, a CORE activist in Madison County, noted the center's "impressive physical structure" and that "inside one forgets that one is in rural Mississippi: it's that good." Prior to the center's construction, mass meetings and citizenship classes bounced between various locations, from empty buildings to homes to churches to the FDP office in Lexington. Upon completion, the center became a movement stronghold.[55]

The center hosted the Mileston and community-wide meetings as well as ad hoc committees, rallies, workshops, and discussions about whether and how to desegregate the public schools. Mass meetings provided a space for local blacks to come together for mutual support and sanctity. Resembling a church service, each Wednesday night assembly included hymns, prayers, scripture readings, and exhortations to register to vote. A local leader often gave an inspirational talk. Hartman Turnbow spellbound participants with his biblical allusions and fire-and-brimstone oratory. Freedom songs also fortified the group and displayed their growing strength. "Go Tell It on the Mountain," "Ain't Gonna Let Nobody Turn Me 'Round," and "We Shall Not Be Moved" were standbys. Another mainstay, "We Shall Overcome," often closed meetings. With their arms crossed and hands clasped, everyone sang with hope and faith. Movement people felt consecrated that "God is on our side," as their favorite verse from "We Shall Overcome" reinvigorated them. They stood in good company with Moses, the other Hebrew prophets, Jesus of Nazareth, and the Almighty.[56]

Other hallmarks of life at the community center featured social events and educational opportunities for adults and children. Sponsored activities included health care, literacy courses, clothing drives, economic cooperatives, welfare aid, and a Head Start program, one of the first in the United States. Blacks relied on the center in emergencies and for legal assistance as well. The center's library stocked its shelves with 10,000 books. Children attended an innovative kindergarten class. Adults enjoyed the Free Southern Theatre, an integrated troupe of actors who performed plays. The center also served as a hangout for activists canvassing the county about school desegregation and voter registration.[57]

Throughout 1964, the county's black citizens continued to appear before the registrars; however, as was true in other Mississippi communities, black voter registration remained low. SNCC and COFO volunteers worked fervently to increase voter participation among blacks in Holmes, but whites curtailed their handiwork. Between April 1963 and December 1964, fewer than five African Americans qualified to vote. Perhaps only 20 of 8,757 eligible black voters had been registered. Comparable figures for the white population highlighted the glaring extent of corruption and discrimination in the voter process. The voter rolls included 4,800 whites.[58]

Blacks still complained that the circuit clerk administered the literacy test unfairly to checkmate them at the courthouse. Another county official proved to be a greater obstacle to registration. Sheriff Andrew Smith did not intend to let any Negroes vote in Holmes County. Traditionally, white reprisals, both personal and pecuniary, convinced most blacks not to vote. When blacks began to push for change and sought the franchise, planters sometimes kicked them off their land. Hostile banks could turn them down for loans and mortgages. Though poverty and fear immobilized many black citizens, some managed to pay their poll taxes. If they did, the sheriff had a simple solution: he would not accept payments from African Americans on their poll taxes. Hazel Brannon Smith once overheard him pledge that "no nigger will ever . . . vote as long as I am sheriff."[59]

Smith made good on his oath, but the sheriff's notoriety finally drew the attention of the Justice Department. A 1963 federal investigation revealed that Sheriff Smith repeatedly violated black voting rights, and government lawyers brought a suit against him. In January 1964, Smith admitted in federal court that he had refused to let blacks pay their prerequisite poll taxes for almost eight years. The only African Americans to furnish their taxes successfully had found a loophole and had mailed the money. When denying blacks the chance to pay the tax failed to quash their interest, Smith had jailed and harassed them. Activist Rosie Head's account of trying to vote in 1964 vividly illustrated the sheriff's intimidation tactics. Smith and his deputies had escorted Head and four other black women into the courthouse with growling police canines. Once inside, Smith locked Rosie Head in a dark closet for four hours with her registration paperwork. Each time she turned the doorknob, a dog snarled at her. The sheriff eventually released her to undergo Henry McClellan's customary interrogation. "I know you know better," McClellan took a turn barking at Head. The clerk knew her grandparents. "I've known your people for years," McClellan fumed. "What are you doing out here anyway?" She began to explain, but he interrupted: "This ain't for black folk." No one ever notified the women whether they passed. Only when federal examiners later arrived to supervise elections at the Lexington post office did blacks in Holmes County start to vote uniformly and en masse.[60]

During the summer of 1965, while blacks campaigned to register voters in Holmes, seismic events occurred in Washington, D.C., that would affect the civil rights movement in the county. On Capitol Hill, opening the ballot booth to blacks had become a priority. President Lyndon B. Johnson addressed the need for voting rights legislation on national television and impelled Congress to assist disfranchised blacks. His bill would automatically suspend literacy tests in states where less than 50 percent of the potential electorate had voted in the last presidential election. The proposed law, therefore, would apply to Mississippi, Alabama, Georgia, Louisiana, South Carolina, and Virginia. In August, the Voting Rights Act flew through Congress with bipartisan support.[61]

While following the gradual evolution of the voting rights measure in Washington, the Holmes County movement magnified its campaign to register voters. The barriers that blacks faced at the ballot box began to erode with federal enforcement of the Civil Rights Act of 1964 and the Voting Rights Act of 1965. With a ban on tests to restrict the franchise and the promise of federal supervisors, blacks registered to vote in droves. In 1964, only a handful of African Americans had qualified to vote. In November 1965, the Justice Department assigned a registrar to Holmes County. Over a four-month period, 2,000 blacks signed the voter rolls. By 1967, the number leaped to over 6,300, or nearly 70 percent of eligible African-American voters. Just as blacks began to grasp their newfound political power, whites noticed the shifting political sand beneath them. "Negroes Dominate in County Voting," gulped a June 1966 headline in the *Holmes County Herald*. Heavy black turnout and banner gains catapulted the Holmes movement into a heady phase of electoral politics.[62]

The Holmes movement benefited from a coalition of grassroots leaders and monthly meetings that glued activists together throughout the county. The FDP chapter held regular countywide meetings and stoked black political participation. After Freedom Summer, FDP acted as the principal organizing force in the Holmes movement, and its executive committee, comprising the wealthier members of the black community, outlined its agenda. MFDP provided Negroes with direction and a scaffold to mobilize the black vote. The FDP's infrastructure endowed a strong sense of cohesion, engendered solidarity, and inspired blacks to further bravery. One SNCC worker, Ed Brown, remarked that "people weren't afraid" in Holmes because "people got reinforcement from each other as a result of having been part of an organizational effort . . . and didn't feel that they were kind of out there taking all the risks by themselves." The Holmes movement enjoyed incremental gains as blacks adopted tactics to expose chinks in the county's white supremacist armor. "It was a situation," Brown ascertained, "where as opposed to placing the emphasis on confrontational politics we had placed the emphasis on organizing so that in the instances where there were confrontations there was sufficient organizational strength behind it to make the whites think, you know, twice before doing anything." With enough confidence to spare, the Holmes movement pursued other objectives.[63]

In the fall of 1967, the movement coordinated a broad-based economic boycott in Lexington. Edgar Love, a local FDP organizer who had been ejected from a plantation for voting, waged a selective buying campaign that tweaked downtown businesses. His lobbying group, the Negro Consumers of Lexington, composed an open letter to white merchants in the *Lexington Advertiser* that requested the formation of a biracial committee to address police brutality and implored the city to take down the Jim Crow "whites only" signs and permit black patrons in white-owned stores and offices. Their manifesto also called for tax-funded allocations to improve public schools and roads and an end to vicious attacks, harassment, and intimidation. Love busily planned marches and sit-ins around the county, and black teenagers joined his demonstrations. By early October, white businessmen and city leaders smarted from the picketing and agreed to some of the Negro Consumers' demands.[64]

Love's sparkplug activism singled him out for punishment and provoked an armed showdown on the streets of Tchula. On a warm autumn night, two Klansmen cornered and interrogated him: "You is that nigger that's in all the civil rights working, ain't you?" Love nodded affirmatively. One of the whites icily assured him, "Okay, nigger, you've had it." Before anybody crept closer, Love reached into his jacket and drew a pistol. Suddenly, other vigilantes lurched at him from the darkness. "These motherfuckers was going to kill me," he panicked. Love darted down the street and knocked on doors for help before he ducked into Anthony Mansoor's shop. As Love hid behind the store counter, Tony Mansoor, a Lebanese merchant, pleaded with the Klansmen to go home. When one shoved inside, Edgar Love popped up and aimed his gun at him. The man froze and yelled for backup. The standoff lasted until a white police officer took Love into custody for his own protection.[65]

Despite the limited success of Love's boycott, white violence lingered and poverty corralled black aspirations. African Americans in Holmes, nevertheless, made considerable advancements. Even though whites continued to control most of the county's wealth, owned the best land, and got the highest-paying jobs, blacks tried to compensate for their lack of economic clout with political power. After the passage of the Voting Rights Act, blacks made up the majority of the electorate and began to leverage their advantage. Holmes blacks were ready for the 1967 local and state elections. Robert G. Clark Jr., the grandson of slaves and a popular teacher and coach from Ebenezer, became Mississippi's first black state representative since the Reconstruction era.[66]

Coming from a long line of schoolteachers and churchmen who owned land in the hills, Clark joined the Holmes movement in 1966. Many activists initially distrusted him because African-American teachers typically answered to white school boards. With exceptions, like him and Bernice Montgomery, black educators in Holmes usually dodged the movement. Movement people warmed to Clark after he caucused with the MFDP about the upcoming 1967 election. Once enough blacks registered to vote, Clark calculated the possibility of winning and decided to run for the Mississippi House of Representatives. Black voters in Holmes and Yazoo counties elected him on the

FDP ticket. His victory over Tchula's white incumbent, J. P. Love, symbolized the growing voting muscle of blacks and their ability to induce reform. After Clark went to the state legislature, African Americans unseated many in the county's traditional white leadership. Whites could not quite fathom the vagaries of the black insurgency. In addition to the "registering and voting" that Holmes blacks initiated, they asserted "some strange new power," one white Lexington woman perceived. By the mid-1970s, blacks would control Holmes County's school board and the superintendent's office. Blacks also claimed twelve of the eighteen other elected county posts. Robert Clark's journey to the state house made national news and solidified the reputation of Holmes as one of the most formidable grassroots movements in Mississippi.[67]

Though they had made progress slowly and welcomed federal arbitration in voter registration, blacks had finally broken the stranglehold of fear in Holmes County and made political strides. After years of white opposition to any tampering with the status quo, blacks had at last mustered the courage to join the civil rights movement. Shedding their apprehension and doubt, they clamored for racial change. Through unceasing collective action, African Americans in Holmes transformed their county in ways that offered grist for optimism. For the first time many could remember, there was a glimmer of hope—as well as the weight of more struggles to come.

Along with their opposition to Jim Crow laws and voter registration drives, blacks contemporaneously pursued school desegregation. With a federal mandate in the 1964 Civil Rights Act to desegregate the public schools, black parents and children in Holmes began to steel themselves for the task. One woman recalled, "We helped the parents decide which of the children were the strongest. We sat each child down and told them all we could, so they would know what was ahead." Cruelty, disruptions, and delays awaited them. The toll exacted on black students would be difficult to bear.[68]

Buttoning up their indignation, black families gathered their strength and committed themselves to surmount another challenge. Directed by able lawyers, they put their trust in the courts of the United States. They would need all the resourcefulness and wherewithal of their community. In the spring of 1965, local leaders and civil rights attorneys combed Holmes County with a petition to enlist parents in school desegregation. Nearly 500 signed up. Shadrach Davis volunteered two children, Linda Jean and Joshua Raymond. Charlie and Alma Carnegie's grandson Robert Jean Jr. appeared on the petition. Rosie Head, a mother of five, listed her son Willie. Eugene and Bernice Montgomery knew their nine kids were as intelligent as white students and eventually enrolled three at Lexington's junior high and high school. When the county school board refused to desegregate, blacks brought a lawsuit in July 1965 that came to the federal district court in Jackson. The case would be formally known as *Alexander v. Holmes County Board of Education*—after the Alexanders, among the hundreds of black families named as plaintiffs. The outcome of the suit would transfigure the South. The injustice it sought to redress had persisted even as segregation withered.[69]

— CHAPTER THREE —

The Grassroots and the Lawyers

❀

Hereditary bondsmen! Know ye not
Who would be free themselves must strike the blow?
—Lord Byron

THE DAY AFTER the Supreme Court handed down *Brown*, attorney Thurgood Marshall told reporters that there would be "no organized resistance" to the Court's order and that schools nationwide would be fully desegregated "in up to five years," ensuring that black children throughout the country would have education that would gain them entry to skilled jobs and colleges on an equal basis with whites. His prediction fell woefully short of his goals. Regardless of the high court's ruling, school systems across the South, including Holmes County's, would perpetuate segregated education.[1]

By 1960, reality tempered Marshall's wishful thinking. Beyond the forty-six school suits propelling through the border states, little desegregation had occurred, especially in the Deep South. "The case by case judicial process moved at a glacial pace," gauged historian James T. Patterson. Even Marshall professed doubts about the force of litigation to crush segregated education. "I consider the lawsuits to be a holding action," a more subdued Marshall later conceded to journalists, "a way of getting things open so that they can operate. But the final solution will only be when the Negro takes his part in the community, voting and otherwise." Only the conjunction between the grassroots level and the bar of justice could bring about the destruction of racial segregation that Marshall and the Court had hoped for in 1954. Thus, in the 1960s, new lawsuits would be filed.[2]

Alexander v. Holmes unfolded in three phases. Filed with the U.S. District Court for Southern Mississippi, the case traveled to the courtroom in Jackson toward a hearing in July 1965. The first rung of *Alexander* started with the plaintiffs' motion and preliminary request for immediate relief from the federal court against county school officials. After a good day in court, a federal judge entered a permanent injunction and ordered the Holmes County school board to draw up a desegregation timetable by August 14, 1965, that would cover four grades during the 1965–66 school term. Another four grades would be desegregated each subsequent year. The school board submitted a plan that permitted a student who did not gain entry to the school of his or her first choice to apply to another school. On August 16, the district court accepted the proposal but affirmed the rights of the plaintiffs to seek a modification as well. When Holmes County whites subverted any meaningful school desegregation, blacks appealed to the Fifth Circuit Court, and the penultimate round began in New Orleans. Teased out for nearly four years, the legal proceedings eventually resulted in an omnibus ruling against Holmes County school officials and boards of education in other Mississippi counties. The appellate court decision also set the third stage by triggering an unanticipated showdown between the Fifth Circuit and the administration of President Richard M. Nixon that the U.S. Supreme Court finally resolved in October 1969.[3]

While the juridical paperwork moved ahead, segregationist judges, lawyers, educators, and antagonists subjected civil rights attorneys and black plaintiffs in Holmes and elsewhere in Mississippi to numerous postponements, maddening red tape, and legal cul-de-sacs. The segregationists' guileful stall tactics demonstrated the white community's foot-dragging, and the litigants' mixed record of successes and setbacks made evident the nonlinear accretion of southern school desegregation. The legal road to the Supreme Court's ruling in 1969 was a long and circuitous one with plenty of twists and turns in the case.

Nearly eleven years before black parents and students petitioned the Holmes County school board in 1965, the Supreme Court's 1954 decision in *Brown v. Board* eliminated separate-but-equal schooling. The Court had knocked out a main pillar of segregation and white supremacy. The ruling stirred racial passions, and many white Mississippians rushed to defend their way of life. Some state lawmakers even vowed overt resistance to *Brown*. State Representative Edwin White justified the frenzied defiance to desegregation because there "is only one thing in the whole [racial] situation which the white man asks for, and that is, the privilege of his children, and his children's children, continuing to be white people." Capitulation to the *Brown* order would take the white race to the edge of the abyss, and "in a few centuries the races would become amalgamated. Thus to put the Supreme Court's decision into effect would operate to violate God's creation and Law, and when any court decision violates His Law it is sinful, unholy and unworthy of obedience."[4]

Throughout Mississippi and in Holmes County, white intransigence had kept the public schools totally segregated for ten years after *Brown*. Of all the southern states, Mississippi held out longest to begin school desegregation. Notwithstanding provisions in the Court's ruling, members of the Holmes County school board had maintained bifurcated white and black schools. By the 1964–65 school year, five of the county's schools accommodated nearly 1,700 white pupils and thirteen educated almost 5,900 African-American students. Most whites viewed *Brown* as a herald of greater threats to segregation and racial orthodoxy. After the Court decision, whites wasted no time in preparing a defense of their time-honored racial privilege. The Citizens' Council mobilized to outfox *Brown*. In Holmes, the segregationist outfit resisted simultaneous challenges by civil rights groups to achieve voting rights and desegregate education. Integration-minded blacks, conversely, mounted efforts to gain voluntary compliance with the *Brown* decree.[5]

After the Supreme Court's bombshell, the burden of initiating school integration fell upon black communities. Although Thurgood Marshall and his legal team had won *Brown*, limited resources had restricted their labors to a fraction of the school districts in the South. Without the capacity to tackle every case, civil rights attorneys instructed black parents to file school desegregation petitions with their respective school boards. During the summer of 1955, a groundswell of nearly sixty petitions surfaced throughout the South. In Mississippi, African Americans called on school boards in Natchez, Vicksburg, Jackson, Yazoo City, and Clarksdale to desegregate. In all five cities, local newspapers published the identities of the petitioners. Under duress, most of the signatories dropped their names from the petitions. Their efforts came to naught when the five school boards dismissed their claims.[6]

Over the next decade, the same fate awaited anyone who tried to invalidate Mississippi's dual-school system. In late February 1965, 250 Negro students in Lexington petitioned their black principal to persuade Holmes County's all-white school board to obey *Brown v. Board* and comply with the 1964 Civil Rights Act. Some 125 students submitted a similar petition in Tchula. Without exception, both black principals shooed them and their petitions away. The reason was simple. School desegregation could mean their jobs. As liaisons between the school board and the black community, whites expected Negro school officials to discourage integration and keep the peace. With that exchange, the battle to desegregate Holmes County's schools had begun.[7]

On April 1, nearly a month later, an ad hoc committee of black parents and movement leaders, including Ralthus Hayes and Howard Taft Bailey, hand-delivered a signed petition on behalf of hundreds of others to the county's school superintendent, Lester R. Thompson, who bore the humorous nickname "Jelly." They asked him to "use his influence with the school board" and follow federal law. The petitioners gave the county school board one month to accept their terms, but just five days later, the board turned down their request. Unlike their response in the past, blacks refused to accept the board's actions. In May, the group demanded a meeting with board members to lay plans for the desegregation of the schools. Again, the board ignored them. Clearly, the Supreme Court's earlier implementation order in *Brown II* (1955) to accomplish school desegregation with "all deliberate speed" had not translated into celerity.[8]

As they dogged the school board, Holmes blacks also contacted civil rights lawyers to file a class-action lawsuit. Incorporated in 1939 as a tax-exempt organization independent of the NAACP, the Legal Defense and Educational Fund (interchangeably referred to as LDF, the Inc. Fund, or the Fund) handled litigation for the NAACP. James Jacob "Jack" Greenberg, a Columbia Law School graduate and director-counsel of the LDF since 1961, managed the organization's overcrowded docket from a tenth-floor suite on New York City's Broadway. By the early 1960s, Greenberg had developed into perhaps the most respected civil rights attorney in America. Anyone who worked beside him agreed on his first-rate intellect and leadership skills: a lively and powerful mind, a talented strategist, an agile student of complex legal issues, a relentless determination to win, and the ability to inspire his staff, drive them, and keep them focused on their clients. Greenberg was a good boss and a sensible judge of which lawsuits to pursue. With hundreds of detailed cases piling up, his job was daunting. Greenberg had a genius for piloting the ballooning caseload and knowing which cases to try before the Supreme Court. Although many of his associates described him as cool and emotionless, Greenberg was neither clinical nor unfriendly. Trustworthy and even-handed with his team, he maintained the high standards established by his predecessor, former LDF director-counsel Thurgood Marshall, and set a professional and fast-paced tone for the office. With Greenberg in charge, the Inc. Fund filed a recrudescent round of school desegregation suits.[9]

The LDF galloped ahead to finish the business of school desegregation and make exigent federal statutes and judicial mandates work. Civil rights laws had been enacted. Color lines had been crossed. The Inc. Fund now intended to hammer *Brown* into every disobedient southern school district and affirm the law of the land. "There was little organized talk about goals and objectives," added one LDF lawyer, because "no one had any reason to doubt that integration was the end sought." Enforcing compliance with *Brown* would be another matter.[10]

Dismantling the apparatus of Jim Crow schools proved a more difficult chore and expansive errand than winning an edict from the Supreme Court. Jack Greenberg observed other impediments to school integration. He noted the power of massive resistance and white-supremacist opposition as well as an inability to bring desegregation suits, since most southern states had very few black lawyers. The Inc. Fund could assist blacks in only a few school districts. A backlog of cases languished under the torpor of segregationist obstinacy and evasive maneuvers that kept desegregation to a bare minimum. Until the mid-1960s, furthermore, a markedly limp social concern for civil rights prevailed in Washington, D.C. "The resources—funds, lawyers, political will—to change that situation were inadequate" for years, Greenberg pointed out, with his usual sangfroid. He described the listless era from *Brown* to the early 1960s as a period of "trench warfare." LDF attorneys "engaged in an agonizingly slow battle to eliminate the vestiges of legal segregation, to enforce the rights won in court, and to protect their own position from attack," commented one staff lawyer. "Not until the American political agenda changed, as a consequence of the civil rights movement, itself partially a product of *Brown*," Greenberg understood, "were the courts—and the country—ready to move to desegregation." Lawsuits may have helped set civil rights in motion, but the political winds had to shift beyond courtrooms to other lawgiving forums, most importantly Congress and the presidency.[11]

By the time of Lyndon Johnson's administration, the mass movement for racial justice was unmistakably thriving and gaining national traction. The Fund benefited from the more favorable political climate, and its star ascended as the preeminent civil rights law firm. The NAACP LDF's role as the legal arm of the black freedom struggle congealed after it defended Martin Luther King and a host of activists and causes. Digging into deeper financial pockets due to greater donor and public support, the Fund hired more lawyers. In 1964, with a bumper budget and more than twenty highly educated young attorneys to choose from, Greenberg picked one of his best and brightest to set up an outpost in Mississippi. On the ground, the Inc. Fund's crusade to accomplish school desegregation came largely through the efforts of one black female lawyer—Marian Elizabeth Wright.[12]

A year out of law school, Wright swapped a lucrative job in the North for civil rights work in Mississippi. Born in 1939 and a native South Carolinian, Marian Wright (now Wright Edelman) attended Spelman College in Atlanta and joined SNCC. She first went to Mississippi as a law student. "I saw those poor people there risking everything they had for change," she remarked. "They had only their wills and their bodies. I felt if they could do so much with nothing, the least one with some skills could do was try to help." As a Merrill Scholar, Wright studied abroad in Paris and Geneva. She also toured the Soviet Union and Eastern Europe on a trip sponsored by a Lisle Fellowship. Wright toyed with the notion of earning a graduate degree in either Russian studies or international relations, but in 1960 she entered Yale Law and finished her JD in 1963. "I do things because I'm angry," she crackled with indignation a few years later, "and I was angry with what was happening in the South. I knew darn well 19th-century Russian literature wasn't going to help me down there." "Once you've decided to be a lawyer," she resolved, "you will be a good one."[13]

After graduation from law school, Wright interned at the Fund's headquarters in New York. For the next year, she learned the inner workings of the legal system and prepared for her fieldwork. At the time, "there was a demonstrated need for more lawyers to do the trenchwork for civil rights," she said, echoing Jack Greenberg's view. "As moving and important as the Montgomery bus boycott was in emotionally galvanizing a city and a nation to end decades of segregated public buses," Wright reflected, "the ultimate victory was in the federal courts where such segregation was outlawed." Proud "to join LDF's ranks with its trailblazing legal legacy," she served "as part of the backup legal machinery for those demonstrating in the streets." Other passions, beyond the law, guided her decision to upend southern race relations. Inspired by Leo Tolstoy's belief that the kingdom of God dwells within each person and by Albert Camus's existentialist philosophy, Wright saw the greatest need in Mississippi. Along with her, she brought a copy of Robert Frost's poem "The Road Not Taken" to hang on her kitchen wall. "Marian Wright was a force of nature," one former LDF associate gushed about her. "She was high energy, very good with clients, multi-talented, and very creative legally and factually."[14]

Black Mississippians badly needed her services. By the 1930s, only six blacks practiced law in the entire state, compared to 1,243 white lawyers. The short list of Negro counsel included Sidney Redmond Sr., a Harvard Law graduate with offices in St. Louis and Jackson; Taylor G. Ewing in Vicksburg; and Ben A. Green, the mayor of Mound Bayou. As in other southern states, black lawyers suffered discrimination in Mississippi's courtrooms. Judges refused them courtesy titles and habitually referred to Negro attorneys by their first names. In criminal proceedings, attorneys often advised their black clients to plead guilty rather than stand trial before an all-white jury. One Jackson lawyer, W. L. Mhoon, who could have passed for white himself, hired whites to advocate for his black clients to get a more favorable outcome. Little prestige and money accumulated from handling usually poor Negro clientele, whose legal problems typically consisted of messy domestic squabbles or banal estate settlements. Most cases paid fifty dollars, barely enough income to scrape together a living. Before the civil rights era, blacks hardly ever brought cases, but by the early 1960s, a few African-American lawyers began to take on the state's racist establishment.[15]

Born and raised in Jackson, Jack Harvey Young was one of three children. The son of a bricklayer, Jack Young earned a college degree at all-black Jackson College. While delivering mail as a postman, a federal job with a steady paycheck and relative independence from whites, his mentor Sidney Redmond taught him the law. In September 1951, Young passed the state bar exam and left the postal service. He opened a law practice and used Redmond's old office, where he stayed for twenty years. When black students at Tougaloo College demonstrated to desegregate Jackson's public library in March 1961, the NAACP hired Young as defense counsel. He paid bond for the restive students and agreed to serve as a full-time NAACP attorney. In May and June 1961, Young and Richard Jess Brown, a Negro lawyer originally from Oklahoma who graduated from Texas Southern University Law School, represented the Freedom Riders, a biracial group of civil rights activists who tested southern compliance with court orders outlawing segregation in interstate travel. Carsie Alvin Hall, another former mailman who studied law with Redmond, passed the bar in 1954 and also assumed a docket of civil rights suits. Hall headed the capital city's NAACP chapter and knew the personal costs of litigation. "To work in Mississippi, you have to be crazy," he chewed over at lunch in 1964. "I don't mean asylum-crazy. I mean crazy so that you stop thinking of things that can happen to you."[16]

As the civil rights caseload snowballed, Hall, Young, and Brown started to receive aid from the LDF as well as assistance from William L. Higgs, a white Jackson attorney who advised James Meredith during the desegregation of the University of Mississippi, and William Kuntsler, a movement lawyer from

New York. For a time, the fraternity of African-American lawyers also got a lift when the LDF assigned Constance Baker Motley—an alumna of the *Brown* campaign and a protégée of Thurgood Marshall—to Jackson. With so much litigation pending, the small cohort of black counselors struggled to keep up. When SNCC announced plans for Freedom Summer in 1964, the prospect of defending thousands of volunteers meant the attorneys would need more help. Anticipating the logjam of race cases, the Inc. Fund asked Marian Wright to hang out her shingle in Jackson.[17]

In 1964, at age twenty-four, Marian Wright opened the LDF's Mississippi office on North Farish Street in the heart of Jackson's Negro district. She ran it from the top floor of the drab two-story Crystal Palace Ballroom, a once-tony dance club for the local black elite. By the 1960s, the building housed a pool hall, a drugstore, a bookstore, and a suite of professional offices. Carsie Hall, Jess Brown, and Jack Young also had their practices on Farish. Within a year, three more civil rights law firms joined the LDF in Jackson. The Lawyers' Committee for Civil Rights Under Law or "President's Committee," created by the American Bar Association (ABA), answered President John F. Kennedy's call in 1963 for attorneys to engage in civic action to ameliorate racial tension. The Lawyers' Constitutional Defense Committee (LCDC), affiliated with the American Civil Liberties Union (ACLU), set up shop across the street from Wright. One block north of the LCDC and the LDF resided the National Lawyers Guild, a leftist organization with Communist sympathies founded in the 1930s. One racist judge in Jackson belittled the menagerie of Negro and civil rights lawyers as the "Farish Street Crowd." They accepted his derision as "a badge we wore with pride," said one black attorney. "In no other state," noted Frank Parker of the Lawyers' Committee for Civil Rights under Law, "did so many national civil rights legal organizations have full-time, staffed offices." Marian Wright got busy and learned from senior black attorneys who cooperated with the LDF.[18]

Jack Young, Jess Brown, and Carsie Hall gave their callow understudy a tutorial in the law. They taught Wright "how to survive and navigate the intricacies of Mississippi's feudal legal system," she wrote, "which no textbook could teach and instructed me in the social etiquette of lawyering." The state required a lengthy residency period of fifteen months before any non-Mississippian—or, more precisely, any outside agitator—could practice. Unlike nonresidents, any graduate of the Ole Miss law program could gain immediate entry to the bar. To begin her litigation career without a license or breaking the law, she clerked for the three older men until she took the

Mississippi bar exam. They signed the official paperwork that she prepared and introduced Wright in local court as their colleague. After she completed the residency term and a three-day examination in December 1965, the state bar admitted her. Wright became the first black woman to pass the test, and her achievement increased the tally of Negro attorneys in Mississippi to six. With more than 900,000 African Americans in the state, the overall Negro population outnumbered black lawyers by a margin of 150,000 to one. Wright knew whites had stacked the deck against blacks, but, she wagered, "these segregationists know they're up against a wall." Coached by her elders, Wright put herself on the legal map in Mississippi. She filed her first civil rights cases in federal district court.[19]

When Wright debuted in federal court, she got a chilly reception. None "of the stony-faced White men sitting around the table would shake my hand as I went around the table to greet them," she recounted in her memoir. "Their shock at my presence and the sustained silence made me feel I'd stumbled into forbidden territory and a closed club. And I had." Unfazed, Wright attended to the monster job in front of her and kept her mind "stayed on freedom." With each passing month, she more keenly understood the plight of Mississippi's black and rural poor. "Down here," she recognized, "a lawyer has more than legal responsibilities. After you get the schools integrated, you're still faced with parents who don't make enough money to buy clothes to send their kids to school. Here you never know when one step forward actually means four backwards" for ordinary black folks. "Granted you have victories," Wright elaborated in her memoir, "many of them superficial, like being able to eat in any restaurant. . . . But the fundamental problems are poverty, jobs, education, and housing. You can't change people's lives on marching and court suits alone." The stupendous task ahead was too much for a single LDF attorney. Another colleague provided vital support.[20]

Often at Wright's side stood Henry M. Aronson, a thirty-one-year-old who shared responsibilities for the Inc. Fund's litigation. Aronson, a Jew and fellow Yale Law graduate, practiced corporate law in Connecticut and lived comfortably until a former classmate, Alan Levine, lured him away to Mississippi. Levine manned the Lawyers' Constitutional Defense Committee office in Jackson and recruited Aronson to serve as an attorney during Freedom Summer. Aronson applied for and received time off to go south. Inundated with volunteers in Mississippi, the LCDC placed him in Alabama and exposed him to Jim Crow justice and segregation. Aronson's first job took him to Selma, in the Black Belt, where he offered legal assistance to protesters.

Resentful of his presence, local lawmen showed him no southern hospitality. Jim Clark, the cattle-prodding sheriff of Dallas County, "beat the living shit out of me," Aronson later winced. "That was the moment in which I knew I had to become more involved in the fight for civil rights and justice." Aronson never returned to corporate litigation. In the wake of Freedom Summer, he left Alabama and arrived in Jackson to take up the cudgels for civil rights clients. During the winter of 1964, he joined Marian Wright's staff as a fast-moving LDF ambassador to black communities throughout Mississippi. Indefatigable and combative, he matched her in prodigious energy. The steadfast pair began their hectic days around 7:00 A.M. and ended at midnight or later. They spent most of their time away from the desk, in court or out in the field consulting with plaintiffs. Splitting the caseload, Aronson and Wright handled a statewide docket brimming with cases, including equal employment and welfare benefits for blacks and integration of public facilities. Education was the nub of their concern. Soon, other lawyers also enlisted in the quest to desegregate Mississippi's schools.[21]

More brainpower flowed into Jackson's LDF branch when Melvyn H. Zarr and Norman Carey Amaker pitched in occasionally. After Zarr received his law degree from Harvard in 1963, he came on board at the Fund's national headquarters. During Freedom Summer, he shuttled between New York City and Mississippi to defend clients. His stated objective in the South "was to become superfluous." Rather than "be another carpetbagger who just came and went," Zarr longed for the day when "southern blacks would stand on their own." Born in 1935 and raised in Harlem, Norman Amaker had been politicized as a black teenager. His hometown hero, Congressman Adam Clayton Powell, influenced Amaker to imbibe community activism and civil rights. He finished college at Amherst in 1956 and earned his JD from Columbia Law three years later. Upon graduation, Thurgood Marshall hired Amaker at the Fund. The Harlemite spent the next decade as a staff attorney and then as first assistant counsel. At age twenty-eight, Amaker represented Martin Luther King in Birmingham and again in Selma. He argued hundreds of cases before state, district, and appeals courts, including the Supreme Court. The Inc. Fund's New York office retained Amaker as a circuit rider or troubleshooter for southern hotspots. If Jim Crow schools would ever disappear in Mississippi, it would depend on the LDF's stable of litigators.[22]

Jackson's enhanced LDF presence buoyed civil rights litigation in Mississippi. The Fund provided Negro plaintiffs with legal expertise to call upon without relying on the Justice Department to defend their rights. Even though the Department of Justice moved on voter registration and harassment cases, black Mississippians did not dictate the government's agenda. Justice Department lawyers also lived far away from Mississippi and did not always fully absorb local conditions. LDF attorneys, on the other hand, worked more closely with plaintiffs, heard their stories, reviewed their struggles, and cultivated camaraderie. By residing in the state and often staying in the African-American community, the Inc. Fund won blacks' respect and trust. Standing alongside their clients in defiance of hostile white Mississippians earned staff lawyers an added level of credibility. Perhaps more importantly, a personal touch kept their eyes on the prize. The education system had to change.[23]

The Fund's legal counsel understood the colossus before them. Except for the 1962 integration of the University of Mississippi, the pattern of strident commitment to segregated education held largely intact. Whites had established the state's educational goals for their own benefit, not for blacks. As one white Baptist minister who had recently relinquished his pulpit in Yazoo City put it, "No matter how much a white person claims he loves 'my nigger,' he doesn't want him to be educated. He thinks a smart-aleck Negro won't be dependent and humble anymore." Many white Mississippians additionally feared that any aperture in segregation would lead, as state legislator Edwin White so apocalyptically divined after *Brown*, to interracial dating, biracial marriage, and mongrelization, the old bugaboo of the white race. Such sentiments chafed LDF attorneys. The timidity and complacency of the federal government also bothered them. According to Marian Wright, skittish bureaucrats from the Office of Education in Washington had too often and too quickly acceded to the assurances of white school officials that desegregation had legitimately occurred. "Until the federal government has the will and staff to implement desegregation in schools, the Negro child will remain the victim of white school boards' delays and evasions of the law," inveighed Wright. While she waited for federal authorities to act, black Holmes Countians contested segregationist wangling.[24]

In the spring of 1965, black parents in Holmes struck back against the county school board's procrastination. The board's unbending opposition to their desegregation petition meant that dissolving the dual-school system would require Negroes to sue. The Holmes movement sent a deputation to confer with NAACP officials and attorneys who ferried their dissatisfaction. Unversed in school lawsuits, Carsie Hall and Jess Brown handed off their case to Marian Wright's LDF staff. Increasingly active in rural, outlying communities, the Fund accepted the Holmes families as clients and motored forward with the frontal attack on segregated education. As plans proceeded to ready a motion in federal district court, Wright and Aronson dispatched a budding law student to scour the county for plaintiffs.[25]

Unfamiliar with the background of Holmes County, Melvyn Rosenman Leventhal got a crash course in Mississippi race relations. In the years ahead, he would witness beatings, endure threats of violence, and shudder at the brutality. The extent of the Magnolia State's bigotry may have hit him hard, but he had known pain and humiliation as a child. Born in 1943, Mel Leventhal was the grandson of Jewish immigrants and was educated in Brooklyn public schools and yeshiva, or Jewish day school. At age nine, his parents divorced, and his mother raised him and his younger brother on a slender bookkeeper's salary. "I don't think I saw my father more than two or three times," Leventhal said of his youth. "One day when I was about twelve, I took my baby brother over to my dad's house, just so he could get a better idea of what his father looked like. The man slammed the door in our face." Shunned by his father, Mel converted his "outsider" status into a rapport with the alienated in general and African Americans in particular as the civil rights movement accelerated in the postwar era. His racial epiphany began in the early 1950s after Jackie Robinson became the first Negro to play Major League Baseball and signed with the Brooklyn Dodgers. Leventhal watched Robinson stoically withstand jeers and racism. "I was outraged and disgusted by the way white people treated Jackie Robinson. I felt his deep hurt in my heart," Leventhal explained, "and vowed right then to end that kind of discrimination and hate." He cast his conviction in personal terms. "I couldn't just be an observer and follow what was happening in the South in the newspapers," his conscience compelled him. "All my life, I had been an empathetic person who could not stand to see anybody mistreated. And what was happening to blacks in Mississippi was as wrong as wrong could be." Reading about civil rights would not suffice. The Brooklynite had to do something.[26]

In June 1965, Mel Leventhal left the hustle and bustle of New York City for the magnolia jungle of Mississippi. The Boston-based Law Students Civil Rights Research Council, through its chapter at New York University, sent the young law student to intern in Jackson. Assigned to the Inc. Fund's office, Leventhal helped draft the numerous complaints filed throughout the state against refusals to comply with desegregation statutes. He also started litigation procedures in Holmes County. Leventhal gathered retainer agreements, interviewed plaintiffs, and heard grievances to compile a case. All summer, he spoke at churches and before community groups in Holmes about the upcoming school year. Leventhal encouraged blacks to win various school

board elections. He urged parents to enroll their children in what LDF attorneys prematurely but confidently referred to as "previously all-white
schools." He met potential litigants several times and counseled them just
as frequently that they did not have to participate. Challenging the school
system could mean losing one's income or even life. With or without their
support, the Fund would take the case to court, he told audiences, but the
people signed up anyway. Their enthusiasm was infectious. Of the nearly
1,000 black Mississippi students who would attend formerly white schools
during the next year, almost 200 came from Holmes County. The contagious
commitment thrilled Leventhal and strengthened his bond with the county's
black residents. "Holmes was very special," he rhapsodized even years later.
"Every county had at least some people like that, but Holmes had a lot of
special people." The esteem was mutual. As a token, local movement people
appointed him as their attorney.[27]

Leventhal made a place for himself in Holmes County. The Jewish boy
from New York seemed unusually at ease in rural Mississippi. Over time, he
could affect a southern drawl with only hints of a Brooklyn accent. Mississippi
novelist and Yazoo City native Willie Morris sketched a vignette of Leventhal
as "a large man with open features who uses the word 'fella' when talking to
you, much as a Kappa Alpha during rush week at Ole Miss would." Morris
pegged the affable law student "as tough—and smart, a shrewd smartness
curiously mingled with a kind of latter-day Southern gentility; as a student
in New York, he spent considerable time at the race track." On a case, lawyer
Leventhal pursued every angle. In the courtroom, he could be outspoken and
passionate. Outside court, Leventhal was cordial and open to people of all
persuasions, as long as they did not try to kill him.[28]

During the summer, Mel Leventhal acculturated to the county in a hurry
and befriended many blacks. He had been tempted to accept invitations to
stay in activists' homes, but he decided not to put them in harm's way. Shelter-
ing a white man ran the risk of bombings and shootings. If anyone got hurt
directly on his behalf, Leventhal could not live with the guilt. Instead, he
bunked at the Holmes County Community Center with Sue and Henry Lorenzi, the white northerners who managed the facility. Leventhal's allegiance
to blacks also tagged him as a race traitor and agitator. The Brooklyn lawyer
came in for caustic criticism from white Mississippians, who slung invectives
at the Yankee Jew. Common synonyms for liberal do-gooders included "Nigger lover," "communist," and "homosexual." The scorn seemed to ricochet
off Leventhal's thick skin. "If I had ever studied up on exactly how dangerous
it was to try to end segregation in Mississippi," he later said wryly, "I might

not have had the courage to go. I could not have imagined the level of racism down there. My ignorance is what saved me." At the time, Leventhal knew the ridicule was no laughing matter. Concerned for his safety, he bought a rifle from a Sears catalog. Leventhal never carried a handgun, but he kept a loaded carbine in his car and at home in case of an emergency. Leventhal largely agreed with Martin Luther King's nonviolent philosophy, but he believed in protecting his right to life too.[29]

Despite the peril, LDF school litigation in Mississippi intrigued Leventhal. He returned every summer to intern for the Inc. Fund and rejoin his clients in Holmes. Leventhal delighted in doing the spadework for *Alexander v. Holmes*. LDF's Jackson office welcomed him back too. Even as a law student, Mel Leventhal impressed Marian Wright as "one's ideal civil rights lawyer. I thought the world of him." What astonished her "was his huge level of energy and absolute insistence that Mississippi must be a just place." When Leventhal later received his law degree in 1967, Wright hired him as a staff attorney. As the astute lawyer settled into life and work in Mississippi, the district court in Jackson heard preliminary motions for his plaintiffs' case.[30]

On July 19, 1965, LDF lawyers and NAACP attorneys entered the federal court building in Jackson, where W. Harold Cox presided as chief judge over the U.S. District Court for the Southern District of Mississippi. With everything in order, they trooped into the courtroom where the judge heard the motion. He ruled in their favor on the merits of the LDF's twelve-page complaint and, on July 28, instructed the Holmes County school board to submit a desegregation plan within thirty days. Cox had based his decision on the recent case of Jerome Singleton, a black student, against Jackson's city schools, which had been filed by the Justice Department and decided in June by the U.S. Court of Appeals for the Fifth Circuit in New Orleans. The Fifth Circuit seized upon guidelines in the 1964 Civil Rights Act that called for "freedom-of-choice" desegregation in the assignment of students, as the minimum anodyne acceptable under the law.[31]

The *Alexander* case listed the Board of Education of Holmes County as defendants, including the superintendent, Lester Thompson; William Bernard "Bill" Kenna, the board's president and a former mayor of Lexington; and members W. H. McKenzie Jr., a Durant banker; Homer E. Chisholm, a prominent farmer from the Coxburg community in the southern part of the county; Martin C. Smith of Tchula; and James Barrett, a cotton planter in Cruger. Local lawyers represented them. Calvin R. King, who practiced law in Durant, joined the defense. Pat M. Barrett Sr., Holmes County's public attorney and Thompson's brother-in-law, also agreed to counsel. Barrett's family had lived in Holmes County for six generations. They started as farmers in Ebenezer and, over the years, acquired substantial landholdings. The Barretts later resettled in Lexington but still raised cattle. Pat Barrett attended college at Southwestern at Memphis with Edwin White and, in 1933, opened a law firm in Lexington. For decades after the Second World War, Barrett served as attorney for the county's board of supervisors. Along with other town fathers, he organized the Lexington chapter of the Citizens' Council and became its first president. After participating in the witch hunt against David Minter and Eugene Cox at Providence Cooperative Farm, he urged them to leave the county. Everyone knew where Pat Barrett stood on integration. In a 1955 open letter to the *Lexington Advertiser*, he reasserted his segregationist bona fides to county residents, "With reference to the tragic and deplorable situation caused by the shameful decision of our Supreme Court . . . I shall continue individually and as your County Attorney to strive unceasingly and unendingly to preserve our Southern way of life."[32]

When blacks filed suit against the county school board, the *Holmes County Herald*, which Barrett supplied with seed money, identified every plaintiff, students and parents alike, on page five. Among the more than 300 blacks singled out by the newspaper, Beatrice Alexander topped the list. Her surname became associated with the lawsuit simply because it headed the roll call of Holmes's black plaintiffs, given in alphabetical order. Enrolled in the ninth grade at the Tchula Attendance Center, eighteen-year-old Beatrice, the eldest of five children, grew up in a black farm family. Her younger siblings— Willie, Floyd, Rosa Linda, and Gereldine—went to school at Mileston Elementary. Their parents, Peter and Mattie, had been convinced by the LDF to exercise their "freedom of choice" and signed up as litigants, along with dozens of others in the Mileston community. In the meantime, the county school board drew plans to meet minimal standards of compliance.[33]

In accordance with the district court's directive, the board grudgingly succumbed to the unavoidable and took baby steps to comply. At a special July session, board members cobbled together a compliance plan and finished their work several weeks later. The county's roadmap to desegregation adopted the "Four-Grades-a-Year, Freedom-of-Choice" model for pupil assignment, a popular option throughout Mississippi and other southern school districts. Federal officials had already approved similar freedom-of-choice approaches for the Jackson schools and the North Panola County district. Beginning in August, the Holmes County school board proposed an end to the dual-school system for Negro and white children in the first four grades. The board also pledged to desegregate at least four additional grades each subsequent school term. Referring to language from Title VII of the 1964 Civil Rights Act, the board stipulated that students would be admitted to a school of their choice "without regard to race, color or national origin." The board's enrollment plan satisfied Title VI of the legislation, which mandated an acceptable degree of school desegregation to qualify for federal funding.[34]

On August 13, the day before the deadline prescribed by Judge Cox for the district to comply, a group of thirteen blacks, including Ozell Mitchell, Alma Carnegie, and other movement people, called on Superintendent Lester Thompson at his office. They asked him to outline the details of the desegregation program. Thompson feigned ignorance, even though the board submitted its plan to court the next day. The superintendent's insincere answer reinforced the perception among many blacks that whites would employ a strategy of indefinite delay and take their sweet time to desegregate the schools. On August 16, Cox, nevertheless, heard and accepted the board's proposal.[35]

School desegregation in Holmes County hit immediate snags. Whites reacted sullenly to the end of school segregation. Most school board members and white parents could not countenance the idea of mixed-race classrooms. County and state officials, many of whom had contemplated ironclad defiance of desegregation, "soon turned to less obvious—and ingenious—devices for delay," noted a LDF brief. One wrench in their toolbox, a "pupil placement" law, "established a labyrinth of administrative procedures to ensnare those Negro students hardy enough to attempt to desegregate white schools." In August, the school board enacted its tortuous version of compliance. It began with an effort to drive Negro students out of the school district. Invoking as a precedent a disputed Mississippi senate bill, SB 1516, under review in the federal courts, the board charged a tuition fee of $225 per year for pupils whose parents resided outside Mississippi. The law also permitted the board to fix an annual fee of $135 for students attending county schools whose parents lived in another school district in the state. Tuition had to be paid in advance. Anyone who could not afford the cost could not attend school.[36]

The board's action adversely impacted nearly 500 mostly black students in the Holmes County district. Inc. Fund and NAACP attorneys pounced and petitioned the federal court in Jackson for a restraining order to prevent districts from using SB 1516. Until LDF and NAACP attorneys won injunctive relief, however, the county school board barred the 500 pupils from school. In late October, the district court finally decided that confiscatory tuition fees for public schools violated the students' state constitutional rights to an education. The ruling also struck down SB 1516. Interrupted from their studies for over a month, the affected students did not begin classes until the last week of October.[37]

An additional board strategy to frustrate desegregation involved the refusal of federal financial assistance. The Holmes County Board of Education had little intention of securing federal money for the district. Declining federal dollars would retard development and stifle the increasingly black public schools. Throughout the academic term, the board obtained only meager funding and even snubbed certain allocations that could help blacks.[38]

The board's encrusted barriers put heavier burdens on black students and their families. Noncompliance and masquerading coarsened into acts of sabotage and retribution. As in other parts of Mississippi, school desegregation encountered considerable opposition. So-called freedom-of-choice plans ostensibly gave parents the right to choose whatever school they wanted for their children. In reality, it put the responsibility on black parents to push for integration even as they and their children faced intimidation and hazarded their jobs and homes for trying to enroll in white schools or for daring to join desegregation lawsuits. African-American parents who sent their children to previously all-white schools suffered from Klan terrorism and other forms of repression. Economic reprisals included evictions from homes and loss of credit and employment. In Durant, on the eastern side of Holmes County, churlish whites posted flyers all over town to advertise the names of the thirty-two black parents and guardians who registered children at Durant Elementary School. The day one of her kids integrated Durant's little brick schoolhouse, Sarah Ruth Hill lost her job as a domestic. As further punishment, Hill's bank in Lexington called her loan. The bills piled up. Unemployed and in debt, the single mother of five went to jail until the LDF got the "total bastards," as one lawyer profaned them, to drop the charges. Around Mileston, local banks, farm equipment suppliers, and gin owners marginalized the economic independence of black landholders by refusing them imprests and service as payback against families who chose white schools. Mild deterrents and a guerrilla campaign of economic and psychological warfare invigorated white resistance to desegregated education across the state and varied in the degree of persecution from school district to school district.[39]

Short-circuiting freedom of choice pervaded Holmes County's public schools as well. White school officials often played on black fears, internalized after years of inferiority under Jim Crow, that their children could not compete academically with white classmates. When Negro parents went to sign up their kids at the all-white Goodman elementary, the principal told them that "any time they wanted to transfer children to the colored school, they would be free to do so." After they enrolled anyway, white teenagers showed up at recess chasing smaller black children with baseball bats and swatting them with sticks. Fighting back gave whites an excuse to expel African-American students, so blacks grit their teeth or hoped that teachers would intervene. At Goodman, no one protected them. "It was like we were just not there," recalled Annie Williams (now Washington), one of the first eighteen black enrollees at Goodman. "They didn't care." Seemingly unaware of the law, white administrators and faculty segregated their new black transferees at every opportunity. They quarantined black children on the playground and seated them apart like pariahs at lunch. In Durant's grammar school, whites and blacks preferred the company of their own race and sat on opposite sides of the lunchroom. The kitchen staff slopped food on the table for Negro students, but the cooks served the white kids on trays and plates. White children also got offered seconds while blacks ate only a single portion.⁴⁰

Intolerant white teachers frequently acted little better than school officials and white students and exhibited rude and unkind behavior toward blacks. At Durant Elementary, the all-white faculty ostracized or avoided Negro pupils. When they did interact, some teachers embarrassed black children by ridiculing their appearance, telling them they stank, and spraying them with deodorant. Others pelted black students with racial pejoratives. White teachers favored white pupils by giving them better grades and denigrated blacks for "bad manners" and "bad character." In Tchula's primary school, teachers ushered black third and fourth graders from the building to the outhouse rather than let them use the indoor toilet. Negro children also drank from separate water fountains and even arrived at school apart from white classmates. The county maintained segregated transportation for black and white students on different bus routes. African Americans sardined into buses so cramped that many black children preferred to trudge a few miles to school. When black parents tried to wave down busloads of whites with empty seats, drivers ignored them. In spite of derogatory treatment, black students had finally desegregated the county school system and pierced a coveted white stronghold.⁴¹

Unhappy with the desegregation of their schools, whites feared for the future and plotted separate, alternative education. Clamor for segregated private schools in Holmes County depended on the level of white concern. Fury and despair about integration revealed considerable enthusiasm and demands for parallel private schools. Preparations for segregationist academies fermented before the fall semester. On August 5, 1965, the *Holmes County Herald* reported "an overflow crowd" of white parents who met in Lexington and hatched plans for a cursory private school. They requested a fifty-dollar membership fee to raise enough money to support a pilot school for the first six grades. Within two months of the court order to desegregate, the white community rigged up a series of three all-white private academies, beginning with the Cruger-Tchula Academy. Between the autumn of 1964 and that of 1966, white students peeled away from the Holmes County public school system. White enrollment evaporated by 500 students, down to 1,000, while black attendance stayed at approximately 6,000. By the fall of 1966, most white students in the hill section of the county returned to desegregated schools. In the blacker Delta, whites stampeded from the public schools.[42]

While nearly 200 black children matriculated in majority-white schools in the fall of 1965, whites did not reciprocate at previously all-Negro schools. Many white parents with youngsters in the first four grades designated for desegregation by court affidavit did not bother to register their children. Others who preregistered their kids before the start of the school year boycotted on the opening day. Of the 172 white pupils enrolled at Lexington Elementary School, only twenty-three showed up for class. By the end of the week, most of them disappeared. In Durant, Mayor C. H. "Junior" Blanton Jr. begged white parents to keep their children in the elementary school. After forty-eight black students appeared on the first day, only five white children remained. Blanton's moderate position invited hate mail and Klan arson. White vigilantes burned an obligatory cross in his yard and set his dry-cleaning business ablaze. The fire did considerable damage. At the other three primary schools slated for desegregation, no white children attended. Many went to the newly chartered private academies. Others, too poor to defect, stayed home—a viable alternative in Mississippi, which did not require compulsory education at the time. During the school year, some white parents withdrew from the boycott and caved in to desegregation, but most ditched the county's public schools altogether.[43]

Beginning in September 1965, the Holmes County school board granted requests from white parents to transfer their children to schools in adjacent Yazoo, Leflore, Carroll, and Attala counties. Federal desegregation law insisted that transfers to another school district could be approbated only for "a valid reason unrelated to race, color, or national origins." Almost without question, board members rubber-stamped the transfer applications, which fueled the mass departure of white students. The board also reorganized school districts and closed certain schools. At the behest of white parents, the board voted to shutter the county's agricultural high school, which exclusively enrolled whites, and authorized transfers to its twenty-seven students.

Between the fall and spring semesters, the school board's artifices continued. When the board met in February 1966, it agreed to return a parcel of private land donated to the Durant school system. Since "circumstances in the district had changed," one member explained, the board wanted to convey the property back to the original owner. The unstated reason must have been the racial writing on the wall. To avoid any mixing of the races, the board scuttled the procurement of land and set aside the real estate to use someday as a separate municipal district run mostly by and for whites.[44]

Maybe the greatest design flaw in the Holmes desegregation plan involved the very premise of freedom of choice for all students. Under freedom of choice, an individual student could ask the county school board for permission to switch to another school. By placing the onus on Negro students to move to the white schools, freedom-of-choice plans meant that, if no black students requested a transfer, then blacks would continue to attend all-black institutions and no desegregation would occur. The plan gave ultimate authority to the Holmes County Board of Education to accept or deny the transfers. Blacks disliked the freedom-of-choice approach because of the strain it placed on them to achieve what should have been their legal right. The system also cast black children in the role of interlopers. Though the impositions of freedom of choice undoubtedly frightened off some registrants, remarkably few black students withdrew their transfer applications. The freedom-of-choice option, in the end, amounted to merely another ploy to prolong Mississippi's dual-school system, a reality increasingly exacerbated by the federal district court in Jackson.[45]

CHAPTER FOUR

Pleading for the Fifth

❧

Racial discrimination
would be eliminated root and branch.
—Justice William J. Brennan

IN THE FOUR YEARS he had been a federal district judge, William Harold Cox had "not exactly endeared himself to civil rights attorneys," noted Bill Minor, the *New Orleans Times-Picayune*'s ace reporter. Infamous for his gamesmanship to buy time for segregation, the judge's sly legal mind fixated on unstinting opposition to integration. Avowedly racist, Cox also spewed antiblack slurs and diatribes from the bench. In a 1964 voter registration case, for instance, when African-American witnesses testified for the Department of Justice, he chided them, "Who is telling these niggers they can get in line to push people around, acting like a bunch of chimpanzees?" Somehow, the case of *Alexander v. Holmes* had to survive Judge Cox's courtroom in Jackson.[1]

Unlike multimember appellate courts, federal trial courts, each presided over by a single judge holding a lifetime appointment, put each jurist's personal idiosyncrasies and prejudices on daily display. When the Supreme Court ruled, by comparison, the bench spoke with the voice of at least five justices and sometimes all nine members. Beneath the high court, the courts of appeals passed edicts with the approval of at least two- and often three-judge panels. Every U.S. district court, however, waded into cases with singular authority. Like their appellate brethren, district judges enjoyed life tenure, in contrast to the state courts. With perpetual sinecure, a federal judge could, in theory, swim against the tide of politics and stand above the whims of the crowd. Federal trial judges operated without any obligation to heed the rulings of other district courts. The district judge conducted the ordinary business of the federal judiciary. He or she established the first trial record in most federal court proceedings. She or he also decided what constituted evidence, hastened or hindered the deliberations, rendered the initial verdict on the law, and prescribed the solutions to a legal problem. Though no federal judge was infallible—all of his or her work was susceptible to rote appeal—it was the judge's trademark blend of independence, job security, and influence without the last word in interpreting the law that generated widely divergent opinions at the district level. A sagacious litigator kept in mind the jurisprudence and disposition of the sitting district judge. Lower-court decisions could be counteracted on remand, but many lawsuits hinged on the outcome in the district courtroom. Arguing before an adversarial district judge could taint a case at the onset.[2]

Probably no southern federal judge played a more off-putting role in *Alexander v. Holmes* than Harold Cox. Born in Indianola, Mississippi, in 1901, he was, in the words of Mel Leventhal, "a force to be reckoned with." One court-watcher described Judge Cox more gravely as "a master of obstruction and delay" who "may well have been the greatest single obstacle to equal justice in the South." Cox grew up in rural Sunflower County, a semifeudal cotton kingdom in the Delta, where his father, Adam C. Cox, served as high sheriff. A large man, at nearly six feet two inches, with an imperious manner, Harold Cox sparred as an amateur boxer in college at Tulane University, abhorred drinking and smoking, and stayed fit and vigorous late into life. In 1924, he graduated from the University of Mississippi School of Law and dabbled in state Democratic politics before President John F. Kennedy appointed him to the federal bench in June 1961. The small contingent of white racial liberals in Mississippi gasped at Cox's nomination because of his rock-ribbed racism. Justice Department officials reported to Kennedy that, despite Cox's noisome racial prejudice, he was a lawyer of above-average intellect and ability. Besides, they conceded, "it is impossible to find a white lawyer of standing in Mississippi who is not publicly committed to segregation. That is the way of white life in Mississippi."[3]

Cox's nomination to the federal bench, Kennedy's first judicial selection, owed less to the president than to Mississippi patronage. Cox's boyhood chum and fellow Sunflower Countian, Senator James O. Eastland, chaired the Senate Judiciary Committee. His father, Woods Eastland, a cotton oligarch and lawyer, and Sheriff A. C. Cox cemented an indissoluble friendship and political alliance inherited by their sons. While Jim Eastland rose in the

Senate ranks, Harold Cox climbed a different greasy pole as a distinguished corporate lawyer and chairman of the Hinds County Democratic Party. Cox always knew that his childhood friend would secure an appointment to a federal judgeship for him at an opportune moment. With a Democrat back in the White House following eight years of Eisenhower's Republican administration, Eastland swooped in fast.[4]

John Kennedy first wanted a background check on Eastland's friend. Nearly two dozen Mississippi judges and attorneys vouched for Harold Cox in American Bar Association interviews. Unconvinced, Bernard Segal, a liberal Republican and national chairman of the ABA's Judicial Selection Review Committee, flew to Jackson to evaluate Cox's racial views. Cox had never belonged to the Citizens' Council, but he also had no public stance on civil rights issues. One lunch with Cox soured Segal on the Mississippi lawyer. After his disconcerting visit, Segal telephoned Attorney General Robert F. Kennedy and relayed his concerns. Kennedy decided to speak with Cox and summoned him to Washington. On a sofa in the attorney general's office, the two men discussed Cox's understanding of the Constitution and his willingness to implement the Supreme Court's edicts. Their colloquy ended when Cox passed Robert Kennedy's initial probe: "He was the only judge, I think, that I had that kind of conversation with. He was very gracious; and he said that there wouldn't be any problem." The attorney general may have consoled himself with that thought.[5]

Harold Cox said what Robert Kennedy had wanted to hear, but the attorney general wondered if the Mississippian had bleached his racial views to get the job. He directed Deputy Attorney General Byron White to broker an alternative arrangement, which worked to the Kennedys' advantage. Broaching the topic through Jim Eastland, the attorney general inquired whether Cox might prefer an appointment to the Fifth Circuit Court of Appeals. Muted by other appellate judges, Cox could inflict himself less on touchy civil rights matters that the Kennedy brothers hoped to finesse. Cox declined the offer. He wanted to stay at home and close to the action. In the putative version of Cox's appointment, Eastland countered Kennedy with some horse-trading of his own. As leverage for Cox's nomination, the senator promised not to block Thurgood Marshall's appointment to the Second Circuit Court of Appeals. Eastland allegedly and devilishly bargained with Robert Kennedy: "Tell your brother that if he will give me Harold Cox, I will give him the nigger." Although factually incorrect, since Cox's confirmation occurred in June, months before the announcement of Marshall's nomination, the anecdote reliably distilled Eastland's state of mind and influence over judicial affairs.[6]

In elevating Cox to the district court in Jackson, John Kennedy installed one of the most unabashedly segregationist judges in the history of the federal judiciary. The announcement of his nomination appalled leading civil rights advocates. Jack Greenberg later decried Cox as "possibly the most racist judge ever to sit on the federal bench." Roy Wilkins, the head of the NAACP, howled, "For 986,000 Negro Mississippians, Judge Cox will be another strand in their barbed wire fence, another cross over their weary shoulders and another rock in the road up which their young people must struggle." Clarence Mitchell, the NAACP's chief lobbyist, worried that the Kennedys' backroom kowtowing to Eastland downgraded the White House to a "dude ranch." Their worst fears materialized quickly as Cox emerged as a foe of civil rights forces. The judge acquired a reputation for vituperation and accrued a shameful record on race. Between 1961 and 1976, superior courts overturned three-fourths of his decisions on civil rights cases. For two decades Harold Cox vitiated the advance of civil rights and harangued movement lawyers.[7]

Judge Cox fought his rearguard action against civil rights from the historic courtroom on the fourth floor of the federal courthouse on Capitol Street in Jackson. Behind the judge's bench, a forty-by-twenty-foot WPA mural, titled *Pursuits of Life in Mississippi*, depicted bucolic scenes of a neatly segregated society. Whites basked happily. Southern belles wore hoopskirts and silk bonnets, escorted by their handsome beaus. Blacks joyfully picked cotton and strummed banjos for everyone's amusement. A tall white preacher held the Bible in one hand. To his left, a group of young white men surveyed blueprints to build their racial utopia. Art imitated Mississippi's way of life and skewed historical memory. The antebellum iconography whitewashed the state's experiment with binary democracy during Reconstruction and resurrected the plantation legend of the Old South. Underneath the mural sat Cox, god-like on a throne. Of course, the judge "thought he *was* God," one nervous attorney recalled.[8]

On the bench, at the height of his power, Cox was a commanding judge. Impatient with legal briefs and more comfortable hearing cases in chambers than in court, his outlandish prerogatives became legendary. The blue-eyed, graying judge maintained a taut grip by hectoring lawyers to abide by his byzantine yet strict code of courtroom conduct. First-time attorneys in Cox's courtroom trespassed on one of his taboos by setting their briefcases on counsel tables. Jackson lawyers often chuckled when Cox dressed down out-of-towners and fined them for violating the "briefcase rule." Casually attired attorneys could also incur sartorial reprimands from the ornery judge. Health problems and pain caused by gout further aggravated Cox's tetchy personality. Splenetic excesses aside, Harold Cox's defense of a rapidly dissipating way of life set him apart.[9]

Judge Cox saved his surliest outbursts for civil rights trials. "Although he was not a pleasant judge for any lawyer to practice law before," attested one LDF staff lawyer, "civil rights attorneys regularly felt his wrath" and his anti-Semitism. Cox, for instance, would not accept papers from Mel Leventhal, the Jewish New Yorker, unless he dated them "A.D.," *Anno Domini*, Latin for "in the year of our Lord." The judge did not require Gentile attorneys to acknowledge the Christian calendar. Harold Cox also regularly referred to Robert Rubin, counsel to the Mississippi Civil Liberties Union, as "that Jew lawyer." When visiting lawyers from other states set foot in his courtroom on a civil rights matter, Cox frequently invoked an arbitrary disclaimer that "outside agitators" could not act as special counsel. The judge waived the rule for any nonresident attorney working for a Mississippi firm on a commercial case. Cox knew the restriction had absolutely no basis in the law, but he got away with the arrant policy for six years and freely admitted the ban applied only to "Jews and niggers from New York."[10]

To behold Cox was to witness a specimen of racial bigotry. The judge ordinarily pronounced the word *negro* as "nigra" in court, but in vulgar flashes of temper, he used the more obscene "nigger." In January 1964, African Americans from Canton, Mississippi, brought a voter registration suit against the local circuit clerk. Judge Cox dismissed the plaintiffs as "a bunch of niggers." On another occasion, Harold Cox extenuated Mississippi's literacy test on the grounds that "the intelligence of the colored people don't [*sic*] compare ratiowise to white people." When a group of Negro teachers filed suit to protect their jobs in a desegregating school system, Cox hooted the remonstrance out of court as "colored people's antics." Only the most heinous crimes could arouse a scintilla of empathy from the judge. In 1967, he presided over a case brought by the Justice Department for the three murdered Freedom Summer volunteers—Schwerner, Chaney, and Goodman—and convicted seven Klansmen for violating the slain men's civil rights. The sentencing stunned Mel Leventhal, who chatted with Cox after the verdict. "Melvyn," the judge confided in chambers, "those guys went too far. If they had beat up those civil rights workers, I could have understood. But killing them—they went too far. They had to go to jail."[11]

Cox's incurable racism and near-total disregard for civil rights statutes drummed up comparisons to a rogue court. In 1964, *Time* magazine referenced Cox and other Kennedy judicial appointees when it opined that "unhappily some of those promising district judges have turned out to be so devoted to segregation that they may be the greatest obstacle to equal rights in the South today." Roy Wilkins questioned Cox's sanity and protested to congressmen, "He is unfit to be a Judge in an American court." Tucked deep within Mississippi, Cox weathered any outside criticisms. The *New York Times* reported, "Judge Cox has shown no sign of being disturbed by such attacks. When asked to disqualify himself in rights cases, he has refused." Repeated calls for his ouster merely "increased the esteem in which he is held by white officials and lawyers in Mississippi," the *Times* commented. Behind his towering rages, there was method to Cox's madness. While the judge's improper behavior in civil rights cases could degenerate into acidulous racism, the overarching impact of his decisions negated the rights of blacks, forestalled racial justice, and inhibited school desegregation. The status quo had to be preserved.[12]

A string of judges on the Southern District of Mississippi—Sidney C. Mize, Harold Cox, Dan M. Russell Jr., and Walter L. Nixon Jr.—looked unfavorably upon civil rights claims and ensured that desegregation shambled through their court at a snail's pace. No federal judge in Mississippi was as bumptious about *Brown* as the inimitable Cox, but the other judges of the southern district could hardly be described as enthusiasts for integration. Sydney Mize served as district judge from 1937 until his death in 1965. His mild-mannered replacement, Dan Russell, practiced corporate and personal injury law on the Mississippi Gulf Coast before President Lyndon Johnson appointed him to the federal bench in October 1965. Russell's father, a former state chancery court judge, taught law at the University of Mississippi and counted James Eastland among his students. Walter Nixon, a Biloxi native and another Johnson appointee, joined the southern district in 1968. Eastland wielded his clout as Senate Judiciary chair to massage the selection of Nixon, Russell, and Cox, who, according to two observers of the South's court beat, "have tended to join in the resistance to change."[13]

Jim Eastland and his junior colleague, Senator John C. Stennis, set the tone and contoured the personalities of Mississippi's district courts. After the momentous 1954 *Brown* verdict, Senator Eastland pilloried the Supreme Court. Maintaining that the "institutions, the culture and the civilization of the South are built" upon racial segregation, he insisted that the "future greatness of America depends upon racial purity and the maintenance of Anglo-Saxon institutions." Eastland argued the Court's "campaign against segregation is based upon illegality" and implored white Mississippians to buck it. The senator did more than rail against the Court and its decision; he shored up Mississippi's southern district as a segregationist vector. Senator

Stennis, on the other hand, approached the race question with a softer touch than his counterpart. Reacting less vocally to *Brown*, Stennis figured that the Court would outline "fairly liberal ground rules" for implementation that would leave white southerners with some wiggle room to compromise. Inflammatory hyperbole, he contended, would only embarrass the South, anger blacks, and make bad matters worse. Rather than fulminating defiance to stiffen Jim Crow's local defenses, Stennis channeled his energies into federal issues in Washington. He tapped the nominees for the more hospitable northern district.[14]

As a result of the variance in the senators' segregationist stripes, Mississippi's two federal judicial districts tackled civil rights litigation in diametric ways. In the northern district, Judges Claude F. Clayton, William C. Keady, and later Orma R. Smith, who replaced Clayton in 1968, regularly scheduled LDF and NAACP motions for hearing. None of them disqualified out-of-state lawyers from appearing in court or flung racial epithets at counsel. LDF attorneys viewed Clayton, Keady, and Smith as fair-minded and conscientious stewards of the law. Because the northern district's judges afforded black plaintiffs a timely hearing, the school districts in that section of the state more readily developed plans for desegregation, in spite of objections by local education officials and white parents. Litigants in the northern jurisdiction, consequently, rarely resorted to appealing to the Fifth Circuit for injunctive relief. The southern district, however, fought integration tooth and nail. While judges considered their responses to civil rights, NAACP LDF litigators monitored school desegregation in Holmes County.[15]

After the maiden year of freedom of choice, school desegregation in Holmes had sunk into a quicksand of counterblows and hostility. Meetings between LDF counsel and their clients unearthed a stratagem of school board equivocation, but the real damage ran deeper. Many blacks remained vigilant, heartened by the breach in a major racial barrier, while others lost faith in the law's ability to alleviate the hassle and hardship of choosing to attend a white school. Segregationists brought to bear economic and other pressure, overtly and covertly, on black students and their families. Whites also continued to bail out on the public school system as the new private academies siphoned off students and teachers. "Extremist segregationist elements," recoiled one LDF memo, had launched "their counter attack." More disturbingly, another Inc. Fund letter divulged, "A common problem in this whole situation is the very limited amount of actual . . . questioning or 'pushing' on the part of the integrating parents. Many things irk the parents, but, on the whole, very few have ever done anything separately or together" to fight back. They and others across the state sacrificed so much only to secure a tiny beachhead in previously all-white schools. Approaching the 1966–67 school year, well under 1 percent of the Negro children in Mississippi, Alabama, and Louisiana attended classes with whites. Faculty desegregation had not even begun. Segregated public education remained entrenched. In the hands of the wrong school administrators and judges, the *Brown* opinion purred like a paper tiger.[16]

Amid the lassitude, Marian Wright appraised the situation. "While cases involving plaintiffs and clear-cut issues test Marian's mettle," *Ebony* magazine noted in June 1966, "ones that seem to move her most, at least emotionally, are those focusing on individual families who dared to register their children in formerly all-white schools." A community of parents in Holmes had gathered with her one night to air grievances about the rabbit hole of problems they had run down. Upon admission of blacks, whites bolted from public schools and sent their children to segregationist academies. Freedom of choice had not met the expectations hyped by LDF lawyers. Black children could attend any school of their choice in their district, but white educators badgered them for "bad manners," "poor records," and "bad character." White teachers too eagerly flunked black students. White bus drivers still rudely refused to pull over for African-American children. Most black kids tramped two to three miles to school. Others, for a variety of reasons, preferred to cap their education where they started, in all-black schools. Only the first four grades, furthermore, had been integrated, thus far. "The worst thing these people live with," Marian Wright pitied them, "is fear. They're afraid that their homes might be burned or they'll be killed or their jobs lost." "Even more devastating," she said, "these people know that most of the time the violators and killers won't even be punished. One has to understand this." In so many respects, white dominance seemed impervious.[17]

Despite winning court cases and registering their children in formerly all-white schools with the help of Inc. Fund attorneys, blacks in Holmes wondered if they would ever unseat the white school board. With county elections still a year off, local movement leaders hoped to gain control of the Holmes County Board of Education. Disappointment for blacks came when state politicians clogged the legal channel to replace white county educators with African Americans. In June 1966, House Bill 183 sailed through the Mississippi legislature, which banned qualified electors in majority-black areas of a county from voting for school superintendent. Though later ruled unconstitutional, HB 183 temporarily paralyzed institutional education reform in Holmes County. Owing to the 1965 Voting Rights Act, blacks notched the right to vote in Holmes, but the law diffused their new power by prohibiting them from selecting a friendly school superintendent. In the upcoming November 1967 election, blacks failed to prevent Lester Thompson's return as chief education official in the county. Blacks and their lawyers did not give up, however. More litigation and judicial intercession could override board hegemony and break the stalemate in school desegregation. The fate of Holmes County's freedom-of-choice plan stood poised for a dramatic development.[18]

In 1966, a ruling by the Fifth Circuit Court of Appeals brought school desegregation and the Holmes County case closer to a climax. A three-judge appellate panel agreed to hear *United States v. Jefferson County Board of Education*. In the New Orleans federal courthouse, Judges Homer Thornberry, Harold Cox, who sat by designation, and John Minor Wisdom convened in December to rule on a suit filed by the Justice Department against the county school system surrounding Birmingham, Alabama. Wisdom had practiced corporate law in New Orleans, his hometown, and had sought job opportunities for African Americans as a member of the Urban League as well as on President Eisenhower's Committee on Government Contracts. Despite Wisdom's liberal tendencies, Eisenhower put him on the Fifth Circuit in 1957. Wisdom earned a reputation as the court's leading legal scholar and apologist for integration. He spent almost a year preparing the appellate panel's *U.S. v. Jefferson County* opinion, which he later considered the most important of his career. In *Jefferson County*, Wisdom declared an end to what he deemed an intolerable gridlock in school desegregation.[19]

In late December, with John Minor Wisdom presiding, the judges voted two to one to convert the "still-functioning dual system to a unitary, nonracial system—lock, stock, and barrel," stated Wisdom, who spoke for the panel. Wisdom composed a daringly innovative statement and dissected the problems inherent in the freedom-of-choice shibboleth and school desegregation. Tired of the federal court system's ambiguity as to whether judicial remedies should mandate "integration" or merely arrest segregation, he reconciled the situation. In his lengthy analysis, Wisdom thoroughly repudiated the inconspicuous position of the courts and scrapped the distinction between "desegregation" and "integration," which some southern judges used to argue that *Brown* required the former but not the latter. "If this process be 'integration,'" Wisdom boldly announced, "so be it." He also harbored doubts about freedom of choice and demolished the popular plan's "serious shortcomings." Wisdom asserted that school boards bore an "affirmative duty" to integrate and facilitate "a bona fide unitary school system where schools are not white schools or Negro schools—just schools."[20]

Without nullifying freedom of choice, Wisdom's opinion produced the sweeping effect of compelling all six states that comprised the Fifth Circuit (Texas, Louisiana, Mississippi, Alabama, Georgia, and Florida) to ratify a uniform set of directives drafted by the federal government by the 1967–68 school year. *Jefferson County* contained a remedial decree giving school boards and district courts meticulous instructions on how to achieve integration of student bodies, faculties, facilities, and programs. Any school district that failed to comply with the strict standards laid down by the Fifth Circuit would suffer the loss of federal funds. School districts could avoid sanctions only by adhering to the minimum guidelines of the Department of Health, Education, and Welfare (HEW)—charged with administering the Civil Rights Act of 1964. Wisdom put wayward school boards on notice and warned that they could no longer expect to hide behind sympathetic judges' robes. His wording took a swipe at the likes of Harold Cox. Though school districts had found "refuge in the federal courts . . . many of these had not moved an inch toward desegregation."[21]

By vindicating HEW criteria, Wisdom's decree also essentially clinched the executive branch of the federal government as the proper enforcement mechanism. On behalf of HEW and the 1964 Civil Rights Act, Wisdom called on the office of the president to direct the Justice Department to bring suits against noncompliant school districts. "A national effort," which he hoped to steer, "bringing together Congress, the executive, and the judiciary may be able to make meaningful the right of Negro children to equal educational opportunities." "*The courts acting alone,*" Wisdom emphasized, "*have failed.*" He had erected an enormously powerful foundation for school desegregation law. "The clock has ticked the last tick for tokenism and delay in the name of 'deliberate speed,'" Judge Wisdom concluded. The courts henceforth would not tolerate the enrollment of a handful of blacks in formerly all-white schools. Within a week of the December 29 release of the opinion in *Jefferson County* and with President Johnson's consent, HEW published its 1967 desegregation guidelines.[22]

Despite Johnson's endorsement, the opinion in *Jefferson County* did not win universal encomia. Although hailed by most legal commentators in the North, many southern politicians, school boards, ordinary white citizens, and some federal judges disdained the decision. Judge Harold Cox, the third member of the *Jefferson County* panel, did not join with Wisdom and Thornberry. Rather than sit in injured silence, he let loose a searing dissent. An adherent to the dictum that desegregation did not imply integration, Cox vociferously objected to Wisdom's formulation and referred to the panel's majority as "impatient... trailblazers." "Surely," Cox lambasted them, "only two of the judges of this Court may not single-handedly reverse those decisions and change such law of this Circuit." He laced Wisdom's "extreme view" and dismissed the opinion as a "harsh and mailed fist decision" that would twist the "rope of liberty... [into] a garrote... in the name of protecting civil rights of some" while stamping out the "civil rights and constitutional liberties of all our citizens, their children and their children's children." Cox's drumbeat of dissent surprised no one at Jackson's LDF office because, according to Mel Leventhal, the irascible judge invariably "marched to his own drummer."[23]

Whereas LDF attorneys tried to snap the tediously slow grind of desegregation for years, *Jefferson County* handed down game-changing orders for compliance that adopted HEW guidelines essentially verbatim. Perturbed by Wisdom's logic, Cox's dissent put him on record as opposing the Fifth Circuit's wishes. On March 29, 1967, the Fifth convened en banc and by a vote of 10–2 affirmed, with only minor clarifications, Judge Wisdom's opinion in *Jefferson County*. The task of enforcing the decision now fell to Dan Russell. In July, Judge Russell issued a strictly worded decree that permanently enjoined the Holmes County Board of Education from "discriminating on the basis of race or color" in the operation of the county school system. The federal court in Jackson ordered complete desegregation of the county's schools by the 1967–68 school term. Russell instructed that the school board "shall take affirmative action to disestablish all school segregation and to eliminate the effects of the dual school system." In keeping with *Jefferson County*, students would exercise their "freedom of choice" annually. Teachers and administrators, Russell admonished, should not attempt to influence student choices in any manner. The decision required desegregated bus transportation, faculties, and student bodies. "Race or color shall not be a factor in the hiring, assignment, reassignment, promotion, demotion, or dismissal of teachers and other staff," his order read.[24]

As another school year got under way in Holmes County, potential racial flare-ups abounded. The battleground in the courts seeped into the home front. The mood of Holmes whites shifted palpably as court-ordered desegregation permeated the rural county and disrupted traditional race relations. Whites and blacks sized each other up apprehensively. Each wondered what the other side intended. A few rabid elements in the white business community responded to desegregation with implacable opposition. The occasional doctor's office or local business defied federal statutes by discriminating against blacks, treating them differently, or refusing to hire them. Most merchants complied with the 1964 Civil Rights Act and covered the words

"WHITE" and "COLORED" at their stores, even though they often segregated the facilities informally. One white Holmes Countian detected that nearly everybody's "nerves were on edge." The perceived downfall of the public schools to Negro students, in particular, grated on many whites, stung them psychologically, and pinched their pocketbooks. They felt driven from the public schools and favored private education over freedom of choice. "Private school tuition had spelled financial strain for most of us," remarked a white woman from a prominent Lexington family, and at "home the parties stopped abruptly." Some affluent whites cashiered their black domestics to save tuition money for the segregationist academies. Across Holmes, she sensed a toxic brew. More attuned to natural rhythms, white farmers and wealthy planters "moaned more loudly about the unpredictable: the weather, the yield, the federal courts." Like other whites, they resented the incursion of desegregation and civil rights into their tranquil little community.[25]

When Lexington's high school opened in the fall of 1967, the freedom-of-choice plan desegregated the upper grades and incensed whites further. "The town had not known a change as sudden as this for years," noticed author Melany Neilson, who grew up in Lexington. "Now that people had to spend money on private school tuition, there was a fervid outbreak of anger." Shrill exchanges marked the white community's outlook. Strong emotions and reactions exposed a deep resentment and suspicion of the countervailing forces arrayed against them. Neilson captured ordinary people's delirium about an epidemic of school desegregation descending upon their county. Explained one accountant:

> The change was temporary and . . . we would get our schools back, come hell or high water. Another [man] said it was the town leaders' duty to devise an admission test which would keep out blacks but which would allow Central Holmes [the new private academy] to keep its tax-exempt status. There was talk of blood, and there were tears, too. A woman who worked a few acres of land outside Coxburg believed that blacks had cheated her children out of their rightful free education; she had five children's tuition to pay—and her life savings in a cookie jar. But these were incidents that barely scratched the surface of the town. Everything had changed. There were rumors of blacks striking to protest unfair chances of employment on the square. Even on the quietest sunny day the people glared and sighed and grumbled. Eyes hardened and mouths turned down at the corners. And by some new sense of habit we shortened our thoughts so that we would not wander out into the uncertainty beyond tomorrow.[26]

The confusion rattled Neilson, but the growing racial acrimony and miasma chilled her. Whites hunkered down, ready to repulse future Negro assaults. Parents taught their children to stay away from blacks. Adults outlined the unsettling conditions to the young:

> We should keep our distance, that was it. Our distance and some kind of dignity, [but the dignity] gave way to anger, and . . . it now seemed all of a sudden that most everyone, even fine families, was using the word "nigger," as often as "colored," as much in anger as unity. . . . And every time we spoke the word "nigger," each time a little more in condescension, we began to feel some power in the word itself. The more we all said it, not about anyone in particular, but about the whole group of them, the more I came to feel that there was nothing wrong with the word itself, so that in the classroom and even at church, if I heard it without expecting it, I felt some kind of obscure, dim satisfaction. . . . There was a darker side to the time, shadows of violence. There were stories of one man on a backroad outside Pickens who shot at blacks from his rocking chair on the front porch, just for the hell of it. There were disappearances and anonymous phone calls. . . . There was the silent fear of uprising among blacks throughout the county.

The Supreme Court's next landmark ruling on race and education confirmed whites' fraught moment.[27]

In early 1968, Holmes County school officials received a notice from the Office for Civil Rights (OCR) in Washington that the county district had failed to meet its desegregation objectives outlined by the *Jefferson County* case. The board met and filed a compliance plan that promised to hire more black teachers and staff, but the OCR rejected the proposal and ordered a substitute. Unwilling to yield to the office's authority, the board developed and submitted its bastardized version of a desegregation plan to the federal court in Jackson. Before the district court could consider the board's itinerary, the Supreme Court rendered a rigorous verdict that fortified Judge Wisdom and the Fifth Circuit.[28]

Decided in May 1968, *Green v. County School Board of New Kent County* conceded that while freedom of choice might be helpful as a means to accomplish desegregation in some situations, "the general experience under 'freedom of choice' to date has been such as to indicate its ineffectiveness as a tool of desegregation." The Court explicitly held that a freedom-of-choice plan used in a rural Virginia county had resulted in no white transfers into black schools and only a 15 percent black crossover. The district's anemic desegregation rate fell short of constitutional requirements because "rather than

further the dismantling of the dual system, the plan has operated simply to
burden children and their parents with a responsibility which *Brown II* placed
squarely on the School Board." Before *Green*, district courts considered only
a school board's intention to desegregate, not the consequences of its actions.
With *Green*, however, impact and effects, not protestations of good faith, became the new edict. Moreover, the high court charged that if a freedom-of-
choice plan "fails to undo segregation, other means must be used to achieve
this end." While many lower courts and school districts still seemed uncer-
tain how much school desegregation was satisfactory, the Supreme Court
clarified that, in several areas—student assignments, faculty and staff com-
position, transportation, extracurriculars, and facilities—southern educators had done precious little to erase the rump forms of school segregation.
There should be no skeletons of the dual-school system—"no black schools
or white schools, just schools." *Green* also expressly required every school
district found in violation of *Brown* to assume an "affirmative duty" to extract
racial identifiability "root and branch" and made that duty urgent. Speaking
for a unanimous bench, Justice William Brennan announced, "The time for
mere 'deliberate speed' has run out. . . . The burden on a school board today is
to come forward with a plan that promises realistically to work, and promises
realistically to work *now*."[29]

Following the *Green* decision, black plaintiffs across the South flooded
district courts with hundreds of requests to grant injunctive relief consistent with the Supreme Court's order that school boards produce a desegregation plan that "promises realistically to work *now*." One renewed petition
to dismember the dual schools came from Holmes County. Together with
Negro supplicants involved in analogous litigation against thirteen other
Mississippi school boards, Inc. Fund and Justice Department attorneys filed
a brief in the district court to demonstrate that "the token results achieved by
these [freedom-of-choice] plans [in the fourteen school districts] were even
less than the results held insufficient by *Green*." Pupil desegregation in the
fourteen school systems sued by the plaintiffs was almost indiscernible. In
Holmes County, the LDF extrapolated that 95 percent of African Americans
would attend all-black schools during the 1969–70 school year. The projected
total of blacks enrolled in predominantly white schools would amount to 4.5
percent. Government and LDF counsel argued that the district courts should
compel school systems to rearrange their classes by the fall of 1968, just three
months away.[30]

Though the Supreme Court frowned upon freedom of choice in *Green*,
the Court's ruling did not explicitly condemn all freedom-of-choice schemes

as ineffective measures to desegregate. The lack of clarity and precision left the lower courts in a conundrum. As a consequence, several district courts, including Mississippi's southern district, disclaimed the petitioners' motions, thereby allowing the 1968–69 school term to begin under the old freedom-of-choice guidelines. In Holmes County, integration remained miniscule. Blacks made up less than 14 percent of the student body in Lexington's schools. Of 533 students in the city's schools, only seventy-four black children attended. Countywide, however, whites accounted for only 14 percent of the net enrollment, or 911 of 6,452 students. No white child attended a majority-black school anywhere in the county. As a result of the district courts' refusal to grant relief, the beleaguered claimants, including the Holmes plaintiffs, asked the Fifth Circuit for a summary reversal of the lower courts. In *Adams v. Mathews*, a September 1968 decision enveloping over forty cases kindred to but separate from the Holmes suit, the Fifth Circuit instructed the district courts to form special three-judge panels, generally composed of one court of appeals judge and two district judges, to give the consolidated cases the "highest priority" and conduct hearings in each case no later than November 4, 1968. The losing party could appeal directly to the Supreme Court.[31]

On remand from *Adams*, the district court panel of Cox, Russell, and Nixon braided together the nine cases brought by the LDF with other suits filed by the Department of Justice against thirty-three Mississippi school boards. The bundled cases, including *Alexander v. Holmes*, proceeded under the title *United States v. Hinds County School Board*. At a hearing in Jackson on Monday, October 7, lawyers for the LDF and the Department of Justice worked hand-in-glove to clear the path for desegregation. The district court flirted with admitting defense testimony about purported disparities between predominantly white and all-black classes and what role social mores played in the desegregation process. Arguing on behalf of the United States, however, Justice Department attorneys objected to the defense's deposition of expert witnesses who wedded academic performance to race. The government counsel had also contended that the Supreme Court insisted that community attitudes toward desegregation—for example, white flight from public schools that had become "too" integrated—should likewise be stricken. Presiding for the district court, Harold Cox overruled them.[32]

At the end of the daylong hearing, the three-judge panel took the case under advisement. The southern district resisted every effort to proceed in a timely manner and deferred action for seven months before handing down an unfavorable ruling. On May 13, 1969, the judges returned from hiatus and issued a unanimous opinion that discredited the plaintiffs' analysis of the issues. Although recognizing that the bracketed appeals would "update the *Jefferson* decree" and conform with *Green*, the panel upheld freedom of choice for all of the defendant school districts on the assumption that it might work sometime in the future. Cox, Russell, and Nixon enlisted an unusual device for managing school desegregation lawsuits for the districts involved in *U.S. v. Hinds County*. Rather than addressing each motion in turn, as mandated by the Fifth Circuit, they scheduled a joint hearing for the constellation of cases. By wrapping more than thirty school desegregation suits into one pronouncement, the judges refused to prescribe an inclusive antidote for the various plans facing districts. The district court was extraordinarily lenient in staving off integration and accepting local freedom-of-choice options that provided for the most fragmentary sort of desegregation. In addition to a continuance of piecemeal desegregation, the court held that, as a matter of law, the plaintiffs and their lawyers had failed to "show a lack of substantial progress toward the disestablishment of a dual-school system and the establishment of a unitary school system of both races." Referencing *Green* to justify the freedom-of-choice arrangements, the court proffered a short dissertation in defense of the school boards: "The facts and circumstances in practically all of these cases . . . show this Court to its entire satisfaction that these schools, operating under the freedom of choice plan, have operated in the very best of good faith with the Court in an honest effort to comply with and conform to all of the requirements of the [*Jefferson*] decree." Unwilling or unable to pinpoint a single occasion where "any colored parent, or colored child did not do exactly what they wanted to do in deciding as to the school which the colored child would attend," the court claimed it had no alternative but to reaffirm freedom of choice. More damning was the court's belief that freedom of choice afforded the best means of fulfilling the desires of black children and their white peers. Besides, they reasoned, "the vast majority of colored children simply do not wish to attend a school which is predominantly white, and white children simply do not wish to attend a school which is predominantly Negro."[33]

In summing up the case, the district judges found that the school boards had not been negligent in discharging their duties. They noted complications caused by a provision in *Jefferson County* that "at no time shall any official, teacher, or employee of the school system influence any parent, or other adult person serving as a parent, or any student, in the exercise of a choice or favor or penalize any person because of the choice made." In the court's rendition of events, each educational official "in every one of these cases . . . testified convincingly . . . that this provision . . . had interfered with a fair and just and proper operation of the freedom of choice plan in these schools." The district judges exonerated the school boards of any wrongdoing. Rather, the lower court upbraided the appeals court, the liability should be with the Fifth Circuit, the germ of the *Jefferson* decree and its odious clause.[34]

Soon after the three-man district court's May 13 ruling, the LDF and Justice Department appealed to the Fifth Circuit for either a summary reversal or an expedited consideration of the cases. In Jackson, Inc. Fund lawyers readied for more legal skirmishing with the district court. Whenever Cox, Russell, or Nixon flouted the Fifth Circuit or trammeled desegregation orders, LDF attorneys fended them off almost reflexively. "We practiced judicial ju-jitsu" with the district court, explained Melvyn Zarr. "Whenever they spouted off at us or the higher courts, we flipped them over and got better relief." On June 25, 1969, the appellate court granted their motion for a rehearing and scheduled oral arguments for July 2. The action moved forward again under the umbrella heading *United States v. Hinds County School Board* and encompassed the *Alexander v. Holmes* suit. With statistical data collated by the U.S. Office of Education, the Department of Justice's brief for the petitioners disputed the district court's approval of the defendants' freedom-of-choice plans. The government also argued that the lower court's ruling contradicted the Supreme Court's decision in *Green* and the direct mandate of the Fifth Circuit in *Adams v. Mathews*. The brief reiterated a disturbing pattern of minimal school desegregation. More than 96 percent of the black students in the districts covered by the *Hinds* case still attended traditionally black schools. The largest percentage of blacks enrolled at any previously all-white school was about 10 percent. School activities remained segregated as well. Black and white schools competed athletically in none of the school districts. Justice Department lawyers requested the court of appeals to remand the case with orders to the district court that desegregation plans must dissolve dual-school systems by the 1969–70 school term.[35]

On appeal, the Fifth Circuit wasted little time vacating the southern district's opinion and resumed authority in the *Hinds* case. In a judgment announced on July 3, 1969, just seven weeks after the district court's ruling, a three-judge panel, comprised of John R. Brown, Homer Thornberry, and Lewis Morgan, gaveled Mississippi's southern district to implement techniques to disestablish dual-school systems. After a thorough review, the Fifth Circuit concurred with the Justice Department's findings that deemed "freedom of choice" constitutionally unsatisfactory. The appeals court noted the total absence of white enrollment in black schools, the token integration of blacks in formerly white schools, and the projected enrollment statistics for

the upcoming school year, which augured little progress toward desegregation. Evaluating the districts sued by the black plaintiffs, the court found that
the highest percentage of black crossover into white schools was 16 percent.
Segregation persisted in school facilities, faculties, and extracurricular activities as well.[36]

The July 3 decision adjudged that the defendant school districts "will no longer be able to rely on freedom of choice as the method for disestablishing their
dual school systems." Acquiescing to the Justice Department's suggestion,
the court enjoined the defendants to coordinate with HEW experts from the
Office of Education to disassemble the dual systems in question. To expedite
the process, the Fifth Circuit ordered school boards to prepare and implement
plans for the district court by the fall semester of 1969. The court set August 11,
1969, as the deadline. In a modified order on July 25, the appeals court amended
its prior mandate and pushed back the date to September 1, 1969.[37]

On August 11, the date originally established by the Fifth Circuit for the
submission of the new plans, the Office of Education supplied a desegregation framework for the thirty-three school boards to the district court.
Thirty complied. Three school boards, including Holmes County's Board
of Education, wriggled free and applied for exempt status due to problems
particular to their districts that required postponement until the beginning
of the 1970–71 school year. Citing expensive construction costs to refurbish
older buildings and to accommodate a larger student body in a unitary school
system, Holmes County's school board filed an alternative plan to stay implementation for one year. HEW officials accepted what they considered an
"educationally and administratively sound" request made in good faith. The
board's last-ditch delay, ultimately, proved no more permanent than its earlier
rejoinders. Time was simply not on its side. The proverbial clock that Judge
John Minor Wisdom alluded to in *Jefferson County* was ticking in Holmes.[38]

In the mid- to late 1960s, the Fifth Circuit handed down decision after decision that followed the course that *Brown* had charted. One study of the Court
of Appeals for the Fifth Circuit described it as "a judicial phalanx that held
firm against the obstructionism, foot-dragging, and outright refusal to begin
the process of school integration that characterized practically every school
district in Georgia, Alabama, Mississippi, and Louisiana." Opinions in favor
of civil rights tumbled out of the appellate court. Black plaintiffs in Holmes
County and their LDF lawyers, understandably, radiated optimism.[39]

Without the robust docket in the Fifth Circuit, integration may not have
been pursued for another decade or more. The court of appeals had punc-
tured "freedom of choice" and punched the accelerator on the judicial speed

limit. "If not for the Fifth Circuit," reflected Reuben Anderson, part of a new crop of attorneys at the Jackson LDF, "we would be years and years behind in terms of what was accomplished in the civil rights movement." So many state and federal judges had opposed civil rights at every turn. Wrested from the lower courts, real change "had to come from a higher court," Anderson apprehended. "[W]hat we had was a lot of federal judges who felt that, yeah, integration's going to happen, but let's let it happen ten years down the road. Let's take this thing one step at a time. And the Constitution doesn't say that, and the Fifth Circuit was able to make sure that the states within its boundaries were integrated and it happened." The "judges on that court were probably more instrumental than anybody else in bringing about that change," Anderson commended them. The Fifth Circuit's vigorous desegregation efforts had encouraged his organization to fight on in the courts. Flushed with victory, Anderson called the appeals court "a Godsend for the movement." Though a landslide of appellate rulings had energized school desegregation, the issue had hardly been settled. Larger forces worked at odds to assist and to thwart integration.[40]

While the Inc. Fund celebrated, the next crucial development in *Alexander v. Holmes* emanated from neither the august marble courthouse in New Orleans nor the Corinthian-columned temple of justice in the Supreme Court but from the Oval Office. LDF attorneys did not mistake Richard Nixon as an ally of the civil rights movement. In 1969, Nixon came to the White House on a platform infused with subtle racism. Nearly every white southerner who backed Nixon for the presidency expected him to stave off the impending catastrophe of court-ordered integration. He would be their tribune. Strong signs that a conservative administration would stymie desegregation gave whites hope that the federal government might still accept some semblance of separate-but-equal schools over unalloyed desegregation. Surreptitiously and sedulously, the president outflanked the activist Fifth Circuit. Before the school bells chimed in September, Nixon threw his thunderbolt.[41]

Day laborers picking cotton on Marcella Plantation, Mileston, Mississippi, October 1939. (Library of Congress/Marion Post Wolcott)

Tchula school, grades 6 and 7, Tchula, Mississippi, 1956. (John E. Phay Collection, Special Collections, University of Mississippi)

Mel Leventhal, 1970.
(Courtesy of Melvyn R.
Leventhal)

Judge Harold Cox outside the federal building in Jackson, Mississippi,
January 11, 1965. (© 1965 The Associated Press/Jack Thornell)

Jack Greenberg, NAACP director-counsel of the Legal Defense and Educational Fund, at a press conference in New York, October 31, 1969. (© 1969 The Associated Press/ Allen Green)

Jerris Leonard (*left*) and John Satterfield outside the Supreme Court, October 31, 1969. (Walter E. Bennett)

A 1969 Herblock cartoon, *Washington Post*, October 29, 1969. (© The Herb Block Foundation; courtesy of the Library of Congress, Prints and Photographs Division, LC-DIG-ppmsca-17205)

A 1969 Herblock cartoon, *Washington Post*, October 31, 1969. (© The Herb Block Foundation/Library of Congress)

— CHAPTER FIVE —

All the President's Mendacity

❀

Watch what we do instead of what we say.
—Attorney General John Mitchell

THE FRENETIC SEVENTEEN-MONTH stretch between *Green v. County School Board of New Kent County* and the Supreme Court's next major decision on race in *Alexander v. Holmes County Board of Education* witnessed a number of far-reaching judicial decrees issued in the waning days of the southern civil rights struggle. In May 1968, *Green* set the new standard for southern school desegregation. Nearly a year and a half later, *Alexander v. Holmes's* unmistakable footprint told southerners that the time to comply had run out. On October 29, 1969, the high court handed down *Alexander* with a peremptory order for immediate desegregation. The case pried open Mississippi's defiantly all-white school districts with shocking effect and triggered an avalanche of implementation directives demanding massive integration across the South. *Alexander* did not reinterpret the law in an imaginative way, but it, along with *Green*, bent the arc of history more toward equality by defeating segregationists in the most recalcitrant southern state and in a set piece with the incoming president.

Richard Nixon was hardly a friend of blacks, but on the 1968 campaign trail he distanced himself from the volcanic disquiet and strident racism of George Corley Wallace, Alabama's former governor and the far-right American Independent Party's presidential candidate. In seeking election, Nixon had deftly given white southerners the sense that he would rescue them from the brink of school desegregation and provide tonic from the deep-seated racial problems gripping the nation. He pursued the presidency on a main plank of lukewarm statements on civil rights and tough talk about dissent. Nixon vowed to end the domestic turmoil in America by restoring "law and order" in the streets and cracking down on protesters and radicals. He also pledged to re-configure the highly activist Warren Court by naming strict-constructionist justices and stated his opposition to "forced integration."[1]

Candidate Nixon's motives were not amoral or purely expedient. His personal convictions matched his political machinations. "The Court was right on *Brown* and wrong on *Green*," Nixon told his speechwriter William Safire in June 1968. Nixon favored freedom-of-choice plans that upheld the requirements of *Brown* to abolish state-sanctioned segregation. He opposed, rather, the *Green* decision's emphasis on compulsory and balanced integration, especially when accomplished by busing students from one school district to another. Nixon's kneejerk conservative reaction tried to keep "government out of the social decisions of the people," Bill Safire deciphered. "Just as government should not enforce the beliefs of those who felt the races should be separated," Safire elaborated, "it should not enforce the beliefs of those who felt the races should not be separated." Nixon acknowledged *Brown* as the irrefutable law of the land and accepted "the responsibility to make certain that desegregation took place wherever racial separation had come about by law"—nothing more, nothing less. Since a president cannot pick and choose which laws and rulings to obey, Nixon cultivated the perception that, if elected, he would find counterweights to contest *Green*.[2]

The impression seduced many white southerners. By insinuating that he would back off on integration, Nixon pandered to disgruntled segregationists and wooed the white South into an emerging Republican alliance with blue-collar workers and business elites. As Mel Leventhal of the Legal Defense Fund explained months after the election, standpat southerners regarded Richard Nixon as a latter-day Rutherford B. Hayes, a president who would "end the modern reconstruction," just as Hayes had abrogated post–Civil War Reconstruction. In November 1968, Nixon snatched Tennessee, Kentucky, Virginia, both Carolinas, and Florida from the once-solidly Democratic South. Buoyed by the president-elect's tepid commitment to civil rights, southern politicians mounted a last-ditch effort against school desegregation just after his inauguration.[3]

Mindful of upsetting powerful southerners on Capitol Hill, Nixon hosted Republican senator J. Strom Thurmond of South Carolina and a coterie of provincial mandarins at the White House. With freedom-of-choice cases pending throughout the region, members of the southern retinue paid Nixon a visit to ventilate their frustrations and demand repayment for their electoral support. If the president wanted to court the South's voters and achieve a new

Republican majority, he would need to uphold his end of the Faustian bargain known as the "Southern Strategy"—the cryptic byword for Nixon's gambit to gain Republican footing in Dixie's already fecund ground for conservatism. Most urgently, the white South sought relief from the Department of Health, Education, and Welfare's unrelenting emphasis on school desegregation. The South's balky leadership began to lean on Nixon to shelve the hated HEW guidelines that would prune federal funds to school districts that failed to dismantle dual systems.[4]

Unremitting rumors that Nixon was under heavy political pressure to rescind the HEW guidelines did not immediately signal a major administrative departure on desegregation. For the first hundred days of Nixon's tenure in office, not all the president's men were of one mind as to how, when, or even whether they ought to tackle the thorny issue of school desegregation. Complicating matters, Nixon allowed his administration to shear into rival camps. An ideological tug-of-war for the bureaucracy's soul played out. On the left side of the dispute were the civil rights and education staff members in HEW, racially progressive Republican lawmakers, and a sprinkling of liberals in the executive branch. They argued that the Supreme Court required a minimum amount of actual racial mixing in the schools. HEW, the watchdog organization over numerous school systems, pushed hard for the enactment of desegregation plans in the South and threatened to withhold funds from holdout districts. Any deviation, the liberal faction feared, would only invite further recalcitrance from the laggard South and more token integration. In the rising starboard wing lurked the arch-segregationist Strom Thurmond, backed by white southern voters; Attorney General John N. Mitchell, Nixon's former campaign manager and law partner; and, it eventually became obvious, the president himself.[5]

After Richard Nixon came into office, the appointment of the secretary of HEW momentarily uplifted civil rights groups. To head up the agency, the president turned to an old pal from California, the man who served as his campaign manager in 1960—Robert H. Finch. Finch had a solid civil rights record and was generally regarded as the most liberal member of Nixon's cabinet. Known for his sympathetic stand on civil rights, Finch set to work enforcing HEW guidelines. During his first weeks in office, Finch trimmed funds for a few school districts despite squeals of protest from the South. Finch tapped thirty-year-old Leon E. Panetta, a fellow Californian and progressive Republican, to run his Office for Civil Rights. Panetta eagerly dedicated HEW to the fall 1969 deadline and tolerated a one-year deferment only for truly extraordinary cases filed in good faith.[6]

John Mitchell's appointment as attorney general, on the other hand, was received less favorably. Whereas Finch committed HEW to bring about a swift end to token integration in the South, Mitchell advised Nixon to decelerate the pace of desegregation. The attorney general edged into Finch's domain and wanted "the onus of school desegregation shifted from the federal bureaucracy (controllable by Nixon) to the federal courts (not controllable by Nixon)," wrote journalists Rowland Evans and Robert Novak. Mitchell's strategy would put the whole question of carrying out the law in the hands of the federal courts and strip HEW of its bailiwick to hack off funds. Besides, the attorney general correctly pointed out, slashing money punished African-American students along with obstructionist whites. Nixon needed to do the political calculus as well. If HEW would not disburse funds, southern whites would cry foul and lash out at the White House. Allowing litigation to drag out in the courts, however, bided time for the administration and scapegoated the judiciary "so that Nixon," according to Evans and Novak, "could tell the South: It's not my fault." In the interim, the president could fulfill his promise to southern delegates at the 1968 Republican National Convention to nominate strict constructionists for the federal bench. Nixon ultimately opted for Mitchell's desegregation policy.[7]

Early on, Nixon hesitated to tell his close friend Finch that he preferred Mitchell's procedural change. In February 1969, Nixon directed the attorney general to "work on what Finch can do." By March, White House chief of staff H. R. "Bob" Haldeman's private meeting notes evinced the president's withering support: "P[resident] wants guidelines changed.... P. feels change in guidelines sh[ou]ld be drastic. [N]o arbitrary guidelines." Not until mid-May did Finch learn that Nixon intended to plot a new course. After an informal chat about the status of delinquent school boards in South Carolina and under pressure from Strom Thurmond's southern clique, Nixon instructed Secretary Finch to back off on HEW yardsticks and grant deferrals for school districts that asked for more time to integrate. In the opinion of one OCR official, the president effectively froze Finch's agency "in a holding pattern."[8]

In the summer of 1969, with school desegregation deadlines looming, the feud between HEW and the Justice Department seemed to simmer down. Giving in to White House blandishments, Finch and Mitchell stitched together a "long-range plan" for desegregation by relying on the lower federal courts. Finch also got marching orders to prepare a statement detailing the policy change. In an effort to edify the public, Mitchell and Finch issued a joint statement on July 3 announcing "new procedures," but not "new guidelines." The resolution even hinted at the possibility of postponing HEW deadlines until 1970 for certain southern school districts. Laying down an invariable date to achieve desegregation, the statement read, was "too rigid to be either workable or equitable." Nixon bet the Mitchell-Finch compromise would muzzle the needling and incessant "right-wing bitching" of his southern critics.[9]

The white South generally greeted the July statement with sighs of relief and pinned their hopes on further delays. Nixon had offered a loophole and slowed desegregation. Headlines reverberated with the region's elation. The *State*, South Carolina's largest newspaper, gleefully proclaimed, "Nixon Delivers Better Deal." The *Savannah Morning News* told readers, "Desegregation Deadlines Won't Be Strictly Enforced." The *Atlanta Journal* correctly recognized the disjointed statement's mixed messages: "Deadlines on Schools Stand, Door Opened to New Delays." Commentators outside the South reacted with either skepticism or dismay. The NAACP interpreted the statement as a major blow to desegregation. Roy Wilkins accused the Nixon administration of "breaking the law." "It's almost enough to make you vomit," he blanched at the NAACP's annual convention. "This is not a matter of too little too late; this is nothing at all." Some papers spotted the elliptical phrasing embedded in the policy. The *Washington Daily News* suspected that the opacity of the statement had been "deliberately calculated to confuse liberals and Southerners alike into believing each had won." The *Saturday Review* dubbed it a "victory" for "Senator Strom Thurmond and his segregationist allies." Jerris Leonard, the new assistant attorney general saddled with civil rights enforcement, brushed off the bulletins: "I assume that there are people who can read it any way they want to read it, and undoubtedly they will."[10]

Not everyone in the administration agreed with Leonard's platitude or to jettison the HEW plan. Leon Panetta would have no part of the backpedaling. The headstrong director of the Office for Civil Rights refused to sound a retreat on desegregation. Panetta pep-talked his demoralized troops at HEW and reassured them the school deadlines would be honored. As far as he cared, nothing had changed. Panetta called the Mitchell-Finch statement "a masterpiece of double-talk," and he reminded staffers of their duty. "It's our job to see that September proves that there is no weakening in our enforcement." Panetta spent the July 4 holiday giving a *Washington Post* journalist his assessment of the statement and indicated that "we intend to send letters to all districts" to clarify that the appointed hour remained intact. The next day, the *Post* announced a "crunch" time for the Nixon administration and predicted "the true test of its intentions would come" in the offing "when Southerners presented themselves in the Capital to demand extensions of the deadline for their individual districts." The reporter asked rhetorically, "Would the Justice Department and the President then stand behind the tough interpretation contained in the Finch letter, or would they force Finch to yield and grant extensions time and again?"[11]

The White House answered petulantly. On the same day that the *Post*'s story ran, John Ehrlichman, the president's top domestic adviser, called Panetta to tell him that Nixon had read the article about his proposed letter. Ehrlichman ordered Panetta not to mail anything and to let the situation "settle now." Furthermore, "blacks are not where our votes are," Ehrlichman chastened him, "so why antagonize the people who can be helpful to us politically?" Finch also advised Panetta to drop the matter. Panetta retaliated by issuing memorandums to the regional offices of the Office for Civil Rights reminding staff personnel to abide by his construal of the July statement. When John Mitchell heard about Panetta's memos, the attorney general supposedly "blew up."[12]

The most downright opposition to Panetta and enforcement emerged not from the U.S. Department of Justice but from the White House. To understand the mind of the South, Nixon consulted his favorite oracle, Harry Dent. Born in 1930, Harry Shuler Dent, a native South Carolinian, served as Strom Thurmond's administrative assistant and personal sycophant. During the senator's record-breaking filibuster against the 1957 Civil Rights Act, Dent reputedly "waited outside his Senate chamber with a bucket just in case Thurmond needed a pot to piss in." Flattery got Dent everywhere. He ingratiated himself with powerful men and arranged the civil union between Thurmond and Nixon prior to the 1968 election. Colluding before Nixon's presidential bid, Dent advised him to win over the senator as the only way to keep George Wallace from poaching Republican votes. When a reporter hounded Nixon about sharing a party with Thurmond, the segregationist Dixiecrats' presidential candidate in 1948, Nixon did not need a week to think about it. "Strom is no racist," then-candidate Nixon replied collegially; "Strom is a man of courage and integrity." President Nixon rewarded Dent with an appointment as White House special counsel. Among other jobs, Dent acted as a liaison between the president and southern Republicans. "Nothing should happen in the South without checking with Harry Dent," Nixon often repeated to White House staff. Civil rights leaders and liberals despised Dent's oleaginous fingerprint on Nixon's Southern Strategy. A 1969 *Time* article joked that critics "considered him a 'Southern-fried Rasputin in the White House.'"[13]

The week after the executive uproar about Leon Panetta's proposed letter, Harry Dent got an alarming report from Clarke Reed, chairman of the

Mississippi Republican Party. Reed assured Dent that his subordinates "were selling the line" in the Magnolia State "that the courts and the last administration were to blame," but "HEW's recent frantic action is shooting that argument down." In the long run, Nixon would pay a penalty in the South. "The HEW people are having a glorious time," Reed continued, "cutting Nixon support in the South with intransigent force mixing with impossible deadlines and making sure Nixon gets the credit instead of the courts. If by doing so, they can strengthen Wallace enough to elect Teddy [Kennedy], they will be heroes in 1972." Reed signed off with a warning: "Harry, the promises of last Fall, Winter and Spring ring hollow now. Our future rests on immediate effective action. I do not have the wisdom to know what can be done. But if the school system must be destroyed, let's be good enough politicians to let the courts get the credit for it instead of the administration."[14]

Dent swung into action. He hastily convened a meeting of southern state Republican chairmen in Washington to muscle the outspoken Panetta into submission. Confronting him in private, they bombarded the young OCR director about his ringing endorsement of the HEW time quotients. Panetta withstood the bullying. Unflappable, he insisted that his office had a duty to obey the law. Georgia's Howard "Bo" Callaway browbeat him: "The law . . . the law, listen here, Nixon promised the South he would change the law, change the Supreme Court, and change this whole integration business. The time has come for Nixon to bite the bullet, for real changes and none of this communicating bullshit." In the coming weeks, the scuffle over the HEW guidelines reached a climax.[15]

Unable to strong-arm Panetta, the Mississippi controversy intensified. HEW drew up new desegregation plans for the district court in Jackson to instate by August 11. During the late summer, expert teams of HEW officials worked feverishly with local school boards and educators named as defendants in the *Hinds* suit. HEW's febrile measures included whatever battery of methods—neighborhood zoning, busing, or "pairing"—it calibrated would produce the most extensive integration of students and faculties. The HEW staff seemed intent on eliminating as many single-race schools, particularly all-black schools, as possible. While four of the thirty-three districts in *Hinds* dodged substantial integration until 1970, the others faced mandatory compliance by early September, just a few weeks away. When Secretary Robert Finch approved the HEW plans prior to their submission to the court, wholesale desegregation seemed unavoidable. Nearly everyone involved expected the demise of Mississippi's dual-school system. Behind the scenes, however, one of Mississippi's most ardent opponents of integration dug deep into his bag of tricks.[16]

On Monday, August 11, the same day the federal court in Jackson awaited the revised HEW plans, Nixon received an ominous memo from Senator John Stennis. In an eleventh-hour reprieve, Stennis, a sixty-eight-year-old conservative Democrat, dashed a four-page, single-spaced letter to Nixon at his "Western White House" in San Clemente, California. Flustered by the Fifth Circuit's July order to implement desegregation in Mississippi, Stennis informed the president, "The plan now proposed will, as a practical matter, destroy our public school system." As chairman of the Senate Armed Services Committee, Stennis had "major responsibilities here in connection with legislation dealing with our national security, but I will not hesitate to leave my duties here at any time to go to Mississippi to do whatever else must be done to protect the people of Mississippi and to preserve our public school system."[17]

The senator's note came at a critical juncture when foreign policy matters preoccupied the president. After Nixon took office, Melvin R. Laird, the secretary of defense, announced a new long-range ballistic missile system—"Safeguard." The Safeguard program defended America's intercontinental ballistic missile silos from Soviet attack. As floor leader, Stennis had herded Safeguard through the Senate. Now, in mid-August, the senator threatened to hold up an appropriation bill to fund the missile program, which Nixon had touted for months, "unless his repeated requests for a delay in Mississippi school desegregation were heeded." Stennis advised Nixon that if HEW did not back off on integration plans, he would leave D.C. and entrust floor management of the multibillion-dollar bill to Senator Stuart Symington of Missouri, a severe critic of military spending. "While I have not yet spoken to Senator Symington," Stennis said forebodingly, "I am sure that as the ranking member . . . he will be glad to assume those committee responsibilities if I am called away." With the defense bill and the white South hanging in the balance, Nixon had to react fast. After conferring with Mitchell, Finch, and Laird, the president instructed them to reach a "workable solution" with the Mississippi political baron. According to the senator's senior staffer, Charles Overby, "It was the closest thing to a quid pro quo situation that I ever saw Senator Stennis involved in." While HEW mavens prepared compliance plans for the opening of school, Nixon knew he could not simply urge Bob Finch to ignore or take it easy on Mississippi. The White House demanded the unthinkable.[18]

Robert Finch took an unprecedented next step. The HEW secretary foisted himself directly into the Mississippi imbroglio. On August 20, John R. Brown, the Fifth Circuit's chief judge, received a hand-delivered letter from

Secretary Finch requesting a delay for the Mississippi districts to file new desegregation plans on December 1. Despite the hard work and assistance of HEW, Finch cited "administrative and logistical difficulties which must be encountered and met in the terribly short space of time remaining." Immediate implementation, he forewarned would open a Pandora's Box of "chaos, confusion, and a catastrophic educational setback to the 135,700 children, black and white alike." Granting the stay would effectively postpone desegregation until August 1970.[19]

Judge John Brown read the letter at home in numbed incredulity. He had never received such a request from a senior cabinet official. Ever since the *Brown* decision, the federal courts had enjoyed wide latitude to consider the feasibility of school desegregation in light of local circumstances and to proceed "with all deliberate speed" toward admitting students to public schools on a racially nondiscriminatory basis. In an anomalous departure, a presidential administration had just asked for a twelve-month delay and thrown up a roadblock to school integration. Caught off guard, Brown groped for answers. The next morning, he contacted Homer Thornberry and Lewis Morgan, the other members of the three-judge panel on the consolidated Mississippi suits. Against their better judgment, the appellate judges sent the case, along with Finch's statement, back to the less benign federal district court in Jackson for a prompt hearing. All parties involved in the lawsuit received copies of the Fifth Circuit's order and excerpts from the HEW secretary's letter. Harold Cox, Dan Russell, and Walter Nixon got instructions to rehear the case and report their findings to the appeals court. The Fifth Circuit's acquiescence to White House intimidation undercut desegregation. Judge Brown later considered remanding the case to the segregationist district court as the "worst mistake" of his judicial career. Compunctious about trampling on the rights of black children, he apologized to Mel Leventhal and confessed, "I knew soon after we took the step that it was wrong."[20]

Finch's interference created a ruckus in both HEW and the Department of Justice. Scheduling a hearing in Jackson that sought school delays meant Justice Department counsel would have to argue against the very implementation orders that they had previously championed. At least one government attorney resigned on the spot. Finch wrote his letter before consulting federal lawyers or informing his employees at HEW. The secretary also acted without asking any experts or visiting the school districts affected by the case. HEW's top civil rights and educational officials reproached Finch and pointed out that his rash analysis lacked the basis for such a calamitous forecast of "chaos" and "confusion." The real welter played out within HEW and the Justice Department. The fracas divided the respective staffs between Nixon loyalists and dissidents. Not everyone in the Office of Education had obliged Finch. Civil rights sympathizers at HEW released a press statement in an effort to tamp down criticisms of their agency's betrayal.[21]

The secretary found himself encircled by insurgents. HEW was "a huge civilian army, guardian of the American welfare state," noted one journalist, and the foot soldiers would not "surrender because a new president wanted to play games with the laws they were dedicated to enforcing." Leon Panetta concluded that Finch's repudiation of the HEW deadline "was not justified by any previous standard." "Worst of all," Panetta rued, Finch "had committed a symbolic act of retreat on school desegregation which couldn't help but infect all such programs."[22]

On August 25, Department of Justice lawyers advocated the school delay in Mississippi's U.S. Southern District Court. Jerris Leonard arrived in Jackson from Washington to argue the Nixon administration's position. Not all the government's officials took part in the two-hour proceeding. A dejected Robert T. Moore, a Justice Department attorney who worked alongside black plaintiffs in numerous civil rights actions across the South, sat silently as his superior in the Civil Rights Division made the motion for a delay. Once, for several minutes, Moore "slumped across the back of an empty chair and buried his face in his folded arms," observed Arkansas reporter Roy Reed of the *New York Times*. Moore probably wished he could crawl under the table. Also sickened by the government's meddling, HEW's Dr. Gregory R. Anrig, who had devised the August 11 desegregation plans, did not appear at the court hearing. In his place, Jerris Leonard substituted a pair of HEW surrogates to testify on the government's behalf.[23]

Relying on Finch's letter and the canned testimony of the two HEW officials, a two-judge panel, consisting of Dan Russell and Walter Nixon, recommended the secretary's request to the appeals court in New Orleans. Judge Russell parroted Secretary Finch's qualms about immediate desegregation. "A smoother plan" would be operable, he assured television viewers in Jackson, "with a little more time." Three days later, the Fifth Circuit Court of Appeals heard Jerris Leonard again present the government's case. During his opening argument, the assistant attorney general admitted feeling "somewhat embarrassed" about the extension, but he asked the Fifth Circuit to affirm and grant the delay. John Brown and the associate judges deferred to HEW's technical expertise, accepted the district court's findings, and ordered an abrupt halt to school desegregation plans until December 1. Sensing they had picked up what one journalist referred to as "a political hot potato," the Fifth

Circuit panel backslid on integration. Caught in a vise, the jittery judges in New Orleans had slackened in their resolve.[24]

NAACP officials and the Inc. Fund correctly suspected White House sabotage. Earlier on August 25, Mel Leventhal, joined in court by LDF deputy counsel Norman Amaker, had already moved that the United States be reassigned as a party defendant in the Legal Defense Fund's cases. "The United States Government for the first time has demonstrated that it no longer seeks to represent the rights of Negro children," he scolded the Justice Department. Even though the district court denied his motion, Leventhal's impassioned speech brought the schism with the Nixon administration into high relief— and with a touch of drama— to gain a national spotlight for the case. In New York, LDF attorneys accused the government of violating black schoolchildren's rights and appealed the Fifth Circuit's delay in a petition to the U.S. Supreme Court. The Fund's discontent made national news. On September 3, the LDF posted a full-page ad in the *New York Times* that featured the photograph of a weeping black child with a single tear. The maudlin caption ran, "On August 25, 1969, the United States Government broke its promise to the children of Mississippi." "We cannot let this happen," the advertisement wailed. "We are the chief legal arm of the Civil Rights Movement. Along with many brave people, we are responsible for the Supreme Court Decision of 1954. We defended Martin Luther King in Birmingham and Selma. We were there at the sit-ins and riots. And the Government was with us too. Until last week."[25]

The Fifth Circuit's sudden retreat elated much of the segregationist South. Perhaps other imperiled school districts could qualify for relief from integration scheduled for that autumn. The *New York Times* reported that within days of the Nixon administration's request for a delay, school boards across the South canceled their plans to implement desegregation in September. Some diehard districts bailed out before telling HEW. In Wheeler County, Georgia, for example, the local newspaper broadcast the return of the region's dual system and freedom of choice for the fall semester. Swamped by calls to intercede in similar cases, Robert Finch receded from public view. Nearly 1,000 HEW employees demanded an explanation from their besieged boss, but he declined a meeting claiming health problems. As Finch withdrew, he became an increasingly isolated and solitary figure.[26]

Secretary Finch's tinkering and the Fifth Circuit's uncharacteristic oscillation appalled at least one member of the Supreme Court. On August 29, Justice Hugo Lafayette Black got word about the LDF's petition at his home in Alexandria, Virginia. Five days later, Solicitor General Erwin Griswold entreated Black to accept the Mississippi school delay. Griswold conceded that any extension "means in most situations, another school year, and that is a tragedy and a default." The postponement, nevertheless, would allow school systems the necessary time to rearrange classes and reassign faculties.[27]

Hugo Black's reaction was predictable. He abhorred the fulsome request. Spry and courtly at the age of eighty-three, Black was the bench's oldest associate justice and senior-most member. Despite his upbringing in backwater Clay County, Alabama, and swearing allegiance to the Ku Klux Klan as a junior lawyer in Birmingham, Black had traded in his white hood for a black robe and had matured into one of the Court's most avid proponents of school desegregation. To his chagrin, the Fifth Circuit Court of Appeals had lost its nerve and caved in to Finch's bidding. As the supervisory justice for the Fifth Circuit, Black wielded the authority to reverse the delay and order immediate integration, but he treaded gingerly. His colleagues on the Court exercised their unilateral power sparingly as circuit justices. Acting as a single justice, Black might irritate his brethren on the bench—who traditionally and unanimously closed ranks on civil rights issues—and unintentionally cause a rift among them.[28]

There was another reason for Black's circumspection. In June 1969, Chief Justice Warren Burger had succeeded the retired Earl Warren. Burger, a strict constructionist named by Eisenhower to the court of appeals in the District of Columbia, had earned Nixon's stamp of approval. On a number of matters, Burger's conservative instincts and ideas, particularly in criminal cases, meshed with Nixon's. The judge's support of "law and order" sealed his nomination. Searching for an ideological counterbalance to the Warren Court in fulfillment of Nixon's campaign promise, the president tapped sixty-one-year-old Burger. The white-pated, broad-shouldered Burger, according to one legal scholar, looked like "a casting director's ideal of a Chief Justice." Many of the liberal justices typecast him as yet another political appointee and warily welcomed Burger. Some justices worried that he might repeal the Supreme Court's hard-fought gains on desegregation. His stance on civil rights, so far, seemed fair, however, and Burger showed no signs of reversing field on the Warren Court's precedents. Rather than a rapid shift to the right, the incoming chief justice chose discretion as the better part of valor. The Court's liberal majority breathed a hopeful sigh. Perhaps sensitive about his image as Nixon's man, Burger seemed a hail-fellow. During the summer, he solicited Hugo Black's input about a slate of issues facing the high bench.[29]

Justice Black reciprocated Burger's conciliatory gesture by practicing judicial restraint with the Fifth Circuit. Writing as a lone justice, on September 5 he responded to the LDF motion for an immediate reversal of the circuit's stay on desegregation. Hugo Black inveighed against the "deplorable" delay granted by the appeals court, but he refused to override the Fifth's order. Since the Court had adjourned for summer recess, Black had suggested that the civil rights plaintiffs seek review by the full Court when the justices returned in early October. Stating his sympathy for the LDF, Black propped the door ajar for further appeal. In an in-chambers decision, he issued a five-page opinion that encouraged the Inc. Fund to present its case to the Supreme Court "at the earliest possible opportunity." The time for "all deliberate speed," he pronounced, had "run out." In their brief, NAACP LDF petitioners heartily agreed: "15 years is enough to tolerate defiance of the Constitution."[30]

The press also assessed the Fifth Circuit's dawdling on school desegregation. In the weeks following the appeals court's suspension of the July 3 order, the story behind Bob Finch's controversial letter broke in newspapers, as did shadowy accounts of Nixon's manipulation. On September 11, Charles Overby, who left Stennis's staff just weeks earlier to join the *Jackson Daily News*, reported that "the Nixon administration's decision to ease desegregation efforts in Mississippi schools was made by President Nixon himself, who intervened after . . . Stennis threatened to quit as floor manager of the controversy-riddled" weapons bill. Overby's article substantiated that Attorney General Mitchell, Secretary Finch, and Defense Secretary Laird had called Stennis within days of his letter to Nixon and cut a deal with the powerful chairman. On the same day, the *Chicago Daily Tribune* corroborated Overby's version of events that the administration "gave in" to Stennis. At a press conference on September 26, Paul Healy of New York's *Daily News* quizzed President Nixon about leaks to the media that Stennis had held the administration's defense bill hostage unless HEW snuffed out the September desegregation plans. The president answered coolly: "Anybody who knows Senator Stennis and anybody who knows me would know that he would be the last person to say, 'Look, if you don't do what I want in Mississippi, I am not going to do what is best for this country.' He did not say that, and under no circumstances, of course, would I have acceded to it.'" Captive to Stennis, Nixon had indeed misled the public and placated the senator and the white South.[31]

Nixon's logrolling with Stennis did not go unchallenged by reporters or Justice Department officials. The scheme to delay integration set off a cascade of events. On school desegregation, the administration's dodgy policy sent more than a tailored message of benign neglect. It proved tortuously obstructionist. The president's hedging on integration and Finch's letter sparked disbelief among many civil rights lawyers in the Department of Justice. Voices of protest emerged when Nixon's administration reneged on the HEW guidelines. Most of the Civil Rights Division's staff opposed Finch. Others fomented rebellion. Senior appeals attorney Gary J. Greenberg "wanted to ascertain whether, under the Constitution, there was any legal argument that might conceivably support the Nixon Administration's request . . . for a delay." After he concluded that no solid basis existed, "the reluctant movement that the press would call 'the revolt' in the Civil Rights Division" took shape.[32]

On August 25, the same day that Jerris Leonard pled the government's case in Jackson's federal court, Greenberg and the other ringleaders summoned their peers to a hasty private meeting. The next night in Washington, forty lawyers squeezed into an apartment to recap the week's portentous news and debated what to do. Several attorneys with direct knowledge of the school desegregation suits in the South briefed the others. After hashing out the legal ramifications of stalling desegregation, Greenberg surmised that the delay request "was not only politically motivated but unsupportable under the law we were sworn to uphold." Staying silent would mean acquiescing to the administration's position. The meeting crested with a unanimous call for action and the selection of a committee to compose a statement of protest. On August 28, after the Fifth Circuit confirmed the delay, the civil rights line attorneys approved a mild resolution. Sixty-five of the seventy-four lawyers in the Civil Rights Division signed the letter. Among other assertions, the collaborators' final two paragraphs read,

> It is our fear that a policy which dictates that clear legal mandates are to be sacrificed to other considerations will seriously impair the ability of . . . the Division, and ultimately the Judiciary, to attend to the faithful execution of the federal civil-rights statutes. . . . We further request that this Department vigorously enforce those laws protecting human dignity and equal rights for all persons and by its actions promptly assure concerned citizens that the objectives of those laws will be pursued.[33]

Greenberg argued that a memo would best articulate the perspectives of so many disenchanted people. He also insisted that Division lawyers should maintain "the appearance of dignity and professionalism if our protest were not to be dismissed as the puerile rantings of a group of unresurrected idealists who, except for their attire, bore a close resemblance to the 'Weathermen' and the 'Crazies.'" Presenting a calm, reasoned position and a unified front would garner the public support "we thought vital to the success of the protest." Speaking in unison "would be a remarkable feat" and show that their "commitment was more important than the words actually used." Greenberg hoped that the statement would demonstrate the lawyers' dissatisfaction and would "imply that 'revolt' was in the air."[34]

In September, the dissenting counsel engaged in bolder overtures. Within weeks of the memo, two veteran Civil Rights Division lawyers, Gary Greenberg and John Nixon, appeared in appellate courts in other school desegregation cases and refused to represent the government's dilatory action in Mississippi. Some attorneys smuggled information to the Inc. Fund to sustain their fight in Mississippi's federal court. Others went public and spoke with the press. Greenberg wanted to "ensure that the public was fully aware of the role political pressures had played in the decision to seek delay."[35]

The lawyers' memo rankled John Mitchell's regime, but instead of recriminations cooler heads prevailed, for the moment. The attorney general and Jerris Leonard respected the right of the line attorneys in the Civil Rights Division to assemble and couch their concerns. The deputy attorney general, Richard G. Kleindienst, in fact, invited the Division lawyers to hold their second meeting at the Department of Justice. Only when the Nixon administration grasped the deep conviction and unanimity of the organized protest did the official stance boomerang from accommodation to admonition.[36]

Mitchell rode herd on the Civil Rights Division and told Leonard to remind the insubordinate line lawyers of their priorities. On September 18, the assistant attorney general offered a potted reply to the Division lawyers' statement and issued a sonorous warning. If any of them disliked the administration's policy, they should resign. Rather than respond to the attorneys' particular grievances about politics intruding in the realm of law enforcement, Leonard digressed into how the administration would pursue school desegregation. His answer frustrated Gary Greenberg. Leonard's pirouettes "completely missed, or avoided, the point of the protest," Greenberg charged. At no time had the lawyers questioned the prerogative of Nixon and Mitchell to set an agenda to achieve school desegregation. What they objected to was the Justice Department's timidity on civil rights. The law required action and an immediate end to dual-school systems.[37]

Alarmed by scuttlebutt that Senator John Stennis had cornered Nixon into sandbagging the HEW school plans in exchange for his support of a defense bill, the whistleblowers in the Civil Rights Division had resolved neither to abide Jerris Leonard's riposte nor to resign. On September 25, they repeated their pledge to uphold the law and informed Mitchell and Leonard of their intention. Accused of political horse-trading, the attorney general refuted allegations that the Mississippi deal had been a payoff to Stennis. The renewed round of inquiry and opposition frayed John Mitchell's threadbare patience. Confronted with disloyalty, the administrative ax fell.[38]

Sensing a mutiny, Mitchell and Leonard doubled down and reaffirmed their authority. Attorney General Mitchell blasted the staff attorneys in the Civil Rights Division and snorted, "Policy is going to be made by the Justice Department, not by a group of lawyers." Three days later, Leonard copied Mitchell and instructed the unhappy lawyers to cease and desist in their protestations. He even cast aspersions on the Supreme Court's ability to settle the matter. At a press conference, he practically dared the justices to adjudicate: "If the Supreme Court were to order instant desegregation nothing would change. Somebody would have to enforce that order." Someone would also have to pay the penalty for embarrassing the president. When Nixon saw the lawyers' petition in his daily news briefing, he lost his temper and exploded at Bob Haldeman: "Get their names! Have their resignations on my desk by Monday." The Department of Justice settled on a more discreet purge.[39]

Fetched to Jerris Leonard's office on October 1, Gary Greenberg had to answer for crossing the administration. Leonard nagged the young lawyer to toe the government's line on the school delays and urged him to acquiesce. "Around here the Attorney General is the law," Leonard clarified. When Greenberg would not heel, the chasm became unbridgeable. Jerris Leonard laid out his options: resign or be fired. Then the assistant attorney general quoted an old Irish adage: "When you start throwing shillelaghs around, you have to expect to get hit by one on the back of your head." Refusing to compromise his principles, Greenberg tendered his letter of resignation. Later that day, Leonard circulated an interoffice memo that prohibited any "further unauthorized statement . . . regarding our work and our policies." The Justice Department's hierarchy would not brook more dissent. Government lawyers got orders to obey the will of John Mitchell without "the dictates of conscience," Greenberg noted in dismay. Speaking to reporters, Gary Greenberg got the last word and uttered a parting shot at the administration. "This rhetoric in and of itself breeds chaos," he told Ed Rogers of United Press International. Leonard "almost invited the reopening of massive resistance," Greenberg bawled him out. "He seemed to make it clear that outright, avowed resistance will receive more consideration than voluntary compliance with the law. There may be other Little Rocks."[40]

Specters of Little Rock hovered in the minds of many in D.C., but the fluid situation dished out more surreal twists. In the fall of 1957, a state governor had disobeyed a federal court order to desegregate. By the autumn of 1969, the executive branch had tabled integration. Another harbinger arose when

Nixon's solicitor general refused to defend the government. Attorney General Mitchell had retained Erwin Griswold, the former dean of Harvard Law School and a leftover appointment from the Johnson presidency. Griswold later explained that he "could not vigorously support" the Nixon administration's position. Once upon a president, Griswold would have gladly pled for more deliberate speed on desegregation. With internal crises erupting by the day, the Justice Department scrambled to prepare for a presumptive showdown in the Supreme Court. In Griswold's notable absence, the unpopular job of opposing school integration went to the president's loyal assistant attorney general. Jerris Leonard faced an uphill battle. The high court had a proven record of spearheading desegregation, and Leonard would have to square off against the freedom movement's best lawyer.[41]

For the last twenty years, Jack Greenberg's client had been civil rights, and he had served the movement brilliantly. Suddenly, however, the skillful LDF attorney's list of allies in the federal government had dwindled. Southern senators and congressmen allergic to integration had found a receptive ally in the White House. Worse, the Fifth Circuit Court of Appeals, until then a bulwark of civil rights, had bailed on immediate school desegregation. During Lyndon Johnson's presidency, the Justice Department had coordinated desegregation suits with the Inc. Fund. At Richard Nixon's behest, John Mitchell and Jerris Leonard had decimated the lawyers' revolt in the Civil Rights Division. The LDF's main office had negligible respect for the new president's men. They reviled Mitchell as a sneaky henchman and Leonard as his crony and a creep. Pressed from nearly all sides, Greenberg "concluded that we had no alternative but to appeal to the Supreme Court immediately." After Hugo Black insinuated that the Court would take up the gauntlet, Jack Greenberg called his staff together in New York to file a petition for a speedy review. He leavened the mood with mock bravado and paraphrased French general Ferdinand Foch at the First Battle of the Marne: "My center is giving way, my right is in retreat . . . I attack."[42]

With Greenberg at the helm, the LDF plunged ahead with its frontal attack on the Fifth Circuit Court's postponement of desegregation. On September 27, the Inc. Fund filed an emergency petition for writ of certiorari and a motion to advance in the Supreme Court. Greenberg asked the justices to accept the cert petition when they reconvened on October 6 and either to review and vacate the Fifth's delay order at once or to schedule oral arguments. Ordinarily, the case would have been heard in December or possibly not until the next year. On October 7, the Justice Department formally urged the high court not to consider the case until after the desegregation plans had been resubmitted on December 1. Hugo Black shepherded the LDF petition through the Court. To resolve the impasse created by the Fifth Circuit's stay, the bench voted to grant the Inc. Fund's request for a prompt hearing. Renaming the Mississippi school suits covered by *Hinds* in alphabetical order under the title *Alexander v. Holmes County Board of Education*, the Court fast-tracked the combined cases to the front of the docket and set a hearing for October 23. *Alexander* would be the first big case of the term and Burger's trial run on civil rights as chief justice. With only two weeks before oral arguments, the parties massed their forces.[43]

The NAACP LDF marshaled a stellar array of legal minds to do battle. Although no longer a novice, Mel Leventhal felt slightly "wet behind the ears" and lacked the gravitas to argue the case in Court. He handed off lead counsel for the plaintiffs to the Defense Fund's chief litigator—Jack Greenberg. Leventhal stayed busy writing the Inc. Fund's brief for *Alexander* and doing legwork for Greenberg. He knew the case inside and out, but his well-versed boss knew the justices and the drill. Greenberg oversaw final preparations. He conducted skull sessions and moot courts to refine the LDF's strategy. The Fund rehearsed for the courtroom by dragooning Columbia law faculty to role-play as certain justices. Each devil's advocate grilled Greenberg to poke holes in his case and spring potential traps set by the bench. Greenberg and LDF staff attorneys, for example, observed a cardinal rule with Justice Byron White never to answer him too quickly. White had a penchant for dangling questions before overzealous counsel to reel them in.[44]

Greenberg also buttressed his case by enlisting lawyers with expertise in the field of civil rights litigation from other organizations. From the Lawyers' Committee for Civil Rights Under Law, the respected group of attorneys in private practice, Louis Oberdorfer, an Alabama attorney and former clerk for Justice Black, joined Greenberg's team. Oberdorfer would present ten minutes of oral argument, and his assistance would signal the American legal establishment's support of the LDF. In an amicus curiae (friend of the court) brief, Oberdorfer's committee disconfirmed Jerris Leonard's statement that the Civil Rights Division lacked the "bodies and people" to enforce school desegregation. The Lawyers' Committee's roster of prestigious attorneys, which boasted John Doar, the old chief of the Division under Kennedy and Johnson, pledged to recruit enough lawyers, if necessary, to handle the job for the supposedly undermanned Justice Department.[45]

Powerful attorneys represented each side. Jerris Leonard kludged together his defense with Mississippi attorney general A. F. Summer and John Creighton Satterfield of Yazoo City, the man whom *Time* magazine anointed "the

most prominent segregationist lawyer in the country." Born in 1904 in Port
Gibson, Mississippi, and a graduate of Ole Miss law school, the sixty-five-year-
old Satterfield would appear in Court as special counsel. The *New York Times*
gave the aberrational pairing of Satterfield and Leonard "the odd couple of the
year award." When novelist Willie Morris once visited Satterfield in his Yazoo
City office, they bantered back and forth. Morris caricatured the lawyer as
"thin and craggy, and if it were not for the unexpected mischief in his eye,
he would look very much like the cartel men in [Charlie] Chaplin's *Modern
Times*." Satterfield was a thorough attorney with a glabrous skull full of legal
knowledge. Jocular in casual conversation, he turned frosty and forensic if the
topic switched to integration. Interviewed by *Times* reporter Roy Reed just
five days before the Supreme Court hearing, Satterfield skewered the plaintiffs' position as the specious "sociological theories of civil rights activists,"
not "true constitutional guarantees."[46]

John Satterfield had achieved notoriety as the foremost legal tactician for
segregated schools in Mississippi. He rubbed shoulders with and befriended
Senators Jim Eastland and John Stennis. Satterfield's defense of white supremacy had also made the lawyer a contentious president of the American
Bar Association in 1961–62. Staunchly conservative, he had used his presidential address as a bully pulpit to vilify the Supreme Court for corroding
states' rights and dangerously hoarding authority in the federal government.
Behind the usurpation of central power, Satterfield detected a pink and "com-
munistic blueprint for conquest drafted by Marx and Lenin, implemented by
Stalin, and being carried forward by every available legal and illegal means
by Khrushchev."[47]

Inc. Fund attorneys had known Satterfield as an unwavering adversary.
Many opposing white counsel, Reuben Anderson of the Jackson LDF later
recalled, "were premier lawyers, good lawyers. For some, this wasn't personal;
they knew segregation wouldn't last." Yet, John Satterfield would not quit.
Of the "out-and-out racists," Anderson bristled, Satterfield "was the worst."
Jack Greenberg and the Yazoo City attorney had already been acquainted
in New Orleans during *Meredith v. Fair*, the 1962 case that had desegregated
the University of Mississippi. Satterfield appeared as a friend of the court on
behalf of Ross Barnett, Mississippi's embattled governor, and came across as
"ever obsequious," as Greenberg inspected him. "Looking like a praying man-
tis, Satterfield tiptoed around the courtroom" as he addressed the Fifth Circuit "in elaborate, deferential tones." When Satterfield violated the appeals
court's explicit instructions not to make any motions or objections or to file
any pleadings, the judges revoked his amicus curiae status.[48]

Seven years after his banishment, John Satterfield still tiptoed in court and
fought desegregation suits brought by the NAACP LDF. In mid-June 1969, he
tried to prevent the Fifth Circuit Court of Appeals from reviewing the *U.S. v.
Hinds* case as it made its halting but gradual way through courtrooms in Jackson and New Orleans. Hired by dual-school systems to salvage "freedom of
choice," Satterfield wrote the motion to dismiss a hearing in the Fifth Circuit
that would ultimately reverse the U.S. District Court for Southern Mississippi's rejection of the *Jefferson* decree. In his brief, he asked the appeals court
to respect, as before, the glacial pace of school desegregation fostered by the
Supreme Court. "It is true that fourteen or fifteen years have elapsed since
Brown I," he pleaded with the judges. "It is also true, however, that the . . . Fifth
Circuit and other courts have recognized the necessity of proceeding with 'all
deliberate speed.'" Satterfield's wily tactics demonstrated his intransigence,
and the Justice Department's acquiescence to Nixon's Southern Strategy
solidified Mississippi's and the government's mutual preference for a joint
defense.[49]

The case brought together strange bedfellows. Although he would not appear in Court, Nashville lawyer Jack Kershaw received amicus curiae status
for the defense. Kershaw represented the Tennessee Federation of Constitutional Government, a segregationist outfit with ties to the Citizens' Council.
In his brief, Kershaw cited a train of studies by scientific racists, like psychologist Audrey M. Shuey, who disputed African Americans' intelligence and the
preparedness of black students to attend integrated schools. "To think that
we could achieve equality of education by massive forced congregation," Kershaw lectured the justices, "and then force-feed the same quantity of learn-
ing upon one and all is a crude attempt." They should preserve freedom of
choice and the "right of self-determination" rather than capitulate to the "cult
of forced equality and forced association."[50]

Ready for Court, the opposing counsel rushed to judgment in Washington.

CHAPTER SIX

Alexander in the High Court

❀

Dear Brethren, the fate of
"all deliberate speed" has been resolved.
—Justice William O. Douglas Jr.

O N THURSDAY, OCTOBER 23, oral arguments began at 12:30 P.M. The Holmes County plaintiffs' legal travail, at long last, had reached the Supreme Court. Seven of the eight justices perched in their high-backed leather chairs that day. Justice William J. Brennan missed the hearing to care for his ailing wife, but he participated in the case by listening to a taped recording. An anxious crowd jammed the ornate chamber. Mel Leventhal and Reuben Anderson watched expectantly. Leon Panetta came to see the Department of Health, Education, and Welfare guidelines restored. The Court allocated an unusually long two hours for oral advocacy. Louis Oberdorfer and Jack Greenberg appeared for the plaintiffs. The unaccustomed trio of John Satterfield, A. F. Summer, and Jerris Leonard shared the government's table.[1]

Greenberg spoke first. At the outset of the hearing, he retraced the history of defiance by Mississippi school officials. Greenberg explained that his clients based their appeal on the Fourteenth Amendment. Adopted during Reconstruction, the law mandated that a state could not deprive any person of life, liberty, or property without due process, nor could it deny to any person the equal protection of the laws. Mississippi's long-held resistance to the Fourteenth Amendment, he jogged the Court's memory, was "second to none." Greenberg also fleshed out the victims of the state's lawlessness. Two people had died during the Ole Miss riot of 1962, and Medgar Evers, a plaintiff who had filed a related school desegregation suit in Jackson, had been gunned down in his driveway the following year. "The question in these cases," Greenberg bored in as he slapped a stack of HEW files, "is whether the children in these school districts, and indeed, the children in any school districts throughout our beloved land, are at last to learn that there is a supreme law of the land, binding upon children and parents; binding upon school boards; binding upon the states; binding upon the United States." The LDF lawyer's plea for Negro rights riveted Leon Panetta. As he listened to Greenberg's passionate oratory, Panetta found it "hard to suppress a chill or a tear."[2]

On the role of the federal district courts, Jack Greenberg's argument grew sharper. "But the sorriest part of the story lies in the exercise of discretion by some United States District Judges in that state." Indeed, Mississippi's southern district had impeded desegregation and exploited "ambiguity—real ambiguities and fancied ambiguities in the decisions of this Court and the Court of Appeals." Then, Greenberg went for the jugular. He pressed the high court to strip the South of its master weapon in the segregationist arsenal of tools to stall. For too long, the lower federal courts heard appeals while the schools stayed segregated. "All of this has had the effect of perpetuating the status quo," Greenberg protested, "and so far in Mississippi the status quo . . . has been racial segregation or minimal token desegregation." His solution was simple. The schools should desegregate at once. The Court, he proposed, should bar the obstructionist district court from interfering in the case. The Fifth Circuit Court of Appeals should supervise implementation of the original HEW plans.[3]

During his closing remarks, Greenberg cautioned that granting further delay would only breed the very southern obstinance that the Court professed to seek to overcome. "So long as [freedom of choice] is the case, there is a premium on litigating *ad infinitum*," he nudged the justices. "There used to be a motto," Greenberg quoted Alabama's bantam former governor George Wallace, "'Segregation forever.'" Mississippi's southern district had swapped Wallace's bombast for "'litigation forever,' making thousands of pages of record on such things as the intelligence of Negro children, delaying the setting of hearings and the entry of orders and effective dates and plans."[4]

When Justice Black probed Greenberg about the practical problems of implementing plans so quickly, the Defense Fund lawyer warned, "That difficulty is preferable to suffer than the difficulty of having the Constitution" desecrated by continued segregation. Mississippi's southern district judges "should not be able to parade respectably under the cloak of complying with the so-called 'deliberate speed' doctrine. It should be indubitably clear that they are law violators, and I think in this country lawfulness counts for something." Black pressed him about what kind of relief he asked of the Court. Greenberg elucidated that he sought a "concrete order" to put an "immediate" end to the dual-school system. Obviously, he assured the Court, instant desegregation would require a little time to "take care of the mechanics"—notifying administrators, teachers, parents, and students. Greenberg did not want the justices bogged down in niceties, however. Since the earlier HEW criteria allowed for eight days to comply between August 23 and September 1, he postulated that no more than eight days after the justices' decision would be necessary to accomplish the Court's decree.[5]

Greenberg took his seat. Oberdorfer rose and briefly addressed the bench. He seconded the LDF's opposition to any desegregation delays and reiterated that the dissolution of the dual-school system, a midyear revolution, could be borne out with only minor disruptions.

Hugo Black butted in on his former clerk. "The thing to do is to say that the dual system is over and that it is to go into effect today ... to go at it now—do you agree?"

"I agree with that, Your Honor," replied Oberdorfer, "without knowing exactly what 'now' is."

"I mean when we issue an order," Black's tongue slipped. The justice fumbled for a moment. "If we do." Some audience members whooped in laughter. "There is no reason to wait on future arguments about 'deliberate speed,'" Black urged on Oberdorfer.

"Correct," the lawyer said, "And furthermore ..."

Black interrupted him again and finished Oberdorfer's thought: "You would like to have us act with all deliberate speed?"

"Faster than that, Your Honor," Oberdorfer answered. His response provoked more snickers in the chamber.[6]

Jerris Leonard opened by imploring the justices to consider the wisdom of the Fifth Circuit's delay order, but he could already read the Court's mind. Hugo Black and the plaintiffs seemed to speak with one voice. Leonard pled with the bench "not to be too caught up in the frustration that counsel have portrayed to the Court today." Against the odds, the assistant attorney general tried to snatch victory from the jaws of defeat. He reminded the Court that it handed down Green almost a year and a half ago, and the previous ruling still needed time to take effect. Many school districts had faithfully, albeit slowly, carried out the justices' wishes. He conceded that Mississippi had straggled behind for fifteen years to implement Brown, but, Leonard stated, "it's more true to say it's been eighteen months since Green, because that's when the important turning point, we feel, came about in substantial progress."

Leonard and the justices clashed from the beginning. He had barely opened his case when Justices William O. Douglas Jr. and Black broke in with an interrogatory. "Why not do it [desegregate] and put it into effect and submit that arrangements be made thereafter?" demanded Black.

The Justice Department attorney noted that serious administrative and logistical challenges muddied the situation.

"What's so complicated?" Black shot back.

Leonard recoiled. He regurgitated Secretary Robert Finch's prognosis of chaos and confusion. "What I'm pleading with this Court is not to do something precipitous."

Riled up, Black spouted off another question. "Could anything be precipitous in this field now?" Hugo Black made no attempt to muffle his dissatisfaction. "With all the years gone by since our order was given?"

Leonard acknowledged the justice's impatience, but he maintained that the plaintiffs' position offered an imprudent way to proceed. "I think it's wrong; I think it's terribly wrong," he plied the Court. "I think there may be some other alternatives to this frustration that—"

Black zeroed in and scalded him. "The frustration has been going on for fifteen years, hasn't it?" Leonard wilted at the justice's hot blast and explained that he meant the frustration experienced by litigants since *Green*, but Hugo Black stumped him: "You want to divide it up into segments?"

"No, I really don't," Leonard spluttered in exasperation as the courtroom burst into another round of laughter.

When the assistant attorney general started to document how many students would be adversely affected by instant desegregation, Black interjected, "Are you arguing for perpetuation of the term 'with all deliberate speed'?"

Leonard denied it.

Justice Thurgood Marshall, Jack Greenberg's mentor, jumped in. "The opinion in which this Court [in reference to *Cooper v. Aaron* (1958)] went out of its way to sign each Justice's name to it. And said that all nine agreed. Wasn't that a slight warning?" Marshall piled on.[7]

Chief Justice Burger extended an olive branch. "Just one question, if I may," he posed to Leonard in his baritone voice. "If there had been no appeal here . . . can you assure us that the plans would have been submitted on December 1?"

Thankful for the reprieve, Leonard nodded yes. With or without any Court mediation, the new desegregation plans would unfold in due time.

Burger seemed content. December was only about a month away. Desegregation would go into effect with or without Court sanction. Byron White and Hugo Black saw no reason to soft-pedal and did not let Jerris Leonard off the hook that easily. They forced Leonard to admit that by delaying the deadline any further, some districts would have to back up desegregation until the 1970–71 school year as school boards resubmitted local plans for review. Another year of dual schools clouded the horizon.

"Too many plans and not enough action," Justice Black squinted at Leonard. More chuckling filled the packed chamber.[8]

John Satterfield and A. F. Summer fared no better with the Court. Summer dredged up the proliferation of de facto segregation in school districts across the country—a hackneyed trope trotted out by southern segregationists. In quick succession, Mississippi's attorney general turned over final arguments to Satterfield, the more experienced litigator. The Yazoo City lawyer began by cribbing Finch's omen about breakneck school desegregation. Satterfield then took umbrage with Greenberg's slights to the district judges in Mississippi. "I have not lost my temper in the last thirty years, and I did not do so today," he defended his kinsmen. "But I am somewhat shocked when I hear the statement made of constitutional defiance by the public officials of Mississippi, and particularly of the schools," Satterfield droned on. "They are law-abiding citizens." In a lawyer's lament, he made a bootless caveat to uphold the original language of the *Brown* decision. He resuscitated the old *Briggs* dictum, which did not insist on integration but merely forbade de jure segregation. Satterfield concluded by citing the low number of racially integrated schools in Chicago. None of his cherry-picked data swayed the Court. Satterfield shifted tack to finagle Mississippi's way out of a final verdict. He asked the justices not to decide the case because the official records had not arrived from Harold Cox's court in Jackson. Unbeknown to the segregationist attorney, Jack Greenberg had left no page unturned and had already acquired the district court's file days before.[9]

In rebuttal, Greenberg parlayed Satterfield's carping about the legal papers into a litany of Mississippi injustices. He clutched the lectern and fired another cannonade: "This is the story of the litigation in this case. Judge Cox doesn't let you have the record, and Mr. Satterfield says you don't belong in this Court if you don't have it." After denouncing the conduct of Cox's court, Greenberg enumerated the Supreme Court's body of civil rights triumphs and gave a précis:

Now, this country has made immense strides in eradicating the stigma of slavery since and largely as a result of this Court's decision in Brown against Board of Education. The principle of those cases has been an important one, not only in theory, but because of actual implementation. ... Conversely, a retreat from the principles of *Brown*, as well as what that retreat would symbolize, would tell the country more than many volumes of mere rhetoric about what the country stands for.

To reverse course now would return the Supreme Court to *Plessy v. Ferguson*, the infamous 1896 ruling that permitted segregation through the doctrine of "separate but equal." Greenberg closed:

> In one of his great opinions ... Mr. Justice Rutledge voiced in dissent, an admonition that has special application today. He said, "It is not too early; it is never too early for the nation steadfastly to follow its great constitutional traditions. It can become too late." Today, we ask this Court to direct the entry of decree ordering desegregation now.[10]

On Friday, October 24, the brethren gathered in their weekly conference to deliberate *Alexander v. Holmes*. Customarily, the chief justice commenced by reviewing the issues at hand and sharing his thoughts. The associate justices would follow suit, and the discussion would then proceed in order of seniority, beginning with Hugo Black and ending with Thurgood Marshall, who had joined the bench in October 1967. In a surprise move that perhaps suggested the magnitude of the case, Chief Justice Burger deferred to Justice Black for an opening synopsis. Black dived in. Talking at length, he revisited the derivation and legacy of the nettlesome phrase "all deliberate speed." In 1955, Hugo Black had nearly voted against the *Brown II* ruling because he feared its indeterminate deadline would encourage whites to jump on the bandwagon of segregationist resistance. It had. The Warren Court had been naive to let the district courts implement *Brown II* when the local level was where segregation had arisen in the first place. Justice Black made it abundantly clear that he would never again be on the wrong side of history or a naïf in an opinion that used "all deliberate speed." *Alexander* symbolized his atonement for "all deliberate speed"—language that had kept another generation of African Americans confined to segregated schools. More deliberation meant inaction. Insistent on immediate desegregation, Black dispensed an ultimatum. "If anybody writes ["all deliberate speed"]," he brusquely announced, "I dissent."[11]

On one end of the spectrum, Justices William Douglas and William Brennan basically supported Black. Both favored action on the race issue, but they also pined for the preservation of unanimity without a thunderous dissent by Black. Acting as supervisory justice for the Tenth Circuit Court in August,

Brennan had overridden that appeals court's stay order on desegregation plans in Denver. Rather than demanding desegregation at once, Brennan suggested giving the Mississippi district a limited window, maybe two weeks, to comply with a directive to desegregate.[12]

At the other end, Justice John Marshall Harlan, one of the rare conservatives on the bench, bridled at his liberal colleagues' enthusiasm. Disconcerted by Black's rumbling of dissent, he stiffened, "You don't give in to blackmail." Harlan agreed that the Fifth Circuit's order should be repealed, but he pushed for greater flexibility with the deadline. The Court should consider practical difficulties linked to desegregating forthwith. He questioned a hard-and-fast cutoff date for rapid desegregation. An order to desegregate "now" would not give school districts enough time to act. Justices Potter Stewart, Byron White, and Thurgood Marshall concurred. The district and appellate courts needed crisp instructions, which meant a written opinion. Chief Justice Burger, who remained complaisant throughout the first day of conference discussion, would prepare a draft opinion.[13]

Over the next four days, the justices bandied about separate draft orders but deadlocked without any consensus. Burger's draft careened between vindicating the Nixon administration and scotching *Brown II*. The chief justice neither deleted "all deliberate speed" nor affixed a firm timetable. Instead, he proposed a vague implementation of "at the earliest possible time" after the Court's verdict. Burger effectively gave the school districts leeway until mid-November to comply, not much different from the December 1 deadline. His ambivalence pleased no one and ran afoul of Justice Black, who circulated his threatened dissent. "There has already been too much writing and not enough action in this field," Black bellowed. "Writing breeds more writing, and more disagreements, all of which inevitably delay action." He added a classic Black peroration: "The duty of this Court and of the others is too simple to require perpetual litigation and deliberation. That duty is to extirpate all racial discrimination from our system of public schools NOW."[14]

In what Byron White chalked up to a "flurry of paper," the justices engaged in an intense debate that nearly splintered the Court—four to four. Some of them hammered out alternatives to Burger's unpopular draft opinion. A simple plurality indicated support for a redraft by Justice Brennan. The brethren annealed their differences, and the judicial phalanx on school desegregation held. Unanimity trumped any misgivings. Harlan submitted to Brennan's revision because the internal divisions had largely boiled down to "pure semantics." Burger and others accepted Brennan's amended version to avoid balkanization and the perception of a retreat from *Brown*.[15]

On Wednesday evening, October 29, the high court announced a judgment. The Court decided unanimously to reverse the Fifth Circuit's August
28 order and implement desegregation plans "effective immediately." The
freedom-of-choice formula and "deliberate speed" standard, the Court declared in a two-page opinion, were "no longer constitutionally permissible."
The justices commanded the Fifth Circuit to direct "every school district . . .
to terminate dual school systems at once and to operate now and hereafter
only unitary schools." With the death knell of the dual-school system, "no
person" would "be effectively excluded from any school because of race or
color." More than fifteen years after *Brown* and more than fourteen years after
Brown II, integration now, not deliberate speed, was undeniably the order of
the day. *Alexander v. Holmes* marked the apogee of the Court's impatience
with southern loitering on school desegregation.[16]

Reactions to *Alexander* by blacks and civil rights forces were, of course,
overwhelmingly sanguine. Norman Amaker, the LDF attorney who argued
the case in Jackson alongside Mel Leventhal on August 25, called the verdict "a
vindication for our position that the Constitution of the United States has to
be obeyed." The decision signaled "a victory for Negro children everywhere."
In Mississippi, Aaron Henry, Clarksdale's NAACP secretary, was jubilant.
Alexander v. Holmes, he mused aloud, "came as fresh water to those of us who
have gotten to the point of wondering where we stood in America." In New
York City, *The Crisis*, the journal of the NAACP, congratulated the Court for
rendering a "great decision and a giant step forward." Emmitt Douglas, president of Louisiana's NAACP, simply stated, "Deliberate speed is dead, dead,
dead." News of *Alexander* gladdened Coretta Scott King, the widow of Martin
Luther King. To her, the ruling "shows that there are still people in America
who believe in justice. Right once again has triumphed." Later remembering *Alexander v. Holmes* as a "huge victory," Reuben Anderson reveled in the
virtues of the American legal system. When the Court acted, "judges follow
their rules. We in America have a great system. When the Supreme Court
speaks, everybody listens. The system works." Anderson's LDF associate in
Jackson, Fred Banks, later declaimed, "The Court sent a clear and forceful
message that political interference, even at the presidential level, would not
be countenanced." Nixon's interposition to hobble the pace of desegregation
had sputtered out. *Alexander* flatly renounced further delay and categorically
rebuffed presidential intransigence. Jack Greenberg expected "that the Justice
Department will come into the case on our side and not oppose the hopes of
Negro school children as they did in the Mississippi cases."[17]

At the upper echelons of the Justice Department, the mood paled by comparison. After the decision, John Mitchell huddled with his deputies. The attorney general then issued a perfunctory statement that acknowledged the authority of the Fifth Circuit to implement the case and dutifully awaited "that court's 'determination.'" When approached by reporters after the ruling, Jerris Leonard said little. One photographer asked for a picture of Leonard with John Satterfield on the Supreme Court's portico steps. Leonard refused to pose with the likes of him. "That is one honor I will decline," he muttered. "His reluctance was understandable," *Time* magazine noted, seeming to poke fun at Leonard. After all, the article sniffed, he "had just become the first Government lawyer ever to ask the high court for a delay in school desegregation."[18]

When Richard Nixon heard about the *Alexander* decision, he responded sardonically. "Let's see how they enforce it," he murmured to Bob Haldeman. One day after the ruling, however, the president vowed publicly to execute the law of the land. "I believe in carrying out the law even though I may have disagreed as I did in this instance with the decree that the Supreme Court eventually came down with," he told reporters. The Court's order bewildered some administration officials. At HEW, Finch's staff sifted through their winnowing options. Robert Mardian, one of Nixon's loyal Californians and a friend of John Mitchell, tilted at windmills and hoped for more trapdoor school delays—given Mississippi's obstinate southern district judges. L. Patrick Gray, Finch's executive assistant, faced facts. "No, this is over," he leveled with the others. "The Supreme Court has spoken. Now we must obey the law." Finch echoed the 1968 *Green* ruling and released a statement that his department would not "tolerate any further delays in abolishing the vestiges of the dual system."[19]

National news stories hailed the ruling as a blow for the Nixon administration. *Newsweek* called the decision "a stinging rebuke to the go-slow tactics of the Nixon administration, which had just installed Warren Burger at the helm of the high tribunal." One of Burger's clerks gave him kudos for bucking the president. No longer could anyone impugn Burger's judicial integrity, he stroked the chief justice's ego, or whisper that Nixon pulled his strings. Taken aback, the justice replied, "Do you think people really think I'm a Nixon puppet?"[20]

Southern segregationists heaped opprobrium on the Burger Court for school desegregation. One of Nixon's advisers counted on making the courts the locus of that churning controversy. Harry Dent salivated at the strategic import and implications of *Alexander v. Holmes.* "The Southern reaction was one of placing blame on the court," he read the electoral tea leaves, "and recognizing that Nixon had tried to be helpful." Nixon could win or lose the presidency based on that outcome. *Alexander* jarred southern extremists. Strom Thurmond railed against the decision but also stoutly defended the president: "The Nixon Administration stood with the South in this case." The Burger Court, George Wallace sizzled, "was no better than the Warren Court." The justices, he seethed, were "a bunch of limousine hypocrites." Georgia's ax-wielding governor, Lester Maddox, cudgeled *Alexander* as a "criminal act by the government." Mississippi's governor, John Bell Williams, groaned, "Once again the school children of our state have been offered as sacrificial lambs on the altar of social experimentation." He warned that the ruling would adulterate "quality public education" and perhaps wreck "public education itself." The Citizens' Council castigated *Alexander* as "Black Wednesday" in its journal, *The Citizen.* Subscribers read an editorial by the council's urbane and cerebral executive director, William J. Simmons, who viewed the Court's opinion as an accelerant "toward national socialism" rendered to "satisfy the demands of inquisitorial liberalism with its obsessive negritude." An anonymous high school student from Jackson, Mississippi, intoned his vitriol in verse set to the tune of "Jingle Bells":

> Riding 'cross the town,
> In a bus half full of blacks.
> Through the hills and vales,
> Across the railroad tracks.

> Jingle Bus, Jingle Bus
> Integration's fun
> At my school I rank 65th,
> at Brinkley number one!

> They have this thing for us in the South,
> The fifth circuit judge has shot off his mouth
> "Mix now" are the words we cannot forget,
> I say, my friend, is that not some shit?[21]

The court of public opinion in Mississippi was predictably dyspeptic. Jackson's *Clarion-Ledger* ran a racially tinged headline: "Supreme Court Orders Immediate State Mix." *Alexander v. Holmes* rudely awakened state officials. State Superintendent of Education Garvin H. Johnston was "very much surprised, amazed and appalled that the court would put such a requirement of school districts in the middle of the year." James Eastland recovered Robert Finch's doomsday scenario: "The decision spells disaster for public education in Mississippi and many parts of the South." Back home in Yazoo City, a still-hopeful John Satterfield swore to file an appeal with the Supreme Court and fight on in the Fifth Circuit with objections to the ruling. Mississippi attorney general A. F. Summer promised state assistance to any school board that requested legal help. "All deliberate speed" meant "now," he told WLBT, Jackson's NBC affiliate. "God help" the school boards "as they try to implement this ruling." The *Memphis Commercial Appeal* struck a more balanced tone and reported, "What happened this week spells the end of one social era and the beginning of another. Surely there will be pragmatic efforts at delay, further frustrations of the intent of the Supreme Court and its interpretation of the constitution. But the gauntlet appears to be down."[22]

Hodding Carter, the liberal editor of Greenville's *Delta Democrat Times*, regarded the Court's ruling as an epochal event and braced his readers for integration:

> The inevitability of school desegregation now stares white Southerners square in the face, and it is equally inevitable that many will seek to flee from it into private schools or away from their communities. Their reaction will not be something uniquely Southern, but typical of White Americans everywhere when faced with the prospect of large numbers of black Americans attending school with their children. . . . The demagogues will seek to capitalize on white fears, even if it means the destruction or serious weakening of the public school system—and consequently of their state's future. Too many moderates will remain silent, although apprehensive about the possibility. For us, the court's decision simply means that more money, more thought and more care must be directed into the public schools so that all our children, black and white, do not have to suffer needlessly because of their elders' mistakes.[23]

Massive integration had finally dawned in the heart of Mississippi. On the ground in Holmes County, Hazel Brannon Smith urged her white neighbors to remain calm. The normally feisty editor appealed to their better angels: "What is needed now from all citizens is a great deal of wisdom, courage and an understanding of what must be done." She dedicated a front-page editorial to the recent visit of the Reverend Hosea Williams, former confidant of the slain Martin Luther King Jr. While the Supreme Court had deliberated *Alexander*, Williams had presented Robert Clark with a civil rights award for becoming the state's only black legislator since Reconstruction. Smith quoted

Williams, who vaulted the people of Holmes to "the brink of history. You can become one of the first counties in America to help redeem its soul. I believe this could be true—but it will take whites and blacks working together—and it will require a degree of integrity and a depth of understanding which has not yet been demonstrated. But I still keep hoping and praying that it will be achieved before it is everlastingly too late."[24]

In court, the LDF had won. Integration's fate, however, would be decided by granular conditions back in the local communities where the case originated.

CHAPTER SEVEN

An Imperfect Revolution:
Enforcing *Alexander*

❀

But we must go further and insist that great
as is this victory, many and long steps
along Freedom Road lie ahead.
—W. E. B. Du Bois

THIRTY YEARS BEFORE the *Alexander* case began, W. E. B. Du Bois, the venerable scholar and peerless civil rights activist, posed a rather blasphemous question in his 1935 essay "Does the Negro Need Separate Schools?" His answer was an unvarnished critique of racial integration: "No general and inflexible rule can be laid down." "Theoretically the Negro needs neither segregated schools nor mixed schools," he continued. "What he needs is Education." Du Bois, a founder of the NAACP in 1909, had grown disenchanted with school desegregation in the North. For many whites, integrated schools conjured visceral reactions against race hybridization. "Race prejudice in the United States," he complained, "is such that most Negroes cannot receive proper education in white institutions." Du Bois despaired that he had "repeatedly seen wise and loving colored parents take infinite pains to force their little children into schools where the white children, white teachers, and white parents despised and resented the dark child, made mock of it, neglected or bullied it, and literally rendered its life a living hell. Such parents want their child to 'fight' this thing out,—but, dear God, at what cost!"[1]

Du Bois urged the NAACP to pressure states to equalize Negro education and upgrade black facilities instead of pushing for racially mixed schools. He disparaged efforts to bulldoze "a rich and powerful majority of the citizens to do what they will not do." Ideally, black children would attend desegregated schools with supportive teachers and friendly classmates. The worst-case scenario would be antagonistic school officials and a hostile reception from white parents and students. Du Bois did not condone segregation, but he had reservations about placing African-American children in white-dominated schools. Confounded by a wall of racism, he warned that integration would improve Negro students' lot only if they enrolled in schools that treated them fairly. Integration unto itself held "no magic."[2]

Neither in 1935 nor later in 1969 did Du Bois's concerns about the talisman of school integration dissuade many black leaders. Proponents of desegregated education threw caution aside and preferred risk-taking to heed-taking. "Education," the NAACP lectured President Nixon in 1970, "is that step ladder out of poverty and anarchism into the mainstream of America and democracy." The long-standing ambition of the NAACP, Inc. Fund attorneys, and other civil rights groups to integrate the schools sallied forth as they imagined a more egalitarian society and sent black children to undertake the greatest experiment in American education. The *Alexander* decree gave them the judicial mandate to achieve their lofty objective and put the federal government squarely on their side. Within a year of *Alexander v. Holmes*, Mississippi and the other southern states under the purview of the Fifth Circuit had transitioned to unitary schools. Dismantling the detritus of the dual-education system in the South, once thought improbable if not insuperable, became a reality relatively peacefully and in a very short span. "The process was not without casualties," admitted Fred Banks, a Mississippi LDF lawyer. Integration, the goal so long desired by many African Americans and contemporary liberals, would not be reached without enormous costs. Black children, teachers, and parents would pay a price for their boldness.[3]

In late October 1969, the Supreme Court remanded *Alexander* to the U.S. Fifth Circuit Court of Appeals. At first, not even the Court's concise and lucid instructions cajoled the Fifth Circuit judges. A majority of the appellate judges still "could not believe that the Supreme Court intended for them to issue orders that required the relocation of hundreds of thousands of school children in the middle of an on-going school year." On November 7, unanimously and en banc, the Fifth Circuit ordered a two-step process. The judges directed Mississippi's school districts to blend their faculty and staffs, transportation, athletics, and other activities no later than February 1, 1970. The midyear consolidation of student bodies seemed too "difficult to arrange," the court prevaricated. "Many students," the Fifth pointed out, "must transfer. Buildings will be put to new use. In some instances it may be necessary to transfer equipment, supplies, or libraries. School bus routes must be reconstituted." The Fifth Circuit postponed massive student integration until the following September. Frustrated by another delay, LDF lawyers appealed. The ball went back to Burger's Court.[4]

The high court once again summarily reversed the Fifth Circuit Court of Appeals. Ruling on January 14, 1970, in *Carter v. West Feliciana Parish School Board*, the Supreme Court routed the Fifth Circuit to integrate all the school districts by February 1. As one legal scholar noted, "The Fifth Circuit—which had been the most diligent court in America in desegregating public school facilities—was wrist-slapped for delaying massive student desegregation." Only Justices Warren Burger and Potter Stewart dissented. The appeals court, they elbowed their fellow justices, "is far more familiar than we with the various situations of these several school districts, some large, some small, some rural and some metropolitan," and interfering with their jurisprudence, moreover, "seems unsound to us." Henceforth, the Fifth Circuit judges informally agreed to avoid en banc hearings and issued opinion-orders to sort out the surfeit of cases before them. "All that can be said about school cases had been said," Chief Judge John Brown counseled his colleagues on the bench; "there is no point in writing further words." *Carter v. West Feliciana* and *Alexander v. Holmes*, taken together, delivered a one-two knockout punch to the dual-school system.[5]

After the *Alexander* ruling, Brown assigned Judge Griffin Bell the awesome task of scudding along implementation. Born in 1918 in Americus, Georgia, to a cotton-planting family, Griffin Boyette Bell joined the Fifth Circuit Court in 1961 as a Kennedy appointee. Well-respected on the appellate court and by civil rights attorneys, Bell brought his considerable administrative talents and charming personality to the Fifth Circuit. One biographer memorably described him as a "cross between Mark Twain and John Marshall . . . plain spoken, witty . . . politically savvy, and extremely intelligent." Embroiled in a period of social kinesis, Judge Bell devoted himself to the job at hand, consulted with white and black community leaders, and sought viable school integration arrangements.[6]

Bell served as a bridge-builder between the opposing parties involved in *Alexander* and its companion cases. He started by summoning civil rights attorneys, defendant school boards, and school superintendents to New Orleans for a conference. Bell spent weeks hearing all sides and finding innovative solutions to accomplish integration. As a judge, Bell did not favor busing plans to achieve racial balance in schools, but he firmly believed in the rule of law and knew the Fifth Circuit must enforce desegregation. If school districts evaded the court or failed to comply, he wanted to negotiate a settlement with them and preferred persuasion to a steamroller solution. Judge Bell often recommended the formation of biracial committees to settle local disputes. His approach struck some skeptics as timorous or too conservative. Others recognized the judge's effectiveness. One admirer claimed Bell could "talk the birds out of the trees to sit on his shoulder." When he brought together LDF counsel and segregationists in his courtroom, Bell did not mince words with white officials who denied African Americans their civil rights. According to one observer, Bell "read the riot act" to the defense attorneys and "told them they were desegregating next month whether they liked it or not." After threatening the "big stick," he demonstrated his ability to reconcile warring factions and arbitrate an entente cordiale. Bell moored compliance by conferring with lawyers, seeking the middle ground, and working out collaborative plans. The nimble judge had amazing success with communities and earned a reputation for his equanimity.[7]

Bell's approach unveiled a radical departure in the way the Fifth Circuit handled school desegregation. Before 1969, if a circuit panel disagreed with a lower court's opinion, it would simply overturn and remand the case with orders to fashion a new plan. Meanwhile, schools would stay segregated. After *Alexander*, however, the criterion became a unitary school system. To avoid bumping up against any uncooperative district courts, Bell handpicked federal judges to implement the Fifth Circuit's instructions. In Mississippi's southern district, he designated Dan Russell, known for his courtesy and fairness, rather than the truculent Harold Cox to hold hearings on local desegregation arrangements and recommend modifications, when and if necessary, to the appeals court. No alteration could occur without Bell's blessing. The judge also vested the LDF with amicus curiae status in all the Justice Department's desegregation cases.[8]

By January 1970, the assault on Mississippi's lingering two-tiered school system was in full swing. The Justice Department, federal judges, and civil rights lawyers continued the yeoman's work of desegregating school districts. Jackson's LDF office assumed the mantle for practically all litigation in the district courts and the Fifth Circuit Court of Appeals. Mel Leventhal supervised the staff attorneys who ensured compliance with *Alexander*. After Marian Wright left Jackson in 1968 to found and run a national defense fund for children, Leventhal became the state's top attorney for the Legal Defense Fund. At age twenty-eight, the hard-driving lawyer had grown increasingly contemptuous of southern racial practices and brazen in his disregard. Since arriving in Mississippi, his actions demonstrated his affinity for blacks. Leventhal fought segregation on his own behalf as well as for his clients. While handling casework in Jackson, he had met the black writer Alice Walker. The two dated, married in New York in March 1967, and moved to Mississippi in July. In 1969, the year before massive integration began, Leventhal passed the Mississippi bar exam and achieved celebrity and public notoriety. Known as "Mr. Civil Rights," he kept a high profile, which brought with it dangers, threats, and intimidation that he wore like badges of honor. For protection, Leventhal still kept a rifle at home and in his Oldsmobile Toronado, a luxury muscle car that did nothing to diminish his visibility. He also relied on Jackson's LDF staff to assist in the fight against school segregation.[9]

Jackson's Inc. Fund hired the first African American to graduate from the University of Mississippi School of Law—Reuben Vincent Anderson. Personable, bright, and laid-back, Anderson joined the handful of black attorneys in the state. In June 1967, just out of law school, he filed his first case for the NAACP. Anderson grew up in Jackson and came of age during Mississippi's freedom struggle. As a child, he befriended Jack Young Jr., whose family practically raised him. Cocooned in the Youngs' household, Reuben Anderson learned about civil rights and even met Roy Wilkins, the NAACP's national secretary. Such early experiences transformed Anderson and set his heart on following his mentor, Jack Young Sr., into the law. Not long after obtaining his JD, Anderson interned with Melvyn Zarr for one year at the LDF's main office in New York. The LDF routinely plucked newly minted lawyers to shadow veteran civil rights attorneys before going south and resuming litigation. As a member of the Mississippi bar, Anderson's credentials proved vital to the Jackson LDF branch, especially in the gaping absence of doyenne Marian Wright. Until Mel Leventhal passed the state bar exam, Anderson argued cases in both the northern and southern district courts of Mississippi. At age twenty-four, the young attorney penetrated the Magnolia State's legal jungle of segregated courtrooms, racist judges, and all-white juries.[10]

To shoulder the titanic task ahead of them, Anderson and Leventhal needed reinforcements and got them in July 1968 when Fred L. Banks Jr. joined the LDF. Banks and Anderson, longtime friends, grew up together in Jackson. Unlike Anderson, Banks studied law out-of-state at Howard University in Washington. Before graduation in June 1968, Banks applied to clerk with Griffin Bell on the Fifth Circuit, but after he met Marian Wright on a visit home, he decided to return to Mississippi and fight for civil rights. Wright recommended the even-keeled Banks to Jack Greenberg, and the LDF snatched him up. During Fred Banks's first year practicing in Jackson, he helped to implement the *Jefferson* and *Green* decrees throughout the state. Obstacles confronted him wherever he went. "Attitudes hadn't changed a whole lot," Banks recalled, but "some things had changed.... There was some school integration based on freedom-of-choice plans.... You were able to get a meal in a restaurant. You were able to get a room in a hotel, and you weren't able to do that when I left." When he entered the courthouse in Noxubee County, "they still had white and colored drinking fountains on the first floor." "So things hadn't changed a whole lot," he laughed. "They were in the process of changing."[11]

As a triumvirate, Jackson's LDF lawyers complemented each other admirably and suffused the undertaking of integration with vigor, dedication, and design. Fred Banks primarily tackled school desegregation and divided the caseload with Anderson and Leventhal. While Banks handled cases filed in Mississippi's pliant northern district, the other two men tussled with the more acerbic southern district. With the full weight of the federal courts now behind them, Banks and his Inc. Fund colleagues felt hopeful for integration. Mel Leventhal called on Mississippians to reconcile "the present and the future. We *will* have quality education for every child."[12]

Wholesale school desegregation now confronted the heartland of the South. Between December 1969 and September 1970, the Fifth Circuit issued a whopping 166 desegregation orders, involving eighty-nine school districts from Georgia through Texas, the cradle of the former Confederacy, at a record pace of four per week. The appeals court handed down fifty-seven opinion-orders in Mississippi alone. *Alexander* "hit" the Magnolia State like a blow from "a sledge-hammer," wrote one journalist. During 1970, 56,000 white children and 67,000 black children would be reshuffled into completely integrated schools. "Perhaps no court in history has responded with such alacrity and such monumental effort to a preemptory reversal," one historian commented. The Fifth Circuit's "judicial blitz had a stunning impact," noted J. Harvie Wilkinson, a law professor and editor of the *Norfolk Virginian-Pilot*. *Alexander v. Holmes* served as the pivotal breakthrough in school desegregation. By 1971, according to HEW statistics, 44 percent of black students attended predominantly white schools in the South, in contrast to 28 percent who did in the North and West. Sixteen years after the *Brown* ruling, Wilkinson remarked, the South finally "became America's most integrated region."[13]

From 1970 to 1972, "speed" superseded "deliberate" as the operative word in school desegregation. The Fifth Circuit and Supreme Court annulled the dual-school systems at once. Desegregation's velocity sometimes outstripped its meaning, however. *Alexander* was far less ambiguous than *Brown* on the timing of implementation, but a uniform code for "desegregation" and what precisely it should consist of proved elusive. Without a proper definition, desegregation could turn into a skin-deep game of numbers and quotas that skidded short of guaranteeing fair treatment for black students and teachers and integrating two cultures and two sets of traditions into one. Onerous questions followed court objectives. As Wilkinson put it, "If freedom of choice was not favored, then what was? What if geographical zoning failed to produce the substantial integration *Green* seemed to require? How much integration did *Green* require? How many all-black schools would be tolerated? How far-reaching an effort was required to desegregate them? Did the Court's approval of racial ratios in faculty assignments . . . impose a similar requirement for student bodies as well?"[14]

During the weeks and months after *Alexander*, such ponderous questions confounded integration's proponents and their segregationist counterparts. Though the courts had acted, a whole raft of perplexing issues had clearly not been settled. From the beginning, various entanglements and kaleidoscopic problems could impair or undermine integration. Federal judges navigated a skein of circumstances when implementing school desegregation. Across the South, state politicians blustered defiance and begged subvention for private academies.

The singular, underlying, and perhaps ironic factor in what hampered the initial wave of integration stemmed from the grassroots level. Rather than taking bold and creative steps to nurture racial reconciliation and sustain school desegregation, myopic, bureaucratic-minded educators and civic boosters too often waited for direction from federal authorities or squandered opportunities to seal integration's long-term success. Supervisory stupor as well as racist headwinds buffeted integration. Many white faculty regarded black students as a nuisance or an intrusion. Black teachers resented white claims about the inferiority of Negro education. Centuries of antiblack discrimination uncorked years of pent-up distrust of whites that could evoke bitterness in the African-American community. White parents strenuously objected to using their children for what Senator James Eastland demonized as "this monstrous sociological experiment." In the hands of the malicious or simply the incompetent, school integration became a piñata for abuse, misunderstanding, and miscommunication—and frittered away.[15]

Local actors did more to shape the outcome of school desegregation than any other catalyst. In 1970, when integration finally became a widespread reality in Mississippi, the abruptness and amplitude of such dramatic change rocked most whites. While initial reactions to *Alexander v. Holmes* varied—the South, after all, was not a monolith—many whites remained firm in their opposition to mixed-race education. Even after decisively losing the legal battle, white Mississippians generally responded to the *Alexander* verdict and the prospect of massive integration as if their world had fallen apart. More than a few frothing letters battered the Supreme Court. One Brookhaven resident cursed the Court for arrogating "tyrannical powers" and flouting "the laws of God. He puts into His creatures instincts to mingle socially and mate with their own." A "place called hell" awaited the justices. Bad blood, fear, and disaffection accompanied the Court's broad mandate.[16]

Hard on the heels of the ruling, tens of thousands of white Mississippians rejected integration with their feet and fled from integrated school systems in the nation's blackest state. As in the decade before *Alexander*, white parents, especially in preponderantly black counties, continued to pull their children out of public education altogether and put them in hastily improvised private segregation academies. In many rural locales, only poor white students who found the escape hatch nailed shut stayed in the public schools with African Americans. Thereafter, scores of school systems desegregated only to "re-segregate." Between 1968 and 1970, total white public school enrollment in the thirty-three districts named in *Alexander* atrophied by 25 percent. In the most heavily black and rural areas, the white exodus from public education hit roughly 90 percent. Statewide, the kudzu-like growth of segregated private schools became an accepted part of the southern educational landscape. From 1966 to 1970, the number of all-white academies had ballooned from 121 to 236, and sixty-one private schools formed within a year after *Alexander*. On WLBT, Bill Simmons, of the Citizens' Council, described Mississippi as a swarming "beehive of activity" following the integration order.[17]

Amid the greatest educational upheaval of the twentieth century, integration became a fact of life in Holmes County. Mirroring other counties, private schools sprang up to cater to white students withdrawing from the public education system. Within two weeks of the *Alexander* decision, nearly 1,600 white students attended segregation academies. The Central Holmes and Cruger-Tchula academies were the largest of three homegrown schools created after the LDF filed *Alexander v. Holmes* back in 1965. By one headcount, only 900 whites remained in the public system, compared with nearly 6,000 African-American students. Reporting from Lexington, *Washington Post* correspondent Philip D. Carter foresaw that white pullout would "leave public schools entirely black by next year" because "white parents will not accept more extensive integration." While wealthier families placed their children in segregation academies, the less affluent either homeschooled or planned to transfer their children to white-majority school districts. Coming up with the money for private school required desperate measures. One poor white remembered families that "mortgaged their homes, sold their land, disposed of one vehicle or any other worldly possessions they could realistically part with, and anything else they could possibly figure out to do" to shirk "the 'shame' and 'degradation' of sending their kids to school with the 'niggers.'"[18]

Such a backlash could have been avoided had Mississippi's leaders not waged a two-decade-long rearguard action to circumvent and hamstring school desegregation. Calvin King, the school board attorney who defended white educators in the 1965 *Alexander* suit, rhetorically asked Carter, "What was the . . . board supposed to do—be tarred and feathered and run out of the community on a rail? That's what would have happened if we had integrated back when [former governor] Ross Barnett was screaming 'never.' I suppose we've lost the battle." The Durant lawyer seemed a man out of time, but he concluded with a reflexive evasion. King pointed out the paucity of integration elsewhere in America: "We can't have a unitary school here any more than they can in Harlem." There was dissonance in Durant.[19]

Almost three months after the *Alexander v. Holmes* ruling, the city acted on behalf of aggrieved whites. On January 26, 1970, Durant's city council adopted an ordinance to reestablish a separate municipal school district. Durant had operated a municipal district from 1902 to 1956, but it had merged with the county school system during a consolidation effort in reaction to the 1954 *Brown* decision. The 1970 reopening of a municipal district in Durant occurred after the mayor and aldermen requested separate status from the state's Educational Finance Commission and Holmes County's board of education. At its March 1970 meeting, school board officials endorsed the petition. Barring any objections from the LDF and the district court in Jackson, Durant could secede. The federal court and Inc. Fund attorneys found no illegality in the plan and granted the city permission to divorce from the county. In July, the Holmes school board authorized the transfer of county buildings and grounds to the new district. Both whites and blacks in all grades could access the Durant schools, but the municipal district also admitted pupils from across Holmes County. The county school board quickly accepted transfers for fourteen white students from seven families living outside the city limits. The black students already enrolled in the Durant schools returned in the fall, but they constituted a small enough presence for the white community to tolerate. When county educators reinstated the Durant district, the school board kept its true motive under wraps. Any poor whites unable to afford tuition at the private academies could attend public school in Durant's less-threatening setting. Durant's separate school system served unofficially as a stopgap or "holding ground" during turbulent times, one black resident observed, until whites could work out the kinks of integration.[20]

Despite wrinkles in desegregation, progressive whites stayed positive. Hazel Brannon Smith insisted on the preservation of the public school system in her editorials. In the *Lexington Advertiser*, she put the responsibility for forming feasible integration plans on county educators. "The challenge to our educators is to find positive constructive solutions for our school problems, unimpeded by further destructive rhetoric of politicians who have brought us to this situation," she editorialized. "The educators must show us how to meet our problems. There can be no more wringing of hands and cowardly retreats. The problem is here, now, and must be solved," Smith implored county officials. Mel Leventhal also kept faith in public education. Time and hard work would restore an integrated public school system. For him, integration was not ideological gas; it was a matter of "character," Leventhal weighed in on Jackson's WLBT. "You learn character and citizenship by growing up with children of different cultural backgrounds and races. I have only pity for the white child who graduates from a private school and is unable to cope with a multi-racial society," he admonished white parents who abandoned public schools. Editor James "Jimmy" Ward of the *Jackson Daily News* had heard enough pieties from Leventhal and the liberal *Washington Post*. In a tirade, he savaged Philip Carter for his coverage of integration and the *Post* "who can so expertly point a finger at Mississippi but fail so miserably in their own backyards where education now counts its curriculum in five 'r's: readin', rightin', 'rithmetic, rape and revolver practice."[21]

The private school movement's cheerleaders also pepped up the defense of segregation academies by trying to preserve their federal tax-exempt status, which helped keep the incipient and financially shaky institutions solvent. Although private schools had long received an automatic exemption from federal taxation because of their standing as nonprofit educational establishments, that policy came under judicial scrutiny after the passage of the Civil Rights Act of 1964, which forbade racial segregation and discrimination. Homing in on the private academies and denying their tax exemption required extensive litigation. Civil rights lawyers and the federal courts whittled away the amount of indirect aid that private schools received from the government.[22]

In January 1970, a group of black plaintiffs from Holmes County and elsewhere in Mississippi pressed a decision for new tax rules when they won a preliminary injunction against David M. Kennedy, Nixon's secretary of the treasury, the cabinet department responsible for the Internal Revenue Service (IRS), and IRS commissioner Randy Thrower. *Green v. Kennedy* banned the IRS from granting tax-exempt status and deductibility of contributions to thirty-nine Mississippi private academies unless the schools issued a statement of nondiscrimination. The federal courts realized the counter-productivity of demanding school integration while simultaneously giving private schools financial relief to skirt desegregation. At first, the Nixon administration dithered about enforcing the ruling, but the White House ultimately proved willing to uphold the court order. In July 1970, the IRS announced that it would no longer vouchsafe tax exemptions for private schools with racially discriminatory policies. Only nine of the offending institutions agreed to issue the declarations. Thirty stubborn schools refused to submit any type of nondiscrimination statement and tried unsuccessfully to appeal the verdict in the high court. In March 1971, the Supreme Court made the injunction permanent and stripped the all-white academies of their tax-exempt status.[23]

As the federal courts required change, school desegregation came to the Deep South grudgingly but mostly nonviolently. One combustible exception in February 1970 involved the burning of a high school in tiny Maben, Mississippi, a black-majority community in the eastern part of the state, on the eve of its scheduled integration. The next month, in Lamar, South Carolina, another small, mostly black town, a mob of white men and women flipped and incinerated two buses loaded with black elementary schoolchildren, who barely escaped grievous injury. In the nick of time, state troopers whisked the students through the schoolhouse door and probably saved their lives. Newspaper drumfire captured the episode. *New York Times* journalist Jon Nordheimer recounted the incident: "Someone in the crowd hollered, 'Stop the buses!' and grim men surged forward with ax handles, broken bottles and rocks. They stood alongside the buses and hammered on them with their long clubs. . . . Not since the bombing in Birmingham had grown men so intimidated children with threats of physical violence."[24]

Still, the predicted chaos, second massive resistance, and bloodbath had not transpired. More southern leaders accepted their responsibility to maintain order, obey *Alexander*, and convert the public schools into a unitary system. Additional fits of resistance were futile. The courts had spoken. As South Carolina's governor Robert McNair reasoned placidly, southerners had "run out of courts" and should pursue "compliance," not "defiance."[25]

President Nixon, likewise, had acted more responsibly to uphold the law and played a constructive albeit behind-the-scenes role in bringing the South into line with *Alexander*. Privately, Nixon doubted the viability of *Alexander's* imperatives. "Integration hasn't worked," he confided to Chief of Staff H. R. Haldeman, and did not point to the "future." White Mississippians shared his view. A mother of three children attending a formerly all-black school in Madison County wrote an open letter to the president in the *Jackson Clarion-Ledger* and beseeched him for help: "Can you imagine yourself as a father of an attractive, intelligent, very dedicated 15 year old girl, forcing her to attend classes with 71 Negroes and only 18 white students?" Nixon sympathized with white parents' dilemma and never personally committed to integration. "Whites in Mississippi can't send their kids to schools that are 90 percent black," he told John Ehrlichman, "They've got to set up private schools." Although many whites held out hope that Nixon would sling them southern comfort, he instead launched a back-channel campaign for school integration.[26]

After endorsing *Green v. Kennedy*, Nixon formed the Cabinet Committee on Education to orchestrate the administration's desegregation strategy and foster interracial cooperation. Coordinating out of the White House and chaired by Secretary of Labor George Shultz, the cabinet committee enlisted biracial groups of moderates and leading citizens, including businessmen, newspaper editors, school board officials, and ministers. After Shultz nursed model civic committees in the southern states most affected by *Alexander*, Nixon met with their emissaries in the Oval Office to accomplish desegregation on a meaningful scale. The number of black students attending integrated schools trampolined—from 600,000 before *Alexander* to 2.6 million in the 1970–71 school year.[27]

The Nixon administration deliberately took no credit for the deed, just what White House spin doctors ordered to deflect flak for desegregation enforcement from the executive to the judicial branch. Richard Nixon had merely carried out the law. The president did more than turn up the political heat on the courts; he made telltale gestures to reassure white southerners. While steering the South toward compliance with *Alexander*, he also gave succor to southern whites by naming conservative judges to the federal bench. Eventually, Nixon assuaged his southern constituency, as his appointees would chip away at the objectives of the liberal activists on the Warren Court. In January 1970, Nixon had announced his nomination of G. Harrold Carswell, a Georgian with a history of white supremacy whom the president had elevated to the Fifth Circuit, to replace Abe Fortas on the Supreme Court.[28]

The staff in Leon Panetta's Civil Rights Division of the Department of Health, Education, and Welfare scoffed at Carswell's choreographed nomination. Panetta had aggressively advocated for compulsory integration and accused the administration of executing a "civil rights retreat." Nixon had not forgotten about the highly vocal thorn in his side at HEW. He characterized Panetta's agency as infested with "eager beavers," "wild young horses," and "pipsqueaks" with "snot-nosed attitudes . . . in the bowels of HEW." Just weeks later in February, Panetta thumbed through a copy of the *Washington Daily News* to find himself out of a job: "Nixon Seeks to Fire HEW's Rights Chief for Liberal Views." On February 15, the Panetta vendetta ended when Nixon terminated the OCR chief. Six of Panetta's colleagues quit in solidarity. Panetta had expected the ax to fall ever since his insubordination during the previous summer's brouhaha over the Finch statement. "The surprise is that Panetta was not fired earlier," wrote historian Raymond Wolters. Nixon could not stomach a partisan "rights zealot" in his administration and told his aide John Ehrlichman, "Firing Panetta is worth dozens of speeches and statements about integrating the schools."[29]

In March 1970, President Nixon further allayed the fears of southern whites with an unusually loquacious 8,000-word policy statement enunciating his views on the school desegregation issue. The president repeated his determination to impose desegregation on the South's public schools, but Nixon also embraced neighborhood schools as "the most appropriate base" for crafting integrated education. Nixon's racial algorithm distinguished between de jure and de facto segregation and drew a sharp line at court-ordered busing. Black Mississippians panted concerns when the president applauded local school officials in the development of integration. For decades, such educators had broken promises to blacks and obstructed desegregation. State Representative Robert Clark "didn't think much of the president's statement," he fired back on Jackson television news. "First of all, he did not say how" school desegregation "was to be done. . . . He said he would put it back in the hands of the local authorities. The president knows as well as I do that the problem will not be solved" under the management of local educators. Without strong federal support, African Americans would have to "go and get on [their] knees in order to get the job done."[30]

Having shored up his southern flank, Nixon counseled against massive resistance to court orders and ensured compliance with *Alexander*. Throughout 1970, he reified desegregation by deploying more than a hundred government lawyers and U.S. marshals to the South. HEW and the Department of Justice also tried to redeem themselves. HEW sequestered federal funds for southern districts that clung to single-race schools. Any straggling school systems that botched integration either invited a HEW probe or incurred a lawsuit from the Justice Department. The legal offensive convinced some civil rights advocates and liberals to recant their criticisms of Nixon. The *New Republic*'s John Osborne cheered the administration's record of enforcement. The president had "brought about more desegregation in the South . . . than anybody had reason to expect," Osborne conceded.[31]

On the right of the political aisle, more sobering and skeptical appraisers played seer with uncanny perfection. Writing in his magazine, *National Review*, William F. Buckley attested to Nixon's knack for backdoor maneuvers and untiring manipulation. Buckley understood the nature of the political beast inhabiting the Oval Office. He suspected that the president had cautiously enabled integration to defuse the race issue and return to his real concern: foreign policy. "The opinion-makers have said that we must have integrated schooling, that any slowdown in that program is nothing less than moral temporizing," Buckley stated. "So, Mr. Nixon has calculated, let's get on with it, and see what happens." Buckley also triangulated "the cynical-realistic" probability "confirmed by all past experience that the desegregated schools will soon be resegregated anyway, so what difference does it make?" Buckley's southern point man, conservative columnist James J. Kilpatrick, fanned the flames of opposition and cast doubts on *Brown*'s progeny and the steady prod of government-induced racially balanced education:

> Jim Crow schools are dead; but Jim Crow schools survive. Segregation is dead as a permissible legal device, but it survives in fact and in human nature. The beacon light of *Brown* now spins erratically; the right of children that shone so bright in 1954 has dimmed. Once *Brown* guided lawmakers and schoolmen clearly. Race could *not* be a factor in school enrollment. We have gone 180 degrees. Today race *must* be a factor in school enrollment. The principle that children must be treated equally has passed through an Orwellian sea change: Some have become more equal than others.[32]

For southern blacks, full-bore integration in 1970 and 1971 represented a pendulum swing. School desegregation marked "a giant step forward in their century-long battle to secure the best-possible education for their children," noted historian Charles C. Bolton, but African Americans "soon recognized the often staggering price exacted for this triumph." As apartheid public education disintegrated throughout the South, blacks experienced a mixture of cautious optimism, disappointment, disruptions, and even trauma. Integration had "no magic," as Du Bois prophesied in 1935, to dispel racial discrimination. Enforcing integration, providing quality education, and protecting black educators were hardly the same. In many communities, whites still held a gross imbalance of power and controlled the school boards. The inception of unitary school systems entailed the closure of black institutions; the firing or demotion of black administrators, teachers, guidance counselors, band directors, and coaches; and the inestimable daily abuses of black students. School integration came at a cost, and African Americans got handed the hardest deal of all.[33]

Despite the burdens of *Alexander*, most blacks remained upbeat. As much as he stewed about the intangibles of desegregation, State Representative Robert Clark, a former teacher, said that "if we can go into this thing shoulder to shoulder, we are willing to try to make a go of it." Not all school systems underwent serious or prolonged dislocations. Some school districts set up biracial committees to consult blacks or to advise school boards. Sometimes, federal judges ordered them to iron out frictions. Results varied.[34]

There were missed opportunities and pockets of success. In southern Mississippi, Hattiesburg's interracial committee became a model of its kind. After some initial trepidation, whites learned to share power with African Americans and sought their input on integration plans. To the north, the university town of Oxford desegregated under the watchful eye of Judge William Keady. New Albany, William Faulkner's birthplace in northeast Mississippi, achieved full integration. The opening day of school breezed through without a major incident in Laurel, the state headquarters of the Ku Klux Klan and home of its imperial wizard, Sam Bowers. In the Delta cotton town of Leland, white moderates and farmers, although not particularly liberal, saved the school system. Civic leaders patched together a biracial coalition of parents and educators that smoothed the way for integration. The alliance passed out stickers at school board meetings that encouraged citizens to "Think Positive." The group also ran a full-page advertisement in the local newspaper with the signatures of more than 200 white parents who vowed that their children would stay in the public school system. In the fall of 1970, nearly half the white students in Leland returned to public school. Considering the town's isolation in a plantation region, it was a monumental accomplishment. Back on the banks of the Pearl River, Columbia's newly desegregated high school beaconed another island of hope. The white student body president said, "If everybody can just treat everybody else as a human being, it might just turn out all right." The black student body president responded with a peace sign and beamed, "We can become a lighthouse in Marion County." In Greenville, however, integration foundered. Blacks lost faith in the city's multiracial committee when whites submitted a zoning plan that led to virtual segregation within the elementary schools. Jackson, the capital, could have served as an exemplar to the state, but 40 percent of its white students deserted the public schools.[35]

Many school districts let racial problems fester, which led to black alienation and disillusionment with integration. The demotion of black principals and dismissal or reassignment of black teachers became a burning issue. Since whites dominated the majority of school boards and superintendents' positions across the state, black administrative personnel, staff, and faculty were vulnerable. Desegregation occurred "primarily on white terms," Fred Banks retrospected, and black educators bore the disproportionate brunt of school integration. When schools melded, white school boards shuttered black institutions to save white ones. Black high school principals found themselves assistant principals serving under whites or demoted to classroom instructors. Between 1970 and 1971, the number of black high school principals in Mississippi shriveled from 168 to nineteen. White school boards, in some instances, downsized black administrators' titles along with their schools. Old black high schools that survived consolidation frequently became junior highs or elementary schools. In Leake County, whites closed all-black Jordan High, but Winnie and Dovie Hudson sent for Mel Leventhal to sue the school board and reopen the school. Whites typically reassigned the most-qualified black teachers to predominantly all-white schools and put the worst white faculty in formerly all-black schools. Statewide, in 1970, 15 percent of black schoolteachers lost their jobs. When Yazoo City's public schools sacked black faculty, observed Willie Morris, a native son and editor of *Harper's* magazine, a white teaching corps replaced them. During the first year of real integration, twenty-six districts in Mississippi hired 800 new teachers. Of them, only 158, or about 20 percent, were African Americans.[36]

That *any* school integration occurred in the wake of *Alexander* seemed incredible and perhaps miraculous. In the patchwork of misanthropic and earnest responses, the South's public school system showed surprising resilience as communities wrestled with desegregation and the endgame of dual schools. Yazoo City's public school system was one of hundreds affected by *Alexander*. On the shivering morning of January 7, 1970, the day of integration arrived. Along with the national press staked out in his hometown, Willie Morris looked on as white and black students eyed each other cagily. Since the *Alexander* ruling, he wrote for *Harper's*, "the white community in Yazoo had been undergoing an agony of survival." For many of Yazoo's nearly 14,000 residents, the prospect of instant integration elicited revulsion and anxiety. One desperate white woman writhed, "If I had a child, I'd go out and collect empty bottles if necessary to send [my son] to private school." Hysteria did not carry the day, however, and the hours ticked by calmly due to the careful preparation of town leaders. The previous November, 200 whites affixed their names to an ad in the *Yazoo City Herald* that pledged their loyalty to the public schools. Even State Senator Herman DeCell, a former member of the Mississippi State Sovereignty Commission, the government agency in charge of defending segregation, promised to keep his daughter in the city's desegregated schools. An impromptu consortium of business-minded whites banded together on economic terms and argued that the town's vitality depended on attracting industry, which required quality public schools, harmonious race relations, and integration.[37]

Integration happened overnight, but not without mischief. The next day, Justice Department attorneys had discovered that local segregationists, including John Satterfield, had played a final and dirty trick. Yazoo City's schools had opened with segregated classrooms. One of the most devious ways for whites to bedevil *Alexander* was to decouple student bodies by race within desegregated schools. Unbeknownst to federal judges and lawyers, city school officials kept most classrooms almost completely segregated. In spite of the subterfuge, an "immense façade was beginning to crack," noted Willie Morris. "It was the little things which were gradually enclosing and symbolizing the promise and the magnitude of what might be taking place here."[38]

In the first month of integration, over 2,000 black and nearly 1,400 white students attended Yazoo City's public schools. Elsewhere in the Delta, the opposite almost always held true as whites beat a retreat into segregation academies. Some 480 of Yazoo's whites enrolled in private schools, but 80 percent stuck with the public system. Students of both races "are groping in pain and innocence toward something new," Morris pondered, "toward" something "blurred and previously unheeded."[39]

Change did not come without detractors. Malcontents continued to choose the path of resistance. Willie Morris caught up with the LDF's old nemesis, John Satterfield, in his downtown law office. The crafty Yazoo City lawyer still held a grudge against the *Alexander* decision. "This was the first time in the history of education in the United States that the Court has declined to follow the recommendations of . . . education authorities . . . the Justice Department, and the attorney general," he noted acidly. Satterfield accused outside agitators of disturbing the peace and intimidating blacks to desegregate the city's schools. Morris countered his claims with a question: "And what if" more defiance warranted "a further Court order?" Satterfield "paused for a moment, puffed on his cigar, and gazed out the window at the flat brown terrain, at the dead cotton stalks stretching toward the horizon. He replied, sternly, 'We won't have any violence here.'" Considering the previous decade of racial violence, the transition to biracial schools in Yazoo City had been fairly smooth and heralded national praise.[40]

Later that year, Morris sat down with Hodding Carter, one of his boyhood heroes. Over dinner and martinis, the two southern liberals reminisced about their journalism and discussed integration. "You're obsessed with the South and went away. I'm not and I stayed," Carter joshed Morris. "It's *insane*," he unloaded on the entire state.

> The one damned place where Yankees and everyone else say this can't work, and it's become the battlefront. It's part of the screwy system in this nation that the one state least equipped, financially and emotion-ally, to deal with all the implications of it is finally havin' to do it first. People like Satterfield could have helped us, maybe could have saved us with their impeccable white Mississippi credentials. They could have helped move things in a civilized way, but they took their refuge in the thickets of the law.

The knot of southern implacability had been tied by *"stupidity! Sheer stupid-ity,"* Hodding Carter added. "Sheer *unyielding conservatism!*" All the segrega-tionists "had to do was talk quietly and try to accommodate, and be a typical hypocritical American state. But there's no halfway measures in *this* place," he said as he polished off a plate of catfish. "Hell, it might just work here someday. Wouldn't *that* surprise 'em?"[41]

While altruistic and law-abiding whites wanted to make the South a better place, the benefits of integration sometimes eluded African-American stu-dents. Entering previously all-white schools, blacks often felt discriminated against both inside and outside the classroom. Although many white educa-tors taught black pupils with professionalism and without animosity, plenty of others did not. Southern school officials, for instance, shunted black stu-dents into remedial classes at disproportionate rates—to limit interfacing with white children. White teachers and administrators also tended to apply a double standard and disciplined blacks more strictly than white classmates or suspended African Americans more readily for behavioral and dress code infractions. Most alarming of all, especially to black parents, was the percep-tion that white teachers graded black students unfairly. Across the state and the wider South, African-American parents claimed that their children, who had performed fine in all-black schools, had now inexplicably fallen behind or struggled to stay in school. In numerous southern school districts, the playing of seditious songs ("Dixie" in particular), naming athletic teams the "Rebels," or unfurling Confederate flags at games periodically roiled controversy as well. Black schoolchildren did not necessarily desensitize to or passively endure such racist conduct. In the years following *Alexander*, as shown in a study by historian David Cecelski, resilient African-American students staged boycotts and protested mistreatment.[42]

Notwithstanding discrimination in the new biracial schools, change had come to the South. *Alexander*'s specific requirements had largely been met. The legally constituted dual-school systems of the South had, reluctantly but inexorably, been unified. Black and white children could enter the same schoolhouse—a Promethean feat in itself. From 1965 to 1968, the ratio of black students who attended majority-white schools hiked from about 2 percent to almost 23 percent. Over the next twenty years, the rate nearly doubled to 43.5 percent in 1988. More astonishingly, between 1968 and 1980, the number of African-American students in essentially all-black schools decreased from 77.5 to 26.5 percent.[43]

Reflecting on civil rights from the panorama of 1998, Fred Banks boasted a record of success, not just notional or symbolic gains. The fight to desegregate education was "the major thrust in breaking the back of governmental apartheid," which vicariously "affected other aspects of our society" and "had ramifications way beyond just education." The ebb tide of dual schooling represented a crucial advancement in black civil rights. After decades of legal scrumming over integrated education, an insidious state-sanctioned system for schooling children had been toppled. To Bill Minor, the Mississippi correspondent for the *Times-Picayune* of New Orleans, the progress in 1970 was undeniable. Errors conceded and limitations duly noted, he told Willie Morris,

> Listen. People who argue that the law can't change a society are crazy. This state is a perfect example of how law can change a place. People down here are out in the bleachers. It's the federal law, the federal government, that's calling the real shots. The politicians down here like Maddox and Wallace and John Bell Williams think they are, but they're not. The changes that have been made in this state in the last few years have been astounding. And it's because of the federal law and the federal government. Even the Nixon Administration can't stop what's been started. All they can do is slow it down.[44]

For the Minor-minded, their kind knew that the struggle had not ended and that manifold injustices remained. Despite the unfinished work of school integration, civil rights agents had proved that even Mississippi could not save segregation. The attorneys, jurists, and ordinary citizens who strived to move the nation closer to the ideals of freedom and equality bestowed school desegregation on future generations as a birthright. Their labors eventually led to the *Alexander v. Holmes* decision that finally snapped official school segregation. Theirs had been no trivial achievement. Writing from Tougaloo College in Jackson, sociologist James Loewen found that integration "did not bring about any racial millennium" but signified a "first step in the upheaval of the old order"—and a profound but imperfect revolution.[45]

Coda

❀

Lord, we ain't what we oughta be.
We ain't what we want to be.
We ain't what we gonna be.
But, thank God, we ain't what we was!
—Former slave preacher

MORE THAN FIFTY years ago, Holmes County blacks brought one of the court suits that culminated in *Alexander v. Holmes*. Since 1965, much has changed. Not everything has. On the once-defiant western end of the county, in the Mississippi Delta hamlet of Tchula, a white-columned mansion looked ready to crumble. The two-story home had belonged to Sara Virginia Jones, heiress of a leading planter family and avid art collector. Nearly 400 paintings by the world's most renowned artists, including Cezanne, Rembrandt, Renoir, Dalí, and Warhol, had adorned the mansion walls. In 1990, Jones died. Her brother and relatives had decamped the area, along with many other wealthy whites who evacuated the Delta in the wake of the civil rights era and left the disadvantaged to cope on their own. The house's current owner, Tchula's former and first black mayor Eddie James Carthan, replaced Jones's fine art with African masks, photographs of himself with U.S. presidents Jimmy Carter, Bill Clinton, and Barack Obama, and a newspaper clipping of the day the Nation of Islam's Louis Farrakhan dedicated the ex-mayor's church across the street.[1]

When interviewed by the *Atlantic*'s Alan Huffman in 2015, Carthan savored the moment. The mansion's change of hands showed more than the ironic imprint of his residence—it indicated an inflection point in who ran

Tchula and the revolution in black rights. In twenty years, he went "from being a second-class citizen to staying in a house where the slave-owners used to live." Carthan grew up in a shack near Mileston on property his family purchased through the New Deal's FSA program. The Jones dynasty had sold land to the federal government for the Mileston project. Ruled by the planter elite for more than a century, Carthan's story and Tchula's transformation augured a shift in political power but not necessarily an abdication of the old race codes or a transfer of money. "I look at the house now, how beautiful it is and well-built it is. I was told slaves built it," Carthan ruminated at his desk in the central hall. "I think about how well they lived back then, and how we lived back then. This house is huge. There are five bedrooms. It has three full bathrooms. We didn't have bathrooms at all," he remarked. "It's something to focus on." It was a poignant pause in a languishing place. The mansion's peeling paint betrayed Tchula's economic plight.[2]

The tiny town of 2,000 recently ranked as the fifth-poorest town in the nation's poorest state. Jobs vanished with the mechanization of plantations. The local coat factory and sawmill shut down long ago. Unemployment soared to 25 percent. "Businesses don't want to come to a town like Tchula," lamented Anthony Mansoor, who, in 1967, shielded Edgar Love from Klansmen in his hardware store. "The people in this town worked so hard to get to where we are today, and in a lot of ways, things are better. But the town is broke. That's the bottom line." Bleak prospects caused many people to keep up with the Joneses and move away.[3]

By 2016, the remaining residents were 97 percent African-American, chronically poor, and increasingly disillusioned. The symptoms of creeping malaise included a fearsome high school dropout rate of four in ten students and an epidemic of drug use and crime. In the Delta bottomlands and the somnolently rural terrain to the east of Tchula, a paralyzing cycle of despair hung over the majority-black communities that once figured so conspicuously in the historic county's movement. Economic troubles continued to hold back blacks. Almost 60 percent of Holmes County families lived below the federal poverty line. Depending on the year, the county earned the disrepute of either the lowest life expectancy in the nation or scraped the bottom.[4]

Although progress had been stunted, the black freedom struggle in Holmes, like the broader movement across the South, had wrought remarkable changes. After the 1960s, blacks voted without restrictions, held elective office, attended desegregated public schools, served on juries, and lived free of the repressive violence of earlier years. African Americans and whites alike seemed to recognize that their county would never return to racial segregation and total white dominance. In Holmes County, black advancement might have been incomplete, with economic problems the most intractable, but at least the great fear of the old days had now largely abated. Without the risks and sacrifices of movement people, life for black Holmes Countians would not have improved. Without them, *Alexander* would have been dead-letter law. Reverend J. J. Russell glowed with pride felt by many veterans of the Holmes movement: "It does something to me when I hear tell of somebody elected in our state or county. . . . Had to stay up late, but we did it." Even if they lacked economic clout, African Americans gained political power.[5]

Integration abraded the segregated dynamics of Holmes County politics. Barely two years after the passage of the Voting Rights Act, the first black representative since the Reconstruction era entered Mississippi's legislature— Robert Clark. Over the following decade, African Americans fielded candidates and elected their race to leadership positions. In 1967, Howard Taft Bailey, a movement alumnus, became county election commissioner. Four years later, Holmes added a black tax assessor, county supervisor, and justice of the peace. In 1977, Eddie Carthan, then a lithe twenty-seven-year-old who wore his hair in a lush Afro, won mayor of Tchula. In 1979, voters elected a black sheriff. One county activist bore witness to the strength of African-American voter mobilization: "Some of the plantation people are waking up. They are not afraid of being kicked off the plantation for voting, marching, registering, or having anything to do with civil rights people."[6]

The steady expansion of black office-holding inspired many African Americans, but the county still reeled from economic disparity. When Carthan became mayor, he tried to "bring the other side up." "Tchula was like most southern towns," he later explained, "with the whites on one side and blacks on the other." Railroad tracks severed the dwellings and trailers of black folks from the grander antebellum manors of whites. On the white side, where Carthan eventually resided, "there were sidewalks, manicured lawns and beautiful homes like this one. But on the other side was dirt roads, shacks, and 75 percent of the houses had no plumbing."[7]

By the end of the 1970s, blacks effectively controlled the Holmes County government, but their civil rights movement involved more than just political action. Carthan sought federal funds to install water and sewer systems, create one of the first day-care centers in Mississippi, pave streets in the black section of town, build public housing, establish a free clinic and nutrition program for the elderly, and begin a transportation system. Community action and federal spending provided services and eighty jobs. Notwithstanding the much-needed infrastructural improvements, a balm to Holmes County's economic misery seemed as distant as ever. The despicable sharecropper system had disappeared, but some 800 blacks still lived on plantations. For three to four months of the year, workers chopped or picked cotton by hand. The other nine months, they subsisted on low-wage menial jobs, government welfare, and individual farming. Whites held on to their wealth and owned most businesses. When the political tables turned in Tchula, whites "didn't take kindly" to Carthan's progressive agenda. "Tchula's a plantation town," he stated, "and they just rejected me. . . . They were accustomed to blacks who'd bow, say 'yes-sir,' boss, that sort of thing." Tchula's whites did not easily surrender the old caste-ridden codes to the young black firebrand.[8]

Eddie Carthan's rise and eventual fall exemplified how local politics changed dramatically in the aftermath of legalized segregation and the shortcomings of the Holmes County movement. Threatened by his assertiveness and the breakthroughs in black independence, the planter elite and Tchula merchants conspired against Carthan. Throughout his stint in office, the *Holmes County Herald* regularly ginned up coverage about Carthan's political quarrels to discredit him. Carthan bickered with Lester Lyon, his white predecessor, and the board of aldermen. In 1980, the town council tried to oust Tchula's black police chief and reinstate Jim Andrews, a white businessman who held the post before Carthan took over. The feuding turned intraracial. Under pressure from whites, two black aldermen backed Andrews's reappointment. Carthan deputized six men to keep the brittle peace. When they confronted Andrews at the municipal building, a fight broke out. In April 1981, the dysfunction and strife forced Carthan to resign. A white judge sentenced him to three years in federal prison for assaulting Andrews. Following what many blacks considered to be a spurious conviction, "the situation spun out of control," said Carthan's administrative assistant.[9]

While in prison, Carthan faced more serious allegations. The police charged him with fraud and capital murder. Authorities indicted Carthan for hiring two career criminals to assassinate his black political rival, Alderman Roosevelt Granderson. The killers jerked Granderson out back of the convenience store where he worked, put him on his knees, and shot him twice in the head. Carthan spent more than a year behind bars before a trial jury acquitted him of homicide in 1982. Carthan defended himself in court and claimed that Tchula's white minority framed him. On the stand, one hit man admitted that the white district attorney promised them abbreviated sentences in exchange for their testimony against Carthan. After his exoneration, Carthan returned to jail on the earlier felony conviction for assault. In the spring of 1983, Governor William F. Winter suspended the remainder of

Carthan's assault sentence, but he served eight more months for fraud before a federal judge freed him. By then, the mayor's office had reverted to Lester Lyon's control. In 1986, NBC aired a segment about Eddie Carthan's saga. His detractors viewed the controversial ex-mayor as "a conniving troublemaker." The black community lionized Carthan as "a folk hero." To African Americans, the message was crystal clear: blacks could enter politics but not push too far or too fast. Racial prejudice proved slower to change. One Catholic nun in Lexington bluntly put it: "Many Whites view Blacks as they do a dog. It's okay for Blacks to work for you, or maybe talk together—if Blacks understand their place—but you *don't* invite your dog to dinner." Eddie Carthan did not know his "place."[10]

If Carthan's legal battles belied any lingering racial discord, Holmes County's public schools offered a similarly checkered and discouraging picture. When the Supreme Court in 1969 mandated the abolition of Mississippi's racially dual system, the white exodus from districts covered by *Alexander v. Holmes* was immediate and all but complete. In the school year before *Alexander*, white student enrollments had already slid by over 15 percent. From the fall of 1969 to the spring of 1970, another 15 percent drifted away. During the next two years, white parents yanked all but three children from Lexington's city schools. To the dismay of incoming black faculty, deserting whites helped themselves to school supplies and even absconded with athletic and shop equipment. By 1989, Holmes County public schools were essentially all black. Only two whites remained among the district's 4,344 students. Six years later, whites made up only 0.1 percent of the county's entire student body. In some ways, it seemed as if *Alexander* had never happened. White flight and the concentration of virtually all-black schools did not represent the official school segregation athwart *Brown* and *Alexander*, but atavistic instincts died hard.[11]

Gyrations in Holmes County's board of education accompanied court orders to desegregate. In 1968, after twenty years as superintendent, Lester Thompson retired from the county school board. H. A. Grisham, a white man, succeeded him, but blacks gradually took control of the school system. In 1968, Arenia C. Mallory, a highly qualified and widely respected educator, became the first black elected to the board. She beat Bill Kenna, one of the original defendants in *Alexander v. Holmes*. Within nine years, African-American candidates, including Eddie Carthan in 1972, replaced the last four white board members. In 1974, William Dean Jr., groomed by Mallory, won school superintendent.[12]

A younger generation of black activists replaced the old guard and combated the county's structural racism in other ways. Instead of pursuing school desegregation and voter registration, they worked for racial dignity and social justice by empowering the community and effacing the degrading reminders of black inferiority. Over the years, blacks pressured white businessmen to end discriminatory practices. The dentist's office in Lexington desegregated its waiting room. The separate drinking fountains for blacks and whites and "whites only" signs disappeared. "We went to the core of the oppressive system we lived in," commented Arnett Lewis, one of the new community organizers. They built institutions, including the rural health center in Lexington, and renamed the "negro attendance centers" after African-American leaders to instill black pride. All manner of Jim Crow laws and customs had fallen alongside the dual-school system, as Holmes, and the nation writ large, struggled to cleanse itself of the scourge journalist Richard Kluger trenchantly termed America's original sin.[13]

The widening of black political opportunities and educational rights could not obscure the painful realities that still mire Holmes County. In Holmes and other locales where the *Alexander* cases exuded from, a major piece of work confronts the black community before claiming complete victory. Nearly fifty years after *Alexander*, Holmes's almost all-black student body points out the inescapably stark racial chasm, but deprivation, ignorance about the past, and an air of resignation present far greater hurdles for African-American citizens than the segregationist heritage of the pre-1969 era. Breaking the shackles of the county's vast rural ghetto has proven a more difficult task than ending state-sponsored racial segregation. Holmes's rocky journey since 1969 shows how desegregation's effects defies precise measurement. Though Holmes blacks won in federal court, *Alexander* amounted to a limited triumph as well as a benchmark case. Nearly one hundred–odd years earlier, Mississippi had criminalized slave literacy and maintained no public school system. After an ensuing century of invidious racism and Jim Crow education, the Supreme Court unified the South's schools and opened them to students of all races. The arc of the moral universe had indeed been long, but *Alexander v. Holmes* bent it more toward elementary justice and reset the nation's clock on achieving what had once been thought an unattainable dream.

The fight for black people's minds has also lasted much longer and produced fateful results. "There are so many people of my color who know *nothing* of what happened," said Sylvia Gist, who left Holmes as a young person but moved back as an educator. "They know little about slavery, migration out of the county, and civil rights. Therefore, there's little or no appreciation for where you came from. If there was more awareness of history, among all populations, black and white, we would not have the problems we have now." What had been lost or forgotten testified to what remained to be done. In his fading mansion, Eddie Carthan shook his head and offered a succinct recapitulation on the community that helped to turn *Alexander v. Holmes* into living law: "We've come a long ways, but we've got a long ways to go."[14]

NOTES

ABBREVIATIONS

JCL—*Jackson Clarion-Ledger*

LA—*Lexington Advertiser*

LOC—Library of Congress, Washington, D.C.

MDAH—Mississippi Department of Archives and History, Jackson

NAACPLDF Litigation Files—NAACP Legal Defense Fund, Inc., Litigation Files, 1961–1972, microfilm, reel 133, Amistad Research Center, Tulane University, New Orleans, La.

NYT—*New York Times*

SNCC Papers—Student Nonviolent Coordinating Committee Papers, Martin Luther King Jr. Center for Nonviolent Change, Atlanta, Ga., microfilm, reel 65

WP—*Washington Post*

INTRODUCTION

1. Loewen, "School Desegregation in Mississippi," 2 (quotation); "Schools Seem Calm under Mix Regime," *JCL*, January 6, 1970, 1; Minchin and Salmond, *After the Dream*, 103.

2. Wicker, *One of Us*, 487; Davies, "Richard Nixon," 368. In important ways, *Brown* amounted to a modest ruling. The Court eliminated narrowly de jure segregation in primary and secondary public education but did without mentioning racial discrimination in other facets of public life or castigating white supremacists (see Kennedy, "Ackerman's *Brown*").

3. Hudson and Curry, *Mississippi Harmony*, xxi, 1; Walker, *In Search of Our Mother's Gardens*, 14 (quotation).

4. Historian J. Mills Thornton has recommended that students of the civil rights era find ways "to understand the profound significance of the local in the lives of people and in the fabric of history, and therefore an appreciation of the capacity of ordinary, and even humble, residents of obscure places to shape their destiny in decisive and world-historical ways" (Thornton, *Archipelagoes of My South*, 195–96).

5. Dittmer, *Local People*, 256; Hudson and Curry, *Mississippi Harmony*, 4; Herbers, "School Test Nears in Harmony, Miss.," 58 (quotation). John Herbers covered Mississippi extensively as a reporter for United Press International. Not every economically independent, all-black community in Mississippi pushed aggressively for civil rights. Mound Bayou in the Delta, for example, never earned a reputation for civil rights leadership (see Payne, *I've Got the Light of Freedom*, 472n28). The interchangeable use of "Negro" and "black" throughout the text reflects, in part, the prevailing terminology favored by the federal courts in the 1950s and 1960s. "Negro" was also what many African Americans called themselves throughout most of U.S. history. Blacks used the word with pride and respect. This book will treat the term in the same way.

6. Hudson and Curry, *Mississippi Harmony*, 39–46 (first quotation on 44; second quotation on 41–42); Dittmer, *Local People*, 256.

7. Hudson and Curry, *Mississippi Harmony*, 52 (quotation); Sanders, *Chance for Change*, 18–19; Douglas Martin, "Winson Hudson, 87, Tireless Civil Rights Activist, Dies," *NYT*, May 9, 2004; Bolton, *Hardest Deal of All*, 99–103; "Leake County Parents File Desegregation Suit," *Mississippi Free Press*, March 16, 1963; *Diane Hudson et al. v. Leake County School Board*, Civil Action No. 3382 (S.D. Miss. 1963). In 1917, philanthropist Julius Rosenwald, the merchant prince and president of Sears, Roebuck and Company, established the Rosenwald Fund. On the history of Rosenwald schools, see Anderson, *Education of Blacks in the South*.

8. Hudson and Curry, *Mississippi Harmony*, 57 (first quotation), 66 (second quotation); Dittmer, *Local People*, 256–57; "Leake Negro Educator Asks Name Removal from Petition," *Jackson (Miss.) Daily News*, April 5, 1963; Bolton, *Hardest Deal of All*, 150–51. Ross Barnett was born in Standing Pine in Leake County. As Mississippi's rural, down-home governor, he gave the Kennedy brothers fits during the 1962 integration crisis at the University of Mississippi. Ironically, tracing Cleo Hudson's family genealogy later revealed that he was related to the white Barnett family (see Eagles, *Price of Defiance*, 281; Bill Minor, "Leake County Civil-Rights Matriarch Pens Memoir," *Clarksdale Press Register*, February 14, 2003). Although four schools accepted black applications, only one student entered Leake County schools in the fall of 1964. The other black parents withdrew their applications under pressure from white businessmen (see Hale, "History of the Mississippi Freedom Schools," 185; "Leake County Enrolls One Negro Pupil," *JCL*, September 2, 1964; Minor, "Leake County Civil-Rights Matriarch Pens Memoir"). Diane Hudson withdrew from Leake High and transferred to a school in Meridian, where she eventually earned enough credit to graduate. Debra Lewis, however, continued her education in the Leake County school system and later graduated high school. As a result, her father, A. J. Lewis, lost his job. Whites also repeatedly tried to burn down the Lewises' home (see Hudson and Curry, *Mississippi Harmony*, 97–99; Minor, "Leake County Civil-Rights Matriarch Pens Memoir").

9. Hudson and Curry, *Mississippi Harmony*, 60 (second quotation), 63 (third quotation); Summers, *I Dream a World*, 160 (first and fourth quotations); von Hoffman, *Mississippi Notebook*, 94–95.

10. Dittmer, *Local People*, 253 (first quotation); Crawford, Rouse, and Woods, *Women in the Civil Rights Movement*, 21–23; Williams, *Eyes on the Prize*, 241 (second quotation). See also Blackwell with Morris, *Barefootin'*.

11. Williams, *Eyes on the Prize*, 242–43 (quotation); Crawford, Rouse, and Woods, *Women in the Civil Rights Movement*, 22–23.

12. Crawford, Rouse, and Woods, *Women in the Civil Rights Movement*, 23; Blackwell with Morris, *Barefootin'*, 3–4 and 137–39; Bolton, *Hardest Deal of All*, 156-57; Morrison, *Black Political Mobilization*, 117–19; *Blackwell v. Issaquena County Board of Education*, 363 F.2d 749 (5th Cir. 1966). Judge Sidney C. Mize presided over *Blackwell v. Issaquena*.

13. Andrews, *Freedom Is a Constant Struggle*, 79; Sojourner, "Got to Thinking," 1–3 (quotation); Wood and Samuel, "'He Was Non-violent, but My Boys Weren't,'" 167; Daniel, *Dispossession*, 76; Payne, *I've Got the Light of Freedom*, 278; Cohen, *Freedom's Orator*, 431. In 1965, SNCC estimated that black Holmes Countians operated 89,875 acres of farmland compared with 306,829 acres owned by whites. The average size of Holmes's 2,340 farms was 170 acres (see "Holmes County Report," SNCC Papers).

14. Youth of the Rural Organizing and Cultural Center, *Minds Stayed on Freedom*, 10 (first quotation); Dittmer, *Local People*, 192 (second quotation); Payne, *I've Got the Light of Freedom*, 278; Gist, "Educating a Southern Rural Community," 106–7. Alan Draper has noted that black landholders enjoyed social status in rural Mississippi. "Whether or not one wants to label them middle-class," he pointed out, "independent farmers were clearly closer to the top of the class structure in rural black communities than they were to the bottom" (Draper, "Class and Politics in the Mississippi Movement," 282n53). See also Weissberg, "Study of the Freedom Movement," 28; Wirt, *Politics of Southern Equality*, 118. Compared with black workers on white-owned plantations, black farm owners were relatively well off. Their land and capital placed them in the upper reaches of Mississippi's rural black communities, especially in a state with so few African-American professionals. The 1960 census, for instance, counted only four black lawyers and fifty-five black doctors in the entire state of Mississippi (see Holloway, *Politics of the Southern Negro*, 33–35). Mileston became the fulcrum of the county's civil rights movement. The area's black farmers were more organized than other African-American communities and very tight-knit (see author's interview with Arnett Lewis).

15. Payne, *I've Got the Light of Freedom*, 278; Andrews, *Freedom Is a Constant Struggle*, 79; Gist, "Educating a Southern Rural Community," 164.

16. King, *Stride toward Freedom*, 199 (first quotation); Martin, Brown v. Board of Education, 7 (second quotation); author's interviews with Melvyn Leventhal (third quotation) and Paul Brest; Kennedy, "Martin Luther King's Constitution," 1064 (fourth quotation). Historian Tim Minchin noted that *Alexander* and similar school desegregation cases "spotlighted how the NAACP's legal work, far from being separate from the grass roots, drew on local activism" (Minchin, "Making the Best Use of the New Laws," 670). On bridging legal and social history as well as local and national perspectives on the civil rights movement, see Brown-Nagin, *Courage to Dissent*, 9–11. Tomiko Brown-Nagin's study adopts a bottom-up view of

the movement and reveals intense intraracial conflict between the NAACP's Legal Defense and Educational Fund (LDF) and Atlanta's black community. Her conclusions about the synergy between the law and social protest fluctuate from ambiguity to contradiction. At one point, Brown-Nagin claims that lawyers and the local movement "interacted dynamically." Later, she insists that legal and direct action "did not have a catalytic effect on each other. . . . The spirit of protest seldom touched the LDF's school desegregation campaign" (Brown-Nagin, *Courage to Dissent*, 8, 210 (first quotation), 309 (second quotation), 321). Historically, social change does not exclusively come from below. There is almost always dialectic between the margins and the seats of power. For a stunning reassessment of social activism in Mississippi, see Draper, "Class and Politics in the Mississippi Movement." See also Draper, "Mississippi Movement." Draper questioned the underlying class basis of studying "local people" in the movement. Contrary to the prevailing literature, he found that local people were disproportionately middle-class blacks and that disputes between the NAACP and other civil rights groups were over power and patronage, not about politics and principles. In Draper's interpretation, movement scholars have often unfairly criticized the black middle class as an inauthentic expression of grassroots activism. Such class-based predilections divulge more about scholars' political biases than an accurate portrayal of substrate struggles for civil rights. Swedish economist and sociologist Gunnar Myrdal would have shared Draper's concern about drawing too fine a line between the black elite and the grassroots. In *An American Dilemma*, Myrdal recounted a story about meeting a distinguished NAACP leader fighting for equal rights in a small capital of the Deep South. When Myrdal asked the gentleman where he might find a representative of the city's more radical Negro organization, the black man told him to look no further; he belonged to both protest groups. "We are all the same people in both organizations," the NAACP activist surprised Myrdal. The anecdote "revealed much of the political shrewdness by which the difficulties are sometimes met," recalled Myrdal (Myrdal, *American Dilemma*, 776–77). African Americans engaged protest pragmatically, kept mixed company, and were less obviously divided along class fault lines. If one civil rights organization ensured victories, blacks backed it. If another group proved effective on another front, African Americans supported it as well. Historian Françoise Hamlin has also warned against assuming that major civil rights organizations did not overlap in memberships and strategies (see Hamlin, *Crossroads at Clarksdale*, 4). For scholarship on the movement that privileges "grassroots" activists at the expense of national civil rights organizations and middle-class blacks, see Dittmer, *Local People*; Payne, *I've Got the Light of Freedom*. Dittmer and Payne inspired a second generation of historians who inherited their meme. See Crosby, *Little Taste of Freedom*; Moye, *Let the People Decide*; Brown-Nagin, *Courage to Dissent*, esp. 431–32.

17. Jacoby, *Someone Else's House*, 3 (quotation). On the need to reinvigorate and reconceptualize civil rights scholarship with bold and iconoclastic theses, see Eagles, "Toward New Histories of the Civil Rights Era," 844. On *Brown*'s inability either to achieve durable integration or to inspire the civil rights movement, see Patterson, Brown v. Board of Education; Irons, *Jim Crow's Children*; Orfield and

Seaton, *Dismantling Desegregation*; Rosenberg, *Hollow Hope*; Klarman, "How *Brown* Changed Race Relations," 81–118; Fairclough, *Race and Democracy*; Thornton, "Challenge and Response in the Montgomery Bus Boycott, 1955–1956." In Rosenberg's work, he argues that the courts "can almost never be effective producers of significant social reform," divert scarce resources, and provide only an "illusion of change" (Rosenberg, *Hollow Hope*, 338 and 341). The very problem with enforcing the 1964 Civil Rights Act, however, was trying cases before segregationist judges in Mississippi and Alabama. Rosenberg forgets that the courts can be forces for both change *and* resistance (see Stern, "Judge William Harold Cox"). Furthermore, as shown in chapter 5, depending on the administration, executive leadership could undercut federal enforcement of the Civil Rights Act. Mark Tushnet and David Garrow have also disputed Rosenberg's conclusions about the effectiveness of *Brown* and the role of the courts. Tushnet traced the NAACP litigation that led to *Brown* and called the decision "a moral resource" that limited resistance to the movement (Tushnet, "The Significance of *Brown v. Board of Education*," 182). In Garrow's rebuttal to Rosenberg, he praised *Brown* as a boon to the movement that encouraged blacks that the law was on their side (see Garrow, "Hopelessly Hollow History"). In 1958, Martin Luther King emphasized that *Brown* "marked a joyous end to the long night of enforced segregation" and "brought hope to millions of disinherited Negroes who had formerly dared only to dream of freedom" (King, *Stride toward Freedom*, 191). On the law's ability to induce social reform, see also Wirt, *Politics of Southern Equality*, chap. 1. Another defect in NAACP litigation was that it did little to attain the larger goal of improving black education (see Bell, "*Brown v. Board of Education* and the Interest-Convergence Dilemma"; Halpern, *On the Limits of the Law*). Other scholars have been kinder to *Brown* and its legal progeny. In journalist Richard Kluger's magisterial study of *Brown*, he conceded that *Brown II*, the Court's 1955 implementation ruling, barely dented segregation. Kluger, however, deemed *Brown II* the best decision under the circumstances and would not indict the Court for its timidity (see Kluger, *Simple Justice*). Law professor J. Harvie Wilkinson III followed Kluger's analysis and acknowledged the Court's critics, but he ultimately concluded, "*Brown II* can be justified, but just barely" (Wilkinson, *From* Brown *to* Bakke, 77). For a thorough historiographical review essay on *Brown*, see Goluboff, "Lawyers, Law, and the New Civil Rights History." In 1984, Raymond Wolters published a slashing appraisal of the *Brown* decision and dissented from the orthodoxy that integration was an unquestionable good (see Wolters, *Burden of* Brown). See also Wolters, *Race and Education*. For a concise history of trends and consequences of school segregation since *Brown*, see Reardon and Owens, "60 Years after *Brown*."

18. Doherty, "'Integration Now.'" Doherty provided a straightforward account just after the Supreme Court ruled on *Alexander*. This book borrowed his pithy title. For extended analyses of *Alexander v. Holmes* within other civil rights and legal histories, see Woodward and Armstrong, *Brethren*, 36–62; Wilkinson, *From* Brown *to* Bakke, 118–26; Minchin and Salmond, *After the Dream*, chap. 4. The 1954 *Brown* ruling outlawed official discrimination based on race, which is exactly what the plaintiffs

desired. The Brown family in Topeka, Kansas, believed in principled opposition to any laws and public institutions that inhibited or disempowered African Americans in their pursuit of education. Interestingly, however, the Browns did not fight against school segregation on the grounds that white schools were superior to black education (see Kluger, *Simple Justice*, 408–11).

19. Cobb, *Most Southern Place on Earth*. For other important studies on the civil rights movement and school desegregation in the rural South, see Hanks, *The Struggle for Black Political Empowerment in Three Georgia Counties*; McPhail, *A History of Desegregation Developments in Certain Mississippi School Districts*; Cecelski, *Along Freedom Road*; and Wirt, *Politics of Southern Equality*.

20. *Eyes on the Prize*, episode 5: "Mississippi: Is This America?" (first quotation); Sojourner with Reitan, *Thunder of Freedom*, 1 (second quotation). "Dark journey" pays homage to Neil McMillen's work on the racial history of Mississippi (see McMillen, *Dark Journey*).

CHAPTER ONE

1. Jane Heggard to Federal Bureau of Investigation, October 28, 1939; O. John Rogge to Heggard, November 14, 1939; and Heggard to Franklin Delano Roosevelt, March 12, 1941, General Records of the Department of Justice, #158260, National Archives and Records Administration, Washington, D.C.; Burnham and Russell, "Cold Cases of the Jim Crow Era"; "Civil Rights and Restorative Justice Project." For more on the background of demagogue James K. Vardaman, see Holmes, *White Chief*.

2. Berman, *House of David in the Land of Jesus*, 6–8; White, *Rise to Respectability*, 26; Gist, "Educating a Southern Rural Community," 44; Whalen, *Maverick among the Magnolias*, 28–29; U.S. Department of Agriculture, *Field Operations of the Bureau of Soils*, 775; Busbee, *Mississippi*, 78; McCain, "The Administrations of David Holmes."

3. Berman, *House of David in the Land of Jesus*, 6–8; Youth of the Rural Organizing and Cultural Center, *Minds Stayed on Freedom*, 4; Gist, "Educating a Southern Rural Community," 44; White, *Rise to Respectability*, 26. Some Choctaw defied removal and escaped into the big swamp along the Black River. For decades, they formed a hidden community that harbored and intermixed with runaway slaves. Many Holmes blacks trace Choctaw Indian lineage (see author's interview with Arnett Lewis). For more on Choctaw tribal history, see O'Brien, *Choctaws in a Revolutionary Age*.

4. Berman, *House David in the Land of Jesus*, 6–8; Youth of the Rural Organizing and Cultural Center, *Minds Stayed on Freedom*, 4; Gist, "Educating a Southern Rural Community," 4; Neilson, *Even Mississippi*, 9; Rowland, *Mississippi, Comprising Sketches of Counties, Towns, Events, Institutions, and Persons, Arranged in Cyclopedic Form*, 876–78; U.S. Department of Agriculture, *Field Operations of the Bureau of Soils*, 773. Deposits of silt and clay from floods formed the loess bluffs along the eastern edge of the Delta in Holmes County.

5. *Durant Plaindealer*, July 1, 1976, 18; White, *Rise to Respectability*, 26; Berman,

House of David in the Land of Jesus, 6–8; U.S. Department of Agriculture, *Field Operations of the Bureau of Soils*, 775.

6. U.S. Bureau of the Census, *Eighth Census*. Antebellum census records also indicate the presence of at least ten free blacks in Holmes.

7. U.S. Bureau of the Census, *Eighth Census*.

8. *Durant Plaindealer*, July 1, 1976, 18; White, *Rise to Respectability*, 26; Morrison, *Black Political Mobilization*, 126; Berman, *House of David in the Land of Jesus*, 6–8; Philip D. Carter, "What Effect on Public Schools in Black Areas?," *WP*, November 3, 1969; U.S. Bureau of the Census, *Eighth Census*; Cobb, *Most Southern Place on Earth*, chap. 1; U.S. Department of Agriculture, *Field Operations of the Bureau of Soils*, 775.

9. Elvira Boles quoted in Rawick, *American Slave*, 336–39; Archer, *Growing Up Black in Rural Mississippi*, 1 (second quotation).

10. Elvira Boles quoted in Rawick, *American Slave*, 336–39 (quotations). Recorded nearly seventy-odd years after her enslavement, Elvira Boles's memory may not have been perfect and thus rendered a contradictory account of her master's sadism and "good" side. The race of the amanuensis could also affect the accuracy of the WPA slave narratives. African Americans tended to speak more candidly with black interviewers. On the accuracy of the WPA slave narratives, see Blassingame, "Using the Testimony of Ex-slaves."

11. Elvira Boles quoted in Rawick, *American Slave*, 337–38.

12. Gist, "Educating a Southern Rural Community," 67; Youth of the Rural Organizing and Cultural Center, *Minds Stayed on Freedom*, 5–6; Bennett, "First Black Governor," 95; Morrison, *Black Political Mobilization*, 126.

13. Gist, "Educating a Southern Rural Community," 25, 40, 63–64; Cobb, *Most Southern Place on Earth*, 49. Before the war, Richland's Freedmen's School building housed the Richland Male and Female Academy. Black students attended the "Colored School" at Richland until a segregated "attendance center" opened at Lexington in 1958. After blacks transferred to Lexington, whites reclaimed the facility and classified it as a historical landmark. Today, the building, known locally as "The Little Red Schoolhouse," sits just off Highway 17 between Lexington and Pickens. After the war, black congregations also opened perhaps thirty-five elementary "church schools" (see Gist, "Educating a Southern Rural Community," 25, 29–31, 72n5). Mississippi's Reconstruction Constitution of 1869 created the state's first public education system. Prior to the Civil War, Mississippi had lacked any statewide public school system because a small, dispersed population made public schools impractical and the wealthy slaveholding elite had little interest in paying taxes to finance public schools for poor whites (see Lucas, "Education in Mississippi," 352–55).

14. Gist, "Educating a Southern Rural Community," 64–65. Some blacks simply did not put a premium on education because dire economic conditions overshadowed their ability to make schooling a priority. In a farm family, every black child was an economic asset. Sylvia Gist, for example, was one of ten children in a black family from the hills of eastern Holmes. By age four, she began to pick cotton, the usual fate of African-American kids in Holmes at the time. Her father believed in

working all ten children to make money. His paternal philosophy was that no black person needed an education beyond the eighth grade. Sylvia's maternal grandfather, Otis Campbell, however, disagreed entirely and provided one of the epigraphs for this book (see author's interview with Sylvia Gist).

15. Gist, "Educating a Southern Rural Community," 65–66; White, *Rise to Respectability*, 26–27.

16. Gist, "Educating a Southern Rural Community," 9, 63–64; Youth of the Rural Organizing and Cultural Center, *Minds Stayed on Freedom*, 5–6. Simmons taught at the school until local whites forced him out of the county around 1898 (see Gist, "Educating a Southern Rural Community," 45).

17. Newton, *Ku Klux Klan in Mississippi*, 11–12; Witty, "Reconstruction in Carroll and Montgomery Counties," 129–30 (quotations).

18. Cobb, *Most Southern Place on Earth*, 50–51; Foner, *Reconstruction*, 199–201.

19. Witty, "Reconstruction in Carroll and Montgomery Counties," 130 (quotations); Youth of the Rural Organizing and Cultural Center, *Minds Stayed on Freedom*, 5–6.

20. Morrison, *Black Political Mobilization*, 126.

21. Gist, "Educating a Southern Rural Community," 68 (quote on 69); White, *Rise to Respectability*, 26.

22. White, *Rise to Respectability*, 26.

23. Woodruff, *American Congo*, 22; Willis, *Forgotten Time*, 128–29. The Tchula Cooperative Store vanished almost as soon as it appeared. By 1897, the store no longer extended credit to farmers, and it disappeared from public records shortly thereafter. The demise of the Colored Farmers' Alliance movement in nearby Leflore County and white opposition certainly hindered the cooperative's existence (see Cobb, *Most Southern Place on Earth*, 85).

24. Cobb, *Most Southern Place on Earth*, 86; Cohen, *Freedom's Orator*, 431; Klarman, *From Jim Crow to Civil Rights*, 32; Kiesel, *She Can Bring Us Home*, 59; Loewen and Sallis, *Mississippi*, 199–201.

25. Darjean, "Mrs. Catherine Jefferson," 33 (quotation).

26. McMillen, *Dark Journey*, 231; "Lynchings" Vertical File, MDAH; "Negro Girl Shot Down by a Mob at Pickens," *Memphis Commercial Appeal*, October 7, 1923; Youth of the Rural Organizing and Cultural Center, *Minds Stayed on Freedom*, 9 (quotation). The full tally of lynchings in Holmes County remains incomplete due to a "wall of silence" erected by whites. In 1919, when county blacks "informed a Memphis newspaper of the lynching of a recently discharged black soldier and young black woman near Pickens," the paper refused to investigate or report the double homicide (McMillen, *Dark Journey*, 228).

27. Morrison, *Black Political Mobilization*, 126.

28. Du Bois, *Black North in 1901*, 2 (quotation); U.S. Department of Agriculture, *Field Operations of the Bureau of Soils*, 772, 776–79.

29. U.S. Department of Agriculture, *Field Operations of the Bureau of Soils*, 773, 779.

30. Ransom and Sutch, *One Kind of Freedom*, 106–70; Cobb, *Most Southern Place on Earth*, chaps. 4 and 5; Litwack, *Trouble in Mind*, 129–31.

31. Youth of the Rural Organizing and Cultural Center, *Minds Stayed on Freedom*, 7; Kiesel, *She Can Bring Us Home*, 55; Darjean, "Mrs. Catherine Jefferson," 38 (quotation).

32. Gist, "Educating a Southern Rural Community," 101 (quotation); U.S. Bureau of the Census, *Fifteenth Census*; U.S. Bureau of the Census, *Sixteenth Census*.

33. Cobb, *Most Southern Place on Earth*, 184, 186–90; Whalen, *Maverick among the Magnolias*, 28; U.S. Bureau of the Census, *Sixteenth Census*; U.S. Bureau of the Census, *Seventeenth Census*; Newman, "Hazel Brannon Smith," 62. In 1939, only eight counties in Mississippi were worth more in crop values than Holmes County (see U.S. Bureau of the Census, *Sixteenth Census*).

34. Suitts, "The Southern Regional Council and the Roots of Rural Change," 6–7; Dunbar, *Against the Grain*, 199–200 (quotation); Cobb, *Most Southern Place on Earth*, 191. See also Gaer, *Toward Farm Security*.

35. Aiken, *Cotton Plantation South since the Civil War*, 161; Youth of the Rural Organizing and Cultural Center, *Minds Stayed on Freedom*, 10; Gist, "Educating a Southern Rural Community," 105–6; Payne, *I've Got the Light of Freedom*, 281; Alcindor, "Mississippi Growing." The federal government acquired much of the land for the Mileston project from Bernard Bryan Jones, whose cotton empire of ten plantations included Marcella. Many plantation owners lost the land deeded to Mileston blacks through foreclosures stimulated by dim economic conditions. By 1960, 110 Mileston farm families owned land as an outgrowth of the FSA program (see Wood and Samuel, "'He Was Non-violent, but My Boys Weren't,'" 167; Daniel, *Dispossession*, 76; Payne, *I've Got the Light of Freedom*, 278).

36. Youth of the Rural Organizing and Cultural Center, *Minds Stayed on Freedom*, 10–11.

37. Gist, "Educating a Southern Rural Community," 105–6 (first quotation); Archer, *Growing Up Black in Rural Mississippi*, 15 (second quotation); Andrews, *Freedom Is a Constant Struggle*, 79; Youth of the Rural Organizing and Cultural Center, *Minds Stayed on Freedom*, 10–11.

38. See Anderson, "Northern Foundations"; Gist, "Educating a Southern Rural Community," chap. 3, 83–86, 93; Archer, *Growing Up Black in Rural Mississippi*, 19–20, chap. 10.

39. Howell, "Undiscovered Country," 8–10; Cobb, *Most Southern Place on Earth*, 222; Newman, *Divine Agitators*, 128. For more on the history of Providence Cooperative Farm, see Campbell, *Providence*; Ferguson, *Remaking the Rural South*.

40. Howell, "Undiscovered Country," 10–11; Ferguson, *Remaking the Rural South*, 161.

41. Kampe and Lindamood, *Underemployment Estimates*, 4–6; *Holmes County Herald*, August 28, 1986, 5C; U.S. Bureau of the Census, *Eighteenth Census*; "Holmes County Report," SNCC Papers; Gist, "Educating a Southern Rural Community," 92–94; McMillen, *Dark Journey*, 72 (quotation).

42. "Holmes County Report," SNCC Papers; Gist, "Educating a Southern Rural Community," 92–94. For more on Mississippi school equalization, see Bolton, "Mississippi's School Equalization Program." With equalization, Holmes County established three new attendance centers for black students. The one near Tchula served blacks in the Delta, but whites built it in the hills, about ten miles east of Tchula, because plantation owners would not release land to build the school on the fertile agricultural soil. Most Holmes whites would probably have preferred *no* public schools for blacks to dual schools. Even in a segregated system, much of the county's limited funds went to black schools because African Americans outnumbered whites by a ratio of three to one. The white minority wanted outsiders to finance black education. If external entities, like the Rosenwald Fund or the Rockefeller Foundation, would spend money on blacks, then whites could earmark state and local revenue for white schools (see author's interview with Sylvia Gist).

43. Gist, "Educating a Southern Rural Community," 35 (quotation). In rural Mississippi, informal white supremacy and planter rule governed race relations more than legal segregation did. As Mills Thornton has pointed out, "The direct, personal control by white landlords of each individual black tenant family rendered the compulsion of the state merely ancillary.... Other than in the public schools, white supremacy in rural [Mississippi] did not express itself in the form of separate institutions, nor was it usually embodied in law. Rather, it was nongovernmental and peremptory, dependent not on political but on economic authority" (Thornton, *Archipelagoes of My South*, 166).

44. Tracy, *Mississippi Moonshine Politics*, 38; Smith, "Looking at the Old South Through Hazel Eyes," http://aliciapatterson.org/stories/looking-old-south-through -hazel-eyes (quotations); Whalen, *Maverick among the Magnolias*, 28–29.

45. Berman, *House of David in the Land of Jesus*, 100; Tracy, *Mississippi Moonshine Politics*, 39; Tracy, *Juke Joint King*, 62–63.

46. Wexler, *Fire in a Canebrake*, 112–13; "Negro Flogged to Death in Mississippi," 1 (quotation); Sokol, *There Goes My Everything*, 28; Patterson, *We Charge Genocide*, 64; Smith, "Looking at the Old South through Hazel Eyes"; Hazel Brannon Smith, "Five Men Freed on Manslaughter in Negro's Death," *LA*, October 24, 1946, 1.

47. Berry, *Jim Crow Routine*, 93–94; Harkey, *The Smell of Burning Crosses*, 21 (quotation). To enforce submission and deference to white authority and the rituals of Jim Crow, southern blacks fell victim to lynchings, wanton acts of violence, and "nigger hunts" (see Litwack, *Trouble in Mind*, 284). The extent of the racial violence in Holmes may never be fully known. Whites killed untold numbers of blacks in the countryside. As older blacks used to say, "If these cotton fields and swamps could talk" (author's interview with Arnett Lewis). For a riveting account of Eddie Noel's story, see Povall, *Time of Eddie Noel*. Al Povall's father, Allie S. Povall Sr., was a co-founder of the Central Holmes Academy, a segregationist private school organized in the fall of 1965 to resist school desegregation (see Gist, "Educating a Southern Rural Community," 207n70).

48. Berry, *Jim Crow Routine*, 93–94; Youth of the Rural Organizing and Cultural

Center, *Minds Stayed on Freedom*, 154–57; Povall, *Time of Eddie Noel*, chaps. 5 and 6; Ferguson, *Remaking the Rural South*, 146.

49. Minor, "Tales of Jim Crow Mississippi," (quotations); Povall, *Time of Eddie Noel*, chap. 7. Eddie Noel (formerly Edmond Noel) was named for the one-term governor, but he altered his name. Noel could have potentially eluded his pursuers indefinitely. Not even a $1,000 bounty could entice Holmes blacks to betray him. Only when the black grapevine telegraphed Noel to turn himself in did he surrender. By November 1954, the Noel case was closed. In 1970, after an appeal by state representative Robert Clark, Noel was released to in-laws, left Mississippi, and lived in Ft. Wayne, Indiana, until his death in 1994 (see Minor, "Tales of Jim Crow Mississippi"). Eddie Noel's defiance made him an almost mythical bandit hero among local blacks for generations. The *Memphis Commercial Appeal* confirmed another local legend about Noel. His marksmanship was supposedly so accurate that he could shoot matches and cigarettes out of his wife's mouth (see Youth of the Rural Organizing and Cultural Center, *Minds Stayed on Freedom*, 11, 157; Ferguson, *Remaking the Rural South*, 146). In Delta dialect, a "slough" is a body of water that might dry up in the summer, a "deadening" is a drowned hardwood forest, and an "oxbow" is an old meander abandoned by a river that had changed course.

50. Weill, *In a Madhouse's Din*, 50 (quotation). Edwin White also wrote a virulent letter about the *Brown* ruling to the *New York Times*. In it, he argued that miscegenation would result without segregated education and lead to the "death of the race which brought civilization to the world" (Edwin White, *NYT*, December 1, 1955, 34).

51. Kempton, "What Have They Got to Live For?," 5 (quotations).

52. Kempton, 5.

53. Kempton, 5 (quotation); Waldron, *Hodding Carter*, 262.

54. Kempton, "What Have They Got to Live For?," 5 (quotations); Cobb, *Most Southern Place on Earth*, 224.

55. Cobb, *Most Southern Place on Earth*, 224 (quotation); Silver, *Mississippi*, 38–39. Scholars have debated the sincerity of Hazel Brannon Smith's dedication to civil rights and racial justice. Journalism professor Arthur Kaul argues that Hazel Smith was never a civil rights advocate. Historian Mark Newman portrays Smith as having a profound conversion away from segregationism (see Kaul, "Hazel Brannon Smith"; Newman, "Hazel Brannon Smith"). See also Whitt, *Burning Crosses and Activist Journalism*, chap. 1. Compared with other whites, Smith was very liberal on race. Still, she was a person of her time. Most blacks liked her, but she observed local racial customs. For instance, Smith made her black lawn boy, Byron Montgomery, and domestic, Miss Margaret, eat meals in the kitchen by the stove rather than at the family table (see author's interview with Byron Montgomery). Though Smith did not support social integration between the races, she fought official segregation. Her first priority as a journalist was to publish the truth at all costs and defend the freedom of the press. Smith was not an ally of the movement per se, but she was sensitive to the plight of blacks. The few sympathetic whites in Holmes mostly stayed in the background rather than provoking white supremacists. More important than what

Hazel Smith said and wrote was *where* she took her stand. Marooned in Lexington and surrounded by the Citizens' Council, Smith enjoyed little insulation from white supremacists. Greenville, the economic and political epicenter of the Delta to the northwest, by contrast, was larger than Lexington and had a patina of liberalism thanks to the satrapy of Hodding Carter, the Alexander and Percy families, and federal judge William C. Keady. Greenville's comparative oasis of tolerance also owed to its diverse community of blacks, whites, Jews, Chinese, and immigrants from Syria and Lebanon.

56. Kaul, "Hazel Brannon Smith," 246, 250; Hazel Brannon Smith, *LA*, November 10, 1960; Silver, *Mississippi*, 39 (quotation); McMillen, *Citizens' Council*, 256; Mississippi State Sovereignty Commission Papers, SCR ID #2–54–1–9–1–1–1, MDAH. Fifteen-year-old Pat "Don" Barrett Jr. and his friends burned the cross on Smith's lawn. The prank nearly caught the house on fire. As the boys sped away, Hazel Smith scribbled down the license plate number. The getaway car belonged to Pat Barrett Sr., the county's public attorney and president of the Lexington Citizens' Council chapter. Barrett Sr., along with fellow shareholders Sheriff Andrew Smith, state senator T. M. Williams, and state representative Wilburn Hooker, put up the seed money for the *Holmes County Herald* (see Kaul, "Hazel Brannon Smith," 250). In February 1964, Don Barrett Jr., then a freshman at the University of Mississippi, shared his racial views with the *New York Times Magazine*, later republished in the *Holmes County Herald*. In addition to defending the benefits of slavery for African Americans and denouncing the federal government for integrating the University of Mississippi in 1962, Barrett questioned school integration. "What's to keep little white Mary from bringing home little black Johnny from school some day," he posed hypothetically to his interviewer, "and that leads to mixed dating and mixed marriages." Barrett saw a solution to racial problems through the migration of blacks to the North "to live on welfare, since the planters and automated land no longer need them" ("Don Barrett Featured in New York Magazine," *Holmes County Herald*, February 6, 1964). In later life, Don Barrett told the author that he had atoned for his racial views due to a heartfelt religious conversion to Jesus Christ (author's interview with Don Barrett Jr.).

57. Cobb, *Most Southern Place on Earth*, 225 (quotation).

58. Whalen, *Maverick among the Magnolias*, 85–86 (quote). For her outspoken opposition to the Citizens' Council, Hazel Brannon Smith's offices and print shop endured bombings, arson, and boycotts. Because of her unpopularity, she jostled to keep the paper going, but the unsinkable Smith withstood the hate campaign for years. In 1964, she became the first woman to win the Pulitzer Prize for Editorial Writing.

59. Dallas, "Delta and Providence Farms," 306; Eagles, *Price of Defiance*, 164–65; Ferguson, *Remaking the Rural South*, 153.

60. Cobb, *Most Southern Place on Earth*, 222; Kerry Taylor, "Dangerous Memories," 6 (quotation).

61. Cobb, *Most Southern Place on Earth*, 222; Kerry Taylor, "Dangerous Memories," 6.

62. Cobb, *Most Southern Place on Earth*, 223 (quotation); Howell, "Undiscovered Country," 30; Silver, *Mississippi*, 36–37.

63. Smith, *Trouble in Goshen*, 137 (first quotation); Cobb, *Most Southern Place on Earth*, 222–23 (second quotation); Eagles, *Price of Defiance*, 120; Campbell, *Providence*, 3–24; Kieran Taylor, "'I Done Made Up My Mind,'" 9–17; "'Liberal' Whites Ordered Out of Miss. County"; Ferguson, *Remaking the Rural South*, 152–53.

64. Ferguson, *Remaking the Rural South*, 153–56 (first quotation on 154; third quotation on 156); Cobb, *Most Southern Place on Earth*, 222–23 (second quotation). "Madhouse din" is a quote from an editorial written during the desegregation of the University of Mississippi by Pulitzer Prize–winning newspaper editor Ira Harkey (see Harkey, "Confusing Times, Dangerous Times," *Pascagoula Chronicle*, September 18, 1962).

65. Edwin White quoted in Silver, *Mississippi*, 37; Carter, "Memo to Some Holmes Countians" (second quotation); Cobb, *Most Southern Place on Earth*, 223–24.

66. Ferguson, *Remaking the Rural South*, 159–60; Dunbar, *Delta Time*, 203; Cobb, *Most Southern Place on Earth*, 223–24; Silver, *Mississippi*, 37 (quotation). Gene Cox continued to work for racial change and eventually joined the National Council of Churches. During the 1960s, he served as director of the Delta Foundation, a group that oversaw poor relief in cooperation with the Rural Development Program of the Kennedy administration (see Howell, "Undiscovered Country," 29). After Cox and Minter abandoned the farm, the federal government purchased the land and set it aside as a wildlife refuge (see Campbell, *Providence*, chap. 15).

67. Kerry Taylor, "Dangerous Memories," 7 (quotation).

68. In his brief history of *Brown*, Waldo Martin acknowledged, "Elite venues— lawyers' offices, courtrooms, judges' chambers—are principal sites of formal legal struggles. Nevertheless, the legal struggle—battles waged from the top down—does not happen in isolation but exists in dynamic mutuality with the social struggle— battles waged from the bottom up" (W. Martin, Brown v. Board of Education, 7).

CHAPTER TWO

1. Daniel, *Dispossession*, 76.

2. Daniel, 76 (first quotation); Brigham, "Writer Recalls 1965 Request for Help"; Campbell, *Robert G. Clark's Journey to the House*, 54–55 (second quotation on 54). Mike Kenney was a Student Nonviolent Coordinating Committee volunteer (see "Holmes County Report," p. 185, SNCC Papers).

3. Cobb, *Most Southern Place on Earth*, 232–33; Sojourner with Reitan, *Thunder of Freedom*, 24.

4. Cobb, *Most Southern Place on Earth*, 232–33; Gist, "Educating a Southern Rural Community," 176–77; Branch, *Parting the Waters*, 633–34; Sojourner with Reitan, *Thunder of Freedom*, 24.

5. Gist, "Educating a Southern Rural Community," 177–78 (quotation); Sojourner with Reitan, *Thunder of Freedom*, 24, 67 (quotation on 67).

6. Gist, "Educating a Southern Rural Community," 179–80; Sojourner with Reitan, *Thunder of Freedom*, 24 (quotation); Youth of the Rural Organizing and Cultural Center, *Minds Stayed on Freedom*, 13. Numbers vary on how many African Americans

had passed the county's registration exam by 1963 (see Stein, "This Female Crusading Scalawag," 59). Several blacks attempted to submit their poll taxes as well. During the 1950s, Ralthus Hayes tried but failed to pay the poll tax (see Wood and Samuel, "'He Was Non-violent, but My Boys Weren't,'" 167). Reverend Willie James Burns married and later divorced Matilda Burns (see author's interview with Arnett Lewis).

7. Sojourner with Reitan, *Thunder of Freedom*, 24, 26; Andrews, *Freedom Is a Constant Struggle*, 80; Youth of the Rural Organizing and Cultural Center, *Minds Stayed on Freedom*, 27. As of January 1, 1964, only twenty blacks had registered to vote (see "Holmes County Report," SNCC Papers).

8. Sojourner with Reitan, *Thunder of Freedom*, 26; "Holmes County Report," SNCC Papers. In 1955, McClellan won election to circuit clerk. He served until 1980 (see Youth of the Rural Organizing and Cultural Center, *Minds Stayed on Freedom*, 160).

9. Stein, "This Female Crusading Scalawag," 59; Sojourner with Reitan, *Thunder of Freedom*, 27–28 (quotations on 27). Scholars interested in the Holmes County struggle will benefit from sifting through Sue Sojourner's memoir as a primary source, especially her oral histories of local movement people, for years to come. For another remarkable trove of interviews with Holmes activists, see Youth of the Rural Organizing and Cultural Center, *Minds Stayed on Freedom*.

10. Neilson, *Even Mississippi*, 32–33.

11. Sojourner with Reitan, *Thunder of Freedom*, 29; Dittmer, *Local People*, 192.

12. Sojourner with Reitan, *Thunder of Freedom*, 29 (first and second quotations), 34; author's interview with Sue Sojourner; Dittmer, *Local People*, 192 (third quotation); Mississippi State Sovereignty Commission Papers, SCR ID #2–54–1–79–1–1–1, MDAH; Wood and Samuel, "'He Was Non-violent, but My Boys Weren't,'" 161–62 (fourth and fifth quotations). See also Andrews, *Freedom Is a Constant Struggle*, 115–16; Terkel, *American Dreams*, 196–97.

13. Sojourner with Reitan, *Thunder of Freedom*, 38–40 (quotation on 39); author's interview with Sue Sojourner. In October 1951, Turnbow had been arrested on a manslaughter charge for killing his wife, Celie, when she had tried to leave him and board a bus out of town. Many people witnessed the heinous crime, including Turnbow's son, Gerow. Parchman Farm discharged Hartman Turnbow after he served five years. Turnbow's violent past gave segregationists ammunition to tarnish him and the local movement's activities. The *Holmes County Herald* reliably pointed out Turnbow's criminal record. Movement actors also considered Turnbow to be a liability and sometimes asked him to stay away from protests (see *Holmes County Herald*, April 11, 1963, 1; Wood and Samuel, "'He Was Non-violent, but My Boys Weren't,'" 161). According to Ralthus Hayes, the sheriff did not threaten anyone, and Turnbow was probably tale-spinning. Hayes also insisted that Dan Wesley walked into the courthouse before Hartman Turnbow while everyone else waited patiently outside. They knew the Justice Department had officials present to survey the situation. The atmosphere felt safe enough. In her memoir, Sue Sojourner did not grapple with the inconsistency between Hayes's and Turnbow's versions of events on April 9 (see Sojourner with Reitan, *Thunder of Freedom*, 39; John Daniel Wesley

Oral History, Civil Rights in Mississippi Digital Archive, University of Southern Mississippi, Hattiesburg.

14. Brief at 147, *United States v. Holmes County, Mississippi et al.*, 385 F.2d 145 (5th Cir. 1967); Dittmer, *Local People*, 192; Mississippi State Sovereignty Commission Papers, SCR ID #2–54–1—79–1-1-1, MDAH; Sojourner with Reitan, *Thunder of Freedom*, 29.

15. *Holmes County Herald*, April 11, 1963, 1 (quotation); Sojourner with Reitan, *Thunder of Freedom*, 29, 31; Hazel Brannon Smith, *LA*, April 11, 1963, 1.

16. Andrews, *Freedom Is a Constant Struggle*, 80 (quotation); Sojourner with Reitan, *Thunder of Freedom*, 31; author's interview with Sue Sojourner.

17. Dittmer, *Local People*, 191–93; Wood and Samuel, "'He Was Non-violent, but My Boys Weren't,'" 162; Andrews, *Freedom Is a Constant Struggle*, 116; Stein, "This Female Crusading Scalawag," 59; Brigham, "Transforming Places," 199n215; Raines, *My Soul Is Rested*, 260; Sojourner with Reitan, *Thunder of Freedom*, 31–33; author's interview with Sue Sojourner; Estes, *I Am a Man!*, 66–67 (first quotation); Hazel Brannon Smith, *LA*, May 9, 1963, 1 (second quotation); Newman, "Hazel Brannon Smith," 80 (third quotation). Although they lived together for years, Hartman and C. Bell "Sweets" Turnbow did not marry until May 1963 (see "Holmes County Report," affidavit, August 11, 1965, SNCC Papers). Many rural blacks established only common-law families and other temporary associations. On the prevalence of black common-law marriages, see Powdermaker, *After Freedom*, 149.

18. Dittmer, *Local People*, 192–93 (quotation); "5 Negroes in Vote Drive Charged with Arson in Mississippi Blasts," *NYT*, May 10, 1963, 14; Wood and Samuel, "'He Was Non-violent, but My Boys Weren't,'" 162; Stein, "This Female Crusading Scalawag," 59; Sojourner with Reitan, *Thunder of Freedom*, 32–33; brief at 4 in *United States v. Holmes County*.

19. Silver, *The Closed Society*.

20. Stein, "This Female Crusading Scalawag," 55–56; Hazel Brannon Smith, *LA*, June 13, 1963, 1.

21. Dittmer, *Local People*, 193; Payne, *I've Got the Light of Freedom*, 279; Sojourner with Reitan, *Thunder of Freedom*, 32–36 (quotations); author's interview with Sue Sojourner. One notable characteristic of the early stages of the Holmes movement was the lack of public protest. Few demonstrations, marches, or boycotts occurred. Groups who pushed for voting rights went individually or in pairs to throw off unwanted attention and lessen retaliation. Perhaps they had learned from the stalled demonstrations in Greenwood to disperse their activities and deploy in smaller units. The Holmes movement instead relied on a loose confederation of local communities to organize bases for activism (see Andrews, *Freedom Is a Constant Struggle*, 82).

22. Dittmer, *Local People*, 191–92. Turnbow was one of many leaders to arise in the early days of the local movement. He acquired a "John the Baptist" reputation for his fiery oratory and audacious personality. The comparison to the biblical prophet derived from a conversation with Mel Leventhal (see author's interview with Melvyn Leventhal).

23. Sojourner with Reitan, *Thunder of Freedom*, 33 (second and third quotations); author's interview with Sue Sojourner; Wood and Samuel, "'He Was Non-violent, but My Boys Weren't,'" 161 (first quotation).

24. Raines, *My Soul Is Rested*, 4 (first quotation), 267 (second and third quotations).

25. Campbell, *Robert G. Clark's Journey to the House*, 55–56 (quotation). After Emmett Till's murder, Arnett Lewis's grandfather moved his shotgun from beside the chifforobe to the bedroom to defend the family. Lewis's family members were not movement people, but they feared for their lives (see author's interview with Arnett Lewis).

26. Rosie Head Oral History, LOC (quotations). SNCC field secretary Lawrence Guyot, who worked in Holmes, remembered Turnbow as a man not to be "messed with." In a 1978 interview, he recalled when not to cross Turnbow: "Now there were some clear no-no's. Hartman Turnbow had a daughter, and it was clearly understood that if ever there was a no-no, that was *the* no-no" (Wood and Samuel, "He Was Non-violent, but My Boys Weren't,'" 160–61). Turnbow's wife also supposedly carried a handgun and kept it close (see Dittmer, *Local People*, 285–86). Hartman Turnbow was the type of man who was "qualified to take care of himself," remarked Arnett Lewis, a distant relative of Turnbow and a county activist in the 1970s and 1980s schooled by elders in the civil rights generation. Turnbow was a "stand-alone guy" and "knew how to handle himself." He also cared deeply about his community and stood ready to fight back if whites got violent. Turnbow adopted a "by-any-means-necessary" attitude about defending himself and the community. Carry a "fast-shootin' shotgun" was his motto (author's interview with Arnett Lewis).

27. Youth of the Rural Organizing and Cultural Center, *Minds Stayed on Freedom*, 153 (first quotation); Daniel, *Dispossession*, 76–77 (second quotation); Payne, *I've Got the Light of Freedom*, 280. If whites tried to sneak up on civil rights meetings, black watchmen would shoot bursts over their heads or in their general direction to scare off would-be attackers. After a few such displays of force, whites and blacks reached a tacit understanding. "They understood each other," said Arnett Lewis. Everybody knew not to disturb the meetings. Blacks also did not bring their guns inside churches where meetings occurred (author's interviews with Sylvia Gist and Arnett Lewis).

28. Author's interview with Melvyn Leventhal (first quotation); Walter Bruce Oral History, LOC (second quotation). Holmes activist Robert Cooper Howard put self-defense this way: "I just didn't want to go out and shoot 'em [whites] up, but I figure like this: If they try to attack me, then I was goin' to protect myself.... I'm not gon' meddle, but I want you to treat me like you want to be treated" (Howard quoted in Youth of the Rural Organizing and Cultural Center, *Minds Stayed on Freedom*, 95). Arnett Lewis noted that many Holmes blacks embraced Martin Luther King's nonviolent philosophy but also kept guns and rifles for home defense and to "keep a level playing field with whites." Furthermore, not every black who owned or packed a gun joined the civil rights movement (author's interview with Arnett Lewis). Very few blacks in Holmes carried weapons during the movement, and most African Americans thought the more militant types like Hartman Turnbow and Eugene

Montgomery were "crazy" (author's interview with Byron Montgomery). According to Sue Sojourner, "Nobody took extreme risks" in the Holmes movement. "People weren't dumb. They were also older people and didn't fly off the handle" (author's interview with Sue Sojourner). Since the 1990s, a series of monographs and journal articles have contended that black southerners and civil rights activists tended to treat nonviolence nonchalantly. Much of this scholarship overstates the importance of armed self-defense, viewing it retroactively and giving it significant credit for any gains in the movement, and caricaturizes nonviolent civil disobedience as a weaker tactic that succeeded only in high-profile instances accompanied by national media coverage. In particular, see Tyson, *Radio Free Dixie*. Influenced by Tim Tyson, several works have tackled the topic of armed black resistance in the civil rights struggle for a variety of organizations and regions. For example, see Umoja, "Eye for an Eye"; Strain, "'We Walked Like Men'"; Hill, *Deacons for Defense*; Jeffries, *Bloody Lowndes*; Crosby, "'You Got a Right to Defend Yourself'"; Cobb, *This Nonviolent Stuff'll Get You Killed*. On the long tradition of black self-defense against white supremacy, see Johnson, *Negroes and the Gun*. For a corrective to this literature, see Wendt, *Spirit and the Shotgun*. Historians who have studied the role of violence in the movement have either celebrated or overblown the importance of armed self-defense groups. In the provocative subtitle of his book, Charles Cobb, for one, asserts that "guns made the civil rights movement possible" but never supports his thesis. Lance Hill focused on the Louisiana-based Deacons for Defense, but it was a marginal presence in the wider southern freedom movement. Perhaps only a few dozen men and women ever belonged to the Deacons, a defensive rather than an offensive organization, as the group's name indicated. By 1968, the Deacons went extinct. Tim Tyson regards Robert F. Williams, president of the NAACP chapter in Monroe, North Carolina, as "one of the best organizers in the black freedom movement." Tyson chalks up Williams's appeals for violence, his call for black soldiers to rise in an insurrection against the U.S. military during the 1962 Cuban Missile Crisis, and his often-bizarre rhetoric and behavior to "the same frustrations and delusions that plagued the rest of the movement" (Tyson, "Robert F. Williams," 568).

29. Raines, *My Soul Is Rested*, 266; Wood and Samuel, "'He Was Non-violent, but My Boys Weren't,'" 162–63 (quotations).

30. Rosie Head Oral History, LOC (first quotation); Dittmer, *Local People*, 192 (second quotation).

31. Dittmer, *Local People*, 191; Sojourner with Reitan, *Thunder of Freedom*, 36–40; author's interview with Sue Sojourner; Gist, "Educating a Southern Rural Community," 178; Payne, *I've Got the Light of Freedom*, 280 (quotations). Payne argued that independent black landholders "were distinctly more likely than the sharecroppers to have been active in the civil rights movement, no matter how activity was measured," and the difference between the two groups only grew as the "degree of danger" associated with different civil rights activities increased (Payne, *I've Got the Light of Freedom*, 281–82). Sue Sojourner also emphasized the receptivity of black landowners to civil rights and referred to the First Fourteen as the "first movers" (Sojourner with Reitan, *Thunder of Freedom*, 27–46 (quotation on 31)). Alan Draper has pointed

out, however, that despite their relative economic independence, "black landowners still depended on white bankers who held their mortgages, on white merchants who extended credit to purchase equipment and seeds, on white wholesalers who marketed their crops, and on white owners who ginned their cotton. Black landowners were independent only in relation to the abject dependence of black farmworkers on white-owned plantations, on the one hand, and the dispiriting vulnerability of black schoolteachers to white school boards, on the other" (Draper, "Class and Politics in the Mississippi Movement," 272–73).

32. John Daniel Wesley Oral History.

33. John Daniel Wesley Oral History; Sojourner with Reitan, *Thunder of Freedom*, 40–43 (quotations on 43); author's interview with Sue Sojourner.

34. Sojourner with Reitan, *Thunder of Freedom*, 61–62; author's interview with Sue Sojourner; Guy Gugliotta, "Dwindling Black Farmers."

35. Sojourner with Reitan, *Thunder of Freedom*, 62–63 (quotations); author's interview with Sue Sojourner.

36. Youth of the Rural Organizing and Cultural Center, *Minds Stayed on Freedom*, 14–15.

37. Youth of the Rural Organizing and Cultural Center, 15 (first and second quotations), 22–34 (fourth quotation on 33); Walter Bruce Oral History, LOC (third quotation); Gist, "Educating a Southern Rural Community," 214–15; Archer, *Growing Up Black in Rural Mississippi*, 135–36.

38. Harvey, *Through the Storm*, 121; Howell, "Undiscovered Country," 50–51; Harvey, *Freedom's Crossing*, 195; interview with Mary Hightower, Tom Dent Oral History Collection, Tougaloo Civil Rights Collection, MDAH. The Second Pilgrim Rest Church functioned as a community center and rallying point for Durant activists. To prevent the Klan from burning the church, local MFDP leaders stationed armed men to stay the night and protect the sanctuary (see Andrews, *Freedom Is a Constant Struggle*, 83). Word spread quickly that Durant blacks would shoot at would-be attackers. Walter Bruce believed that whites figured, "We [sic] not going to go back out there no more. Them Niggers got all kinds [of guns] out there" (Howell, "Undiscovered Country," 51).

39. Andrews, *Freedom Is a Constant Struggle*, 84–85 (first quotation); Sojourner with Reitan, *Thunder of Freedom*, 77 (second quotation); author's interview with Sue Sojourner.

40. Sojourner with Reitan, *Thunder of Freedom*, 78 (quotations); author's interview with Sue Sojourner.

41. Payne, *I've Got the Light of Freedom*, 278; Dittmer, *Local People*, 191; John Daniel Wesley Oral History; Sojourner with Reitan, *Thunder of Freedom*, 98–99; author's interview with Sue Sojourner. Alma Mitchell Carnegie suffered repeatedly for her activism. In 1965, authorities jailed her in a cattle pen for participating in a Jackson protest. In 1966, during the Meredith March, the police tear-gassed her and other marchers (see Sojourner with Reitan, *Thunder of Freedom*, 99).

42. Sojourner with Reitan, *Thunder of Freedom*, 127; author's interview with Sue Sojourner; Youth of the Rural Organizing and Cultural Center, *Minds Stayed on*

Freedom, 68; author's interview with Byron Montgomery; Gist, "Educating a Southern Rural Community," 180; interview with Zelpha Montgomery Whatley, *The Story*, PBS, June 18, 2013, www.thestory.org/stories/2013–06/voting-rights-act-1965. Sue Sojourner described the humble black farmers of the hills as living in "run-down old shacks disconnected and isolated from each other and, seemingly, the world. The houses may have had a TV set, but no indoor toilet or running water. In some outhouses, the maggots sifted through shit within a foot of the seat" (Sojourner with Reitan, *Thunder of Freedom*, 46). The land in the hillier section of the county was prone to erosion and soil depletion. Black farmers bought property that whites deemed unsuitable for cultivation. Dating back to the early twentieth century, the Montgomery family owned hundreds of acres, which made them the largest black landholders on the eastern end of the county. The Montgomery men loomed large physically as well. Each brother stood over six feet tall (see Youth of the Rural Organizing and Cultural Center, *Minds Stayed on Freedom*, 10; author's interview with Sylvia Gist). Eugene Montgomery, unlike his wife, did not counsel nonviolence, carried a .38 pistol, and refused to take disrespect from whites, including the sheriff's deputies and police. If anyone threatened his boys, Eugene told them to hit back. Both parents taught their children not to use the word "can't." Eugene liked to say, "The man who invented 'can't' should be shot" (author's interview with Byron Montgomery). Dependency of black teachers and ministers on white financial support and of black businessmen on segregated business practices had been nearly ubiquitous since the beginning of Jim Crow. Black educators, in particular, did not like to rock the boat. They were "totally dependent upon the school district for means of survival," according to Sylvia Gist (Gist, "Educating a Southern Rural Community," 178). Sylvia Gist and Eugene Montgomery were first cousins on her father's side. She informed the author that although Bernice Montgomery was a vocal exception among black teachers, other educators supported the movement but not outwardly for fear of putting their jobs and lives in jeopardy (see author's interview with Sylvia Gist).

43. Sojourner with Reitan, *Thunder of Freedom*, 34–35 (first quotation); author's interview with Sue Sojourner; Andrews, *Freedom Is a Constant Struggle*, 80–81 (second quotation).

44. Sojourner with Reitan, *Thunder of Freedom*, 127–28 (quotation); author's interview with Sue Sojourner; Youth of the Rural Organizing and Cultural Center, *Minds Stayed on Freedom*, 72. Other blacks confirmed the practice used against Bernice Montgomery. Her daughter, Zelpha Montgomery Whatley, claimed McClellan would tell aspiring black voters, "You know it's illegal for niggers to vote in Holmes County or in Mississippi." If the person insisted, McClellan would demand payment of the poll tax. If paid, he would then hold up a bar of soap and ask for the number of bubbles. "Smart niggers," said Whatley, had to recite the U.S. Constitution (interview with Zelpha Montgomery Whatley, *The Story*). Bernice Montgomery's account, however, should not be taken entirely at face value. Her rote memorization of the federal constitution and ability to quote it verbatim seems improbable, if not impossible. The romanticized lore surrounding her registration has since been erroneously recorded in other places and attributed to the family's proud retelling of the story

over the years (see author's interviews with Sylvia Gist and Byron Montgomery). On January 29, 1965, the county registrar logged Bernice Montgomery as a voter (see Voter Registration sheet, Office of the Holmes County Circuit Court, Lexington, Miss). Sue Lorenzi Sojourner discussed most aspects of the county's movement history, but she often relied on and uncritically accepted oral histories (see Sojourner with Reitan, *Thunder of Freedom*, 127–28). One should always be skeptical of conversations recreated from memory.

45. Dittmer, *Local People*, 239–52.

46. Cohen, *Freedom's Orator*, 50 (quotation).

47. Cohen, 53–54 (quotations on 54). Other Freedom Summer volunteers reported similar incidents during their first few weeks in Holmes. Eugene Nelson wrote home to his parents about scare tactics and terrorism that included "the bombed car, the pistol packing Whites at the local store, and the bombing attempt in the next town." Instead of breaking the movement, the violence galvanized the black community. Nelson remarked, "Particularly the bombing in Tchula can only help: the man they did it to was not in the Movement, and it showed everyone that cowardice was no escape either" (Nelson quoted in Andrews, *Freedom Is a Constant Struggle*, 82).

48. Cohen, *Freedom's Orator*, 54 (first quotation), 55 (second quotation).

49. Cohen, 55.

50. Cohen, 55.

51. Payne, *I've Got the Light of Freedom*, 282–83 (first quotation); Cohen, *Freedom's Orator*, 55 (second quotation).

52. Cohen, *Freedom's Orator*, 55–56 (first quotation); Sojourner with Reitan, *Thunder of Freedom*, 48–49 (second quotation).

53. Cohen, *Freedom's Orator*, 56 (quotations).

54. Cohen, 56–58 (quotations).

55. Andrews, *Freedom Is a Constant Struggle*, 81 (quotation); Sojourner with Reitan, *Thunder of Freedom*, 48–49. Building the community center would not have been possible without the labor of Abraham Osheroff, a white carpenter and veteran of the Abraham Lincoln Brigade in the Spanish Civil War. In 1964, Osheroff arrived from Los Angeles to begin construction of the Mileston center. On his first day in Holmes County, whites greeted him with placards that read "White Nigger" and bombed his car. Osheroff pursued a variety of leftist causes. In the 1980s, he aided the Sandinista government in Nicaragua by constructing homes for peasants. For more on Osheroff's life, see Carroll, *Odyssey of the Abraham Lincoln Brigade*, 354; Douglas Martin, "Abe Osheroff, Veteran of the Abraham Lincoln Brigade, Dies at 92," *NYT*, April 11, 2008. Located in Lexington's black Pecan Grove neighborhood, the FDP office was a ramshackle building with a wood-burning stove.

56. Sojourner with Reitan, *Thunder of Freedom*, 63, 67–68, 275; author's interview with Sue Sojourner; Youth of the Rural Organizing and Cultural Center, *Minds Stayed on Freedom*, 15; "Holmes County Report," Letter from the Director, Holmes County Community Center, no date, and FDP Minutes, February 27, 1966, SNCC Papers. Turnbow had a tremendous facility with language and could create vivid images with biblical references (see author's interview with Melvyn Leventhal).

One observer of the countywide mass meetings noted their lack of discipline. Arnett Lewis, then a high school student, described the meetings as "organized chaos." Without proper rules of order, one person would rise to speak but another would interrupt. Lewis never left a meeting with a sense of being involved or accomplishment (see author's interview with Arnett Lewis).

57. Sojourner with Reitan, *Thunder of Freedom*, 70–71; author's interview with Sue Sojourner; Andrews, *Freedom Is a Constant Struggle*, 86; "Holmes County Report," Letter from the Director, Holmes County Community Center, no date, SNCC Papers.

58. Gist, "Educating a Southern Rural Community," 179–80; "Holmes County Report," 1965 Information Sheet, SNCC Papers.

59. Andrew Smith quoted in Fleming, *Son of the Rough South*, 293.

60. Youth of the Rural Organizing and Cultural Center, *Minds Stayed on Freedom*, 97; Rosie Head Oral History, LOC (quotations). In 1963, John Doar sought injunctive relief in Jackson, Mississippi, against Smith, county attorney Pat M. Barrett, and other public officials for voter intimidation (see brief at 2, 3, 6 in *United States v. Holmes County*; Silver, *Mississippi*, 86–87; Wood and Samuel, "'He Was Non-violent, but My Boys Weren't,'" 162). Not until the federal government enforced the 1965 Voting Rights Act did most blacks in Holmes County register to vote. Within days of the law's enactment, the number of black voters countywide more than tripled from eighty-seven to 312 (see Gist, "Educating a Southern Rural Community," 185–86).

61. See Lawson, *Black Ballots*, 288–321.

62. Andrews, *Freedom Is a Constant Struggle*, 85; *Holmes County Herald*, June 9, 1966, 1 (quotation); Sojourner with Reitan, *Thunder of Freedom*, 289.

63. Andrews, *Freedom Is a Constant Struggle*, 84, 86 (quotation). Kenneth Andrews argues that the MFDP's ability to provide organizational leadership prevented the kind of rivalry and balkanization that marred civil rights activities in many other southern communities (see Andrews, *Freedom Is a Constant Struggle*, 84). Andrews's study of Bolivar, Holmes, and Madison Counties focused more on statistics than on local people's stories and never really explains how grassroots organizing occurred. Sue Sojourner, who lived and worked in Holmes, noted fault lines within the black community defined by income, assets, and education that Andrews missed. Class tensions emerged between black farm owners at the top of the class structure and the throngs of plantation wage laborers below them (see Sojourner with Reitan, *Thunder of Freedom*, 230). "Wealthier members of the black community" included prominent black farmers, like Ralthus Hayes, elected chairman of the county's FDP chapter in January 1965; Ozell Mitchell; T. C. Johnson; and Howard Taft Bailey, the vice chairman of the FDP. John Henry Malone of Pickens served as treasurer, and Bernice Montgomery acted as secretary (see "Holmes County Report," Information Sheet, p. 3, no date, SNCC Papers). By 1965, Holmes activists held FDP meetings across the county in Lebanon, Tchula, Mileston, Mount Olive, Lexington, Goodman, Second Pilgrim Rest, and Sunny Mount. On the third Sunday of each month, the countywide meeting occurred at the Holmes County Community Center in Mileston (see "Holmes County Report," Information Sheet, p. 4, no date, SNCC Papers).

64. Sojourner with Reitan, *Thunder of Freedom*, 249; author's interview with Sue Sojourner; Andrews, *Freedom Is a Constant Struggle*, 86. The boycott's leaders also demanded the firing of Lexington's token black police officer, W. C. "Fats" Jordan—hired in 1965 to keep blacks in their place. In October 1967, the chamber of commerce convinced the mayor to fire Jordan. He resigned and left town. Local merchants did not agree to hire more blacks, however (see Gist, "Educating a Southern Rural Community," 185–86; Hazel Brannon Smith, *LA*, September 21 and October 10, 1967).

65. Sojourner with Reitan, *Thunder of Freedom*, 251–53 (quotations); author's interview with Sue Sojourner; Huffman, "How White Flight Ravaged the Mississippi Delta."

66. Gist, "Educating a Southern Rural Community," 13. In 1967, a slate of eight black landowners, including Robert Clark, ran for local and state offices. Clark served for thirty-six years in the state legislature and eventually rose to speaker pro tempore. In 2003, his son, Wandrick Bryant Clark, succeeded him (see Sojourner with Reitan, *Thunder of Freedom*, 228–30, 275).

67. Gist, "Educating a Southern Rural Community," 13, 15; Neilson, *Even Mississippi*, 37 (quotation); Campbell, *Robert G. Clark's Journey to the House*, 99; Sojourner with Reitan, *Thunder of Freedom*, 231–37; author's interview with Sue Sojourner; Andrews, *Freedom Is a Constant Struggle*, 88; Payne, *I've Got the Light of Freedom*, 350; Sewell and Dwight, *Mississippi Black History Makers*, 80. After the end of slavery, Robert Clark's family had owned 350 acres of land. When Clark advocated for an adult education program, county school officials fired him and banned him from running for superintendent of schools. As a result, he decided to campaign for state legislator (see Orey, "Robert Clark and the Ascendancy to Black Power," 230–50). Under threat of losing their jobs or through the misapplication of the politics of respectability, black teachers and school administrators were typically among the most ruthless enemies of the civil rights movement. Currying favor with local school boards, black principals, in particular, shunned the civil rights movement. African-American educators often cast aspersions on black dissidents as disgraceful lawbreakers and tattled on their subversive activities to white authorities. A 1961 Mississippi State Sovereignty Commission memo illuminated the extent of white control over black teachers in Holmes County. Superintendent of Education Lester Thompson informed a commission investigator that "none of his teachers belonged to the NAACP and he considered all of his principals to be good Negro instructors and loyal." If he suspected any black teachers of participating in civil rights, Thompson muzzled or fired the offender. The board of education "would not tolerate retaining an agitator," he assured a commission investigator (Mississippi State Sovereignty Commission Papers, SCR ID #2-54-1-48-2-1-1, MDAH). Robert Clark's campaign inspired a new generation to further the cause of black rights in Holmes. Drafted as a marine in 1966 and sent to Vietnam, Arnett Lewis watched news of Clark's victory on television. His election "made 1954 [*Brown*], 1964 [the Civil Rights Act], and the Constitution *real*," remembered Lewis (author's interview with Arnett Lewis).

68. Sojourner with Reitan, *Thunder of Freedom*, 103 (quotation); author's interview with Sue Sojourner.

69. Sojourner with Reitan, 104; "Holmes County Report," Messages from the Staff, SNCC Papers; inter-office memo, *Alexander v. Holmes County Board of Education*, NAACPLDF Litigation Files. Byron Montgomery, a student at Saints Industrial, was the first of the Montgomery children to attend Lexington's previously all-white schools. In the summer of 1966, he was staying in Chicago with his father's extended family and happily looking forward to starting as tailback on the Saints' football team. When he came home, however, his mother broke the news that she had enrolled him at Lexington High School. A disappointed Byron accepted his fate: "If mom said you had to do something; you did it." In September, Byron started his sophomore year as one of two incoming black students at Lexington High. His older cousin Fannie Jean Archer entered as a senior and graduated in the spring of 1967. For the next two years, barely any whites spoke to Byron. The white students had met before the opening of school and threatened to ostracize anyone who talked to the unwelcome black arrivals. One particularly aggressive white classmate sprayed Byron's pants with gasoline and almost lit him on fire. His chemistry teacher made him work alone without a lab partner. In 1968, Byron graduated and intentionally went to college far away from Mississippi at the University of Illinois. He lives in California today (see author's interview with Byron Montgomery).

CHAPTER THREE

1. "N.A.A.C.P. Sets Advanced Goals," *NYT*, May 18, 1954 (quotation); Kluger, *Simple Justice*, 902. Thurgood Marshall's blueprint to use the courts to achieve emancipation for blacks was a gradual and daring strategy. Other civil rights leaders recommended direct-action protest and even political theater to accomplish racial equality. One gnawing criticism of Marshall's approach was that winning lawsuits did not necessarily change whites' hearts and minds. Racism could and did persist in spite of the law. More precisely, the Supreme Court chose to locate the harm of segregation in the psyche of black children, and *Brown v. Board*, therefore, failed to shift the conversation from the individual-level effects of discrimination to institutional and structural racism. Working through the legal system presented another difficulty. Courts, it is said, are only as good as their judges. Southern federal district judges often reflected the racial attitudes of the majority white population (see Brown-Nagin, *Courage to Dissent*, 1–7, chap. 1; Tushnet, *NAACP's Legal Strategy*, 29–32, 55, 100; McNeil, *Groundwork*, 131–36, 140–41, 152, 155, 198–99, 216–18).

2. Patterson, Brown v. Board of Education, 118 (first quotation); Thurgood Marshall quoted in *NYT*, January 3, 1960 (second quotation); Greenberg, *Crusaders in the Courts*, 254–55, 304, 391; Dittmer, *Local People*, 70; Rosenberg, *Hollow Hope*, 90–93; Tushnet, *Making Civil Rights Law*, 234–35, 268, 305–6.

3. "Beatrice Alexander," *Race Relations Law Reporter*, 1089; Gist, "Educating a Southern Rural Community," 195. Davison Douglas makes clear that the legal cases stretching from *Brown v. Board of Education* to *Swann v. Charlotte-Mecklenburg Board of Education* (1971) did not form an unbroken or unchallenged string of victories. Disparate judges regarded desegregation differently. Situations in various lower courts

and judicial circuits were often at odds with one another. The push for the 1964 Civil Rights Act and federal mandates to comply with desegregation were countered by Richard Nixon's political machinations. Only in hindsight is it possible to observe a straight line from *Brown* to *Alexander* (see Douglas, *Reading, Writing, and Race*).

4. Edwin White quoted in the *Jackson (Miss.) Daily News*, August 12, 1954. See also Ferguson, *Remaking the Rural South*, 153–54.

5. Brief for petitioners at 4, *Alexander v. Holmes County Board of Education*, 396 U.S. 1218 (1969); Gist, "Educating a Southern Rural Community," 190; Parker, "Protest, Politics, and Litigation," 690; Bolton, "Last Holdout," 125–26.

6. Fairclough, *Race and Democracy*, 435–36; Bolton, "Last Holdout," 125–26.

7. Gist, "Educating a Southern Rural Community," 162; Minutes, February–March 1965, "Official Minutes of the Holmes County Board of Education," 1950-80.

8. Petition, reel 133, NAACPLDF Litigation Files (quotation); Gist, "Educating a Southern Rural Community," 162–64; Parker, "Protest, Politics, and Litigation," 690; Bolton, "Last Holdout," 125–26; brief for petitioners at 1, *Alexander v. Holmes County Board of Education*, Civil Action No. 3779 (S.D. Miss 1965). In what is commonly referred to as *Brown II* (1955), the Court advised the lower courts and local school boards to implement school desegregation with "all deliberate speed" (see *Brown v. Board of Education of Topeka, Kansas*, 349 U.S. 294 (1955)). For the next decade, southern school boards and state officials devised evasive maneuvers to minimize integration (see Irons, *Jim Crow's Children*, 188–89).

9. Minchin, "Making the Best Use of the New Laws," 674; author's interview with Melvyn Zarr; Meltsner, *Making of a Civil Rights Lawyer*, 95; Kluger, *Simple Justice*, 436. Meltsner worked under Greenberg and credited his former boss with cultivating mutual respect, dedication, and collegiality among the LDF staff (see Meltsner, *Making of a Civil Rights Lawyer*, 118, 120). Jack Greenberg died on October 12, 2016. To the author's knowledge, no southern newspaper published an obituary for him (see Richard Severo and William McDonald, "Jack Greenberg, a Courthouse Pillar of the Civil Rights Movement, Dies at 91," *NYT*, October 12, 2016).

10. Meltsner, *Making of a Civil Rights Lawyer*, 92 (quotation).

11. Meltsner, 92 (second and third quotations); Greenberg, *Crusaders in the Courts*, 390 (first and fourth quotations); Irons, *Jim Crow's Children*, 188–89. The problem during the Eisenhower years was that the conservative president supported states' rights and did not regard civil rights as a personal matter (see Mayer, "With Much Deliberation and Some Speed").

12. Greenberg, *Crusaders in the Courts*, 390; Meltsner, *Making of a Civil Rights Lawyer*, 112. For more on Lyndon Johnson's civil rights accomplishments and the Great Society, see Zeitz, *Building the Great Society*.

13. Zarr, "Recollections of My Time in the Civil Rights Movement," 373n19; Pierce, "Mission of Marian Wright," 94, 96 (quotations on 96).

14. Edelman, *Lanterns*, 74–75 (first and second quotations); author's interview with Melvyn Zarr (third quotation).

15. R. Jess Brown Oral History, Civil Rights in Mississippi Digital Archive, University of Southern Mississippi, Hattiesburg; author's interview with Reuben Anderson;

Sewell and Dwight, *Mississippi Black History Makers*, 115–16; "Wide Opportunities for Negro Lawyers"; Motley, *Equal Justice under the Law*, 72; Smith, *Emancipation*, 300; Epp, *Rights Revolution*, 56–58; Spriggs, *Voices of Civil Rights Lawyers*, 205. Ben A. Green grew up in Mound Bayou, received his BA from Fisk University in Nashville, and, in 1914, earned his law degree from Harvard (see Somerville, *Dear Boys*, 88).

16. Sewell and Dwight, *Mississippi Black History Makers*, 112–13, 115–16; Edelman, *Lanterns*, 74–75; Orr-Klopfer with Klopfer and Klopfer, *Where Rebels Roost*, 298; Spriggs, *Voices of Civil Rights Lawyers*, 205–6; Carsie Hall quoted in Gale, "Southern Front," n.p. The arrival of the Freedom Riders brought the larger civil rights movement directly into the heart of Mississippi. By summer's end, more than 300 Freedom Riders had been arrested, tried, convicted, and jailed in the state. For more on the Freedom Rides, see Arsenault, *Freedom Riders*; Dittmer, *Local People*, 90–99. Jess Brown had been a teacher at Lanier High School in Jackson before he lost his job and became a lawyer (see Dittmer, *Local People*, 35). On the importance of federal post office jobs to blacks, see Rubio, *There's Always Work at the Post Office*.

17. Dittmer, *Local People*, 229–30; Eagles, *Price of Defiance*, 225, 227–28.

18. Sweet and Bradley, *Church Street*, 50, 53; Runnels, "Trailblazers of the Mississippi Legal Frontier," 16 (second quotation); Babson, Elsila, and Riddle, *Color of Law*, 358 (first and third quotations); Trillin, *Jackson*, 5; Dittmer, *Local People*, 229–30; Hilbink, "Filling the Void." With so few civil rights attorneys around, the various legal organizations often split the workload to concentrate their energies on particular aspects of the law. The Lawyers' Constitutional Defense Committee, for example, assumed primary responsibility for defending civil rights activists, especially ones arrested during voter-registration campaigns. The LDF took up school desegregation suits (see author's interviews with Reuben Anderson and Fred L. Banks Jr.; Charles Bolton interview with Fred Banks, Civil Rights in Mississippi Digital Archive; Wasby, *Race Relations Litigation*, 182–83). Farish Street intersects with Capitol Street, downtown Jackson's main business corridor. Unwelcome in white stores, blacks formed a separate business hub adjacent to the white downtown and carved out a six- to eight-block area. The neighborhood boomed after World War II and acted as a cultural oasis for black Mississippians and a safe haven from white control. The street was named for Walter Farish, a former slave who lived on the corner of Davis and what is now Farish. The descendants of slaves built the entire thoroughfare. On the history of the Farish District, see Sweet and Bradley, *Church Street*. Despite their offices' proximity and shared commitment to civil rights, the LDF and the National Lawyers Guild did not associate with each other. Marian Wright and Jack Greenberg did not cooperate with the guild because of its Communist affiliation. Infighting and misgivings never escalated into internecine turf warfare and only infrequently divided movement activists and lawyers. In 1964, for example, Greenberg threatened to withdraw LDF support from the Mississippi Freedom Summer Project after the Council of Federated Organizations and SNCC announced that the Lawyers Guild would participate (see Dittmer, *Local People*, 229–30; Babson, Elsila, and Riddle, *Color of the Law*, 358; Spriggs, *Voices of Civil Rights Lawyers*, 152, 207–9). In their disdain for the Guild, NAACP LDF lawyers reflected Thurgood Marshall's

politics of respectability. Greenberg's LDF office inherited Marshall's belief in steering clear of radical groups and in picking reputable main plaintiffs—individuals, professionals, or others who seemed beyond reproach—when bringing civil rights lawsuits. On the politics of respectability and black civil rights, see Mack, *Representing the Race*, 295; Brown-Nagin, *Courage to Dissent*, 32; Higginbotham, *Righteous Discontent*, 185–229; Kennedy, "Lifting as We Climb." Otherwise, relations between the LDF and the Lawyers' Constitutional Defense Committee were good. The different organizations operated in separate spheres with occasional overlap. The LDF largely focused on school desegregation with some lawsuits to challenge housing and employment discrimination. The LCDC, under chief counsel Frank R. Parker, took the lead in voting rights cases. The Lawyers' Constitutional Defense Committee mainly handled protest demonstrations and threats. It also represented Robert Clark in Holmes County (see author's interview with Armand Derfner).

19. Edelman, *Lanterns*, 78–79 (first quotation); Zarr, "Recollections of My Time in the Civil Rights Movement," 373n19; Pierce, "The Mission of Marian Wright," 94 (second quotation); Spriggs, *Voices of Civil Rights Lawyers*, xv. Wright had a secret weapon to pass the state bar exam. One of the federal district court's law clerks, Ed Wright, a Harvard Law School graduate, shared his notes and stock of knowledge about the questions and statutes that might appear on the test (see Edelman, *Lanterns*, 78–79).

20. Edelman, *Lanterns*, 76–77 (first, second, and third quotations); Pierce, "Mission of Marian Wright," 100 (fourth and fifth quotations).

21. Honigsberg, *Crossing Border Street*, 12; Pierce, "Mission of Marian Wright," 96, 100, 104; author's interview with Melvyn Zarr; Hudson, *Let the Students Speak!*, 148 (quotation); Sarat and Scheingold, *Cause Lawyers and Social Movements*, 76.

22. Author's interview with Melvyn Zarr (quotations); Branch, *Parting the Waters*, 728; James Janenga, "Norman Amaker, 65, Key Civil Rights Figure," *Chicago Tribune*, June 11, 2000; Reuben Anderson Oral History, Civil Rights in Mississippi Digital Archive. Zarr would also sign his name to the 1965 *Alexander* brief. Paul and Iris Brest were two other additions to the Jackson LDF office. The black freedom struggle and the sit-in movement, in particular, attracted Paul Brest, and he decided to become a civil rights lawyer. He attended Harvard Law. After graduation, he clerked for Chief Judge Bailey Aldrich of the U.S. Court of Appeals, First Circuit. In 1966, Paul Brest came to Mississippi with his wife, Iris. They worked at the Inc. Fund and litigated school desegregation in and around Greenville. In 1968, Paul Brest clerked for Justice John Marshall Harlan. In 1969, Brest accepted a teaching position at Stanford Law (see author's interview with Paul Brest).

23. Parker, *Black Votes Count*, 81–82.

24. Pierce, "Mission of Marian Wright," 102–3 (quotations).

25. Gist, "Educating a Southern Rural Community," 194–95. When a lawsuit turned toward a major legal challenge to segregation, the LDF usually sent highly trained litigators to help local black lawyers make decisions. In many southern states, local cooperating attorneys could handle a case all the way to the federal district court. In Mississippi, however, LDF staff attorneys had to appear even at the lower

rungs of federal court because of the shortage of experienced legal counsel. Jack Young, Carsie Hall, and Jess Brown, furthermore, had more expertise as defense attorneys, not as school litigators, and they generally represented demonstrators and argued in state, rather than federal, courts (see Wasby, *Race Relations Litigation*, 266, 312). The trajectory from Holmes County to NAACP representatives to LDF attorneys followed a typical path. Often, Aaron Henry, Clarksdale's NAACP secretary, would tip off the LDF about a recalcitrant school system, and the Fund targeted that district (see author's interview with Reuben Anderson).

26. Morris, *Yazoo*, 143–44; White, *Alice Walker*, 135–36 (quotations).

27. White, *Alice Walker*, 135–36; author's interviews with Melvyn Leventhal (quotations) and Reuben Anderson; Walter Bruce Oral History, LOC. In many instances, civil rights organizations encountered difficulty finding desirable or willing plaintiffs. NAACP attorneys usually struggled to convince parents to initiate cases on behalf of their children. In Holmes, the opposite held true. Scores of parents eagerly signed up, thanks to the strength of the local movement (see Wasby, *Race Relations Litigation*, 211).

28. Morris, *Yazoo*, 143–44 (quotations); author's interview with Sue Sojourner; author's interview with Melvyn Leventhal. Leventhal acculturated quickly. Surrounded by Mississippians, he picked up an accent easily. Paul and Iris Brest remembered him speaking to one group of plaintiffs like a "Baptist preacher" (author's interviews with Paul Brest and Iris Brest).

29. White, *Alice Walker*, 136 (quotations); Harris, *Gifts of Virtue*, 38; author's interview with Melvyn Leventhal. Sue Lorenzi (now Sojourner) changed her last name to Sojourner years after the movement.

30. White, *Alice Walker*, 135–36, 156–57 (quotations); author's interview with Melvyn Leventhal.

31. *Alexander v. Holmes* (1965); Aronow, "Special Master in School Desegregation Cases," 746; Bolton, "Last Holdout," 129–30; Parker, "Protest, Politics, and Litigation," 690; Doherty, "'Integration Now,'" 491; *Holmes County Herald*, July 29, 1965, 1; *Singleton v. Jackson Municipal Separate School District*, 348 F.2d 729 (5th Cir. 1965).

32. Author's interview with Don Barrett Jr.; Kaul, "Hazel Brannon Smith," 246, 250; Bryan, *These Few Also Paid a Price*, 73; "Holmes County Report," p. 2, SNCC Papers; Ferguson, *Remaking the Rural South*, 154 (quotation). Jim Barrett was not related to Pat Barrett. Lester Thompson played football for Mississippi State University in the 1920s, and, in 1933, he coached Lexington High School's only undefeated football team. In the 1950s, he won election to superintendent of county schools. He married Pat Barrett's older sister, Rachel, and lived next door (see author's interview with Don Barrett Jr.; "U.S. Social Security Death Index, 1935–2014," Family Search, https://familysearch.org/search/collection/1202535). Abraham "Abe" Fortas also attended Southwestern at Memphis and graduated in 1930. In 1965, Fortas joined the Supreme Court and served until May 1969, almost six months shy of hearing *Alexander v. Holmes* (see Woodward and Armstrong, *Brethren*, 17–19).

33. Docket sheet, case file of *Alexander v. Holmes County Board of Education*, Record Group #3779, National Archives and Records Administration—Southeast

Region, Atlanta, Ga.; interoffice memo, reel 133, NAACPLDF Litigation Files; author's interview with Reuben Anderson; *Holmes County Herald*, July 29, 1965, 1; Wirt, *Politics of Southern Equality*, chaps. 9 and 10. Born around 1920, Peter Alexander worked as a farm laborer and eventually acquired land in the Mileston vicinity. Like many black farmers, he received minimal education and went to school only through the first grade (see U.S. Bureau of the Census, *Sixteenth Census of the United States*).

34. Gist, "Educating a Southern Rural Community," 193–94, 196 (quotation); LDF memo, no date, reel 133, NAACPLDF Litigation Files. Under "freedom of choice," the races resumed their segregated schooling. Eventually, a few courageous black families began to send their kids to all-white schools (see author's interview with Paul Brest). To compel southern school districts to desegregate, Lyndon Johnson's administration utilized what historian Joshua Zeitz described as "a carrot-and-stick method." If a school system complied with desegregation, it could partake in the federal endowment for public schools that expanded from $2.7 billion in 1964 to $14.7 billion in 1971. If, however, local officials clung to segregated education, they faced more than Justice Department lawsuits. The administration could also punitively withhold funding (see Zeitz, "What Everyone Gets Wrong About LBJ's Great Society").

35. Gist, "Educating a Southern Rural Community," 197, 205n53.

36. Brief for petitioners at 4, in *Alexander v. Holmes County Board of Education*, 396 U.S. 1218 (1969) (quotations); Gist, "Educating a Southern Rural Community," 198–99.

37. Gist, "Educating a Southern Rural Community," 198–99. In July 1964, the state legislature had passed SB 1516. Over the next year, civil rights attorneys appealed to the Fifth Circuit for injunctive relief (see Doherty, "'Integration Now,'" 491).

38. In early 1967, for example, Robert Clark brought the school board an application for a job-training program worth $750,000. When black parents petitioned the board to request the money, its members brushed off their plea. Superintendent Thompson did not deem it "in the best interest of the public schools." The terse reasoning dumbfounded Clark and the group of parents (Gist, "Educating a Southern Rural Community," 204–5). Lester Thompson likely had twin motives in obstructing school desegregation: one racial, the other economic. As federal arbitration in the school system intensified, Thompson and the school board fought to keep planter domination of the social and economic order fundamentally intact. Thompson, after all, like other board members, was a planter. In Holmes, white planters adjusted the academic calendar to coincide with the cotton harvest. During September and October, many black children picked cotton alongside their parents and siblings rather than attend school. Court orders to begin desegregation in late August interrupted the harvest and interfered with the planters' labor (see Cobb, *Most Southern Place on Earth*, chaps. 7 and 8; author's interview with Sylvia Gist).

39. Author's interview with Melvyn Leventhal; Andrews, *Freedom Is a Constant Struggle*, 82–83; Sue and Henry Lorenzi to Jean Fairfax and Melvyn Zarr, March 21, 1966, reel 133, NAACPLDF Litigation Files (quotation); "Holmes County Report,"

flyer, no date, SNCC Papers. Other school systems consolidated into the *Alexander* case experienced similar white retaliation against blacks who participated in freedom of choice. In Issaquena County, for example, black children rode on separate school buses, ate apart from whites in the cafeteria, and sat in segregated classrooms (see Dittmer, *Local People*, 390).

40. Bolton, "Last Holdout," 133–34; Andrews, *Freedom Is a Constant Struggle*, 162; Motion for Supplemental Relief, September 1965, reel 133, NAACPLDF Litigation Files (first quotation), Sue and Henry Lorenzi to Fairfax and Zarr, March 21, 1966, reel 133, NAACPLDF Litigation Files; Annie Washington quoted in Youth of the Rural Organizing and Cultural Center, *Minds Stayed on Freedom*, 104.

41. Fairclough, *Race and Democracy*, 438; Bolton, *Hardest Deal of All*, 160–61; Jean Fairfax to Sue and Henry Lorenzi, February 23, 1966, and Sue and Henry Lorenzi to Fairfax and Zarr, March 21, 1966, reel 133, NAACPLDF Litigation Files; Robert G. Clark Oral History, Civil Rights in Mississippi Digital Archive.

42. U.S. Commission on Civil Rights, "Racial Isolation in the Public Schools," 76; Crespino, "Civil Rights and the Religious Right," 93; *Holmes County Herald*, August 5, 1965, 1; Gist, "Educating a Southern Rural Community," 206–7; Fuquay, "Civil Rights and the Private School Movement," 169. In the fall of 1965, whites opened the Central Holmes Academy and hired eight teachers, some of whom had recently been released from contracts with the county school system. Before the construction and completion of a new school, grades 1 and 2 met in Lexington's Methodist church; third and fourth graders gathered in the Baptist annex; and, in 1966, grades 5 through 8 assembled in the Presbyterian manse. Church indulgences for segregation came in several denominations (see *Holmes County Herald*, August 28, 1986, 5C).

43. Bolton, *Hardest Deal of All*, 108–9; Gist, "Educating a Southern Rural Community," 199–201. Initially, Blanton was more racially liberal than blacks expected from Durant's white establishment. After the backlash against his moderate position, however, he fell back in line and later became a proponent of Durant's separate school district. Chapter 7 examines Durant's separate municipal school system (see author's interview with Sylvia Gist).

44. Gist, "Educating a Southern Rural Community," 201–4 (quotation on 202). Julian Brown had given 7.7 acres of his estate to the Durant city school system for an athletic field. In February 1966, the board returned the gift of land (see Gist, "Educating a Southern Rural Community," 203–4).

45. Banks, "United States Court of Appeals for the Fifth Circuit," 277; Parker, "Protest, Politics, and Litigation," 691; Bolton, "Last Holdout," 132–33, 135; Irons, *Jim Crow's Children*, 189. Frederick Wirt's study of desegregation in Panola County, Mississippi, also noted similar limitations about freedom-of-choice plans. In Panola, freedom of choice as "a formula for change was futile, because all the resources for making it work had to be provided by the black. He was told an option now lay open for him if he chose to exercise it, but fear of reprisals and concern for his children rendered the option quite meaningless" (Wirt, *Politics of Southern Equality*, 204–7, 213–14).

CHAPTER FOUR

1. W. F. Minor, "Judge in Rights Case," *NYT*, February 26, 1965, 14 (quotations); author's interview with Melvyn Leventhal. Wilson Floyd "Bill" Minor's "Eyes on Mississippi" column ran in the *New Orleans Times-Picayune* for more than two decades. His intrepid reporting on the civil rights struggle in Mississippi was sensible and invaluable. Minor died in March 2017. For more on his legacy, see Sam Roberts, "Bill Minor, Journalist Who Was Called Conscience of Mississippi, Dies at 94," *NYT*, March 28, 2017; Bart Barnes, "Wilson 'Bill' Minor, 'Conscience' of Mississippi Journalism during Civil Rights Era, Dies at 94," *WP*, March 28, 2017.

2. Richard Kluger's work proved helpful and descriptive on the role of federal district courts (see Kluger, *Simple Justice*, 294–95). See also Freyer, *Little Rock on Trial*, 53–54.

3. Author's interview with Melvyn Leventhal (first quotation); Lyles, *Gatekeepers*, 84–85 (second quotation); Bass, *Unlikely Heroes*, 164; Barnes, "Embattled Judges," 6–7 (third quotation). Kennedy was not the first president to consider Cox for the federal bench. In 1955, a vacancy opened on the Fifth Circuit Court of Appeals, and President Dwight Eisenhower considered appointing Cox to win favor with white southerners. When the Justice Department sought input from the Senate Judiciary Committee, Mississippi senator James Eastland submitted Cox's name. Deputy Attorney General William Rogers, however, apparently laughed at the recommendation and told Eastland that he wanted "reasonable suggestions, not impossible ones" (William Rogers quoted in Barnes, "Embattled Judges," 7). On June 20, 1961, Kennedy nominated Cox. A week later, the Senate confirmed his appointment.

4. Bass, *Unlikely Heroes*, 164–65.

5. Bass, 165–66 (quote on 165).

6. Bass, 166–68; James Eastland quoted in Zelden, *Thurgood Marshall*, 127; Ball, *Murder in Mississippi*, 23; author's interview with Melvyn Leventhal; Alston and Dickerson, *Devil's Sanctuary*, 69; Read and McGough, *Let Them Be Judged*, 408; Martin, *Count Them One by One*, 57–58. On Robert Kennedy's meeting with Cox, Judge Elbert P. Tuttle of the Fifth Circuit remarked, "The trouble with that interview is that they were talking different languages. When Bobby asked him if he would uphold the law of the land, he was thinking about *Brown v. Board of Education*. But when Cox said yes, he was thinking about lynching. When Cox said he believed Negroes should have the vote, he meant two Negroes" (Elbert Tuttle quoted in Bass, *Unlikely Heroes*, 167–68). The conversation revealed the Kennedy brothers' lack of familiarity with southern code language. Cox sat and nodded politely while Kennedy questioned him. In private, Cox and Eastland probably gloated about outmaneuvering the highborn, Harvard-bred Massachusetts Yankees.

7. Jack Greenberg quoted in Zelden, *Thurgood Marshall*, 127; Roy Wilkins quoted in Bass, *Unlikely Heroes*, 166–67; Clarence Mitchell quoted in Bryant, *Bystander*, 286–87; Read and McGough, *Let Them Be Judged*, 408; Parker, *Black Votes Count*, 84. Time and again, the Fifth Circuit overturned Cox's rulings, but he "did *not care* if the senile old men in New Orleans reversed him," one lawyer heard him repeat with

pride (author's interview with Thomas L. Kirkland Jr.). Cox delighted in the Fifth Circuit's reversals. He liked to say that the Fifth "has a big ole bat down there, and I know they're going to send this back!" (Spriggs, *Voices of Civil Rights Lawyers*, 26).

8. Author's interview with Melvyn Leventhal; Ball, *Murder in Mississippi*, 119–20; Motley, *Equal Justice under the Law*, 76; author's interview with Thomas L. Kirkland Jr. (quotation). During the Great Depression, the WPA constructed several new courthouses, including the one in Jackson. In 1938, Russian-born artist Simka Simkhovitch completed the mural. The eccentric and troubled Mississippi artist Walter Anderson had been turned down for the commission (see Alston and Dickerson, *Devil's Sanctuary*, 302). When Judge Tuttle from the Fifth Circuit visited Cox in Jackson, he reprimanded the district judge for allowing such an obscenely racist picture to grace a federal courtroom. Any time Tuttle sat as chief judge, Cox covered the mural whenever the appellate judges came to Jackson. Otherwise, he presided beneath it. In 1972, Frank Parker finally succeeded in getting a court order to cover the mural with a curtain (see Spriggs, *Voices of Civil Rights Lawyers*, 26). The curtain was reopened only on February 25, 1988, during a ceremony to hang a portrait of Judge Harold Cox (see Bass, *Unlikely Heroes*, 167; *JCL*, May 2, 1989, 1). When the Fifth Circuit ordered the mural to be draped, Cox allegedly "pitched a fit" (author's interview with Thomas L. Kirkland Jr.). Cox preferred hearing motions to legal briefs and usually met with lawyers privately "in chambers" at a long table with the American flag on one side and the Mississippi state flag on the other. Mel Leventhal found Cox to be simultaneously a "terrible" and a "fascinating" judge. Leventhal harbored no hard feelings toward Cox and admired the judge's facility with language. He even detected a good sense of humor underneath Cox's severity. Cox, however, regularly frustrated civil rights attorneys with his militant ardor. Presiding over civil rights cases, the judge knew the cases would ultimately wind up in the Fifth Circuit and adopted a "do whatever the hell you want to do" posture toward the LDF, remarked Leventhal (author's interview with Melvyn Leventhal). Other lawyers who appeared in Cox's courtroom doubted anything risible about the judge. In fact, they thought Cox was either scary or possibly crazy (see author's interview with Kenneth Rutherford).

9. Author's interviews with Melvyn Leventhal and Kenneth Rutherford; Read and McGough, *Let Them Be Judged*, 409.

10. Read and McGough, *Let Them Be Judged*, 409; author's interview with Melvyn Leventhal; Banks, "United States Court of Appeals for the Fifth Circuit," 275n1 (first quotation); Spriggs, *Voices of Civil Rights Lawyers*, 26 (second quotation); Greenberg, *Crusaders in the Courts*, 348 (third quotation). The Lawyers' Committee for Civil Rights Under Law eventually challenged Cox about out-of-state staff lawyers and volunteers in his court. In 1968, the Fifth Circuit finally struck down his rule. When Armand Derfner, who worked for Jackson's Lawyers' Constitutional Defense Committee, visited Cox in chambers on another court matter, the surly judge offhandedly asked about the pending case against his procedural rule in the Fifth Circuit. Derfner fully expected the Fifth to overturn Cox's pro hac vice rule. The judge, half-teasing and half-serious, replied, "But they probably won't deal with my new

order about personal appearances." Unaware of any provision about a dress code, the lawyer wanted to know where to read the new rule. "Well, I haven't published it yet," Cox nettled him (Spriggs, *Voices of Civil Rights Lawyers*, 174–75 and 250–51). Cox remained a thorn in the side of civil rights lawyers for years, but his ability to stop desegregation diluted over time. Despite Cox's gamesmanship, the Fifth Circuit overruled him again and again. Civil rights attorneys, however, could not so easily sidestep or simply ignore Cox. Even a weakened federal judge may still exert power (see author's interview with Armand Derfner).

11. Author's interview with Melvyn Leventhal; Spriggs, *Voices of Civil Rights Lawyers*, 26; Alston and Dickerson, *Devil's Sanctuary*, 302–3 (first quotation); Lyles, *Gatekeepers*, 84–85 (second quotation); Bass, *Unlikely Heroes*, 166–67 (third and fourth quotations). Since homicide is a crime usually covered by state law, the federal government cannot bring murder charges. Instead, Justice Department lawyers, led by John Doar, charged the Klansmen responsible for the murders with conspiring to violate the three slain men's civil rights (see Ball, *Murder in Mississippi*, 119). In 1968, the LDF finally got an order from the Fifth Circuit against Cox that invalidated his restrictions on out-of-state lawyers (see Greenberg, *Crusaders in the Courts*, 348). On Cox's mistreatment of civil rights attorneys, see Landsberg, "Symposium."

12. "Those Kennedy Judges," *Time*, November 6, 1964, 44 (first and second quotations); Barnes, "Embattled Judges," 33–35; *NYT*, February 26, 1965 (third quotation); Read and McGough, *Let Them Be Judged*, 409–10.

13. Parker, *Black Votes Count*, 84–85 (quotation); Eagles, *Price of Defiance*, 240. The Southern District in Jackson truly belonged to Harold Cox. Walter Nixon and Dan Russell typically stuck to the Gulf Coast and ruled on cases in Biloxi and Hattiesburg (see author's interview with Thomas L. Kirkland Jr.). Russell exhibited the run-of-the-mill racial sensibilities of a white Mississippian. Although he rarely ruled in favor of civil rights claims, Russell was not as caustically racist as Judge Cox (see author's interview with Armand Derfner). In November 1989, Walter Nixon would be impeached and convicted on perjury charges (see Neil A. Lewis, "Senate Convicts U.S. Judge, Removing Him from Bench," *NYT*, November 4, 1989).

14. James Eastland quoted in the *Jackson Clarion-Ledger*, May 18, 1954 (first quotation); *Oxford Eagle*, June 3, 1954 (second quotation); John Stennis quoted in Crespino, *In Search of Another Country*, 18. Stennis drew his support from northern Mississippi, including the university town of Oxford and Tupelo, an industrial city with a reputation for racial moderation. Eastland's power base, conversely, was in southern Mississippi and the Delta, home of the White Citizens' Council. Eastland's pugnacious racism derived from personal and even traumatic experiences, including the murder of his paternal uncle by a disgruntled African-American man. Eastland's father orchestrated the killer's gruesome lynching. The lynch mob also executed the black man's lover. Throughout his tenure in the Senate, James Eastland thought in more parochial terms than John Stennis. Eastland, for example, frequently micromanaged local appointments of judges and sheriffs. On Eastland's life, views, and career, see Zwiers, *Senator James Eastland*. On Stennis's more "practical segregation," see Crespino, *In Search of Another Country*, chap. 1.

15. Parker, *Black Votes Count*, 84–85, 161, 220n9; Banks, "United States Court of Appeals for the Fifth Circuit," 278. Judge William Keady conscientiously applied federal law because his moral compass was straight—he knew right from wrong. This observation is drawn from conversations with Ken Rutherford, a long-practicing Mississippi lawyer, and Paul Brest (see author's interviews with Kenneth Rutherford and Paul Brest). In 1967, President Johnson elevated Claude Clayton to the Fifth Circuit. Judge Orma Rinehart "Hack" Smith, a Corinth lawyer and honorable man, replaced Clayton (see Eagles, *Civil Rights*, 176).

16. Jean Fairfax to Sue and Henry Lorenzi, February 23, 1966 (first quotation), and Sue and Henry Lorenzi to Jean Fairfax and Melvyn Zarr, March 21, 1966 (second quotation), Report on Holmes County schools, May 1967, reel 133, NAACPLDF Litigation Files; Bass, *Unlikely Heroes*, 299; Wilkinson, *From Brown to Bakke*, 126; Dittmer, *Local People*, 390; Andrews, *Freedom Is a Constant Struggle*, 158. In 1966, the problem in Grenada went well beyond a "paper tiger." On Monday, September 12, black children tried to desegregate the local public schools, but white thugs attacked them while law enforcement ignored the riot (see Bolton, *Hardest Deal of All*, 3). Among other problems embedded in *Brown* was the Warren Court's non-accusatory language that purposefully avoided identifying the perpetrators of white supremacy in an effort to create good faith and compliance with the law in segregated communities. As a result, *Brown* omitted the story of segregation's origins, ideology, impulses, and goals. Harvard legal scholar Randall Kennedy notes that the *Brown* opinion basically excused segregationists of any wrongdoing and had "all the moral grandeur of a bill of lading," as the historian Richard Hofstadter once said of another iconic document of racial freedom, the Emancipation Proclamation. On the shortcomings of *Brown*, see Kennedy and Foner, "*Brown* at 50" (quotation); Kennedy, "Ackerman's *Brown*."

17. Pierce, "Mission of Marian Wright," 103 (quotations). The LDF dealt with outcries in many black-majority counties about horrible schools, split-session academic calendars that dismissed students to pick cotton during the harvest, and one-room schoolhouses (see author's interview with Reuben Anderson). In numerous situations, Marian Wright made contacts with local leaders and built trust because of her race. Then, other LDF lawyers began work with plaintiffs (see author's interview with Paul Brest).

18. Gist, "Educating a Southern Rural Community," 225–26.

19. Bass, *Unlikely Heroes*, esp. 296–97; Peltason, *Fifty-Eight Lonely Men*, esp. 26; Fairclough, *Race and Democracy*, 438–39; Irons, *Jim Crow's Children*, 195; *United States v. Jefferson County Board of Education*, 372 F.2d (5th Cir. 1966). On Thornberry and Wisdom, see Read and McGough, *Let Them Be Judged*; Emanuel, "Forming the Historic Fifth Circuit." Because of Wisdom's liberal leanings, Eisenhower vowed that his nominee would never reach the Supreme Court (see Irons, *Jim Crow's Children*, 195).

20. Fairclough, *Race and Democracy*, 438–39; Bass, *Unlikely Heroes*, 299–301 (first and second quotations on 299; third quotation on 302); Barrow and Walker, *Court Divided*, 122; Wasby, *Race Relations Litigation*, 15. Known as the "*Briggs* dictum,"

after one of the original cases that made up *Brown*, segregationist judges interpreted desegregation to mean only an end to segregation, not mandatory integration. In practice, *Briggs* permitted and encouraged the continuation of a dual, segregated school system because it failed to address, let alone cure, educational apartheid (see Garrow, "Visionaries of the Law," 1223; Kluger, *Simple Justice*, 751–53). In a footnote, Wisdom added that "desegregation" and "integration" would, henceforth, be used interchangeably. For the entirety of Wisdom's opinion, see Opinion of the Court, *U.S. v. Jefferson County Board of Education*. Although Wisdom warned about the problems with freedom of choice, he decided not to torpedo it. Instead, he chose a compromise solution to win his colleagues on the Fifth Circuit and left freedom of choice intact while insisting on tougher indices of compliance from the lower courts (see Fairclough, *Race and Democracy*, 438–39; Bass, *Unlikely Heroes*, 299–302).

21. Bass, *Unlikely Heroes*, 301 (quotation); Friedman, *Champion of Civil Rights*, 220–22. Lloyd Henderson, HEW's point man in Mississippi, doubted the HEW guidelines could work without better court enforcement. "It seems incredible now," he wrote from the vantage point of 1975, "that anyone could seriously have believed that an economically dependent class of people could assume the burden of bringing about compliance with the federal law. Under such circumstances choice could never be free" (Curry, *Silver Rights*, 25).

22. Bass, *Unlikely Heroes*, 302 (quotations); Irons, *Jim Crow's Children*, 195; author's interview with Melvyn Leventhal. Three months after *U.S. v. Jefferson County Board of Education*, with John Doar of the Justice Department and assisting LDF attorneys present, the Fifth Circuit issued an en banc affirmation of Wisdom's opinion and decree. "En banc" means applying or petitioning the whole court, not just a panel, to hear a case. Typically, the losing counsel requests an en banc hearing. In the case of *Jefferson County*, the Fifth Circuit's aptly named Judge John R. Brown, a judicial activist and a supporter of civil liberties, called for an en banc ruling to solidify Wisdom's position. One year later, the Supreme Court endorsed some of Wisdom's language in rendering its *Green v. County School Board of New Kent County* decision (see Garrow, "Visionaries of the Law," 1226).

23. Friedman, *Champion of Civil Rights*, 222–23; Read and McGough, *Let Them Be Judged*, 441 (first, second, and third quotations); author's interview with Melvyn Leventhal (fourth quotation). See also *U.S. v. Jefferson County Board of Education* (Cox dissenting).

24. "Full Integration Ordered for Holmes County Schools," *Holmes County Herald*, July 6, 1967, 1.

25. Neilson, *Even Mississippi*, 35.

26. Neilson, 34–35.

27. Neilson, 38–39.

28. Gist, "Educating a Southern Rural Community," 226–30.

29. Brief, *Green v. County School Board of New Kent County*, 391 U.S. 430, 438–440 (1968), (quotations); Doherty, "'Integration Now,'" 493; Couch, *History of the Fifth Circuit*, 141; Wilkinson, *From Brown to Bakke*, 115–18; Kluger, *Simple Justice*, 766; Minchin and Salmond, *After the Dream*, 83; Irons, *Jim Crow's Children*, 204–5; Sokol,

There Goes My Everything, 169–70; Read, "Judicial Evolution," 28; Tushnet, *Making Constitutional Law*, 69–70. Raymond Wolters pointed out one more critical factor about the *Green* ruling: "Martin Luther King was assassinated on the day after the Supreme Court heard the oral argument in *Green*, and the nation experienced one of its worst periods of racial rioting during the weeks when the Justices considered the case. Once again, the Justices decided, it was time for decisive judicial leadership" (Wolters, *Race and Education*, 139). Paul Brest described most of the LDF's school litigation until the *Green* ruling as a "holding action"—a waiting period to get rid of freedom of choice. Desegregating school systems piecemeal was not a very effective strategy (see author's interview with Paul Brest).

30. Plaintiffs' petition at 391 in *Green v. County School Board of New Kent County* (first quotation); Doherty, "'Integration Now,'" 493–94 (second quotation on 493).

31. Couch, *History of the Fifth Circuit*, 141; Munford, "White Flight," 14 (quotation); Doherty, "'Integration Now,'" 494; Wasby, D'Amato, and Metrailer, *Desegregation from* Brown *to* Alexander, 398–99; Parker, *Black Votes Count*, 82–83; Tushnet, *Making Constitutional Law*, 70; "Additional Response to Motion for Summary Reversal," July 1, 1969, box 4161, folder #28030 and 28042, Record Group 276, Records of the U.S. Court of Appeals Fifth Circuit, National Archives and Records Administration—Southwest Region, Fort Worth, Tex.; *Adams v. Mathews*, 403 F.2d 181 (5th Cir. 1968).

32. Plaintiffs' brief, *United States v. Hinds County School Board*, Civil No. 4075 (J) (S.D. Miss., May 13, 1969); Doherty, "'Integration Now,'" 495. During the civil rights era, the LDF and Justice Department had a complicated relationship because the government typically approached desegregation far more cautiously (see author's interview with Paul Brest). To provide evidence of black inferiority and poor student performance, the defense relied on testimony from some of the nation's leading scientific racists and critics of the *Brown* decision, including Frank C. J. McGurk, Henry E. Garrett, and Ernest Van Den Haag. For a complete transcript of the court hearing, see court reporter's transcript, box 48, "Hinds County School Suit," John C. Satterfield/American Bar Association Collection, University of Mississippi, J. D. Williams Library, Archives and Special Collections, Oxford, Miss. Courts typically consolidated multiple cases under a single title for convenience to settle the same question.

33. Doherty, "'Integration Now,'" 496 (quotations); Banks, "United States Court of Appeals for the Fifth Circuit," 278; Munford, "White Flight," 14; *United States v. Hinds County School Board*; court transcript, box I: 220, folder 2, William J. Brennan Papers, LOC (hereafter cited as Brennan Papers). Civil rights attorneys understood right away that the district court panel meant to delay as long as possible, but they also knew time was on their side. Patience "was required" of any civil rights litigator in the South, commented LDF staff attorney Michael Meltsner; "it was not work for anyone who couldn't delay gratification" (Meltsner, *Making of a Civil Rights Lawyer*, 179).

34. Doherty, "'Integration Now,'" 497 (quotations); *United States v. Hinds County School Board*.

35. Doherty, "'Integration Now,'" 497–500; brief for plaintiffs, *United States v. Hinds County School Board*; "Brief for the U.S.," June 1969, box 4161, folder #28030

and 28042, Record Group 276, Records of the U.S. Court of Appeals Fifth Circuit; author's interview with Melvyn Zarr. The premise in jujitsu is to use your opponent's aggression against him.

36. Banks, "United States Court of Appeals for the Fifth Circuit," 278; Doherty, "'Integration Now,'" 500. Lewis Morgan was Lyndon Johnson's final appointment to the Fifth Circuit (see Bass, *Unlikely Heroes*, 312).

37. Doherty, "'Integration Now,'" 501; per curiam opinion at 12, *United States v. Hinds County School Board*, 417 F.2d 852 (1969) (quotation).

38. Doherty, "'Integration Now,'" 501 (quotation).

39. Irons, *Jim Crow's Children*, 194–95 (quotation); Barrow and Walker, *Court Divided*, 122–23. On the Fifth Circuit's hectic school-desegregation docket after *Brown*, see Bass, *Unlikely Heroes*, chap. 2.

40. Irons, *Jim Crow's Children*, 189–90; Read and McGough, *Let Them Be Judged*, 476; Reuben Anderson Oral History, Civil Rights in Mississippi Digital Archive (first, second, and third quotations); author's interview with Reuben Anderson (fourth quotation). Reuben Anderson assisted Justice Department lawyers during the *Hinds* case as well.

41. Fairclough, *Race and Democracy*, 441.

CHAPTER FIVE

1. Kluger, *Simple Justice*, 763–66 (quotation on 766); Hodgson, *America in Our Time*, 451; Wolters, *Race and Education*, 143–44. Justice Douglas quoted in memorandum, October 29, 1969, box I: 220, folder 2, Brennan Papers, LOC. In 1968, Wallace won five Deep South states. For details on the politics of race in the careers of George Wallace and Richard Nixon, see Carter, *From George Wallace to Newt Gingrich*.

2. Safire, *Before the Fall*, 232 (quotations); Reichley, *Conservatives in an Age of Change*, 179; Wolters, *Race and Education*, 144.

3. Melvyn Leventhal quoted in Bolton, *The Hardest Deal of All*, 129. In 1972, Nixon followed up on his campaign to whiten the GOP below the Mason-Dixon Line and swept the whole South.

4. Schulman, *Seventies*, 36–37; Perlstein, *Nixonland*, 464; Hodgson, *America in Our Time*, 451; McMahon, *Nixon's Court*, 92–93; Read and McGough, *Let Them Be Judged*, 479; Davies, "Richard Nixon," 367.

5. McMahon, *Nixon's Court*, 92–93; Hodgson, *America in Our Time*, 451; Ackerman, *We the People*, 242–43.

6. Read and McGough, *Let Them Be Judged*, 480; Pacelle, *Between Law and Politics*, 110; Ackerman, *We the People*, 242–43; Reichley, *Conservatives in an Age of Change*, 180; Grose, *South Carolina at the Brink*, 270. Finch's choice of Panetta as the OCR director signaled the secretary's liberal leanings on race. Panetta had served as a legislative aide to former senator Thomas H. Kuchel, a progressive California Republican who pushed the 1964 Civil Rights Act and 1965 Voting Rights Act through the U.S. Senate (see Barker, *Federal Retreat in School Desegregation*, 5–6). Calling

Robert Finch a "liberal," in the Nixon scheme of things, really just meant "he wasn't an arch-conservative but would still do bad things," said Armand Derfner (author's interview with Armand Derfner).

7. Evans and Novak, *Nixon in the White House*, 171–72 (quotations); Hoff, *Nixon Reconsidered*, 84; Pacelle, *Between Law and Politics*, 110; Kotlowski, *Nixon's Civil Rights*, 27, 29; O'Reilly, *Nixon's Piano*, 299–300; Lyles, *Gatekeepers*, 94–95; Maxwell, *Indicted South*, 243; Mason, *Richard Nixon*, 52; Ackerman, *We the People*, 243; Clayton, *Politics of Justice*, 138. As Nixon's campaign manager, John Mitchell deployed the Southern Strategy, and one of his assistants, Kevin Phillips, popularized the Republican Party's new approach to race and the white South. For many liberals, Phillips put an analytical finger on a peculiar phenomenon—the melding between conservative blue-collar workers and white-shoe economic royalists (see Lawson, *Civil Rights Crossroads*, 127; Phillips, *Emerging Republican Majority*, 1969).

8. Kotlowski, *Nixon's Civil Rights*, 29 (first and second quotations); Hoff, *Nixon Reconsidered*, 84–85; Lyles, *Gatekeepers*, 95 (third quotation); Bass, *Unlikely Heroes*, 312; Rosen, *Strong Man*, 129–32. On May 15, Nixon sent Finch a one-page memo telling him to monitor desegregation plans "in such a manner as to be inoffensive to the people of South Carolina" (Reeves, *President Nixon*, 117). Under pressure from the president, Finch backed off terminating funds to implement school desegregation. Referring to integration in schools, he told one reporter, "You can't do it with a sledge hammer, and you can't do it overnight—without tearing a community to pieces" (Halpern, *On the Limits of the Law*, 85). Finch's stance indicated the administration's chary approach to desegregation.

9. Kotlowski, *Nixon's Civil Rights*, 29 (first quotation); McMahon, *Nixon's Court*, 94 (second quotation); Read and McGough, *Let Them Be Judged*, 480 (third quotation); Davies, "Richard Nixon," 372 (fourth quotation).

10. McMahon, *Nixon's Court*, 94 (first, second, and third quotations); Read and McGough, *Let Them Be Judged*, 481 (fourth, fifth, and sixth quotations); Barker, *Federal Retreat in School Desegregation*, 9 (seventh quotation); Reeves, *President Nixon*, 118; O'Reilly, *Nixon's Piano*, 300; Davies, "Richard Nixon," 371. Jerris Leonard got his appointment after running Nixon's campaign in Wisconsin. Upon Leonard's arrival in D.C., he sat down with the president and Attorney General Mitchell. Leonard asked Nixon for his marching orders, and the president replied: "Jerris, very simply, I want you to enforce the law, but I want you to use your head." Leonard "took that to mean . . . we had to be vigorous in enforcing the Civil Rights Laws, but we had to try to do it without rhetoric . . . try to bring about solutions rather than simply saying that, 'Well, we want another lawsuit'" (interview with Jerris Leonard, Eyes on the Prize Interviews, Henry Hampton Collection, Washington University, Washington University Libraries, Film and Media Archive, St. Louis, Mo.). Nixon also told Leonard, "Get that god damn school desegregation over before the '72 election" (Jere Nash interview with Jerris Leonard, Nash and Taggart Collection, University of Mississippi, J. D. Williams Library, Archives and Special Collections, Oxford). The president wanted race off the table as a political issue (see Davies, "Richard Nixon," 369).

11. McMahon, *Nixon's Court*, 94–95 (first quotation); Read and McGough, *Let Them Be Judged*, 481 (second, third, and fourth quotations); Panetta and Gall, *Bring Us Together*, 229; Ackerman, *We the People*, 243.

12. McMahon, *Nixon's Court*, 95; Read and McGough, *Let Them Be Judged*, 482 (first and third quotations); Reeves, *President Nixon*, 118 (second quotation); Reichley, *Conservatives in an Age of Change*, 184. Whatever their differences, Panetta held a grudging respect for John Mitchell. "He did not give us a runaround," Panetta later said. "Although it was not a position I agreed with, I admired him for being candid about his objectives." His boss, Robert Finch, however, "did not have strong philosophic convictions on the issue, one way or another," Panetta concluded. "He was under heavy pressure from the White House, and he wished chiefly to do what the White House wanted him to do" (Reichley, *Conservatives in an Age of Change*, 183–84). See also Rosen, *Strong Man*, 131.

13. Reichley, *Conservatives in an Age of Change*, 182–83 (third quotation); Langeveld and Langeveld, "The Downfall Dictionary," (first, second, and fourth quotations). Harry Dent literally wrote the book on the Southern Strategy. His 1978 memoir, *The Prodigal South Returns to Power*, claimed that the Southern Strategy was not about racism but returning the South to national political power. Toward the end of his life, Dent recanted and expressed regret about devising the racist strategy (see Hoff, *Nixon Reconsidered*, 79).

14. McMahon, *Nixon's Court*, 95 (quotations).

15. Kalk, *Origins of the Southern Strategy*, 91 (quotations).

16. Read and McGough, *Let Them Be Judged*, 483. A "pairing" plan designated specific locales in a city to pairs of black and white schools (see Bolton, *Hardest Deal of All*, 165).

17. John Stennis quoted in Reeves, *President Nixon*, 119; Perlstein, *Nixonland*, 465; Banks, "United States Court of Appeals for the Fifth Circuit," 278–79.

18. Smith, *Camille*, 31–32 (first quotation); Reeves, *President Nixon*, 119 (second quotation); Panetta and Gall, *Bring Us Together*, 382n58 (third quotation); interview with Charles Overby, John C. Stennis Oral History Project, Mississippi State University, University Libraries, Digital Collections, Starkville (fourth quotation); Ackerman, *We the People*, 244; Bass, *Unlikely Heroes*, 313. After the delivery of Stennis's letter to Nixon, there followed a telephone conference between the senator, Mitchell, Finch, and Laird (see Robert S. Allen and John A. Goldsmith, "Stennis Threat to Nixon Credited in Postponement," *LA*, September 25, 1961, 2). Pleased with the bargain, Senator Stennis voted to pass the antiballistic missile program. The bill scraped by the Senate 51 to 50 (see Kotlowski, *Nixon's Civil Rights*, 30–31).

19. Ackerman, *We the People*, 244; Irons, *Jim Crow's Children*, 205; Reeves, *President Nixon*, 119; Read and McGough, *Let Them Be Judged*, 483–84 (quotation on 484).

20. Bass, *Unlikely Heroes*, 313 (first quotation); Banks, "United States Court of Appeals for the Fifth Circuit," 279n20 (second quotation); Read and McGough, *Let Them Be Judged*, 484–85.

21. Reeves, *President Nixon*, 119; Ackerman, *We the People*, 244; Read and McGough, *Let Them Be Judged*, 484; Reichley, *Conservatives in an Age of Change*, 185;

author's interview with Armand Derfner. The HEW plans submitted to the court on August 11 had been prepared by professional educators who had spent time in each of the school districts. Finch never set foot in any of them to assess the situation (see Barker, *Federal Retreat in School Desegregation*, 34–35).

22. Reeves, *President Nixon*, 118 (first quotation); Read and McGough, *Let Them Be Judged*, 485 (second quotation); Reichley, *Conservatives in an Age of Change*, 181–82; Greenberg, "Revolt at Justice," 199–200. Within weeks of Finch's request for delay, three top officials in HEW, including Gregory R. Anrig, asked for and received reassignments. The loss of experienced professionals further undercut desegregation efforts and revealed mounting dissatisfaction with administrative policies on school integration (see Barker, *Federal Retreat in School Desegregation*, 34; *WP*, September 23, 1969).

23. Read and McGough, *Let Them Be Judged*, 485; Reed, "U.S. View Alienates the N.A.A.C.P. Fund On Pupil Integration," 24 (quotation); author's interviews with Melvyn Leventhal and Armand Derfner. Unlike Anrig, Jesse J. Jordan, a HEW regional director in Atlanta, and Howard Sullins, from HEW's regional branch in Charlottesville, Virginia, each agreed to testify for Leonard. Both ciphers got promotions soon thereafter. Neither official had worked on drafting the Mississippi desegregation plans (see Read and McGough, *Let Them Be Judged*, 485). For years after the August 25 hearing in Jackson, Jerris Leonard stuck with a fiction that the devastation of Hurricane Camille, not politics, blew in the administration's decision to delay school desegregation. He told one Mississippi interviewer, "Everything was going fine until Camille hit." Finch allegedly called Mitchell and said, "You gotta go down and postpone desegregation in Mississippi. There's no way this can be done when things are so in shambles." In his letter, however, Finch mentioned nothing about the tropical storm (Jere Nash interview with Jerris Leonard).

24. WLBT, August 28, 1969, MP 1980.01, WLBT Newsfilm Collection, MDAH (first quotation); Read and McGough, *Let Them Be Judged*, 485 (second quotation); Bass, *Unlikely Heroes*, 313–14 (third quotation); Irons, *Jim Crow's Children*, 205; Woodward and Armstrong, *Brethren*, 37; Perlstein, *Nixonland*, 464–65.

25. Reed, "U.S. View Alienates the N.A.A.C.P. Fund on Pupil Integration," 24 (first quotation); Wilkinson, *From Brown to Bakke*, 119 (second and third quotations); *NYT*, September 3, 1969; Banks, "United States Court of Appeals for the Fifth Circuit," 279n19; Barker, *Federal Retreat in School Desegregation*, 31.

26. Read and McGough, *Let Them Be Judged*, 485–86, 490. According to Read and McGough, Finch's intrusive letter "boomeranged. It resulted in more integration, not less, and in more 'do it now' orders, not more deliberation. It destroyed Secretary Finch's strong civil rights reputation and led to his eventual resignation as HEW secretary. It also led to charges that in domestic affairs there were no matters, not even the civil rights of black children, that were not 'up for sale' by a politically sensitive administration" (Read and McGough, *Let Them Be Judged*, 491).

27. Woodward and Armstrong, *Brethren*, 39 (quotation); Durr, *Outside the Magic Circle*, 307.

28. Woodward and Armstrong, *Brethren*, 39, 61–62. See also Suitts, *Hugo Black of*

Alabama, chap. 1, 88, 428–32; Newman, *Hugo Black*, 601. Carrying over from the Warren Court, the justices voted unanimously on civil rights matters, especially involving school segregation (see Ball, *Murder in Mississippi*, 104). Historian David Garrow
disagreed with Suitts's and Newman's rosy depiction of Black's conversion on race.
Garrow deemed Hugo Black one of the least praiseworthy justices of the twentieth
century—"simple-minded" and "supposedly liberal"—who never adequately atoned
for his Klan membership or private racism (Garrow, "Doing Justice," 280). "When
he lived in Alabama," wisecracked Thomas Noland, Hugo Black "wore a white robe
and scared the blacks to death. When he got to Washington, he wore a black robe and
scared the whites to death" (Noland, "Dying Memory of Hugo Black"). Doing some
basic psychoanalysis, Justice Black probably joined so many path-breaking decisions
from *Brown* through *Alexander* to redeem himself. Black, however, never completely
transcended his racial prejudices, as most people of his generation failed to do. It is
inconclusive whether he ever endorsed social equality, a step beyond civil rights,
for African Americans. Growing up in rural Alabama allowed for only so much personal growth on race. If any single factor or person changed his beliefs, it probably
resulted from his marriage to Josephine Foster, the sister of racial liberal Virginia
Foster Durr (see Durr, *Outside the Magic Circle*). Mills Thornton attributed Hugo
Black's egalitarianism to his study and embrace of Jeffersonian democracy and civil
libertarianism (see Thornton, *Archipelagoes of My South*, 148–62).

29. Patterson, Brown v. Board of Education, 148, 152–53; Schwartz, *The Unpublished Opinions of the Burger Court*, 5 (quotation); Tushnet, "Supreme Court," 481n47.
When Burger came on the bench, the reformist justices worried about him on civil
rights. Earl Warren's vacancy had already left a void that many had doubted Burger
could ever fill. With Abe Fortas's departure, the Court was missing another strong
liberal voice. Burger, however, had a credible record on race. Before his elevation to
Chief Justice, he served on an appellate court panel that ruled against Mississippi's
largest and racist television station, WLBT in Jackson. The panel's ruling blocked
renewal of WLBT's license for failure to serve the region's black community (see
Ernest Holsendolph, "Blacks May Soon Direct Big Mississippi TV Station," *NYT*,
November 20, 1978, 23; Mills, *Changing Channels*, 101–3).

30. Read and McGough, *Let Them Be Judged*, 486 (second quotation); Bass, *Unlikely Heroes*, 313–14 (first and third quotations); Wasby, D'Amato, and Metrailer, *Desegregation from Brown to Alexander*, 399 (fourth quotation); Woodward and Armstrong, *Brethren*, 36 and 39–40; Tushnet, *Making Constitutional Law*, 71; Schwartz,
Swann's Way, 68; application to vacate suspension order, box 47, "CCA Rehearing En
Banc" folder, John C. Satterfield/American Bar Association Collection, University of
Mississippi, J. D. Williams Library, Archives and Special Collections, Oxford. Each
member of the Supreme Court was assigned to one or more of the eleven federal
appellate courts and responsible for dealing with special and emergency appeals. In
Hugo Black's appellatory capacity as supervisory justice, any motion filed in a case
from any state within the Fifth Circuit was automatically assigned to him for consideration and disposition. On September 5, Justice Black denied the motion to vacate the postponement that the Fifth Circuit had entered. Black, however, instantly

recognized "the administration's move as Nixon's payoff to the South," wrote journalist Bob Woodward (Woodward and Armstrong, *Brethren*, 37). See also author's interview with Melvyn Leventhal.

31. Read and McGough, *Let Them Be Judged*, 488 (first quotation), 489 (second quotation); "Nixon Denies School 'Deal' with Stennis," *Delta Democrat Times*, September 26, 1969, 1 (third quotation); Perlstein, *Nixonland*, 464–65; Reeves, *President Nixon*, 131. Other observers took a different perspective on the deal between Nixon and Stennis. Ultimately, Stennis could only postpone but not prevent school desegregation. Hazel Brannon Smith's *Lexington Advertiser* acknowledged, "While the publicity in his home state serves the senator's short-term interests, it has created another problem. Now that it has been reported . . . that Stennis forced the President to back down, it will be pretty hard for Nixon to accommodate Stennis again when the new deadline rolls around. Like the vaudevillian at a loss for an encore, the senator will really have to pull a rabbit from his hat when the 90-day extension expires" (Smith quoted in Allen and Goldsmith, "Stennis Threat to Nixon Credited in Postponement," 2). Richard Nixon's ambiguity on desegregation tended to muddy policy issues and sent mixed signals from Washington. As a result, the pursuit of real integration lumbered along awkwardly and tentatively. Thus began what Nixon's in-house liberal intellectual, Daniel Patrick Moynihan, summed up as the administration's "schizophrenic" conduct on desegregation (Rosen, *Strong Man*, 130). For months, Nixon ducked the hard questions and hedged his bets on civil rights to placate the millions of moderate and suburban Republicans who helped put him in the White House. The enigmatic Nixon prolonged the mystery about his own stance until late September 1969, when he announced at a White House news conference a "middle course" between the "two extremes" of "instant integration" and "segregation forever" (Hodgson, *America in Our Time*, 451). An uncanny political animal, Nixon "sensed that most moderates would agree with him," noted historian Raymond Wolters, and even diehard segregationists "would understand that Nixon's position would salvage as much as was possible in the circumstances" (Wolters, *Race and Education*, 144). See also Barker, *Federal Retreat in School Desegregation*, 68; Langeveld and Langeveld, "The Downfall Dictionary"; Read and McGough, *Let Them Be Judged*, 480; Grose, *South Carolina at the Brink*, 270.

32. Greenberg, "Revolt at Justice," 195–97 (quotations); Jack Anderson, "Mitchell Warns 'Rights' Lawyers"; Douglas, *Reading, Writing, and Race*, 163–64.

33. Greenberg, "Revolt at Justice," 197–98 (quotations).

34. Greenberg, 204–5 (quotations).

35. Greenberg, 205–6 (quotations); Delmont, *Why Busing Failed*, 121.

36. Greenberg, "Revolt at Justice," 206–7. "Boomerang" plays on Read and McGough's description of the events leading up to Finch's delay request (see Read and McGough, *Let Them Be Judged*, 491).

37. Wilkinson, *From Brown to Bakke*, 119; Greenberg, "Revolt at Justice," 207 (quotation); Barker, *Federal Retreat in School Desegregation*, 4–5.

38. Greenberg, "Revolt at Justice," 207–8; "Nixon Aide Warns Quick Integration Can't Be Enforced," *NYT*, September 29, 1969; O'Reilly, *Nixon's Piano*, 299.

39. Greenberg, "Revolt at Justice," 207–8 (first quotation); Ackerman, *We the People*, 245 (second quotation); Halpern, *On the Limits of the Law*, 89 (third quotation); Clayton, *Politics of Justice*, 139; "Nixon Aide Warns Quick Integration Can't Be Enforced." California's *Sacramento Bee* upbraided Leonard for his "asserted inability to enforce the law of the land. Seen in its simplest terms, it is a surrender of law to social anarchy" ("High Court Refuses to Go Along with More Desegregation Delays," *Sacramento Bee*, October 15, 1969).

40. Greenberg, "Revolt at Justice," 208–9 (first, second, and fourth quotations); Barker, *Federal Retreat in School Desegregation*, 32–34; Jack Anderson, "Mitchell Warns 'Rights' Lawyers," 12 (third quotation); Ed Rogers, "Nixon's 'Southern Strategy' on Schools," *LA*, October 1, 1969, 2 (fifth quotation). In 1998, Jerris Leonard told one interviewer that his decision to purge the lawyers in the Civil Rights Division would ensure that they "would not treat [desegregation] as a *carte blanche* for them to run wild through the South enforcing compliance with extreme or punitive requirements they had formulated in Washington" (Pacelle, *Between Law and Politics*, 115). See also "Leonard Defends U.S. School Policy," *NYT*, October 2, 1969. After Gary Greenberg's stilted resignation, another head rolled in the Civil Rights Division. The administration also expelled the revolt's other rebel leader—John Nixon.

41. McMahon, *Nixon's Court*, 96 (quotation); Ackerman, *We the People*, 245; "Civil Rights: The Apologist," 77. In a bipartisan gesture, Lyndon Johnson appointed Griswold, a moderate Republican, as solicitor general. He held the job from 1967 until 1973 (see Dennis Hevesi, "Erwin Griswold Is Dead at 90; Served as a Solicitor General," *NYT*, November 21, 1994).

42. Greenberg, *Crusaders in the Courts*, 384 (quotations); author's interview with Melvyn Zarr. Jerris Leonard acquired a pathetically low reputation among civil rights lawyers. Gary Greenberg later wrote of him, "He was insensitive to the problems of black citizens and other minority-group victims of discrimination. Almost from the beginning, he distrusted the attorneys he found in the Division. He demonstrated that distrust by isolating himself from the line attorneys. Still another element was the shock of his ineptitude as a lawyer. In marked contrast to the distinguished lawyers who had preceded him in his job, Leonard lacked the intellectual equipment to deal with . . . legal problems" (Greenberg, "Revolt at Justice," 199). Mel Zarr likened Jerris Leonard to a toady for John Mitchell. According to Zarr, Leonard was "no John Doar. John Doar had been a legal scholar as well as a legal practitioner" (author's interview with Melvyn Zarr). Doar, a Wisconsinite, like Leonard, joined the Civil Rights Division under Eisenhower and served under Kennedy and Johnson. Involved in local negotiations and litigation in the South, he was known as a friend of the civil rights movement. The description of Doar derives from copious sources that mention him and praise his work.

43. Greenberg, *Crusaders in the Courts*, 385; "Civil Rights: The Apologist," 81; Woodward and Armstrong, *Brethren*, 40; Jack Greenberg Oral History, LOC. Even from afar, Judge Harold Cox could put a crimp in the LDF's preparations for Court. When asked to send the case records to the Supreme Court, Cox's clerk refused unless the LDF paid fifty cents per page for thousands of pages. Jack Greenberg then

asked John F. Davis, the clerk of the Supreme Court, to intervene and order Cox's clerk to mail the records. The clerk obeyed and shipped eight boxes to D.C. (see Greenberg, *Crusaders in the Court*, 385). A "writ of certiorari" means a lawyer petitions the court to hear a case. Under the Supreme Court's internal rules, four votes—one less than a majority—are required to consider a case.

44. Author's interviews with Melvyn Leventhal (quotation) and Melvyn Zarr; Wasby, *Race Relations Litigation*, 64. Mel Leventhal later confessed he was momentarily "in the dumpster" when Jack Greenberg took over as direct counsel. Leventhal hoped to be second chair to Greenberg, but he never expected to argue the case in Court. The LDF's mastermind, Greenberg, "of course" should handle oral arguments, Leventhal said (author's interview with Melvyn Leventhal). LDF staff attorney Mel Zarr and Yale law professor Charles L. Black Jr. helped Leventhal prepare the brief and Greenberg for *Alexander*. Black, a native of Austin, Texas, taught constitutional law at Columbia and Yale, possessed an adroit legal mind, and worked alongside the LDF for decades. Years earlier, he and Thurgood Marshall crafted the brief for *Brown* (see Robert D. McFadden, "Charles L. Black, Jr., 85, Constitutional Law Expert Who Wrote on Impeachment, Dies," *NYT*, May 8, 2001).

45. Wasby, *Race Relations Litigation*, 64, 267; "Civil Rights: The Apologist," 77. After graduating from Yale Law, Oberdorfer clerked for fellow Alabamian justice Hugo Black. Oberdorfer was very bright and worked as a corporate lawyer before serving in the Justice Department during the Kennedy administration (see author's interview with Armand Derfner; Matt Schudel, "Louis F. Oberdorfer, Federal Judge in D.C. Court," *WP*, February 23, 2013).

46. "Civil Rights: The Apologist," 81 (first quotation); Crespino, *Strom Thurmond's America*, 233 (second quotation); Morris, *Yazoo*, 72–73 (third quotation); *New York Times*, box 47, "School Material" folder, John C. Satterfield/American Bar Association Collection (fourth quotation). Friends and colleagues described Satterfield as a thorough lawyer, a consummate southern gentleman who would doff his hat to women, and a man who loved telling stories and joking. He even collected jokes in a little book that he carried. Satterfield also kept extremely busy. He typically worked seven days a week, even after church. In briefs, he insisted on citations and precedents. There had to be a platform and a basis for everything presented in court (see author's interview with Thomas L. Kirkland Jr.).

47. Morris, *Yazoo*, 71–72; Satterfield, "Law and Lawyers in a Changing World," 922 (quotation). Only a respected and intelligent lawyer could become president of the American Bar Association. Satterfield met both criteria. "He wasn't just a Mississippi lawyer," said an associate who worked with Satterfield in the late 1970s. "He was a lawyer of great stature, a legendary lawyer, and a legal scholar" (author's interview with Thomas L. Kirkland Jr.). Satterfield held himself and others to high professional standards, but his ideological convictions also revealed a deep commitment to defending southern traditions.

48. Author's interview with Reuben Anderson (first quotation); Eagles, *Price of Defiance*, 328; Greenberg, *Crusaders in the Courts*, 326–27 (second quotation), 385–86.

49. Motion to dismiss and memorandum brief in response to motion for summary

reversal by the plaintiffs-appellants (*Harris v. Yazoo*) at 19, box 4160, Record Group 276, Records of the U.S. Court of Appeals Fifth Circuit.

50. Amicus curiae brief, box 9477, folder 632 OT 1969, Record Group 267, Records of the U.S. Supreme Court, National Archives and Records Administration, Washington, D.C. (quotations). John Karl "Jack" Kershaw went on to defend James Earl Ray, Martin Luther King's assassin. Kershaw represented Ray after his June 1977 prison break and concocted a bogus story that a mysterious figure named "Raul" had actually killed King. Kershaw argued that Ray was merely an unwitting participant in a conspiracy (see Douglas Martin, "Jack Kershaw Is Dead at 96; Challenged Conviction in King's Death," *NYT*, September 24, 2010).

CHAPTER SIX

1. Schwartz, *Swann's Way*, 68; Woodward and Armstrong, *Brethren*, 41; Greenberg, *Crusaders in the Court*, 386; Stern and Wermiel, *Justice Brennan*, 332; court transcript, box I: 220, folder 2, Brennan Papers, LOC. In October 1969, only eight justices sat on the bench. Nixon had not yet replaced Abe Fortas, who had resigned in May 1969. In the fall of 1969, Nixon nominated South Carolinian Clement Haynsworth to the Supreme Court, but Congress blocked his appointment (see Perlstein, *Nixonland*, 465). Typically, the Court allotted only an hour for oral arguments. In *Alexander*, considerable questioning punctuated the counsels' arguments (see Wasby, D'Amato, and Metrailer, *Desegregation from* Brown *to* Alexander, 400).

2. Woodward and Armstrong, *Brethren*, 41; Irons, *Jim Crow's Children*, 206; Wasby, D'Amato, and Metrailer, *Desegregation from* Brown *to* Alexander, 401; court transcript, box I: 220, folder 2, Brennan Papers (first quotation); Greenberg, *Crusaders in the Courts*, 386 (second and third quotations). By the time the Supreme Court heard *Alexander*, "everything was just legal stuff and already on record," explained Mel Zarr. "Nobody needed to come and testify from Holmes. No new evidence was being introduced. They were simply going over trod legal ground and getting the Court to enforce immediate desegregation and the prior rulings" (see author's interview with Melvyn Zarr).

3. Woodward and Armstrong, *Brethren*, 41; Bass, *Unlikely Heroes*, 314; court transcript, box I: 220, folder 2, Brennan Papers (quotations). While preparing for Court, the LDF staff batted about whether to press the justices for a remand order to the Fifth Circuit. Ordinarily, the case would revert to the district court. Dismayed by that prospect, Mel Leventhal feared Cox, Nixon, and Russell "would figure out a way to screw us." At that point, Charles Black hit upon a novel idea: "Why don't we ask the Court to direct jurisdiction away from the Southern District?" Leventhal was dumbstruck. His mind kept telling him that, given precedent, the lower court would oversee any implementation order. "No way," Black reassured him in his Texas drawl. In oral arguments, Jack Greenberg followed Black's suggestion and asked the Court to grant the Fifth Circuit judicature. The bench complied. Leventhal praised Black's command of the psychology of the law: "He understood where the Court was historically and that they were way out ahead. The Justices were ready to end the era of 'all

deliberate speed'" (author's interview with Melvyn Leventhal). See also Robert D. McFadden, "Charles L. Black, Jr., 85, Constitutional Law Expert Who Wrote on Impeachment, Dies," *NYT*, May 8, 2001.

4. Wasby, D'Amato, and Metrailer, *Desegregation from* Brown *to* Alexander, 399, 401; court transcript, box I: 220, folder 2, Brennan Papers (quotations).

5. Court transcript, box I: 220, folder 2, Brennan Papers, (quotations).

6. Court transcript, (quotations); Woodward and Armstrong, *Brethren*, 42; Schwartz, *Swann's Way*, 86; Wasby, D'Amato, and Metrailer, *Desegregation from* Brown *to* Alexander, 402.

7. Court transcript, box I: 220, folder 2, Brennan Papers (quotation). Justice Marshall referred to the earlier Court opinion in *Cooper v. Aaron*—the Little Rock school case. *Cooper v. Aaron* was the first time in the history of the Court in which all nine justices cosigned as authors to emphasize their unity in demanding that Little Rock (and Governor Orval Faubus) yield to the requirements of the federal constitution (see *Cooper v. Aaron*, 358 U.S. 1 (1958)). The 1968 *Green* decision was unanimous as well, but only Justice Brennan signed as its author.

8. Court transcript, box I: 220, folder 2, Brennan Papers (quotations); Woodward and Armstrong, *Brethren*, 42. Woodward and Armstrong provided a riveting behind-the-scenes account of the Court's proceedings and deliberations in the *Alexander* decision. The typed court transcript is available at the Library of Congress.

9. Court transcript, box I: 220, folder 2, Brennan Papers (quotations); Greenberg, *Crusaders in the Courts*, 386; Wasby, D'Amato, and Metrailer, *Desegregation from* Brown *to* Alexander, 403. Satterfield believed that whenever you win something in court, it is time to leave immediately. Perhaps his last-ditch maneuvers were a way to get a minor concession from the Court in a losing situation (see author's interview with Thomas L. Kirkland Jr.).

10. Greenberg, *Crusaders in the Courts*, 386 (first quotation); court transcript, box I: 220, folder 2, Brennan Papers (second and third quotations). Greenberg quoted a famous dissent by Justice Wiley Blount Rutledge. In 1943, Franklin Roosevelt appointed Rutledge to the Supreme Court. A reliably liberal justice and ardent defender of the Fourteenth Amendment's "equal protection" clause, Rutledge dissented in *Yamashita v. Styer* (1946). Japanese general Tomoyuki Yamashita filed for habeas corpus to appeal his conviction for war crimes in World War II (see "Justice Wiley Rutledge Dies of Brain Hemorrhage at 55," *NYT*, September 11, 1949). Justice Byron White may have squirmed a bit in his seat at the uttering of Cox's name. In 1961, as Robert Kennedy's deputy attorney general, he recommended Cox for the district court (see Bass, *Unlikely Heroes*, 149, 168).

11. Woodward and Armstrong, *Brethren*, 43 (quotation); Schwartz, *Swann's Way*, 69. The "all deliberate speed" language derived from a draft decree in *Brown II* written by Justice Felix Frankfurter. Frankfurter argued for leeway in implementing school desegregation. Otherwise, the Court might push white southern society too far, too fast. Hugo Black, on the other hand, did not want to shunt off desegregation. Unlike the Viennese-born Frankfurter, who never lived in the American South, Black knew that any discretion from the Court would only encourage white

southerners to sidestep meaningful desegregation. The Court needed a strong implementation order. Black's foresight proved prescient. Except for dramatic instances of overt resistance, southern school districts proceeded as they saw fit (see Newman, *Hugo Black*, 440; Klarman, "How *Brown* Changed Race Relations," 81, 84, 103–5; Feldman, *Scorpions*, 376–85).

12. Tushnet, *Making Constitutional Law*, 71; Schwartz, *Swann's Way*, 69; Woodward and Armstrong, *Brethren*, 43.

13. Patterson, Brown v. Board of Education, 153–54 (quotation); Schwartz, *Swann's Way*, 69–70; Tushnet, *Making Constitutional Law*, 71; Woodward and Armstrong, *Brethren*, 44–47. Paul Brest, who clerked for Harlan the year before *Alexander* arrived in the Supreme Court, described the justice as a conservative in the older sense of the term. Harlan usually deferred to states' rights in the tradition of Felix Frankfurter, but he was sympathetic to desegregation (see author's interview with Paul Brest). Burger was probably so agreeable in the conference discussions because liberals outnumbered him. In his first few years on the Court, Burger had not yet emerged as a conservative leader. Not until Justices Lewis Powell and William Rehnquist joined the Court did Burger deviate from civil rights causes. Rehnquist, in particular, taught Burger to move right on race. In 1952, as one of Justice Robert Jackson's clerks, Rehnquist wrote an infamous advisory memo titled "A Random Thought on the Segregation Cases" that defended *Plessy v. Ferguson*, the 1896 ruling in which the Supreme Court upheld the constitutionality of a Louisiana statute that required separate but equal accommodations for whites and blacks on railroad cars (see Kluger, *Simple Justice*, 605; Kennedy, "Ackerman's *Brown*").

14. Patterson, Brown v. Board of Education, 153–54 (first quotation); Stern and Wermiel, *Justice Brennan*, 333–34; Tushnet, *Making Constitutional Law*, 71–73; Schwartz, *Swann's Way*, 70–75; Black's dissent, box 428, folder 5, Hugo LaFayette Black Papers, LOC (hereafter cited as Black Papers); memorandum, October 26, 1969, box I: 220, folder 2, Brennan Papers (remaining quotations).

15. Patterson, Brown v. Board of Education, 153–54; Schwartz, *Swann's Way*, 76–86 (first quotation on 84); Stern and Wermiel, *Justice Brennan*, 333–34; Woodward and Armstrong, *Brethren*, 42–56; Tushnet, *Making Constitutional Law*, 71–74 (second quotation on 73). Hugo Black admitted that no one on the bench actually thought desegregation would happen by an exact cutoff date. The Court's best hope was to pronounce "all deliberate speed" dead, use the word "immediate," and support the lower courts (Tushnet, *Making Constitutional Law*, 72–73).

16. Opinion of the Court in *Alexander v. Holmes County Board of Education* (1969), (quotations at 20); Bass, *Unlikely Heroes*, 314–15; Wilkinson, *From* Brown *to* Bakke, 119–20; Irons, *Jim Crow's Children*, 206; Read, "Judicial Evolution," 31n105; Fairclough, *Race and Democracy*, 443; Wasby, D'Amato, and Metrailer, *Desegregation from* Brown *to* Alexander, 406; "Notes on *Alexander v. Holmes*," box I: 220, folder 2, Brennan Papers; Harlan memo, box 428, folder 5, Black Papers. Effective forthwith, *Alexander* relegated "all deliberate speed" to the jurisprudential junk heap.

17. *JCL*, October 30, 1969, 14A (first, second, and seventh quotations); Patterson,

Brown v. Board of Education, 154 (third and fourth quotations); "Court Refuses Delay in School Integration," *San Diego Union*, October 30, 1969, A1 (fifth quotation); author's interview with Reuben Anderson (sixth quotation); Banks, "United States Court of Appeals for the Fifth Circuit," 279 (eighth quotation). Norman Amaker appeared beside Mel Leventhal in Jackson's federal district court when Jerris Leonard made the motion to delay school desegregation. Otherwise, Amaker rarely argued cases in Mississippi and played little role in *Alexander* or any of the affiliated school desegregation cases in Mississippi. Jack Greenberg decided to send Amaker, one of his two top deputies, to add gravitas to the case. Leventhal briefed Amaker and primarily handled the presentation of the case that day in court (see author's interview with Melvyn Leventhal).

18. *JCL*, October 30, 1969, 14A (first quotation); "Civil Rights: The Apologist," 77 (second quotation).

19. Kotlowski, *Nixon's Civil Rights*, 31 (first quotation); McMahon, *Nixon's Court*, 96–97 (second quotation); Ackerman, *We the People*, 246; Reichley, *Conservatives in an Age of Change*, 182–85 (third and fourth quotations on 185); Barker, *Federal Retreat in School Desegregation*, 67–68. Both Mardian and Gray had forcefully extolled the administration's position on the school delays. Nixon rewarded Mardian by promoting him to assistant attorney general when Jerris Leonard stepped down (see Hodgson, *America in Our Time*, 451; O'Reilly, *Nixon's Piano*, 302–3).

20. "Yes, Virginia, There Is a Constitution," *Newsweek*, November 10, 1969, 35 (first quotation); Woodward and Armstrong, *Brethren*, 56 (second quotation).

21. Grose, *South Carolina at the Brink*, 274–75 (first quotation); McMahon, *Nixon's Court*, 96–97; Woodward and Armstrong, *Brethren*, 56 (second, third, and sixth quotations); Patterson, Brown v. Board of Education, 154 (fourth and fifth quotations); "'Public Schools' Future Pondered," *Delta Democrat Times*, November 2, 1969, 2 (seventh quotation); Simmons, "Black Wednesday," 2 (eighth quotation); Bolton, *William F. Winter*, 151; unknown author and date, "Jingle Bus," box 428, folder 6, Black Papers (ninth quotation); Kalk, *Origins of the Southern Strategy*, 92; Kotlowski, *Nixon's Civil Rights*, 31–32; Halpern, *On the Limits of the Law*, 92; O'Reilly, *Nixon's Piano*, 296–97. White House adviser John Ehrlichman shared Dent's enthusiasm about a surge of southern support: "The President is looking good down in Dixie because the Supreme Court shot him down with the state of Mississippi" (Lassiter, *Silent Majority*, 244).

22. *JCL*, October 30, 1969, 1 (first and second quotations), 14A; A. F. Summer quoted in WLBT, October 27, 1969, MP 1980.01, WLBT Newsfilm Collection, MDAH; Jerry DeLaughter, "Stunning, but What Will It Mean?," *Memphis Commercial Appeal*, November 1, 1969 (fourth quotation).

23. Hodding Carter, "The Inevitable Occurs," *Delta Democrat Times*, November 2, 1969, 6A (quotation).

24. Hazel Brannon Smith, *LA*, October 30 (quotation) and November 13, 1969. Smith provided lively coverage of the decision, whereas the *Holmes County Herald* waited nearly two weeks to comment on *Alexander* and offered only a blasé account (see *Holmes County Herald*, November 13, 1969, 1).

CHAPTER SEVEN

1. Du Bois, "Does the Negro Need Separate Schools?," 328–29 (first and second quotations), 330–31 (third quotation); Patterson, Brown v. Board of Education, 8–9; Lewis, *W. E. B. Du Bois: The Fight for Equality and the American Century, 1919–1963*, 2. Du Bois's objections to integrated education had support among lawyers who later worked on school desegregation cases in the 1960s. Derrick Bell, a Harvard law professor and former LDF litigator, argued that blacks would have been better served if the Supreme Court in 1954 moved to enforce the "separate but equal" doctrine rather than mandate integrated education (see Bell, *Silent Covenants*). On the mid-1930s as a turning point in Du Bois's thinking, see Lewis, *W. E. B. Du Bois: A Reader*, 5–6.

2. Du Bois, "Does the Negro Need Separate Schools?," 329 (first quotation); Kluger, *Simple Justice*, 691 (second quotation); Wolters, *Race and Education*, 38.

3. NAACP quoted in Minchin and Salmond, *After the Dream*, 83; Banks, "United States Court of Appeals for the Fifth Circuit," 282 (second quotation); Bolton, *Hardest Deal of All*, 166; Wolters, *Race and Education*, 38. Litigation to achieve school integration may not have improved black education, but, as Charles Bolton has reminded scholars, neither did southern educational equalization programs (see Bolton, "Mississippi's School Equalization Program," 781–82).

4. Bass, *Unlikely Heroes*, 315; Wilkinson, *From Brown to Bakke*, 120 (quotations); author's interview with Melvyn Zarr; Irons, *Jim Crow's Children*, 206–7; Barker, *Federal Retreat in School Desegregation*, 64–65; court reporter's transcript, November 6, 1969, box 4163, folder #28030 and 28042, Record Group 276, Records of the U.S. Court of Appeals Fifth Circuit, National Archives and Records Administration—Southwest Region, Fort Worth, Tex. In conference, Judges John Minor Wisdom and Irving Goldberg warned the other judges that the Supreme Court would not allow any more delays on integration, but neither of them dissented. They knew the high court would reverse the Fifth Circuit (see Bass, *Unlikely Heroes*, 315). It seems that neither the LDF nor Mississippi state officials were pleased with the en banc hearing. On November 21, Attorney General A. F. Summer, who appeared before the Fifth Circuit alongside John Satterfield, petitioned the judges for a rehearing. In his defense petition, Summer wrote, "Being completely frank with this Court, when the announcement was made from the bench at the pre-order conference . . . the attorneys present were so stunned they were in a state of mental shock and literally speechless. The order entered here has dealt a crippling blow to public education in the United States. It is resulting in untold waste of human resources. Chaos and confusion exist in the education of thousands of children" (Petition for rehearing en banc by the Court of Appeals for the Fifth Circuit, November 1969, box 4163, folder #28030 and 28042, Record Group 276, Records of the U.S. Court of Appeals Fifth Circuit).

5. Read, "Judicial Evolution," 31–32 (first quotation on 32; third quotation on 32n106); Wilkinson, *From Brown to Bakke*, 120 (second quotation); Irons, *Jim Crow's Children*, 206–7; Bass, *Unlikely Heroes*, 315; *Carter v. West Feliciana Parish School Board*, 396 U.S. 290 (1970) (per curiam).

6. Dillard, "Bell," 59 (quotation); Banks, "United States Court of Appeals for the Fifth Circuit," 279n25; Bass, *Unlikely Heroes*, 162; Bolton, *Hardest Deal of All*, 195. Griffin Bell helped initiate the Sibley hearings to desegregate Atlanta's public schools and became a storied figure in Georgia politics. On the Sibley Commission, see Roche, *Restructured Resistance*, 90–94, 158–59. For the most part, Bell was a middle-of-the-road judge on race. He was nowhere near John Minor Wisdom and the other crusading judges on the Fifth Circuit, but he also was not in league with many of Nixon's right-wing court appointees.

7. Bass, *Unlikely Heroes*, 162–64; Dillard, "Bell,"60 (quotations); Bolton, *Hardest Deal of All*, 195. Bolton noted a record of mixed success for school districts that used biracial committees. In Hattiesburg, Mississippi, for instance, the black-majority committee got bogged down in multiple and sometimes conflicting desegregation plans. In Greenville, the education committee "was mere window dressing, adopted by a school board under duress." Whites dominated the Greenville school board and maintained single-race schools as long as possible (Bolton, *Hardest Deal of All*, 196–97).

8. Dillard, "Bell"; Banks, "United States Court of Appeals for the Fifth Circuit," 279–80; Aronow, "Special Master in School Desegregation Cases," 743–44, 756–75; author's interviews with Fred L. Banks Jr. and Melvyn Leventhal.

9. White, *Alice Walker*, 157; Banks, "United States Court of Appeals for the Fifth Circuit," 277n14; author's interview with Reuben Anderson. In June 1967, the Supreme Court invalidated segregation at the marriage altar. Striking down state miscegenation laws allowed Leventhal and Walker to move to Mississippi. In August 1970, Roger Mills, a LDF summer intern, and Berta Linson, a black student at Jackson State University, became the first interracial couple to marry legally in Mississippi (see Spriggs, *Voices of Civil Rights Lawyers*, 94–96). Alice Walker and Mel Leventhal endured constant harassment but found some solace among friends in Jackson's small liberal community. For additional home security, the couple kept dogs. They owned a mutt, Myshkin, named for an incorruptible character in Dostoyevsky's novel *The Idiot*. After someone stole Myshkin, they adopted Andrew, a German shepherd. Just weeks after the *Alexander* ruling, Alice Walker gave birth to their daughter, Rebecca. In 1976, the couple divorced amicably (see White, *Alice Walker*, 135–36, 157–58, 179, 280). In the spring of 1978, Mel Leventhal left the NAACP LDF to join President Jimmy Carter's administration as deputy director of the Office of Civil Rights in the Department of Health, Education, and Welfare. Today, he practices law in New York City and is an op-ed contributor to the *New York Times*. In 1973, Marian Wright Edelman founded the Children's Defense Fund. She continues to advocate for children's rights, the poor and homeless, and people with disabilities.

10. Author's interview with Reuben Anderson; Runnels, "Trailblazers of the Mississippi Legal Frontier," 15–16; Banks, "United States Court of Appeals for the Fifth Circuit," 277n14; Reuben Anderson Oral History, Civil Rights in Mississippi Digital Archive, University of Southern Mississippi, Hattiesburg; Zarr, "Recollections of My Time in the Civil Rights Movement," 375. It was standard LDF practice for fresh batches of African-American lawyers to spend a year in New York City, hone their

legal skills, and then join a law practice in the South. New York was boot camp for becoming a civil rights lawyer. From 1963 to 1969, Mel Zarr worked for the LDF. His job in Mississippi, as he understood it, was to make himself "superfluous." He "didn't want to be another carpetbagger who just came and went—Southern blacks needed to stand their own on the ground. The Reubens [Andersons] of the world would take over." The LDF's business in Mississippi was to go out of business, so to speak (author's interview with Melvyn Zarr). After Marian Wright left Jackson, Leventhal and Anderson became the local LDF staff attorneys. Their office conducted almost all of the LDF work in Mississippi, with occasional help from the national office in the appellate courts. Reuben Anderson enjoyed a long and distinguished judicial career in Mississippi. In 1981, he became a state circuit judge. In 1985, Governor William Allain appointed Anderson as the first African-American supreme court justice in Mississippi. He served until 1991. Today, Anderson is a senior partner with Phelps Dunbar, LLP, in Jackson.

11. Charles Bolton interview with Fred Banks, Civil Rights in Mississippi Digital Archive (quotations); author's interview with Fred L. Banks Jr.; Runnels, "Trailblazers of the Mississippi Legal Frontier," 15; Banks, "United States Court of Appeals for the Fifth Circuit," 277. Fred Banks's family also experienced racial violence and tragedy. In July 1938, a white mob lynched Claude Banks, Fred's uncle, in Canton, Mississippi. Earlier in the day, a white man claimed to have been attacked and robbed by an African-American man. Local whites, including the police, set up a roadblock and ambushed Claude Banks in his car. Without warning, they shot him. Law enforcement arrested no suspects for the murder (see Payne, *I've Got the Light of Freedom*, 12). During the early 1970s, Banks, Anderson, and Leventhal opened the state's first interracial law firm in Jackson. In 1971, they hired Nausead Stewart, an Ole Miss law graduate, and John A. Nichols, a 1968 graduate of Emory University Law School. Stewart was the second black woman to graduate from the Ole Miss law school and the first African-American student to serve on the law journal. In 1970, Leventhal, Anderson, Banks, and Nichols started a private firm—the state's first integrated law firm (see Banks, "United States Court of Appeals for the Fifth Circuit," 277n14). In 1976, Banks entered politics and joined Robert Clark in the state legislature. From 1991 to 2001, he served on the Mississippi Supreme Court. After Banks stepped down, he resumed private practice and is currently a senior partner at Phelps Dunbar, LLP, in Jackson.

12. Author's interview with Fred L. Banks Jr.; Banks, "United States Court of Appeals for the Fifth Circuit," 277; White, *Alice Walker*, 157 (quotation).

13. Minor, "Mississippi's Schools in Crisis," 32 (first quotation); Wolters, *Burden of Brown*, 163; Bass, *Unlikely Heroes*, 315; Read, "Judicial Evolution," 32n108 (second quotation); Irons, *Jim Crow's Children*, 208; Wilkinson, *From Brown to Bakke*, 120–21 (third and fourth quotations); Couch, *History of the Fifth Circuit*, 149–50; Clotfelter, *After Brown*, 26; author's interview with Reuben Anderson; Minchin and Salmond, *After the Dream*, 84; Douglas, *Reading, Writing, and Race*, 164; Minchin, "Making the Best Use of the New Laws," 683. By 1972, despite losing white students to private

schools, the South "had the most racially mixed public schools in the nation," added historian Gavin Wright (Wright, *Sharing the Prize*, 160).

14. Wilkinson, *From* Brown *to* Bakke, 120–22 (quotation on 122).

15. James Eastland quoted in Asch, *Senator and the Sharecropper*, 274; Grose, *South Carolina at the Brink*, 269–70; Bolton, *Hardest Deal of All*, 206. Integration often overwhelmed educators' limited capacity for creative thinking to the point of paralysis. An ardent critic who blamed the timidity of the education system for the failures of school integration was psychologist and educator Kenneth B. Clark. In 1954, his famous "doll study" helped the LDF to convince the Court of segregation's nefarious effects on black children (see Keppel, "Kenneth B. Clark in the Patterns of American Culture"). For a poignant reminiscence about integration in a small Mississippi Delta town, see Blackmon, "Resegregation of a Southern School." For an extensive overview of school integration's spotty record in Mississippi, see Bolton, *Hardest Deal of All*, chaps. 7 and 8. Mills Thornton cautioned against trying to understand the civil rights movement without "attending to the extraordinary variety of both its municipal and rural expressions and consequences." During integration, the "diverse patterns of race relations in southern towns and cities, not to mention the quite different structures in the countryside," noted Thornton, "determined the forms that the new order would take. . . . A portrait of the civil rights movement that fails to capture how greatly its outcomes differed from place to place fundamentally distorts its history. Just as segregation expressed itself in different forms in different communities, so too did integration" (Thornton, *Archipelagoes of My South*, 212).

16. M. R. Carpenter, "A Look at Our Supreme Court," open letter, box 428, folder 6, Black Papers (quotation). The vitriol aimed at Hugo Black, in particular, was raw, especially in Alabama. Because of his controversial and unpopular pro–civil rights stances, Black's family moved to New Mexico.

17. Wilkinson, *From* Brown *to* Bakke, 121; Patterson, Brown v. Board of Education, 154–55, 164–65; Bolton, *Hardest Deal of All*, 173; Andrews, *Freedom Is a Constant Struggle*, 163–74; Wright, *Sharing the Prize*, 159–60; Sokol, *There Goes My Everything*, 171–72; Minchin and Salmond, *After the Dream*, 92–94; WLBT, December 12, 1969, MP 1980.01, WLBT Newsfilm Collection, MDAH (quotation). By 1970, 42,000 white students enrolled in private academies (see Parker, "Protest, Politics, and Litigation," 693). Across the South, an estimated 300,000 white children attended one of the nearly 400 segregation academies (see McMillen, *Citizens' Council*, 302).

18. Philip D. Carter, "What Effect on Public Schools in Black Areas?," *WP*, November 3, 1969 (first quotation); Upchurch, *White Minority*, 9 (second quotation); Sokol, *There Goes My Everything*, 173; Andrews, *Freedom Is a Constant Struggle*, 161–69. Today, Central Holmes Academy is the Central Holmes Christian School.

19. Carter, "What Effect on Public Schools in Black Areas?" (quotations). State leaders employed quixotic tactics in their initial reaction to *Alexander*. Shortly after the ruling, A. F. Summer, at the behest of Governor John Bell Williams, dispatched letters to 2,800 Mississippi lawyers asking them to file school desegregation suits in northern and western states (see Bolton, *Hardest Deal of All*, 172).

20. Board minutes, March 1970 and July 1970, Durant Separate School District, Sylvia Gist Archives, private collection, Durant, Miss.; Julia Matilda Burns Oral History, LOC; Upchurch, *White Minority*, 9. Sylvia Gist generously shared her research on the Durant city school board meetings. Her examination of board minutes indicated that Durant's municipal school district acted as "a holding ground." When city officials proposed the new Durant separate school district, Mel Leventhal met with Calvin King in the LDF's office in Jackson. King pitched the creation of a separate Durant school system. Leventhal then met with a group of black community leaders, headed by Mary Hightower, who all supported the change. Thereupon, the district court approved the change because children of both races in all grades could attend school (see author's interview with Melvyn Leventhal).

21. Hazel Brannon Smith, "Public School System Must Be Preserved," *LA*, November 6, 1969, 2 (first quotation); Carter, "What Effect on Public Schools in Black Areas?"; WLBT, June 3, 1970, MP 1980.01, WLBT Newsfilm Collection, MDAH (second quotation); James Ward, "Poor Example by Washington," *Jackson (Miss.) Daily News*, January 21, 1970, 12 (third quotation). Mississippi's House of Representatives only recently reined in Durant's separate school district. In 2016, the Mississippi legislature passed House Bill 926 to consolidate the Holmes County School District and the Durant Public District into one on or before July 2017 (see House Bill 926, http://www.billstatus.ls.state.ms.us/documents/2016/html/HB/0900–0999/HB 0926IN.htm).

22. Banks, "United States Court of Appeals for the Fifth Circuit," 281.

23. John Sparks, "14 Additional Schools Lose Tax Exemption," *JCL*, October 6, 1970; "End of Tax Exemption Ordered for 23 Mississippi Academies," *NYT*, March 27, 1971; Bolton, *Hardest Deal of All*, 177–79; Crespino, "Civil Rights and the Religious Right," 90–94; Parker, "Protest, Politics, and Litigation," 693–94. In May 1969, Frank Parker's Lawyers' Committee for Civil Rights Under Law filed *Green v. Kennedy* on behalf of black schoolchildren in Mississippi (see *Green v. Kennedy*, 309 F. Supp. 1127 (D.D.C. 1970)).

24. Wilkinson, *From Brown to Bakke*, 122–23; Minchin and Salmond, *After the Dream*, 88–89 (quotation); "Mississippi School Destroyed by Fire," *NYT*, February 11, 1970, 16; Kluger, *Simple Justice*, 767; Bolton, *Hardest Deal of All*, 181–82; Munford, "White Flight," 22; Minor, *Eyes on Mississippi*, 250. For an account of white southern reactions to *Alexander*, see Minchin and Salmond, *After the Dream*, 81–94.

25. Robert McNair quoted in Minchin and Salmond, *After the Dream*, 82; Wilkinson, *From Brown to Bakke*, 123; Davies, "Richard Nixon," 387. In Mississippi, Garvin Johnston, the state superintendent of education, encouraged white parents to stick with the public schools and make integration work for the sake of economic growth. In 1978, he noted that a poor state like Mississippi "will not survive economically or culturally without a strong public school system." For his example of strong leadership, Bill Minor called Johnston an "unsung hero of his time" (Minor, "Hopefully Wright Will Stand Up to Politicians," *JCL*, January 1, 2015).

26. Davies, "Richard Nixon," 373–77 (first quotation on 373–74), 382–86, 388–89;

Mrs. Matt J. Schmidt, letter to the editor, box 428, folder 6, Black Papers (second quotation).

27. Wolters, *Burden of* Brown, 163–64; Shultz, "How a Republican Desegregated the South's Schools"; Leuchtenberg, "White House and Black America," 121–45; Garment, *Crazy Rhythm*, 204–6, 214–15; Mason, *Richard Nixon*, 52; Reichley, *Conservatives in an Age of Change*, 188–89; Kotlowski, *Nixon's Civil Rights*, 36–37; Ackerman, *We the People*, 249–50; Halpern, *On the Limits of the Law*, 90–91; Patterson, Brown v. Board of Education, 155; Roy Reed, "Both Sides in South Mistrust Nixon Actions on School Integration," *NYT*, July 16, 1970, 22. Gareth Davies suggests that Nixon chose compliance with *Alexander* to control the tenor of desegregation, downplay the race issue, and stave off a third-party challenge from George Wallace in the 1972 presidential election (Davies, "Richard Nixon," 377). In his account of the "Republican" who "desegregated the South's schools," George Shultz defended Richard Nixon's contributions. Joseph Califano, a former aide to Lyndon Johnson, accused Shultz of rewriting history and Nixon of undermining civil rights laws (Califano, "Race and the Party of Lincoln").

28. Wolters, *Race and Education*, 146–47, O'Reilly, *Nixon's Piano*, 303; Haldeman, *Haldeman Diaries*, 126.

29. Reeves, *President Nixon*, 160–67 (first quotation on 167); Leon Panetta quoted in Grose, *South Carolina at the Brink*, 274 (second quotation); Schell, *Time of Illusion*, 81; Haldeman, *Haldeman Diaries*, 126; O'Reilly, *Nixon's Piano*, 303; Perlstein, *Nixonland*, 459; Davies, "Richard Nixon," 381 (third quotation); Minchin and Salmond, *After the Dream*, 64; Panetta and Gall, *Bring Us Together*, ix, 60, 126; Wolters, *Race and Education*, 146–47 (fourth quotation); Delmont, *Why Busing Failed*, 123–24 (fifth and sixth quotations). Nixon fired Panetta on February 15, the day before he announced the creation of Shultz's new subcommittee to find ways to assist school districts undergoing school desegregation (see Reichley, *Conservatives in an Age of Change*, 187–88). Robert Finch did not want Panetta to quit because he worried about the demoralization of his department. In the spring of 1970, Finch resigned from HEW (see Hoff, *Nixon Reconsidered*, 86–87). In addition to Panetta's departure, one-fourth of the attorneys in the Civil Rights Division quit during the first six months of 1970 (see Clayton, *The Politics of Justice*, 139).

30. Bolton, *Hardest Deal of All*, 195 (first and second quotations); WLBT, March 24, 1970, MP 1980.01, WLBT Newsfilm Collection, MDAH (third quotation); Wolters, *Race and Education*, 146; Garment, *Crazy Rhythm*, 208–9; Ackerman, *We the People*, 248–49; Orfield, "1964 Civil Rights Act and American Education," 111; Kotlowski, *Nixon's Civil Rights*, 32–33; Lassiter, *Silent Majority*, 245. The *New York Times* reprinted the entire text of Nixon's statement ("Text of President's Statement Explaining His Policy on Desegregation," *New York Times*, March 25, 1970, 26).

31. Evans and Novak, *Nixon in the White House*, 174; Wolters, *Race and Education*, 146–48; Read and McGough, *Let Them Be Judged*, 491; Ackerman, *We the People*, 249; Kluger, *Simple Justice*, 764–65; Osborne, *Third Year of the Nixon Watch*, 85–89 (quotation). In 1970, Jerris Leonard returned to Mississippi to enforce compliance with

Alexander. Some school districts refused to deal with Justice Department attorneys. They had "simply thrown up their hands and said 'sue us,'" recalled Leonard. Nixon instructed him to bring forceful federal action. "This is the end of the negotiations," he told stonehearted school boards. "Negotiating time is over with" (WLBT, June 6, 1970, MP 1980.01, WLBT Newsfilm Collection, MDAH). On the swath of Justice Department suits, see Norman, "Strange Career." Nixon retroactively encouraged compliance with court orders to desegregate, but he never led the way on integration. The Nixon administration never pushed for any more integration than what the Court required and consistently opposed the use of busing for desegregation. Nixon, furthermore, appointed four justices who voted to limit the reach of desegregation (see Davies, "Richard Nixon and the Desegregation of Southern Schools," 388–89; Wilkinson, *From* Brown *to* Bakke, 217).

32. Wolters, *Race and Education,* 148; William F. Buckley, *National Review,* September 22, 1970, 986–88 (second quotation), 1016 (first quotation); Kilpatrick, "Back to Segregation," 611 (third quotation). For one of the best explanations of Nixon's racial conservatism, see Schulman, *Seventies,* chap. 1. LDF lawyers did not share the victory of school desegregation with Richard Nixon. On Nixon and school desegregation, Mel Leventhal said, "The Republicans have tried to revise the history of Nixon and that he advanced school desegregation. What a fallacy. Because desegregation happened during his administration doesn't mean he gets credit. Those advances happened *despite* Nixon, not because of him" (author's interview with Melvyn Leventhal).

33. Banks, "United States Court of Appeals for the Fifth Circuit," 280; Asch, *Senator and the Sharecropper,* 274–75; author's interview with Reuben Anderson; Minchin and Salmond, *After the Dream,* 94–95; Wirt, *Politics of Southern Equality,* 224–27; Bolton, *Hardest Deal of All,* 194, 199–200 (quotation). "The hardest deal of all" pays homage to Bolton's work on the subject. In Bolton's bleak assessment, school integration in Mississippi "represented a pyrrhic victory" (Bolton, *Hardest Deal of All,* 194). Unintended consequences accompanied integration. One problem with the earlier *Brown* ruling was its emphasis on segregation's psychological damage to black children. *Brown* said nothing about black teachers, however. As a result, few people anticipated the need to defend black faculty and administrators during the era of school desegregation. On the psychological harm inflicted by segregation, see Keppel, *Work of Democracy,* chap. 4. Another side effect of integration was the loss of black culture and history in the transition to desegregated schools. When integration occurred, black teachers in formerly all-white schools were usually too afraid to mention black history. White teachers, of course, typically knew nothing about the subject. Consequently, black faculty stopped passing down generations of oral history to their students. The cultural preservation of the black past disappeared along with the dual-school system. One former student of segregated schools in Holmes remarked, "The 'beauty' within the tragedy [of segregation] was that we learned about our heritage" (author's interview with Sylvia Gist).

34. Bolton, *Hardest Deal of All,* 195–97 (quotation on 195).

35. Bolton, 200; Marsh, *Last Days*, 259–60; Blackmon, "Resegregation of a Southern School"; Morris, *Yazoo*, 122–23; Loewen, "School Desegregation in Mississippi," 2 (quotations). In spite of early and assertive community leadership, Leland's public schools resegregated as the spirit of integration "slowly melted away" (Blackmon, "Resegregation of a Southern School"). In Clinton, a suburb of Jackson, school superintendent Virgil Belue adopted a community school system rather than neighborhood schools, which tended to reinforce segregation. As a result, in 1970, blacks made up 15 percent of the student body in the unified school system. Today, Clinton's schools are 54 percent African-American and a kind of model system for integrated education (see Mader, "How One Mississippi District Made Integration Work"). Many school districts in Mississippi did not follow Clinton's lead. A Southern Regional Council report of February 28, 1970, remarked that school desegregation in the Deep South worked most effectively when white community leaders had laid the groundwork (see Wirt, *Politics of Southern Equality*, 220n6).

36. Charles Bolton interview with Fred Banks, Civil Rights in Mississippi Digital Archive (quotation); Fairclough, *Class of Their Own*, 402; Morris, *Yazoo*, 127–28; Patterson, Brown v. Board of Education, 165; Bolton, *Hardest Deal of All*, 200, 204–7, 214–15; Hudson and Curry, *Mississippi Harmony*, 98–99; author's interview with Reuben Anderson; Banks, "United States Court of Appeals for the Fifth Circuit," 281. For an examination of integration's harmful effects on black teachers and administrators, see Fairclough, *Class of Their Own*, chap. 10; Cecelski, *Along Freedom Road*. For a survey of school integration's successes and fiascos across the wider South, see Minchin and Salmond, *After the Dream*, 94–101. For a provocative essay on black teachers who lost out in the newly integrated order and black nostalgia for segregation, see Winner, "Doubtless Sincere," 157–58, 165–66. Jackson's LDF lawyers shouldered some of the blame for the failure to protect black educators. Reuben Anderson thought they had done what "was best during that time. We did not put a lot of emphasis on retaining the black leadership in the schools. Our main emphasis . . . was getting these schools integrated. And a lot of the philosophies during that time was that if you got enough black kids into the white schools that they would get a better education because of the better facilities and the better teachers and all. . . . We should have probably looked at making sure that some of the black schools stayed in existence and that the black leadership stayed there" (interview with Reuben Anderson, Civil Rights in Mississippi Digital Archive).

37. Sokol, *There Goes My Everything*, 173 (quotation); Morris, *Yazoo*, 111–12; Katagiri, *Mississippi State Sovereignty Commission*, 194.

38. Bolton, *Hardest Deal of All*, 203; Boman, *Original Rush Limbaugh*, 200. See also Munford, "Black Gravity," 165–67; Berry, "Dynamics of White Resistance."

39. Morris, *Yazoo*, 42, 89, 103–4 (second quotation), 133 (first quotation); Sokol, *There Goes My Everything*, 174–75.

40. Morris, *Yazoo*, 73–74 (quotations), 112–13; Bolton, *Hardest Deal of All*, 203. Satterfield met a sad and violent end. Ill with Parkinson's disease, he rehearsed his obsequies with the Methodist bishop of Mississippi and confessed that he had been

on the wrong side of the segregation battle. In 1981, he committed suicide to spare his family from having to take care of him (see Hustwit, *James J. Kilpatrick*, 247n68; author's interview with Thomas L. Kirkland Jr.). Like so many other public schools in Mississippi, Yazoo City's experiment in racial diversity ended in the 1990s as the education system slowly and unofficially resegregated (see "'Yazoo Revisited: Integration and Segregation in a Deep Southern Town' Documentary Screening," *Jackson Free Press*, February 18, 2016, www.jacksonfreepress.com/. . . yazoo-revisited -integration-and-segregation-deep-s/?et=21371).

41. Morris, *Yazoo*, 189–90 (quotations).

42. Bolton, *Hardest Deal of All*, 206–12; Cecelski, *Along Freedom Road*, 170-72; author's interview with Reuben Anderson; Minchin and Salmond, *After the Dream*, 96.

43. Zeitz, "What Everyone Gets Wrong about LBJ's Great Society." Not even Nixon's conservative appointments to the Supreme Court reversed course on school desegregation. In *Swann v. Charlotte-Mecklenburg Board of Education* (1971), the Court reaffirmed the duty of school officials to dismantle the dual system.

44. Fred Banks quoted in Bolton, *Hardest Deal of All*, 215; Bill Minor quoted in Morris, *Yazoo*, 120–21.

45. Loewen, "School Desegregation in Mississippi," 2 (quotation). Despite conflicting views about the reality of desegregation, Frederick Wirt notes that "what is interesting is that, over time, this region had adjusted to an educational change, any small part of which was dangerous to discuss—much less to start—barely a quarter century ago. Few people disagree that only a national court could have started a national policy change for the region" (Wirt, *"We Ain't What We Was,"* 34–35).

CODA

1. Huffman, "How White Flight Ravaged the Mississippi Delta" (quotations); McGreal, "Poorest Town in Poorest State"; Wood and Samuel, "'He Was Nonviolent, but My Boys Weren't,'" 167; Daniel, *Dispossession*, 76; Payne, *I've Got the Light of Freedom*, 278.

2. Huffman, "How White Flight Ravaged the Mississippi Delta" (quotations).

3. Huffman, "How White Flight Ravaged the Mississippi Delta" (quotations).

4. Huffman, "How White Flight Ravaged the Mississippi Delta"; McGreal, "Poorest Town in Poorest State"; Youth of the Rural Organizing and Cultural Center, *Minds Stayed on Freedom*, 17; "Holmes County, Mississippi," Bureau of the Census, http://www.census.gov. Long-past conditions pulled Holmes in certain directions, even generations after deleterious events like slavery and segregation. Studies have shown that the deeper a southern county's immersion in slavery, the greater the black-white inequality in the twenty-first century (see Fischer, "Slavery's Heavy Hand"). Much of today's electoral politics focuses on the "forgotten Americans," the white working-class Rust Belt voters and non-coastal elite. The real forgotten Americans, however, inhabit out-of-the-way communities, like the rural Black Belt of the American South, where conditions are truly dire. In Holmes County, columnist Leonard Steinhorn reports, "43.3 percent of residents live below poverty, median

household income is a mere $20,732—and households in one of its nearly all black towns, Tchula, make an unconscionable $13,273 per year" (Steinhorn, "Real Forgotten Americans").

5. J. J. Russell quoted in Andrews, *Freedom Is a Constant Struggle*, 76–77.

6. Gist, "Educating a Southern Rural Community," 189; Andrews, *Freedom Is a Constant Struggle*, 120–24 (quotation on 120).

7. Huffman, "How White Flight Ravaged the Mississippi Delta," (quotations); Bolton, *Hardest Deal of All*, 215–16; Cobb, *Most Southern Place on Earth*, 273; Scott Rodd, "A Man 'Elected before His Time' in Mississippi Gives Politics One More Go," *WP*, August 3, 2015; Kaul, "Hazel Brannon Smith," 259; Neilson, *Even Mississippi*, 42–43.

8. Huffman, "How White Flight Ravaged the Mississippi Delta" (quotations); Youth of the Rural Organizing and Cultural Center, *Minds Stayed on Freedom*, 18; Andrews, *Freedom Is a Constant Struggle*, 146–48; Harris, "Myth of the 'New South,'" 60.

9. Youth of the Rural Organizing and Cultural Center, *Minds Stayed on Freedom*, 17–18; Huffman, "How White Flight Ravaged the Mississippi Delta"; McGreal, "Poorest Town in Poorest State"; Cheers, "Battle Rages In Tchula, Miss."; Rodd, "Man 'Elected before His Time'" (quotation).

10. Huffman, "How White Flight Ravaged the Mississippi Delta" (first and second quotations); Harris, "Myth of the 'New South,'" 62 (third quotation); Rodd, "Man 'Elected before His Time'"; McGreal, "Poorest Town in Poorest State"; Youth of the Rural Organizing and Cultural Center, *Minds Stayed on Freedom*, 18; Kincaid, "Beyond the Voting Rights Act," 155–72; "Eddie Carthan: Fallen Star," November 20, 1986, *NBC Sunday Today*, NBC News, NBC University Archives, New York; Reginald Stuart, "Trial of Mississippi Ex-mayor Raises Wide Black Anxieties," *NYT*, October 20, 1982. For more on Carthan's legal problems, see Sheehan, *People's Advocate*. Roosevelt Granderson was also a schoolteacher and successful basketball coach. His murder may have been the result of one of two unfortunate scenarios unrelated to any conspiracy against Carthan by local whites. Some blacks who helped Carthan fight for his freedom knew about Granderson's involvement in drug trafficking. He may have been executed for failing to pay off a transaction. Others suspected that Granderson had an affair with his boss's wife. When his employer discovered it, he paid men to kill Granderson (see author's interview with Arnett Lewis; Wojcik, "Eddie Carthan"). A careful and gifted politician, Democratic governor William F. Winter gradually shed most of his segregationist baggage. In Mississippi's 1967 gubernatorial campaign, he pandered to white supremacists in his first and unsuccessful attempt to win the governor's office. By the 1980s, Winter positioned himself as more of a racial liberal (see Bolton, "William F. Winter," 335–36).

11. Andrews, *Freedom Is a Constant Struggle*, 164–65; Bolton, "Last Holdout," 138; Holmes County School District 1995 Report Card, State of Mississippi, Department of Education, Office of Accountability Reporting, http://mdereports.mdek12.org /Account/report/HOLMES.HTM.

12. Gist, "Educating a Southern Rural Community," 191, 213, 216, 218–19, 223–24;

Archer, *Growing Up Black in Rural Mississippi*, 113. Holmes whites and blacks both embraced Arenia Mallory. From 1926 until her death in 1977, she administered the Saints Industrial and Literary School in Lexington, a black private academy affiliated with the Pentecostal Church of God in Christ. In 1897, minister and denominational founder Charles Harrison Mason led a revival in Lexington that formed the basis for the Church of God in Christ's first church, St. Paul Church (see Ownby et al., *Mississippi Encyclopedia*, 584). Over the course of fifty years, Mallory educated an estimated 20,000 black students, including classmates Sylvia Gist and Arnett Lewis. Gist described Mallory as the most apposite black to join the school board because of her stature among African Americans and her impressive ability to bring in outside money to fund Saints, which kept the school segregated and pleased area whites. She was a "bridging black" between the races (author's interviews with Sylvia Gist and Arnett Lewis). For fifteen years prior to his election, William Dean worked under Mallory at Saints. For more on Mallory's life and career, see Butler, "Peculiar Synergy"; White, *Rise to Respectability*; Johnson, *Down behind the Sun*.

13. Like many Vietnam veterans, Arnett Lewis returned from the war radicalized. He was ready to fight for black dignity. In 1978, after white policemen sexually assaulted a black woman, Shirley Boyd, in Lexington, Lewis decided the county had to change. When Boyd refused to have sex with the officers, they beat and then released her. Mentally traumatized, Boyd committed suicide a year later. This "could not happen," Lewis resolved. Through boycotts, demonstrations, and political mobilization, he, Eddie Carthan, and others targeted the albatross of institutional racism in the county. They successfully renamed the county attendance centers because, Lewis insisted, "an attendance center *is not* a school. A school should have the identity of a school." They also founded new organizations to make improvements in the black community, like the Concerned Citizens of Holmes County and the United League of Holmes County, and built the Arenia C. Mallory Health Center in Lexington. Dr. Martha Davis became the health center's executive director. By the late 1980s, the United League evolved into the Rural Organization and Cultural Center (author's interview with Arnett Lewis). See also Shepard, *Rationing Justice*, 208–17; United League Subject File, MDAH; Eddie Carthan Oral History, Civil Rights in Mississippi Digital Archive, University of Southern Mississippi, Hattiesburg; Howell, *Hazel Brannon Smith*, 183–87; *Holmes County Herald*, January 9, 2008; Kluger, *Simple Justice*, chap. 2.

14. Author's interview with Sylvia Gist (first quotation); Huffman, "How White Flight Ravaged the Mississippi Delta" (second quotation); Cobb, *Most Southern Place on Earth*, 251. Eddie Carthan returned to politics and recently won election as county supervisor. Perhaps Randall Kennedy put it best on the unfulfilled promise of integration today: "To address adequately the crises we confront will require more than habitual incantations of *Brown* and other landmarks of prior struggles. It will require forging altogether *new* laws, *new* doctrines, and *new* understandings pertinent to the demands of our own time" (Kennedy, "Ackerman's *Brown*").

BIBLIOGRAPHY

ARCHIVES AND MANUSCRIPT COLLECTIONS

Atlanta, Georgia
    National Archives and Records Administration—Southeast Region
        Case file of *Alexander v. Holmes County Board of Education*
        Records of the District Courts of the United States
College Park, Maryland
    National Archives and Records Administration
        Case file of *Alexander v. Holmes County Board of Education*
        Richard M. Nixon Presidential Materials, Staff Member Office Files
            Robert H. Finch Papers
Durant, Mississippi
    Migration Heritage Center
        Sylvia Gist Archives, private collection
Fort Worth, Texas
    National Archives and Records Administration—Southwest Region
        Case file of *Alexander v. Holmes County Board of Education*
        Case file of *U.S. v. Hinds County School Board*
        Records of the U.S. Court of Appeals Fifth Circuit
Hattiesburg, Mississippi
    University of Southern Mississippi, Civil Rights in Mississippi Digital Archive
        Reuben Anderson Oral History
        R. Jess Brown Oral History
        Eddie Carthan Oral History
        Robert G. Clark Oral History
        Ralthus Hayes Oral History
        The Holmes County Movement Oral History
        Jerris Leonard Oral History
        John Daniel Wesley Oral History
Jackson, Mississippi
    Mississippi Department of Archives and History
        Assistant Attorneys General Files, 1967–1975
        Freedmen's Bureau Records
        Holmes County Board of Education Minutes
        Holmes County Subject File
        Holmes County WPA File

   "Lynchings" Vertical File
   Mississippi State Sovereignty Commission Papers
   Tougaloo Civil Rights Collection
      Civil Rights Cases
      Robert G. Clark Jr. Collection
      Tom Dent Oral History Collection
      Lawyers' Committee for Civil Rights Under Law Collection
      Aurelia Norris Young Papers
   United League Subject File
   WLBT Newsfilm Collection
   Works Progress Administration Scrapbooks
Lexington, Mississippi
   Office of the Holmes County Circuit Clerk
   Office of the Superintendent of Education
   "Official Minutes of the Holmes County Board of Education," 1950–80
Madison, Wisconsin
   Wisconsin Historical Society
      Freedom Summer Collection
New Orleans, Louisiana
   Tulane University
      Amistad Research Center
         Southern Civil Rights Litigation Records for the 1960s
            NAACP Legal Defense Fund, Inc., Litigation Files, 1961–1972,
               microfilm, reel 133
      Law School
         John Minor Wisdom Papers
Oxford, Mississippi
   University of Mississippi, J. D. Williams Library, Archives and Special Collections
      Citizens' Council Collection
      A. Eugene Cox Papers
      Nash and Taggart Collection
      John C. Satterfield/American Bar Association Collection
Starkville, Mississippi
   Mississippi State University, University Libraries, Digital Collections
      Allen Eugene Cox Papers
      John C. Stennis Oral History Project
St. Louis, Missouri
   Washington University, Washington University Libraries, Film and Media Archive
      Henry Hampton Collection
Tuscaloosa, Alabama
   University of Alabama, University Libraries, Digital Collections
      NAACP Papers
Washington, D.C.
   Library of Congress

Hugo LaFayette Black Papers
William J. Brennan Papers
Walter Bruce Oral History
Julia Matilda Burns Oral History
Robert G. Clark Jr. Oral History
William O. Douglas Papers
Jack Greenberg Oral History Interview
John Marshall Harlan Papers
Rosie Head Oral History
Thurgood Marshall Papers
Byron White Papers
National Archives and Records Administration
General Records of the Department of Justice (DOJ)
Jerris Leonard Collection
Richard Nixon Presidential Archives
White House Special Files: Staff Member and Office Files
Records of the U.S. Supreme Court
Case file of *Alexander v. Holmes County Board of Education*
Records of the Works Progress Administration (WPA)

GOVERNMENT PUBLICATIONS

Adams v. Mathews, 403 F.2d 181 (5th Cir. 1968).
Alexander v. Holmes County Board of Education, Civil Action No. 3779 (S.D. Miss. 1965).
Alexander v. Holmes County Board of Education, 396 U.S. 1218 (1969).
Alexander v. Holmes County Board of Education, 396 U.S. 19 (1969).
Blackwell v. Issaquena County Board of Education, 363 F.2d 749 (5th Cir. 1966).
Brown v. Board of Education of Topeka, Kansas, 347 U.S. (1954).
Brown v. Board of Education of Topeka, Kansas, 349 U.S. (1955).
Carter v. West Feliciana Parish School Board, 396 U.S. 290 (1970).
Cooper v. Aaron, 358 U.S. 1 (1958).
Diane Hudson et al. v. Leake County School Board, Civil Action No. 3382 (S.D. Miss. 1963).
Green v. County School Board of New Kent County, 391 U.S. 430, 438–440 (1968).
Green v. Kennedy, 309 F. Supp. 1127 (D.D.C. 1970).
Singleton v. Jackson Municipal Separate School District, 348 F.2d 729 (5th Cir. 1965).
United States v. Hinds County School Board, Civil No. 4075 (J) (S.D. Miss., May 13, 1969).
United States v. Hinds County School Board, 417 F.2d 852 (1969).
United States v. Holmes County, Mississippi et al., 385 F.2d 145 (5th Cir. 1967).
United States v. Jefferson County Board of Education, 372 F.2d (5th Cir. 1966).
U.S. Bureau of the Census. *Eighteenth Census of the United States, 1960.* Vol. 1,

Characteristics of the Population, Mississippi. Washington, D.C.: Government
   Printing Office, 1963. http://mapserver.lib.virginia.edu. Accessed 19 November
   2015.
———. *The Eighth Census: Population of the United States in 1860.* Washington,
   D.C.: Government Printing Office, 1864. http://mapserver.lib.virginia.edu.
   Accessed March 15, 2015.
———. *Fifteenth Census of the United States, 1930.* Vol. 2, Population. Washington,
   D.C.: Government Printing Office, 1931. http://mapserver.lib.virginia.edu.
   Accessed April 30, 2015.
———. *Fourteenth Census of the United States, 1920.* Vol. 6, Agriculture. Washington,
   D.C.: Government Printing Office, 1921.
———. *Ninth Census, 1870.* Vol. 1, *The Statistics of the Population of the United
   States.* Washington, D.C.: Government Printing Office, 1872.
———. *Seventeenth Census of the United States, 1950.* Vol. 7, *Characteristics of the
   Population, Mississippi.* Washington, D.C.: Government Printing Office, 1952.
   http://mapserver.lib.virginia.edu. Accessed May 7, 2015.
———. *Sixteenth Census of the United States, 1940.* Vol. 2, *Population.* Washington,
   D.C.: Government Printing Office, 1943. http://mapserver.lib.virginia.edu.
   Accessed September 10, 2016.
U.S. Commission on Civil Rights. "Racial Isolation in the Public Schools." Wash-
   ington, D.C.: Government Printing Office, 1967.
U.S. Department of Agriculture. *Field Operations of the Bureau of Soils, 1908.* Vol. 10.
   Washington, D.C.: Government Printing Office, 1911.
U.S. Department of Commerce. *Census of Agriculture: 1925—Mississippi.* Washing-
   ton, D.C.: Government Printing Office, 1926.

SELECTED NEWSPAPERS

Holmes County Herald
Jackson Clarion-Ledger
Lexington Advertiser
Memphis Commercial Appeal
New York Times
Washington Post

MICROFILM

Facts on Film
Student Nonviolent Coordinating Committee Papers, 1959–1972

MEDIA AND NEWS FILM

Blackside Media, Washington University Film and Media Archive, St. Louis
   Henry Hampton Collection

Eyes on the Prize, episode 5: "Mississippi: Is This America?," 1987
NBC News, NBC Universal Archives, New York
   NBC Sunday Today
      "Eddie Carthan: Fallen Star," November 20, 1986

INTERVIEWS

Reuben Anderson
Fred L. Banks Jr.
Don Barrett Jr.
Iris Brest
Paul Brest
Armand Derfner
Sylvia Gist
Thomas L. Kirkland Jr.
Melvyn Leventhal
Arnett Lewis
Byron Montgomery
Kenneth Rutherford
Sue [Lorenzi] Sojourner
Melvyn Zarr

ARTICLES, CHAPTERS, AND WEB SOURCES

Abney, Glenn. "Legislating Morality: Attitude Change and Desegregation in Mississippi." *Urban Education* 11, no. 3 (October 1976): 333–38.
Alcindor, Habiba. "Mississippi Growing: An African-American Community with New Deal Roots Finds Some Hope in a Farmers' Market." *The Nation*, September 2, 2009.
Anderson, Jack. "Mitchell Warns 'Rights' Lawyers." *Spartanburg Herald-Journal*, October 19, 1969, 12.
Anderson, James D. "Northern Foundations and the Shaping of Southern Black Rural Education, 1902–1935." *History of Education Quarterly* 18 (Winter 1978): 371–96.
Aronow, Geoffrey F. "The Special Master in School Desegregation Cases: The Evolution of Roles in the Reformation of Public Institutions through Litigation." *Hastings Constitutional Law Quarterly* 7 (Spring 1980): 739–75.
Banks, Fred L. "The United States Court of Appeals for the Fifth Circuit: A Personal Perspective." *Mississippi College Law Review* 16, no. 2 (Spring 1996): 275–88.
"Beatrice Alexander, et al. v. The Holmes County Board of Education, et al., etc." *Race Relations Law Reporter* 10 (1965): 1089–92.
Bell, Derrick A., Jr. "*Brown v. Board of Education* and the Interest-Convergence Dilemma." *Harvard Law Review* 93 (1980): 518–33.
Bennett, Lerone, Jr. "The First Black Governor." *Ebony*, October 1982, 94–97.

Bishop, Jim. "Thunder over Dixie: Mississippi's Lexington Full of Knotted Hatred." *Washington Post*, March 26, 1956.

Blackmon, Douglas A. "The Resegregation of a Southern School." *Harper's Magazine*, September 1, 1992, 14–21.

Blassingame, John W. "Using the Testimony of Ex-slaves: Approaches and Problems." *Journal of Southern History* 41 (November 1975): 473–92.

Bolton, Charles C. "The Last Holdout: Mississippi and the *Brown* Decision." In *With All Deliberate Speed: Implementing Brown v. Board*, edited by Brian J. Daugherity and Charles C. Bolton. Fayetteville: University of Arkansas Press, 2008.

———. "The Last Stand of Massive Resistance: Mississippi Public School Integration, 1970." *Mississippi History Now*, February 2009. http://mshistory.k12.ms.us/articles/305/the-last-stand-of-massive-resistance-1970. Accessed May 24, 2015.

———. "Mississippi's School Equalization Program, 1945–1954: A Last Gasp to Try to Maintain a Segregated Educational System." *Journal of Southern History* 66 (November 2000): 781–814.

———. "William F. Winter and the Politics of Racial Moderation in Mississippi." *Journal of Mississippi History* 72 (Winter 2008): 335–82.

Bosisio, Matthew J. "Hazel Brannon Smith: Pursuing Truth at Her Peril." *American Journalism* 18, no. 4 (2002): 69–83.

Bridges, Billy G., and Wendy E. Walker. "The Forty Year Fight to Desegregate Education in the Fifth Circuit and in Particular, Mississippi." *Mississippi College Law Review* 16, no. 2 (1996): 289–308.

Brigham, Jeremy. "Writer Recalls 1965 Request for Help." *The Gazette*, March 20, 2015.

Brumby, J. "Holmes County—Today and Yesterday." *Lexington Advertiser*, August 28, 1986 (sesquicentennial ed.).

Burnham, Margaret A., and Margaret M. Russell. "The Cold Cases of the Jim Crow Era." *New York Times*, August 28, 2015, A21.

Califano, Joseph A., Jr. "Race and the Party of Lincoln." *New York Times*, January 10, 2003.

Carter, Hodding. "Memo to Some Holmes Countians." *Greenville Delta Democrat Times*, September 30, 1955.

Cheers, D. Michael. "Battle Rages in Tchula, Miss.: Black Mayor Locked Out of City Hall." *Jet*, September 13, 1979, 28–31.

"Civil Rights and Restorative Justice Project: Year End Report 2014." http://nuweb9.neu.edu/civilrights/wp-content/uploads/CRRJ-YearEndReport-2014.pdf. Accessed August 30, 2015.

"Civil Rights: The Apologist." *Time*, October 31, 1969, 77, 81.

Crespino, Joseph. "Civil Rights and the Religious Right." In *Rightward Bound: Making America Conservative in the 1970s*, edited by Bruce J. Schulman and Julian E. Zelizer. Cambridge, Mass.: Harvard University Press, 2008.

Crosby, Emilye J. "'It Wasn't the Wild West': Keeping Local Studies in Self-Defense Historiography." In *Civil Rights History from the Ground Up: Local Struggles, a*

National Movement, edited by Emilye J. Crosby. Athens: University of Georgia Press, 2011.

———. "'You Got a Right to Defend Yourself': Self-Defense and the Claiborne County, Mississippi Civil Rights Movement." *International Journal of Africana Studies* 9, no. 1 (Spring 2003): 133–64.

Dallas, Jerry W. "The Delta and Providence Farms: A Mississippi Experiment in Cooperative Farming and Racial Cooperation, 1936–1956." *Mississippi Quarterly* 40 (Summer 1987): 283–308.

Daniel, Philip T. K. "The Not So Strange Path of Desegregation in America's Public Schools." *Negro Educational Review* 56, no. 1 (January 2005): 57–66.

Darjean, John. "Mrs. Catherine Jefferson: 'Seems Like I Just Been a Slave.'" *Bloodlines* 1 (Summer 1988): 33–38.

Davies, Gareth. "Richard Nixon and the Desegregation of Southern Schools." *Journal of Policy History* 19, no. 4 (2007): 367–94.

Dillard, Stephen Louis A. "Bell, Griffin." In *Great American Judges: An Encyclopedia*, edited by John R. Vile. Santa Barbara, Calif.: ABC-CLIO, 2003.

Doherty, Patric J. "'Integration Now': A Study of *Alexander v. Holmes County Board of Education*." *Notre Dame Law Review* 45 (Spring 1970): 489–514.

Draper, Alan. "Class and Politics in the Mississippi Movement: An Analysis of the Mississippi Freedom Democratic Party Delegation." *Journal of Southern History* 82, no. 2 (May 2016): 269–304.

———. "The Mississippi Movement: A Review Essay." *Journal of Mississippi History* 60 (Winter 1998): 355–66.

Du Bois, W. E. B. "Does the Negro Need Separate Schools?" *Journal of Negro Education* 4 (July 1935): 328–35.

Eagles, Charles W. "Toward New Histories of the Civil Rights Era." *Journal of Southern History* 66 (November 2000): 815–48.

Edelman, Marian Wright. "Southern School Desegregation, 1954–1973: A Judicial-Political Overview." *Annals of the American Academy of Political and Social Science* 407 (May 1973): 32–42.

Edwards, Willard. "Capitol Views: Stennis Works Out a Deal." *Chicago Tribune*, September 11, 1969, 18.

Emanuel, Anne S. "Forming the Historic Fifth Circuit: The Eisenhower Years." *Texas Forum on Civil Liberties and Civil Rights* 6 (Winter 2002): 233–59.

Fischer, Claude S. "Slavery's Heavy Hand." *Made in America*. May 28, 2012. https://madeinamericathebook.wordpress.com/2012/05/28/slaverys-heavy-hand/.

Fuquay, Michael W. "Civil Rights and the Private School Movement in Mississippi, 1964–1971." *History of Education Quarterly* 42, no. 2 (Summer 2002): 159–80.

Gale, Bell. "The Southern Front: 2 Weeks in Mississippi." *Village Voice*, July 16, 1964.

Garland, Phyl. "A Taste of Triumph for Black Mississippi." *Ebony*, February 1968, 25–28, 30, 32.

Garrow, David J. "Brennan Helped Shape U.S. Justice." *Atlanta Journal-Constitution*, July 27, 1997, 1F.

———. "Doing Justice." *The Nation*, February 27, 1995, 278–81.

———. "Hopelessly Hollow History: Revisionist Devaluing of *Brown v. Board of Education*." *Virginia Law Review* 80 (February 1994): 151–60.

———. "The Tragedy of William O. Douglas." *The Nation*, April 14, 2003, 25–30.

———. "Visionaries of the Law: John Minor Wisdom and Frank M. Johnson, Jr." *Yale Law Journal* 109 (April 2000): 1219–36.

Goluboff, Risa. "Lawyers, Law, and the New Civil Rights History." *Harvard Law Review* 126 (June 2013): 2312–35.

Graham, F. P. "President Vows to Enforce Edict on Desegregation." *New York Times*, October 31, 1969, 1.

Green, Winifred. "The Children of the South: School Desegregation and Its Significance." *Journal of Law and Education* 4 (January 1975): 18–24.

Greenberg, Gary J. "Revolt at Justice." In *Inside the System: A Washington Monthly Reader*, edited by Charles Peters and Timothy J. Adams. New York: Praeger, 1970.

Gugliotta, Guy. "Dwindling Black Farmers Fight Formidable Odds for Future." *Washington Post*, December 30, 1990.

Harris, Ron. "The Myth of the 'New South': It's the 'Old South' with a Smile." *Ebony*, February 1979, 54–56, 58, 60, 62.

Herbers, John. "School Test Nears in Harmony, Miss." *New York Times*. August 16, 1964, 58.

"High Court Denies Louisianans' Plea." *New York Times*, December 20, 1969, 20.

Holmes, William F. "The Leflore County Massacre and the Demise of the Colored Farmers' Alliance." *Phylon* 34 (3rd Qtr., 1973): 267–74.

Horowitz, Michael. "In Memoriam: Dean Joshua Morse III." *Mississippi Law Journal* 82, no. 7 (2013): 1229–31.

Horwitz, Morton J. "The Jurisprudence of *Brown* and the Dilemmas of Liberalism." In *Have We Overcome? Race Relations since Brown*, edited by Michael V. Namorato. Jackson: University Press of Mississippi, 1979.

Huffman, Alan. "How White Flight Ravaged the Mississippi Delta." *The Atlantic*, January 6, 2015.

Jacklin, Thomas M. "Mission to the Sharecroppers: Neo-Orthodox Radicalism and the Delta Farm Venture, 1936–40." *South Atlantic Quarterly* 78 (Summer 1979): 302–16.

Kaul, Arthur J. "Hazel Brannon Smith and the *Lexington Advertiser*." In *The Press and Race: Mississippi Journalists Confront the Movement*, edited by David R. Davies. Jackson: University Press of Mississippi, 2001.

Kempton, Murray. "What Have They Got to Live For?" *New York Post*, November 16, 1955, 5.

Kennedy, Randall L. "Ackerman's *Brown*." *Yale Law Journal* 123 (June 2014): 3064-3075.

———. "Lifting as We Climb: A Progressive Defense of Respectability Politics." *Harper's Magazine*, October 2015. http://harpers.org/archive/2015/10/lifting-as-we-climb. Accessed February 20, 2016.

————. "Martin Luther King's Constitution: A Legal History of the Montgomery Bus Boycott." *Yale Law Journal* 98 (April 1989): 999–1067.

Kennedy, Randall L., and Eric Foner. "*Brown* at 50." *The Nation*, April 15, 2004.

Keppel, Ben. "Kenneth B. Clark in the Patterns of American Culture." *American Psychologist* 57 (January 2002): 29–37.

Kilpatrick, James J. "Back to Segregation, by Order of the Courts." *National Review*, June 16, 1970, 611–26.

Kincaid, John. "Beyond the Voting Rights Act: White Responses to Black Political Power in Tchula, Mississippi." *Journal of Federalism* 16 (Fall 1986): 155–72.

Klarman, Michael J. "How *Brown* Changed Race Relations: The Backlash Thesis." *Journal of American History* 81 (June 1994): 81–118.

Lamanna, Richard. "The Negro Teacher and Desegregation: A Study of Strategic Decision Makers and Their Vested Interests in Different Community Contexts." *Sociological Inquiry* 35 (1965): 26–40.

Landsberg, Brian K. "Symposium: Voices of the Civil Rights Division: Then and Now." *McGeorge Law Review*, October 28, 2011, 1–40.

Langeveld, Martin, and Dirk Langeveld. Comment on Harry Dent. "Harry S. Dent: The Bad Footnote." *The Downfall Dictionary Blog*, July 9, 2010. http://downfalldictionary.blogspot.com. Accessed August 11, 2014.

Leuchtenburg, William E. "The White House and Black America: From Eisenhower to Carter." In *Have We Overcome? Race Relations since Brown*, edited by Michael V. Namorato. Jackson: University Press of Mississippi, 1979.

"'Liberal' Whites Ordered Out of Miss. County." *Jet*, October 13, 1955, 11.

Lucas, Aubrey Keith. "Education in Mississippi from Statehood to the Civil War." In *A History of Mississippi*, edited by Richard Aubrey McLemore. Hattiesburg: University and College Press of Mississippi, 1973.

MacLeod, Jay. "Bloodlines: A Case Study of Educational Empowerment." *Southern Changes*, November 1991, 6–9.

Mader, Jackie. "How One Mississippi District Made Integration Work." *Huffington Post*, April 19, 2016.

Martin, Douglas. "Joshua Morse III, Law School Dean Who Defied Segregation, Dies at 89." *New York Times*, September 19, 2012, A27.

Mayer, Michael S. "With Much Deliberation and Some Speed: Eisenhower and the *Brown* Decision." *Journal of Southern History* 52 (February 1986): 43–76.

McAndrews, Lawrence. "The Politics of Principle: Richard Nixon and School Desegregation." *Journal of Negro History* 83 (Summer 1998): 187–200.

McCain, William D. "The Administrations of David Holmes, Governor of the Mississippi Territory, 1809–1817." *Journal of Mississippi History* 29 (1967): 328–47.

McGreal, Chris. "Poorest Town in Poorest State: Segregation Is Gone but So Are the Jobs." *The Guardian*, November 15, 2015. http://www.theguardian.com. Accessed January 5, 2017.

Milius, P. "Decision Denounced in South." *Washington Post*, October 31, 1969, A1.

Minchin, Timothy J. "Making the Best Use of the New Laws: The NAACP and the Fight for Civil Rights in the South, 1965–1975." *Journal of Southern History* 74 (August 2008): 669–702.

Minor, Bill. "Are Charter Schools a Scheme?" *Jackson Clarion-Ledger*, August 15, 2013.

———. "Mississippi Schools in Crisis." *New South* 25, no. 1 (1970): 31–36.

———. "Powerful New Book Examines Race, Schools." *Jackson Clarion-Ledger*, January 19, 2006.

———. "Tales of Jim Crow Mississippi Continue Unfolding in Book." *Jackson Clarion-Ledger*, August 12, 2010.

Munford, Luther. "White Flight from Desegregation in Mississippi." *Integrateducation* 11 (1973): 12–26.

"Negro Flogged to Death in Mississippi." *The Militant*, August 10, 1946, 1.

Newman, Mark. "Hazel Brannon Smith and Holmes County, Mississippi, 1936–1964." *Journal of Mississippi History* 54 (March 1992): 59–87.

Noland, Thomas. "The Dying Memory of Hugo Black." *Southern Changes*, no. 3 (1978): 20.

Norman, David L. "The Strange Career of the Civil Rights Division's Commitment to *Brown*." *Yale Law Journal* 93, no. 6 (May 1984): 983–89.

Norrell, Robert J. "One Thing We Did Right: Reflections on the Movement." In *New Directions in Civil Rights Studies*, edited by Armstead L. Robinson and Patricia Sullivan. Charlottesville: University Press of Virginia, 1991.

Nussbaum, Dave. "A Conversation with Malcolm Gladwell: Revisiting *Brown v. Board*." *Behavioral Scientist*, July 12, 2017. http://behavioralscientist.org/conversation-malcolm-gladwell-revisiting-brown-v-board/. Accessed August 10, 2017.

Orey, Byron D'Andra. "Robert Clark and the Ascendancy to Black Power: The Case of the Mississippi Black State Legislators." In *The Civil Rights Movement in Mississippi*, edited by Ted Ownby. Jackson: University Press of Mississippi, 2013.

Orfield, Gary. "The 1964 Civil Rights Act and American Education." In *Legacies of the 1964 Civil Rights Act*, edited by Bernard Grofman. Charlottesville: University of Virginia Press, 2000.

———. "The Politics of Resegregation." *Saturday Review*, September 20, 1969, 58–60.

Parker, Frank R. "Protest, Politics, and Litigation: Political and Social Change in Mississippi." *Mississippi Law Journal* 57 (December 1987): 677–704.

Payne, Charles M. "'The Whole United States Is Southern!': *Brown v. Board* and the Mystification of Race." *Journal of American History* 91 (June 2004): 83–91.

Pierce, Ponchitta. "The Mission of Marian Wright." *Ebony*, June 1966, 94–108.

Podhoretz, Norman. "My Negro Problem—and Ours." *Commentary*, February 1963, 93–101.

Rachal, John R. "The Long Hot Summer: The Mississippi Response to Freedom Summer, 1964." *Journal of Negro History* 84 (Autumn 1999): 315–39.

Read, Frank T. "Judicial Evolution of the Law of School Integration since *Brown v.*

Board of Education." In *The Courts, Social Science, and School Desegregation*, edited by Betsy Levin and Willis D. Hawley. New Brunswick, N.J.: Transaction Books, 1975.

Reardon, Sean F., and Ann Owens. "60 Years after *Brown*: Trends and Consequences of School Segregation." *Annual Review of Sociology* 40 (July 2014): 199–218.

Reed, Roy. "U.S. View Alienates the N.A.A.C.P. Fund on Pupil Integration." *New York Times*, August 26, 1969, 24.

Rosenthal, Jack. "In Washington: Showdown by the Administration." *New York Times*, August 31, 1969, 1.

———. "Stennis Linked to Desegregation Delay." *New York Times*, September 13, 1969, 36.

Runnels, Susan L. "Trailblazers of the Mississippi Legal Frontier." *Mississippi Lawyer*, February 2003, 14–34.

Russell, Margaret. "De Jure Revolution?" *Michigan Law Review* 93 (1995): 1173–95.

Rustin, Bayard. "The Role of the Negro Middle Class." *The Crisis*, June–July 1969, 237–42.

Sallis, Charles, and John Quincy Adams. "Desegregation in Jackson, Mississippi." In *Southern Businessmen and Desegregation*, edited by David R. Colburn and Elizabeth Jacoway. Baton Rouge: Louisiana State University Press, 1982.

Satterfield, John C. "Law and Lawyers in a Changing World: President's Annual Address." *American Bar Association Journal* 48 (October 1962): 922–35.

Shultz, George. "How a Republican Desegregated the South's Schools." *New York Times*, January 8, 2003.

Sides, W. Hampton. "Interview: Richard Ford." *Memphis* 10 (February 1986): 42.

Simmons, William J. "Black Wednesday." *The Citizen*, December 1969, 2.

———. "Court Disaster." *The Citizen*, February 1970, 11.

———. "How to Start a Private School." *The Citizen*, September 1964, 4–5.

Smith, Hazel Brannon. "Hartman Turnbow Enjoys His Day." *Lexington Advertiser*, May 11, 1978.

———. "Looking at the Old South through Hazel Eyes." 1984. http://aliciapatterson.org/stories/looking-old-south-through-hazel-eyes. Accessed July 26, 2015.

Solomon, John Otto. *The Final Frontiers, 1880–1930: Settling the Southern Bottomlands*. Santa Barbara, Calif.: Praeger, 1999.

Stein, Bernard. "This Female Crusading Scalawag: Hazel Brannon Smith, Justice and Mississippi." In *Profiles in Journalistic Courage*, edited by Robert H. Giles, Robert W. Snyder, and Lisa DeLisle. Livingston, N.J.: Transaction, 2001.

Steinhorn, Leonard. "The Real Forgotten Americans." January 19, 2017. http://billmoyers.com/story/real-forgotten-americans/. Accessed January 31, 2017.

Stern, Gerald M. "Judge William Harold Cox and the Right to Vote in Clarke County, Mississippi." In *Southern Justice*, edited by Leon Friedman. Cleveland, Miss.: World, 1965.

Strain, Christopher B. "'We Walked Like Men': The Deacons for Defense Justice." *Louisiana History* 38, no. 1 (1997): 43–62.

Suitts, Steve. "The Southern Regional Council and the Roots of Rural Change."
    Southern Changes 13, no. 3 (1991): 5–12.

Sullivan, Patricia. "Jerris Leonard, 75; Oversaw the Desegregation of Schools under
    Nixon." *Washington Post*, August 7, 2006.

Taylor, Kerry. "Dangerous Memories: The Legacy of the Providence Cooperative
    Farm." *Mississippi Folklife* 31 (Fall 1998): 5–11.

Thornton, J. Mills. "Challenge and Response in the Montgomery Bus Boycott of
    1955–1956." *Alabama Review* 33 (July 1980): 163–235.

Tushnet, Mark V. "The Significance of *Brown v. Board of Education*." *Virginia Law
    Review* 80 (February 1994): 173–84.

———. "The Supreme Court and Race Discrimination, 1967–1991: The View from
    the Marshall Papers." *William and Mary Law Review* 36, no. 2 (1995): 473–545.

Tyson, Timothy B. "Robert F. Williams, 'Black Power,' and the Roots of the Afri-
    can American Freedom Struggle." *Journal of American History* 85 (September
    1998): 540–70.

Wax, Mel. "A Center of Hope and Pride in Mississippi." *San Francisco Sunday
    Chronicle*, February 7, 1965.

Webb, Clive. "A Continuity of Conservatism: The Limitations of *Brown v. Board of
    Education*." *Journal of Southern History* 70, no. 2 (May 2004): 327–36.

Weill, Susan. "Hazel and 'Hacksaw': Freedom Summer Coverage by the Women of
    the Mississippi Press." *Journalism Studies* 2, no. 4 (2000): 545–61.

"Wide Opportunities for Negro Lawyers." *The Crisis*, December 1964, 371.

Wilson, Charles Reagan. "Mississippi Delta." *Southern Spaces*. April 4, 2004. http://
    southernspaces.org/2004/mississippi-delta. Accessed March 22, 2015.

Winner, Laura F. "Doubtless Sincere: New Characters in the Civil Rights Cast."
    In *The Role of Ideas in the Civil Rights South*, edited by Ted Ownby. Jackson:
    University Press of Mississippi, 2002.

Witty, Fred M. "Reconstruction in Carroll and Montgomery Counties." In *Publica-
    tions of the Mississippi Historical Society*, edited by Franklin Lafayette Riley. Ann
    Arbor: University of Michigan, 1909.

Wojcik, J. "Eddie Carthan and the Struggle for Black Empowerment in the Deep
    South." *People's World*. February 20, 2009. http://www.peoplesworld.org
    /article/eddie-carthan-and-the-struggle-for-black-empowerment-in-the-deep
    -south/. Accessed May 27, 2017.

Wood, Spencer D., and Ricardo Samuel. "'He Was Non-violent, but My Boys
    Weren't': The Hegemonic Myth of Non-violence and the Construction of a
    Black Identity." *Arkansas Review: A Journal of Delta Studies* 41 (December 2010):
    155–69.

Woodruff, Nan Elizabeth. "African-American Struggles over Citizenship in the
    Arkansas and Mississippi Deltas in the Age of Jim Crow." *Radical History Review*
    55 (Winter 1993): 33–52.

"'You Have a Right ...' Voices from the Movement in Mississippi." *Southern
    Changes* 12, no. 2 (1990): 10–14.

Zarr, Melvyn. "Recollections of My Time in the Civil Rights Movement." *Maine Law Review* 61, no. 2 (2009): 366–76.

Zeitz, Joshua. "What Everyone Gets Wrong about LBJ's Great Society." *Politico.* January 28, 2018. https://www.politico.com/magazine/amp/story/2018/01/28/lbj-great-society-josh-zeitz-book-216538. Accessed January 29, 2018.

BOOKS

Ackerman, Bruce. *We the People.* Vol. 3, *The Civil Rights Revolution.* Cambridge, Mass.: Harvard University Press, 2014.

Aiken, Charles S. *The Cotton Plantation South since the Civil War.* Baltimore: Johns Hopkins University Press, 2003.

Alston, Alex A., Jr., and James L. Dickerson. *Devil's Sanctuary: An Eyewitness History of Mississippi Hate Crimes.* Chicago: Chicago Review Press, 2009.

Ambrose, Stephen E. *Nixon.* New York: Simon and Schuster, 1987.

Anderson, James D. *The Education of Blacks in the South, 1860–1935.* Chapel Hill: University of North Carolina Press, 1988.

Andrews, Kenneth T. *Freedom Is a Constant Struggle: The Mississippi Civil Rights Movement.* Chicago: University of Chicago Press, 2004.

Archer, Chalmers, Jr. *Growing Up Black in Rural Mississippi: Memories of a Family, Heritage of a Place.* New York: Walker, 1992.

Arsenault, Raymond. *Freedom Riders: 1961 and the Struggle for Racial Justice.* New York: Oxford University Press, 2006.

Asch, Chris Myers. *The Senator and the Sharecropper: The Freedom Struggles of James O. Eastland and Fannie Lou Hamer.* Chapel Hill: University of North Carolina Press, 2011.

Babson, Steve, David Elsila, and Dave Riddle. *The Color of the Law: Ernie Goodman, Detroit, and the Struggle for Labor and Civil Rights.* Detroit: Wayne State University Press, 2010.

Baldwin, Sidney. *Poverty and Politics: The Rise and Decline of the Farm Security Administration.* Chapel Hill: University of North Carolina Press, 1968.

Ball, Howard. *Murder in Mississippi: United States v. Price and the Struggle for Civil Rights.* Lawrence: University Press of Kansas, 2004.

Barker, Horace. *The Federal Retreat in School Desegregation: Special Report.* Atlanta: Southern Regional Council, 1969.

Barrow, Deborah J., and Thomas G. Walker. *A Court Divided: The Fifth Circuit Court of Appeals and the Politics of Judicial Reform.* New Haven: Yale University Press, 1988.

Bass, Jack. *Unlikely Heroes: The Dramatic Story of the Southern Judges of the Fifth Circuit Who Translated the Supreme Court's* Brown *Decision into a Revolution for Equality.* New York: Simon and Schuster, 1981.

Baughman, E. Earl, and W. Grant Dahlstrom. *Negro and White Children: A Psychological Study in the Rural South.* New York: Academic Press, 1968.

Beckwith, David W. *A New Day in the Delta: Inventing School Desegregation as You Go*. Tuscaloosa: University of Alabama Press, 2009.

Beito, David T., and Linda Royster. *Black Maverick: T. R. M. Howard's Fight for Civil Rights and Economic Power*. Urbana: University of Illinois Press, 2009.

Bell, Derrick. *Silent Covenants:* Brown v. Board of Education *and the Unfulfilled Hopes for Racial Reform*. New York: Oxford University Press, 2004.

Berman, Robert Lewis. *A House of David in the Land of Jesus*. Gretna, La.: Pelican, 2007.

Berry, Stephen A. *The Jim Crow Routine: Everyday Performances of Race, Civil Rights, and Segregation in Mississippi*. Chapel Hill: University of North Carolina Press, 2015.

Blackwell, Unita, with Joanne Prichard Morris. *Barefootin': Life Lessons from the Road to Freedom*. New York: Crown, 2006.

Bolton, Charles C. *The Hardest Deal of All: The Battle over School Integration in Mississippi, 1870–1980*. Jackson: University Press of Mississippi, 2005.

———. *William F. Winter and the New Mississippi: A Biography*. Jackson: University Press of Mississippi, 2013.

Boman, Dennis K. *The Original Rush Limbaugh: Lawyer, Legislator, and Civil Libertarian*. Columbia: University of Missouri Press, 2012.

Branch, Taylor. *Parting the Waters: America in the King Years, 1954–1963*. New York: Simon and Schuster, 1988.

Brandfon, Robert L. *Cotton Kingdom of the New South: A History of the Yazoo Mississippi Delta from Reconstruction to the Twentieth Century*. Cambridge, Mass.: Harvard University Press, 1967.

Brown, Sarah Hart. *Standing against Dragons: Three Southern Lawyers in an Era of Fear*. Baton Rouge: Louisiana State University Press, 1998.

Brown-Nagin, Tomiko. *Courage to Dissent: Atlanta and the Long History of the Civil Rights Movement*. New York: Oxford University Press, 2011.

Bryan, G. McLeod. *These Few Also Paid a Price: Southern Whites Who Fought for Civil Rights*. Macon, Ga.: Mercer University Press, 2001.

Bryant, Nick. *The Bystander: John F. Kennedy and the Struggle for Black Equality*. New York: Basic Books, 2006.

Bullock, Henry A. *A History of Negro Education in the South*. Cambridge, Mass.: Harvard University Press, 1967.

Busbee, Westley F., Jr. *Mississippi: A History*. Hoboken: N.J.: John Wiley & Sons, Inc., 2015.

Butler, Anthea D. *Women in the Church of God in Christ: Making a Sanctified World*. Chapel Hill: University of North Carolina Press, 2012.

Campbell, Will D. *Providence*. Waco, Tex.: Baylor University Press, 2002.

———. *Robert G. Clark's Journey to the House: A Black Politician's Story*. Jackson: University Press of Mississippi, 2003.

Carroll, Peter N. *The Odyssey of the Abraham Lincoln Brigade: Americans in the Spanish Civil War*. Redwood City, Calif.: Stanford University Press, 1994.

Carter, Dan. *From George Wallace to Newt Gingrich: Race in the Conservative Counterrevolution, 1963–1994*. Baton Rouge: Louisiana State University Press, 1996.

Carter, Hodding. *First Person Rural*. Greenwood, Miss.: Greenwood Press, 1977.

Cecelski, David S. *Along Freedom Road: Hyde County, North Carolina, and the Fate of Black Schools in the South*. Chapel Hill: University of North Carolina Press, 1995.

Classen, Steven D. *Watching Jim Crow: The Struggles over Mississippi TV, 1955–1969*. Durham: Duke University Press, 2004.

Clayton, Cornell W. *The Politics of Justice: The Attorney General and the Making of Legal Policy*. Armonk, N.Y.: M. E. Sharpe, 1992.

Clotfelter, Charles T. *After* Brown: *The Rise and Retreat of School Desegregation*. Princeton: Princeton University Press, 2011.

Cobb, Charles E., Jr. *This Nonviolent Stuff'll Get You Killed: How Guns Made the Civil Rights Movement Possible*. New York: Basic Books, 2014.

Cobb, James C. *The Most Southern Place on Earth: The Mississippi Delta and the Roots of Regional Identity*. New York: Oxford University Press, 1992.

Cohen, Robert. *Freedom's Orator: Mario Savio and the Radical Legacy of the 1960s*. New York: Oxford University Press, 2009.

Coles, Robert. *Children of Crisis: A Study of Courage and Fear*. Boston: Little, Brown, 1967.

Couch, Harvey C. *A History of the Fifth Circuit, 1891–1981*. Washington, D.C.: Government Printing Office, 1984.

Crawford, Vicki L., Jacqueline Anne Rouse, and Barbara Woods, eds. *Women in the Civil Rights Movement: Trailblazers and Torchbearers, 1941–1965*. Bloomington: Indiana University Press, 1990.

Crespino, Joseph. *In Search of Another Country: Mississippi and the Conservative Counterrevolution*. Princeton: Princeton University Press, 2007.

———. *Strom Thurmond's America*. New York: Hill and Wang, 2012.

Crosby, Emilye. *A Little Taste of Freedom: The Black Freedom Struggle in Claiborne County, Mississippi*. Chapel Hill: University of North Carolina Press, 2005.

Curry, Constance. *Silver Rights: The Story of the Carter Family's Brave Decision to Send Their Children to an All-White School and Claim Their Civil Rights*. Chapel Hill, N.C.: Algonquin Books, 2014.

Daniel, Pete. *Dispossession: Discrimination against African American Farmers in the Age of Civil Rights*. Chapel Hill: University of North Carolina Press, 2013.

———. *The Shadow of Slavery: Peonage in the South, 1901–1969*. Urbana: University of Illinois Press, 1990.

Daugherity, Brian J., and Charles C. Bolton. *With All Deliberate Speed: Implementing* Brown v. Board of Education. Fayetteville: University of Arkansas Press, 2008.

Davis, Allison, and John Dollard. *Children of Bondage*. New York: Harper and Row, 1964.

Delmont, Matthew F. *Why Busing Failed: Race, Media, and the National Resistance to School Desegregation.* Berkeley: University of California Press, 2016.

Dittmer, John. *Local People: The Struggle for Civil Rights in Mississippi.* Urbana: University of Illinois Press, 1994.

Douglas, Davison M. *Reading, Writing, and Race: The Desegregation of the Charlotte Schools.* Chapel Hill: University of North Carolina Press, 1995.

Du Bois, W. E. B. *The Black North in 1901: A Social Study.* 1901; repr., New York: Arno Press, 1969.

Dunbar, Anthony P. *Against the Grain: Southern Radicals and Prophets, 1929–1959.* Charlottesville: University Press of Virginia, 1981.

———. *Delta Time: A Journey through Mississippi.* New York: Pantheon Books, 1990.

Durr, Virginia Foster. *Outside the Magic Circle: The Autobiography of Virginia Foster Durr.* Edited by Hollinger F. Barnard. Tuscaloosa: University of Alabama Press, 1985.

Eagles, Charles W. *Civil Rights, Culture Wars: The Fight over a Mississippi Textbook.* Chapel Hill: University of North Carolina Press, 2017.

———. *The Price of Defiance: James Meredith and the Integration of Ole Miss.* Chapel Hill: University of North Carolina Press, 2009.

Edelman, Marian Wright. *Lanterns: A Memoir of Mentors.* Boston: Beacon Press, 1999.

Egerton, John. *Shades of Gray: Dispatches from the Modern South.* Baton Rouge: Louisiana State University Press, 1991.

Ehrlichman, John. *Witness to Power: The Nixon Years.* New York: Simon and Schuster, 1982.

Engel, Stephen M. *American Politicians Confront the Court: Opposition Politics and Changing Responses to Judicial Power.* New York: Cambridge University Press, 2011.

Epp, Charles R. *The Rights Revolution: Lawyers, Activists, and Supreme Courts in Comparative Perspective.* Chicago: University of Chicago Press, 1998.

Estes, Steve. *I Am a Man! Race, Manhood, and the Civil Rights Movement.* Chapel Hill: University of North Carolina Press, 2006.

Evans, Rowland, Jr., and Robert D. Novak. *Nixon in the White House: The Frustration of Power.* New York: Random House, 1971.

Fairclough, Adam. *A Class of Their Own: Black Teachers in the Segregated South.* Cambridge, Mass.: Harvard University Press, 2007.

———. *Race and Democracy: The Civil Rights Struggle in Louisiana, 1915–1972.* Athens: University of Georgia Press, 1995.

Federal Writers' Project of the Works Progress Administration. *Mississippi: The WPA Guide to the Magnolia State.* New York: Viking, 1938.

Feldman, Noah. *Scorpions: The Battles and Triumphs of FDR's Great Supreme Court Justices.* New York: Grand Central Publishing, 2010.

Ferguson, Robert Hunt. *Remaking the Rural South: Interracialism, Christian*

Socialism, and Cooperative Farming in Jim Crow Mississippi. Athens: University of Georgia Press, 2018.

Fleming, Cynthia Griggs. *In the Shadow of Selma: The Continuing Struggle for Civil Rights in the Rural South.* New York: Rowman and Littlefield.

Fleming, Karl. *Son of the Rough South: An Uncivil Memoir.* New York: PublicAffairs, 2005.

Flucker, Turry, and Phoenix Savage. *African Americans of Jackson.* Chicago: Arcadia Publishing, 2008.

Foner, Eric. *Reconstruction: America's Unfinished Revolution, 1863–1877.* New York: Harper and Row, 1988.

Freyer, Tony Allan. *Little Rock on Trial:* Cooper v. Aaron *and School Desegregation.* Lawrence: University Press of Kansas, 2007.

Friedman, Joel William. *Champion of Civil Rights: Judge John Minor Wisdom.* Baton Rouge: Louisiana State University Press, 2009.

Gaer, Joseph. *Toward Farm Security: The Problem of Rural Poverty and the Work of the Farm Security Administration.* Washington, D.C.: Government Printing Office, 1941.

Galbraith, John Kenneth. *The Affluent Society.* Boston: Houghton Mifflin Harcourt, 1958.

Garment, Leonard. *Crazy Rhythm: My Journey from Brooklyn, Jazz, and Wall Street to Nixon's White House, Watergate, and Beyond . . .* New York: Times Books, 1997.

Genovese, Eugene D. *The Political Economy of Slavery: Studies in the Economy and Society of the Slave South.* New York: Pantheon Books, 1965.

George, Carol V. R. *One Mississippi, Two Mississippi: Methodists, Murder, and the Struggle for Racial Justice in Neshoba County.* New York: Oxford University Press, 2015.

Goudsouzian, Aram. *Down to the Crossroads: Civil Rights, Black Power, and the Meredith March.* New York: Macmillan, 2014.

Grant, Richard. *Dispatches from Pluto: Lost and Found in the Mississippi Delta.* New York: Simon and Schuster, 2015.

Greenberg, Jack. *Crusaders in the Courts: How a Dedicated Band of Lawyers Fought for the Civil Rights Revolution.* New York: Basic Books, 1994.

Grose, Philip G. *South Carolina at the Brink: Robert McNair and the Politics of Civil Rights.* Columbia: University of South Carolina Press, 2006.

Hahn, Steven. *A Nation under Our Feet: Black Political Struggles in the Rural South from Slavery to the Great Migration.* Cambridge, Mass.: Harvard University Press, 2003.

Haldeman, H. R. *The Haldeman Diaries: Inside the Nixon White House.* New York: G. P. Putnam's Sons, 1994.

Halpern, Stephen C. *On the Limits of the Law: The Ironic Legacy of Title VI of the 1964 Civil Rights Act.* Baltimore: Johns Hopkins University Press, 1995.

Hamlin, Françoise N. *Crossroads at Clarksdale: The Black Freedom Struggle in the*

Mississippi Delta after World War II. Chapel Hill: University of North Carolina Press, 2012.

Hanks, Lawrence J. *The Struggle for Black Political Empowerment in Three Georgia Counties.* Knoxville: University of Tennessee Press, 1987.

Harkey, Ira B., Jr. *The Smell of Burning Crosses: The Autobiography of a Mississippi Newspaperman.* Jacksonville, Ill.: Harris-Wolfe & Company, 1967.

Harris, J. William. *Deep Souths: Delta, Piedmont, and Sea Island Society in the Age of Segregation.* Baltimore: Johns Hopkins University Press, 2001.

Harris, Melanie L. *Gifts of Virtue, Alice Walker, and Womanist Ethics.* New York: Palgrave Macmillan, 2010.

Harvey, Paul. *Freedom's Crossing: Religious Culture and the Shaping of the South from the Civil War through the Civil Rights Era.* Chapel Hill: University of North Carolina Press, 2005.

———. *Through the Storm, through the Night: A History of African American Christianity.* Lanham, Md.: Rowman and Littlefield, 2011.

Higginbotham, Evelyn Brooks. *Righteous Discontent: The Women's Movement in the Black Baptist Church, 1880–1920.* Cambridge, Mass.: Harvard University Press, 1994.

Hill, Lance. *The Deacons for Defense: Armed Resistance and the Civil Rights Movement.* Chapel Hill: University of North Carolina Press, 2006.

Hodgson, Godfrey. *America in Our Time: From World War II to Nixon—What Happened and Why.* New York: Doubleday, 1976.

Hoff, Joan. *Nixon Reconsidered.* New York: Basic Books, 1994.

Holloway, Harry. *The Politics of the Southern Negro.* New York: Random House, 1969.

Holmes, William F. *The White Chief: James Kimble Vardaman.* Baton Rouge: Louisiana State University Press, 1970.

Honigsberg, Peter Jan. *Crossing Border Street: A Civil Rights Memoir.* Berkeley: University of California Press, 2000.

Horn, Teena F., Alan Huffman, and John Griffin Jones. *Lines Were Drawn: Remembering Court-Ordered Integration at a Mississippi High School.* Jackson: University Press of Mississippi, 2016.

Hothschild, Jennifer L. *Thirty Years after* Brown. Washington, D.C.: Joint Center for Political Studies, 1985.

Howell, Jeffrey B. *Hazel Brannon Smith: The Female Crusading Scalawag.* Jackson: University Press of Mississippi, 2017.

Hudson, David L. *Let the Students Speak! A History of the Fight for Free Expression in American Schools.* Boston: Beacon Press, 2011.

Hudson, Winson, and Constance Curry. *Mississippi Harmony: Memoirs of a Freedom Fighter.* New York: Palgrave Macmillan, 2002.

Hustwit, William P. *James J. Kilpatrick: Salesman for Segregation.* Chapel Hill: University of North Carolina Press, 2013.

Inscoe, John C. *Writing the South through the Self: Explorations in Southern Autobiography.* Athens: University of Georgia Press, 2011.

Irons, Jenny. *Reconstituting Whiteness: The Mississippi State Sovereignty Commission*. Nashville: Vanderbilt University Press, 2010.

Irons, Peter. *Jim Crow's Children: The Broken Promise of the Brown Decision*. New York: Viking, 2002.

Jacoby, Tamar. *Someone Else's House: America's Unfinished Struggle for Integration*. New York: Free Press, 1998.

Jeffries, Hasan Kwame. *Bloody Lowndes: Civil Rights and Black Power in Alabama's Black Belt*. New York: New York University Press, 2010.

Johnson, Dovie Marie. *Down behind the Sun: The Story of Arenia C. Mallory*. Memphis: Riverside Press, 1973.

Johnson, James Weldon. *Negro Americans, Now What?* New York: Viking, 1934.

Johnson, Nicholas J. *Negroes and the Gun: The Black Tradition of Arms*. Amherst, N.Y.: Prometheus Books, 2014.

Jonas, Gilbert. *Freedom's Sword: The NAACP and the Struggle against Racism in America, 1909–1969*. New York: Routledge, 2004.

Kalk, Bruce H. *The Origins of the Southern Strategy: Two-Party Competition in South Carolina, 1950–1972*. New York: Lexington Books, 2001.

Kampe, Ronald E., and William A. Lindamood. *Underemployment Estimates by County, United States, 1960*. Washington, D.C.: Government Printing Office, 1969.

Katagiri, Yasuhiro. *The Mississippi State Sovereignty Commission: Civil Rights and States' Rights*. Jackson: University Press of Mississippi, 2001.

Keppel, Ben. *The Work of Democracy: Ralph Bunche, Kenneth B. Clark, Lorraine Hansberry, and the Cultural Politics of Race*. Cambridge, Mass.: Harvard University Press, 1995.

Kiesel, Diane. *She Can Bring Us Home: Dr. Dorothy Boulding Ferebee, Civil Rights Pioneer*. Lincoln: University of Nebraska Press, 2015.

King, Martin Luther, Jr. *Stride toward Freedom: The Montgomery Story*. New York: Harper and Brothers, 1958.

Klarman, Michael J. *From Jim Crow to Civil Rights: The Supreme Court and the Struggle for Racial Equality*. New York: Oxford University Press, 2004.

Kluger, Richard. *Simple Justice: The History of Brown v. Board of Education and Black America's Struggle for Equality*. New York: Vintage Books, 1975.

Kotlowski, Dean J. *Nixon's Civil Rights: Politics, Principle, and Policy*. Cambridge, Mass.: Harvard University Press, 2001.

Lassiter, Matthew D. *The Silent Majority: Suburban Politics in the Sunbelt South*. Princeton: Princeton University Press, 2013.

Lau, Peter F., ed. *From the Grassroots to the Supreme Court: Brown v. Board of Education and American Democracy*. Durham: Duke University Press, 2004.

Lawson, Steven F. *Black Ballots: Voting Rights in the South, 1944–1969*. New York: Columbia University Press, 1976.

———. *Civil Rights Crossroads: Nation, Community, and the Black Freedom Struggle*. Lexington: University Press of Kentucky, 2003.

Lewis, David Levering, ed. *W. E. B. Du Bois: A Reader*. New York: Henry Holt and Company, 1995.

———. *W. E. B. Du Bois: The Fight for Equality and the American Century, 1919–1963*. New York: Henry Holt and Company, 2000.

Litwack, Leon F. *Trouble in Mind: Black Southerners in the Age of Jim Crow*. New York: Vintage Books, 1998.

Loewen, James W., and Charles Sallis. *Mississippi: Conflict and Change*. New York: Pantheon Books, 1974.

Lomax, Alan. *The Land Where the Blues Began*. New York: Pantheon Books, 1993.

Lyles, Kevin L. *The Gatekeepers: Federal District Courts in the Political Process*. Westport, Conn.: Greenwood, 1997.

Mack, Kenneth W. *Representing the Race: The Creation of the Civil Rights Lawyer*. Cambridge, Mass.: Harvard University Press, 2012.

MacLean, Nancy. *Freedom Is Not Enough: The Opening of the American Workplace*. Cambridge, Mass.: Harvard University Press, 2006.

Maltz, Earl M. *The Chief Justiceship of Warren Burger, 1969–1986*. Columbia: University of South Carolina Press, 2000.

Maris, Paul V. *"The Land Is Mine": From Tenancy to Family Farm Ownership*. New York: Greenwood Press, 1950.

Marsh, Charles. *The Last Days: A Son's Story of Sin and Segregation at the Dawn of a New South*. New York: Basic Books, 2001.

Marshall, James P. *Student Activism and Civil Rights in Mississippi: Protest Politics and the Struggle for Racial Justice, 1960–1965*. Baton Rouge: Louisiana State University Press, 2013.

Martin, Gordon A. *Count Them One by One: Black Mississippians Fighting for the Right to Vote*. Jackson: University Press of Mississippi, 2011.

Martin, Waldo E., Jr. Brown v. Board of Education: *A Brief History with Documents*. Boston and New York: Bedford / St. Martin's, 1998.

Mason, Robert. *Richard Nixon and the Quest for a New Majority*. Chapel Hill: University of North Carolina Press, 2004.

Maxwell, Angie. *The Indicted South: Public Criticism, Southern Inferiority, and the Politics of Whiteness*. Chapel Hill: University of North Carolina Press, 2014.

McMahon, Kevin J. *Nixon's Court: His Challenge to Judicial Liberalism and Its Political Consequences*. Chicago: University of Chicago Press, 2011.

McMillen, Neil R. *The Citizens' Council: Organized Resistance to the Second Reconstruction, 1954–64*. Urbana: University of Illinois Press, 1971.

———. *Dark Journey: Black Mississippians in the Age of Jim Crow*. Urbana: University of Illinois Press, 1989.

McNeil, Genna Rae. *Groundwork: Charles Hamilton Houston and the Struggle for Civil Rights*. Philadelphia: University of Pennsylvania Press, 1983.

McPhail, James H., ed. *A History of Desegregation Developments in Certain Mississippi School Districts*. Hattiesburg: University of Southern Mississippi Press, 1971.

Meltsner, Michael. *The Making of a Civil Rights Lawyer*. Charlottesville: University of Virginia Press, 2006.

Mertz, Paul E. *New Deal Policy and Southern Rural Poverty.* Baton Rouge: Louisiana State University Press, 1978.

Mills, Kay. *Changing Channels: The Civil Rights Case That Transformed Television.* Jackson: University Press of Mississippi, 2004.

Minchin, Timothy J., and John A. Salmond. *After the Dream: Black and White Southerners since 1865.* Lexington: University Press of Kentucky, 2011.

Minor, Bill. *Eyes on Mississippi: A Fifty-Year Chronicle of Change.* Jackson, Miss.: J. Prichard Morris Books, 2001.

Morris, Aldon D. *The Origins of the Civil Rights Movement: Black Communities Organizing for Change.* New York: Free Press, 1984.

Morris, Willie. *Yazoo: Integration in a Deep-Southern Town.* New York: Harper's Magazine Press, 1971.

Morrison, Minion K. C. *Black Political Mobilization: Leadership, Power, and Mass Behavior.* Albany: State University of New York Press, 1987.

Motley, Constance Baker. *Equal Justice under the Law: An Autobiography.* New York: Macmillan, 1999.

Moye, J. Todd. *Let the People Decide: Black Freedom and White Resistance Movements in Sunflower County, Mississippi, 1945–1986.* Chapel Hill: University of North Carolina Press, 2004.

Myrdal, Gunnar. *An American Dilemma: The Negro Problem and Modern Democracy.* New York: Harper & Brothers, 1944.

Nash, Jere, and Andy Taggart. *Mississippi Politics: The Struggle for Power, 1976–2006.* Jackson: University Press of Mississippi, 2006.

Neilson, Melany. *Even Mississippi.* Tuscaloosa: University of Alabama Press, 1989.

Newman, Mark. *Divine Agitators: The Delta Ministry and Civil Rights in Mississippi.* Athens: University of Georgia Press, 2004.

Newman, Roger K. *Hugo Black: A Biography.* New York: Pantheon Books, 1994.

Newton, Michael. *The Ku Klux Klan in Mississippi: A History.* Jefferson, N.C.: McFarland, 2010.

Noblit, George W., ed. *School Desegregation: Oral Histories toward Understanding the Effects of White Domination.* Rotterdam, Netherlands: Sense Publishers, 2015.

O'Brien, Greg. *Choctaws in a Revolutionary Age, 1750–1830.* Lincoln: University of Nebraska Press, 2002.

O'Reilly, Kenneth. *Nixon's Piano: Presidents and Racial Politics from Washington to Clinton.* New York: Free Press, 1995.

Orfield, Gary. *The Reconstruction of Southern Education.* New York: John Wiley and Sons, 1969.

Orr-Klopfer, Susan, with Fred Klopfer and Barry Klopfer. *Where Rebels Roost: Mississippi Civil Rights Revisited.* Lulu.com, 2005.

Osborne, John. *The Third Year of the Nixon Watch.* New York: Liveright, 1971.

Osgood, Kenneth, and Derrick E. White, eds. *Winning while Losing: Civil Rights, the Conservative Movement, and the Presidency from Nixon to Obama.* Gainesville: University Press of Florida, 2014.

Ownby, Ted, Charles Reagan Wilson, Ann J. Abadie, Odie Lindsey, and James G. Thomas, eds. *The Mississippi Encyclopedia.* Jackson: University Press of Mississippi, 2017.

Pacelle, Richard L., Jr. *Between Law and Politics: The Solicitor General and the Structuring of Race, Gender, and Reproductive Rights Litigation.* College Station: Texas A&M University Press, 2003.

Panetta, Leon E., and Peter Gall. *Bring Us Together: The Nixon Team and the Civil Rights Retreat.* Philadelphia: Lippincott, 1971.

Parker, Frank R. *Black Votes Count: Political Empowerment in Mississippi after 1965.* Chapel Hill: University of North Carolina Press, 1990.

Patterson, James T. Brown v. Board of Education: *A Civil Rights Milestone and Its Troubled Legacy.* New York: Oxford University Press, 2001.

Patterson, William L., ed. *We Charge Genocide: The Historic Petition to the United Nations for Relief from a Crime of the United States Government against the Negro People.* Ann Arbor: University of Michigan Press, 1952.

Payne, Charles M. *I've Got the Light of Freedom: The Organizing Tradition and the Mississippi Freedom Struggle.* Berkeley: University of California Press, 1995.

Peltason, J. W. *Fifty-Eight Lonely Men: Southern Federal Judges and School Desegregation.* Urbana: University of Illinois Press, 1971.

Perlstein, Rick. *Nixonland: The Rise of a President and the Fracturing of America.* New York: Scribner, 2008.

Perman, Michael. *Struggle for Mastery: Disfranchisement in the South, 1888–1908.* Chapel Hill: University of North Carolina Press, 2001.

Phillips, Kevin P. *The Emerging Republican Majority.* New Rochelle, N.Y.: Arlington House, 1969.

Posner, Richard A. *How Judges Think.* Cambridge, Mass.: Harvard University Press, 2008.

Povall, Allie. *The Time of Eddie Noel.* Concord, N.C.: Comfort Publishing, 2010.

Powdermaker, Hortense. *After Freedom: A Cultural Study in the Deep South.* New York: Viking, 1939.

Raines, Howell. *My Soul Is Rested: Movement Days in the Deep South Remembered.* New York: G. P. Putnam's Sons, 1977.

Ransom, Roger L., and Richard Sutch. *One Kind of Freedom: The Economic Consequences of Emancipation.* New York: Cambridge University Press, 1977.

Raper, Arthur. *Preface to Peasantry: A Take of Two Black Belt Counties.* Chapel Hill: University of North Carolina Press, 1936.

Rawick, George P., ed. *The American Slave: A Composite Autobiography.* Vol. 2, *Texas Narratives,* part 1. West Point, Conn.: Greenwood Press, 1979.

Read, Frank T., and Lucy S. McGough. *Let Them Be Judged: The Judicial Integration of the Deep South.* Metuchen, N.J.: Scarecrow Press, 1978.

Reeves, Richard. *President Nixon: Alone in the White House.* New York: Simon and Schuster, 2002.

Reichley, A. James. *Conservatives in an Age of Change: The Nixon and Ford Administrations.* Washington, D.C.: Brookings Institution, 1981.

Reid, Debra A., and Evan P. Bennett. *Beyond Forty Acres and a Mule: African American Landowning Families since Reconstruction*. Gainesville: University Press of Florida, 2012.

Roberts, Gene, and Hank Klibanoff. *The Race Beat: The Press, the Civil Rights Struggle, and the Awakening of a Nation*. New York: Alfred A. Knopf, 2006.

Roche, Jeff. *Restructured Resistance: The Sibley Commission and the Politics of Desegregation in Georgia*. Athens: University of Georgia Press, 2010.

Rosen, James. *The Strong Man: John Mitchell and the Secrets of Watergate*. New York: Doubleday, 2008.

Rosenberg, Gerald N. *The Hollow Hope: Can Courts Bring About Social Change?* Chicago: University of Chicago Press, 1991.

Rowland, Dunbar. *Mississippi: Comprising Sketches of Counties, Towns, Events, Institutions, and Persons, Arranged in Cyclopedic Form*. Atlanta: Southern Historical Publishing Association, 1907.

Rubio, Philip F. *There's Always Work at the Post Office: African American Postal Workers and the Fight for Jobs, Justice, and Equality*. Chapel Hill: University of North Carolina Press, 2010.

Ryan, Yvonne. *Roy Wilkins: The Quiet Revolutionary and the NAACP*. Lexington: University of Kentucky Press, 2014.

Safire, William. *Before the Fall: An Inside View of the Pre-Watergate White House*. Garden City, N.Y.: Doubleday, 1975.

Sanders, Crystal R. *A Chance for Change: Head Start and Mississippi's Black Freedom Struggle*. Chapel Hill: University of North Carolina Press, 2016.

Sarat, Austin, and Stuart A. Scheingold. *Cause Lawyers and Social Movements*. Stanford: Stanford University Press, 2006.

Schell, Jonathan. *The Time of Illusion*. New York: Vintage Books, 1976.

Schulman, Bruce J. *The Seventies: The Great Shift in American Culture, Society, and Politics*. Cambridge, Mass.: Da Capo Press, 2001.

Schwartz, Bernard. *Swann's Way: The School Busing Case and the Supreme Court*. New York: Oxford University Press, 1986.

———. *The Unpublished Opinions of the Burger Court*. New York: Oxford University Press, 1988.

Schweninger, Loren. *Black Property Owners in the South, 1790–1915*. Urbana: University of Illinois Press, 1990.

Scott, Daryl Michael. *Contempt and Pity: Social Policy and the Image of the Damaged Black Psyche, 1880–1996*. Chapel Hill: University of North Carolina Press, 1997.

Sewell, George A., and Margaret L. Dwight. *Mississippi Black History Makers*. Jackson: University Press of Mississippi, 1984.

Sheehan, Daniel. *The People's Advocate: The Life and Legal History of America's Most Fearless Public Interest Lawyer*. Berkeley: Counterpoint Press, 2013.

Shepard, Kris. *Rationing Justice: Poverty Lawyers and Poor People in the Deep South*. Baton Rouge: Louisiana State University Press, 2009.

Shoemaker, Don, ed. *With All Deliberate Speed: Segregation-Desegregation in Southern Schools*. New York: Harper and Brothers, 1957.

Silver, James W. *Mississippi: The Closed Society*. New York: Harcourt, Brace and World, 1966.

Slade, Peter. *Open Friendship in a Closed Society: Mission Mississippi and a Theology of Friendship*. New York: Oxford University Press, 2009.

Smith, Fred C. *Trouble in Goshen: Plain Folk, Roosevelt, Jesus, and Marx in the Great Depression South*. Jackson: University Press of Mississippi, 2014.

Smith, J. Clay, Jr. *Emancipation: The Making of the Black Lawyer, 1844–1944*. Philadelphia: University of Pennsylvania Press, 1999.

Smith, Mark M. *Camille, 1969: Histories of a Hurricane*. Athens: University of Georgia Press, 2011.

Sojourner, Sue [Lorenzi], with Cheryl Reitan. *Thunder of Freedom: Black Leadership and the Transformation of 1960s Mississippi*. Lexington: University Press of Kentucky, 2013.

Sokol, Jason. *There Goes My Everything: White Southerners in the Age of Civil Rights, 1945–1975*. New York: Alfred A. Knopf, 2006.

Somerville, Mrs. Keith Frazier. *Dear Boys: World War II Letters from a Woman Back Home*. Jackson: University Press of Mississippi, 1991.

Southern Regional Council. *The South and Her Children: School Desegregation, 1970–1971*. Atlanta: Southern Regional Council, 1971.

Spriggs, Kent, ed. *Voices of Civil Rights Lawyers: Reflections from the Deep South, 1964–1980*. Gainesville: University Press of Florida, 2017.

Stern, Seth, and Stephen Wermiel. *Justice Brennan: Liberal Champion*. Boston: Houghton Mifflin Harcourt, 2010.

Suitts, Steve. *Hugo Black of Alabama: How His Roots and Early Career Shaped the Great Champion of the Constitution*. Montgomery, Ala.: New South Books, 2005.

Sullivan, Patricia. *Lift Every Voice: The NAACP and the Making of the Civil Rights Movement*. New York: New Press, 2009.

Summers, Barbara, ed. *I Dream a World: Portraits of Black Women Who Changed America*. New York: Stewart, Tabori, and Chang, 1989.

Sweet, Grace Britton, and Benjamin Bradley. *Church Street: The Sugar Hill of Jackson, Mississippi*. Charleston, S.C.: History Press, 2013.

Terkel, Studs. *American Dreams: Lost and Found*. New York: Pantheon Books, 1980.

Thornton, J. Mills, III. *Archipelagoes of My South: Episodes in the Shaping of a Region, 1830–1965*. Tuscaloosa: University of Alabama Press, 2016.

Tracy, Janice Branch. *The Juke Joint King of the Mississippi Hills: The Raucous Reign of Tillman Branch*. Mt. Pleasant, S.C.: History Press, 2014.

———. *Mississippi Moonshine Politics: How Bootleggers and the Law Kept a Dry State Soaked*. Mt. Pleasant, S.C.: Arcadia Publishing, 2015.

Trillin, Calvin. *Jackson, 1964: And Other Dispatches from Fifty Years of Reporting on Race in America*. New York: Random House, 2016.

Tushnet, Mark V. *Making Civil Rights Law: Thurgood Marshall and the Supreme Court, 1936–1961*. New York: Oxford University Press, 1994.

———. *Making Constitutional Law: Thurgood Marshall and the Supreme Court, 1961–1991*. New York: Oxford University Press, 1997.

———. *The NAACP's Legal Strategy against Segregated Education, 1925–1950*. Chapel Hill: University of North Carolina Press, 1987.

Tyson, Timothy. *Radio Free Dixie: Robert F. Williams and the Roots of Black Power.* Chapel Hill: University of North Carolina Press, 1999.

Upchurch, Thomas Adams. *A White Minority in Post–Civil Rights Mississippi*. Lanham, Md.: Hamilton Books, 2005.

Vance, Rupert B. *Human Geography of the South: A Study in Regional Resources and Human Adequacy.* Chapel Hill: University of North Carolina Press, 1932.

von Hoffman, Nicholas. *Mississippi Notebook*. New York: David White, 1964.

Waldron, Ann. *Hodding Carter: The Reconstruction of a Racist*. Chapel Hill: Algonquin Books, 1993.

Walker, Alice. *In Search of Our Mother's Gardens*. New York: Harvest/HBJ Book, 1983.

Ward, Jason Morgan. *Hanging Bridge: Racial Violence and America's Civil Rights Century.* New York: Oxford University Press, 2016.

Wasby, Stephen L. *Race Relations Litigation in an Age of Complexity*. Charlottesville: University Press of Virginia, 1995.

Wasby, Stephen L., Anthony A. D'Amato, and Rosemary Metrailer. *Desegregation from Brown to Alexander.* Carbondale: Southern Illinois University Press, 1977.

Weill, Susan. *In a Madhouse's Din: Civil Rights Coverage by Mississippi's Daily Press, 1948–1968.* Westport, Conn.: Greenwood, 2002.

Wendt, Simon. *The Spirit and the Shotgun: Armed Resistance and the Struggle for Civil Rights.* Gainesville: University Press of Florida, 2007.

Wexler, Laura. *Fire in a Canebrake: The Last Mass Lynching in America*. New York: Simon and Schuster, 2013.

Whalen, John. *Maverick among the Magnolias: The Hazel Brannon Smith Story.* Bloomington, Ind.: Xlibris Press, 2000.

Wharton, Vernon Lane. *The Negro in Mississippi, 1865–1890*. Chapel Hill: University of North Carolina Press, 1947.

White, Calvin, Jr. *The Rise to Respectability: Race, Religion, and the Church of God in Christ.* Fayetteville: University of Arkansas Press, 2012.

White, Evelyn C. *Alice Walker: A Life*. New York: W. W. Norton, 2004.

Whitt, Jan. *Burning Crosses and Activist Journalism: Hazel Brannon Smith and the Mississippi Civil Rights Movement.* New York: University Press of America, 2010.

Wicker, Tom. *One of Us: Richard Nixon and the American Dream*. New York: Random House, 1991.

Wilkins, Roy, and Tom Mathews. *Standing Fast: The Autobiography of Roy Wilkins.* New York: De Capo Press, 1982.

Wilkinson, J. Harvie, III. *From Brown to Bakke: The Supreme Court and School Integration, 1954–1978.* New York: Oxford University Press, 1979.

Williams, Juan. *Eyes on the Prize: America's Civil Rights Years, 1954–1965.* New York: Penguin Books, 2002.

Williams, Tennessee. *Five Plays: Cat on a Hot Tin Roof, The Rose Tattoo, Something*

Unspoken, Suddenly Last Summer, Orpheus Descending. London: Secker and War-
burg, 1962.

Willis, John C. *Forgotten Time: The Yazoo-Mississippi Delta after the Civil War.*
Charlottesville: University Press of Virginia, 2000.

Wirt, Frederick M. *Politics of Southern Equality: Law and Social Change in a Mississippi County.* Chicago: Aldine, 1970.

———. *"We Ain't What We Was": Civil Rights in the New South.* Durham: Duke
University Press, 1997.

Wolters, Raymond. *The Burden of* Brown: *Thirty Years of School Desegregation.*
Knoxville: University of Tennessee Press, 1984.

———. *Race and Education, 1954–2007.* Columbia: University of Missouri Press,
2008.

Woodruff, Nan Elizabeth. *American Congo: The African American Freedom Struggle
in the Delta.* Cambridge, Mass.: Harvard University Press, 2003.

Woodward, Bob, and Scott Armstrong. *The Brethren: Inside the Supreme Court.*
New York: Simon and Schuster, 1979.

Wright, Gavin. *Sharing the Prize: The Economics of the Civil Rights Revolution in the
American South.* Cambridge, Mass.: Belknap Press, 2013.

Wynne, Ben. *Mississippi's Civil War: A Narrative History.* Macon, Ga.: Mercer University Press, 2006.

Youth of the Rural Organizing and Cultural Center. *Minds Stayed on Freedom: The
Civil Rights Struggle in the Rural South, an Oral History.* Boulder, Colo.: West-
view Press, 1991.

Zeitz, Joshua. *Building the Great Society: Inside Lyndon Johnson's White House.* New
York: Viking Press, 2018.

Zelden, Charles L. *Thurgood Marshall: Race, Rights, and the Struggle for a More Perfect Union.* New York: Routledge, 2013.

Zwiers, Maarten. *Senator James Eastland: Mississippi's Jim Crow Democrat.* Baton
Rouge: Louisiana State University Press, 2015.

UNPUBLISHED WORKS

Barnes, Louie Burton. "The Embattled Judges: Cox, Mize, and Cameron, 1960–
1965." M.A. thesis, Mississippi State University, 1974.

Berry, John Patrick. "The Dynamics of White Resistance to Court-Ordered School
Desegregation in Selected Mississippi Districts." Honors thesis, Harvard College, 1971.

Brigham, Jeremy John. "Transforming Places." Ph.D. diss., University of Iowa,
1998.

Butler, Anthea D. "A Peculiar Synergy: Matriarchy and the Church of God in
Christ." Ph.D. diss., Vanderbilt University, 2001.

Callaway, Michelle Elizabeth. "Mississippi's Segregation Academy Movement,
1954–1970." M.A. thesis, University of Mississippi, 1993.

Cora, Spiro Pete. "A History of Holmes County, Mississippi." M.A. thesis, Mississippi College, 1969.

Edwards, J. Daniel. "Antebellum Holmes County, Mississippi: A History." M.A. thesis, Mississippi State University, 1992.

Emmons, David. "Black Politics in the South." M.A. thesis, University of Chicago, 1965.

Gist, Sylvia Reedy. "Educating a Southern Rural Community: The Case of Blacks in Holmes County, Mississippi, 1870 to Present." Ph.D. diss., University of Chicago, 1994.

Hale, Jon N. "A History of the Mississippi Freedom Schools, 1954–1965." Ph.D. diss., University of Illinois at Urbana-Champaign, 2009.

Hilbink, Thomas. "Filling the Void: The Lawyers' Constitutional Defense Committee and the 1964 Freedom Summer." Senior thesis, Columbia University, 1993.

Howell, Jeffery Brian. "The Undiscovered Country: The Civil Rights Movement in Holmes County, Mississippi 1954–1968." M.A. thesis, Mississippi State University, 2005.

Loewen, James W. "School Desegregation in Mississippi." Monograph, Tougaloo College, 1973.

Middleton, Jeanne. "The History of *Singleton v. Jackson Municipal Separate School District*: Southern School Desegregation from the Perspective of the Black Community." Ed.D. thesis, Harvard University, 1978.

Munford, Luther. "Black Gravity: Desegregation in 30 Mississippi School Districts." Senior thesis, Princeton University, 1971.

Pye, David Kenneth. "Legal Subversives: African American Lawyers in the Jim Crow South." Ph.D. diss., University of California, San Diego, 2010.

Shafer, Carlie C. "A Study of Historical and Legal Factors Influencing the Desegregation Process of the Public Schools in Mississippi." Ph.D. diss., University of Southern Mississippi, 1971.

Sojourner, Sue [Lorenzi]. "Got to Thinking: How the Black People of 1960s Holmes Co., Mississippi, Organized Their Civil Rights Movement." Praxis International, Exhibit, Duluth, Minn.

Spivack, John Michael. "Race, Civil Rights, and the United States Court of Appeals for the Fifth Judicial Circuit." Ph.D. diss., University of Florida, 1978.

Taylor, Kieran W. "'I Done Made Up My Mind': The Legacy of the Providence Cooperative Farm." M.A. thesis, University of Mississippi, 1993.

Umoja, Akinyele K. "Eye for an Eye: The Role of Armed Resistance in the Mississippi Freedom Movement." Ph.D. diss., Emory University, 1997.

Upchurch, Thomas Adams. "Race Relations in Holmes County, Mississippi: The First Hundred Years, 1893–1933." M.A. thesis, Delta State University, 1997.

Weissberg, Karel M. "A Study of the Freedom Movement in Cotton County, Mississippi." Honors thesis, Radcliffe College, 1966.

Wolinsky, Alex. "From the Brink of Death: Judicial Legitimacy and the Supreme Court's Retreat from Abolition of Capital Punishment in the 1970s." Honors thesis, University of California, Berkeley, 2014.

Wood, Spencer D. "The Roots of Black Power: Land, Civil Society, and the State in the Mississippi Delta, 1935–1968." Ph.D. diss., University of Wisconsin, 2006.

INDEX

www.ingramcontent.com/pod-product-compliance
Lightning Source LLC
Chambersburg PA
CBHW030346270326
41926CB00009B/986